Sport and
Criminal Behavior

Sport and Criminal Behavior

Edited by

Jason W. Lee

Jeffrey C. Lee

Carolina Academic Press / Durham, North Carolina

Library of Congress Cataloging-in-Publication Data

Lee, Jason W.
Sport and criminal behavior / Edited by Jason W. Lee, Jeffrey C. Lee.
   p. cm.
Includes bibliographical references and index.
ISBN 978-1-59460-502-4 (alk. paper)
1. Sports--Corrupt practices--United States. 2. Athletes--Drug use--United States.
3. Athletes--Alcohol use--United States. 4. Doping in sports--United States. 5.
Sports betting--United States. 6. Gambling--United States. 7. Organized crime--
United States. 8. Criminal behavior--United States. I. Lee, Jeffrey C. II. Title.
GV718.2.U6L44 2009
306.4'830973--dc22

                                        2009012393

Carolina Academic Press
700 Kent Street
Durham, North Carolina 27701
Telephone 919/489-7486
Fax 919/493-5668
E-mail: cap@cap-press.com
www.cap-press.com

Printed in the United States of America.

Contents

Preface

Sport is filled with paradox. Sport, by nature, is inherently based on athleticism, fitness, strength, and other seemingly healthful benefits. Though such benefits are common, unhealthy and inappropriate associations also exist. This dichotomy is quite prevalent in contemporary sport. Among the most troubling is the increasingly visible prevalence of criminal behaviors associated with sport. This text seeks to examine some of the most relevant and thought provoking occurrences of criminal behavior in sport. Through identifying pertinent issues, including motives and causes associated with such actions, this work aims to present a comprehensive view of these issues while providing ways such matters can be effectively dealt with in contemporary society. The topics addressed in this work include: drug issues, violence, gambling, ticket scalping, hazing, fraud in nonprofit sport, homeland security issues and disaster preparedness in sport, intellectual property (trademark law, copyright misappropriation, and criminal implications), and beyond.

Part I

Introduction

1

Sport and Criminal Behavior: An Introduction

Jeffery C. Lee, Troy University
Jason W. Lee, University of North Florida

The Intersection of Criminal Justice and Sport

This chapter provides a foundation for the rest of the text by addressing the interface between the criminal justice system and sport (as well as sport management). Information pertaining to the field of criminal justice, the American justice system, the justice process, the sport industry, the field of sport management, and the intermingling of these areas will be discussed, including an introduction to concepts addressed in the remainder of this text.

Introduction to Criminal Justice

The term "criminal justice system" often refers to the collective body of agencies that deal with the management of crime. Many people have some knowledge of how our justice system works; however, there are few that have an in-depth understanding of the criminal justice systems' structures, functions, and processes. This segment of the introduction chapter is intended to provide a brief overview of the American criminal justice system.

Crime

Fuller (2006) describes crime as an action that violates the rules of society. This action may harm other citizens or society as a whole. The Federal Bureau of Investigations (FBI) annually publishes data on crime called the Uniform Crime Report (UCR). This report measures crime in two categories: Type I offenses (index crimes) and Type II offenses.

3

Type I offenses include:

1. **Murder and non-neglect manslaughter**: the willful killing of a human being by another.
2. **Forcible rape**: the carnal knowledge of a person, forcibly and/or against that person's will; or not forcibly or against that person's will where the victim is incapable of giving consent.
3. **Robbery**: taking or attempting to take anything of value under confrontational circumstances from the control, custody, or care of another person by force or threat of force or violence and/or by putting the victim in fear of immediate harm.
4. **Aggravated assault**: an assault where the assailant flourishes a deadly weapon or attempts to cause serious bodily injury to another intentionally, knowingly, purposely, or recklessly, while demonstrating extreme indifference for human life.
5. **Burglary**: unlawful entry into a building or other structure with the intent to commit a felony or theft.
6. **Larceny/theft**: unlawful and intentional taking of another's property, without his or her consent and with the intent to permanently deprive.
7. **Motor vehicle theft**: theft or attempted theft of a motor vehicle, including joyriding.
8. **Arson**: to unlawfully and intentionally damage, or attempt to damage, any real or personal property by fire or incendiary device (Falcone, 2005).

Type II offenses include numerous other crimes that range from drug offenses to simple assaults and batteries. Many justice policies are based on the FBI's Uniform Crime Report. However, almost all criminal justicians recognize that this report captures only a small amount of the "actual" crime in the U.S. since it is based on crimes reported to law enforcement (Neubauer, 2005).

Fuller (2006) points out that there is also a "dark figure of crime." This term refers to crime that goes unreported to law enforcement and criminal justice officials, which is never quantified. The National Incident Based Reporting System (NIBRS) and the National Crime Source (NCS) are computerized crime data collection tools that attempt to capture the "dark figure of crime," which may provide a more accurate reflection on the amount of crime in our society.

Goals of the Criminal Justice System

In general, the American criminal justice system is comprised of three components: law enforcement, criminal courts, and corrections. Criminal justice personnel that work in these agencies are expected to perform their duties with justice and fairness, professionalism, and integrity at every stage of the criminal justice process. Specifically, the courts are charged with the duty of ensuring these expectations are met. The criminal justice system has two primary goals:

1. Enforcing the law and maintaining public order.
2. Protecting individuals from injustice, especially by the criminal justice system.

This first goal is derived from the crime-control model. This model suggests that the criminal justice system should emphasize the efficient arrest and conviction of offenders (Schmalleger, 2009). In other words, this model places the primary emphasis on the right of citizens, as well as society at large, to be protected from crime. Furthermore, the benefits of lower crime rates outweigh any potential costs to individual rights (Gaines & Miller, 2008).

The second goal is derived from the perspective that emphasizes individual rights at all stages of the criminal justice process; specifically, the right of an individual to be protected from the power of the government (Gaines & Miller, 2008). Throughout history, these models have appeared to be in consistent and unavoidable opposition to each other. However, our system of administering justice attempts to balance these goals through due process (Schmalleger, 2009).

Components of the Criminal Justice System

The American criminal justice system is comprised of three interrelated components: law enforcement, courts, and corrections. There are over one million men and women employed in this system. On the front line of the system is the law enforcement component. Law enforcement officers are typically viewed as the "gate-keepers" to the criminal justice system. In other words, they decide which defendants enter the system by their detection, diligence, and discretion. Law enforcement officers' duties extend beyond making arrests. They also obtain information and evidence, write detailed reports, identify witnesses, and provide testimony in court (Worbleski & Hess, 2003).

The organization of American law enforcement has a multi-layered approach that includes federal, state, and local agencies. At the federal level, most people think of the FBI (Federal Bureau of Investigations); however, there are approximately sixty federal law enforcement agencies. Most of these agencies are organized under the Department of Justice (DOJ), Department of the Treasury, or the Department of Homeland Security (DHS). Federal law enforcement agencies have national jurisdiction, but typically focus on specific categories of crimes. For example, special agents of the Drug Enforcement Administration (DEA) are involved with drug interdiction and large-scale drug investigations. The United States Secret Service is authorized to investigate counterfeiting and certain types of fraud, in addition to their executive protection responsibilities (Fuller, 2006).

State level law enforcement agencies are sometimes organized in a similar manner to the federal system. However, no two states are organized identically. Most states have various law enforcement agencies that regulate and enforce specific types of laws. For example, all states, except Hawaii have highway patrol departments (Fuller, 2006). Also, Fish and Wildlife Departments will regulate and enforce state hunting and fishing laws. Additionally, alcohol and tobacco enforcement agencies are another example. These agencies may enforce laws related to alcohol and investigate violations on premises licensed to sell alcohol in addition to collecting revenue from the sale of alcoholic beverages and tobacco products. Most states have a general investigative branch of law enforcement; some examples include the Alabama Bureau of Investigations (ABI), the Florida Department of Law Enforcement (FDLE), and Pennsylvania State Police.

Most crime, however, is handled by local law enforcement agencies. Municipal police departments and county sheriffs' offices make up the local level of law enforcement. Officers at the local level have the broadest authority to investigate crime and apprehend offenders. They also have the wide-ranging responsibility to provide services to their community. Whether an agency is urban (like the New York City Police Department or Los Angeles County Sheriffs' Office) or rural (like the Kinston, Alabama Police Department or the Baker County Florida Sheriffs' Office) they have an obligation to the citizens in their jurisdiction to respond to requests for service, crime, and other community problems.

Courts

The second component of the American criminal justice system is the court system. The U.S. court system is unique because it is a dual court system, which means that is made up of both state and federal courts. In the court system, the term "jurisdiction" refers to the courts' legal authority to try a case. Another "duality" of the court refers to the jurisdiction as being original or appellate; courts with original jurisdiction have the legal authority to try and hear a case. Courts with appellate jurisdiction have the authority to hear an appeal. The United States Supreme Court has both original and appellate jurisdiction (Worbleski & Hess, 2003).

In addition to state and federal courts, there are many "specialized courts" that address specific types of criminal justice cases. For example, drug courts are treatment based. This type of court allows offenders with substance abuse problems to get treatment as soon as they enter the court system as opposed to getting it as a component of the corrections phase of the criminal justice process. Community courts are an alternative to traditional courts. These courts seek to utilize community resources and create partnerships with community groups, government agencies, and service providers to address crime-related problems within a community (Worbleski & Hess, 2003).

In the United States, courts are based on the adversarial system. This system is characterized as a contest between the initiating party (prosecutor for criminal cases) and the responding party (defendants in criminal cases) (Falcone, 2005). Innocence is presumed — the prosecutor has the entire burden of proving the elements of the alleged criminal offense at trial. This burden is proof beyond a reasonable doubt. The defense has no obligation to prove innocence. However, each side may challenge evidence and testimony that is presented. A judge or jury then determines the guilt or innocence of the accused.

There are several key players in the court system, often referred to as members of the courtroom workgroup. These include:

- **Prosecutor:** the official who represents the state or government and conducts the prosecution in a criminal trial.
- **Defense Attorney:** the lawyer who represents the accused at trial.
- **Defendant:** the one who is criminally accused.
- **Judge:** the judicial officer presiding over a court.
- **Jury:** a group of citizens selected to hear evidence in a trial and to reach a decision based on the evidence (Falcone, 2005).

- **Clerk of the Court:** the official record keeper, and responsible to jury pools.
- **Court Reporter:** makes verbatim transcripts of the court proceeding.
- **Bailiff:** maintains order in the courtroom (Neubauer, 2005).

The Justice Process

While the justice system exists to control and prevent crimes, the justice process involves the agencies and procedures that are in place to manage both crimes and the people that are accused of committing them. There are many steps in this process. Once law enforcement is made aware of a crime, a criminal investigation is conducted. Investigative techniques involve examining the crime scene, searching for physical evidence, interviewing witnesses and victims, and identifying the suspect. Once a suspect has been identified, law enforcement seeks to obtain a warrant for the offender's arrest or takes the offender directly into custody. Either way, the standard for their action is probable cause. While no court has rendered an exact definition, probable cause is commonly viewed as a set of circumstances that would lead a reasonable person to conclude that a crime has been committed and that a particular suspect is responsible for the crime in question. When the accused is taken into custody, he or she goes through a process known as booking. This is the administrative processing of an arrested person; it includes taking fingerprints, mug shot, and logging the defendants' name and the official charge. Inciardi (1999), outlines the formal justice process.

Initial Appearance

The accused is brought before a judge or magistrate within a reasonable time and given a formal notice of the charge called an initial appearance. At this time, the defendant will be notified of their legal rights and an appropriate bail determined. Some defendants may be granted a release of recognizance (ROR) in lieu of bail on the promise that they will appear for trial.

Preliminary Hearing

During this hearing, the court determines whether the one charged with a crime should be held for trial. For felony cases, the state must establish probable cause during this hearing.

Formal Charge

The next step in the justice process is the formalization of the charges. This may be done through a grand jury. The grand jury is a group of people impaneled for the purpose of determining whether there is sufficient cause to bind a defendant over for trial. The prosecutors guide the grand jury and ask for an indictment of the defendant. The indictment comes in the form of a "true bill" that contains the following:

- Type and nature of the offense;
- Specific statute that has been violated;
- Time and place of the crime;

- Name and address of the accused;
- Grand jury foreman's signature; and
- Names of any co-defendants.

If the grand jury fails to get the majority vote to indict, the accused is then released. This is referred to as a "no bill."

The most common method of bringing formal charges to the accused is an "information"—a formal criminal accusation against the defendant that is prepared by the prosecutor and presented to the court. Note that in federal cases, a grand jury indictment is required of all felony prosecutions (Falcone, 2005).

Arraignment

This is the first phase of the trial process. During this hearing, the formal charges are read to the defendant. The defendant is then required to enter a plea. There are four common pleas:

1. Not guilty;
2. Guilty;
3. *Nolo Contendre* or no contest; and
4. Standing mute (results in a not guilty plea).

Plea Bargaining

The vast majority of cases—approximately 90 percent—do not make it to trial (Neubauer, 2005). Instead, they are disposed of as a result of a plea bargaining process. This is a process of negotiation between the state and the defendant, generally resulting in a plea of guilty by the defendant in exchange for a more favorable sentence or a reduction in charges, a deviation from the adversarial system. However, most criminal justice practitioners acknowledge that this deviation is necessary when dealing with an over burdened court system. Defendants who enter a plea of guilty will go straight to the sentencing phase.

Pretrial Motion

Pretrial motions are hearings before the trial, usually initiated by the defendant. Some common pretrial motions include:

1. Motion to suppress evidence;
2. Motion to relocate the trial;
3. Motion for discovery (to see the nature of the states evidence); and
4. Motion to postpone the trial.

Jury Selection

Selecting a jury involves a series of procedural steps that begins with a master list of eligible jurors. This list is often obtained form voter registration polls. Names are randomly selected from the master list for "venire." Venire is a writ that summons jurors to report for service. These summoned jurors make up the jury pool. Pool members are randomly selected to become a jury panel. Panel members are subjected to the *voir dire* process, which involves questioning by the prosecutor, defense attorney, and judge, each of whom may challenge a panel member's acceptability to serve on the jury. Members that remain after this process serve as the jury on the case.

Trial

The trial process begins with the prosecution's opening statements. The prosecution presents an outline of the state's case and introduces its witnesses and evidence. Then, the defense makes its opening statement. Again, they will outline the evidence that may be presented on their own behalf and introduce any witnesses. Next, the state will present its case. The prosecution will call witnesses to establish the elements of the crime and introduce any physical evidence through "direct" examination of the witnesses. The defense is entitled to cross-examine the prosecution's witnesses. The defense then has an opportunity to present its case. If the defense feels that the state has failed to prove its case beyond a reasonable doubt, they can make a motion for dismissal. Otherwise, they present their case much as the state has done.

Prosecutors may then have the opportunity for "rebuttal." At this point, they may introduce new witnesses or evidence. The defense then can have a chance at "surrebuttal," making another motion to dismiss or present new evidence or testimony. After this stage, both the prosecution and the defense make their closing arguments. They summarize their arguments and suggest conclusions that may be drawn from the evidence.

Next, the judge will "charge the jury." This refers to the instructions given to the jury: the order to retire to the jury room and return with a verdict. When a decision has been reached, the jury returns to the courtroom and the verdict is announced. Upon a guilty verdict, the court renders a sentence.

Corrections

Corrections is the third component of the criminal justice system. This component is responsible for carrying out the orders (sentence) rendered by the court. The primary purposes of the corrections system include retribution, deterrence, incapacitation, and rehabilitation.

Retribution is the punishment for crimes, which implies that a debt must be paid to society for the defendant's acts (Falcone, 2005). It is based on the premise of *lex talionis*, or an eye for an eye.

Deterrence refers to the justice concept of preventing future criminal acts through fear of swift, severe, and certain punishment. Punishment should be sufficient to convince the offender not to repeat the criminal conduct. Deterrence may also be general. This type of deterrence seeks to prevent criminal behaviors through fear of punishment directed toward those who have not been arrested, but may be tempted to commit crimes (Falcone, 2005).

Incapacitation refers to making it impossible for offenders to commit future crimes. In the American criminal justice system, this typically is achieved by incapacitating them in prison or jail. An example of an extreme form of incapacitation is the death penalty.

Rehabilitation is the correction of deviant behavior (Falcone, 2005). This concept is rarely found in prisons because it is in conflict with the other, more dominant purposes of retribution, deterrence, and incapacitation.

The corrections component may be institutional, community, or both. Institutional corrections are sentences that involve terms of incarceration in prisons or jails. Prisons are state or federal penal institutions that house offenders convicted of felonies who are sentenced to more than a year of confinement. Jails are custodial or detention facilities that house the accused awaiting trial or offenders sentenced to terms of incarceration less than one year. Community corrections refer to programs that are provided to offenders in an open community setting, including halfway houses, residential treatment facilities, or probation services. Probation is a conditional release of an offender who is convicted of a crime into the community to be supervised by a probation officer in lieu of incarceration. Offenders who have served a portion of their sentence in prison may be granted parole. Parole is the conditional release from prison of an offender under the authority of a parole board. The parolee is under the supervision of a parole officer and may be returned to prison to finish the sentence if the terms of parole are violated (Falcone, 2005).

Courts often use a document called a presentence investigation to determine an appropriate sentence for an offender. This investigation is typically conducted by a probation officer. This report describes the crime in question, suffering and costs of the victim, offender's prison record, the offender's education and employment history, residential history, and any other relevant personal or background information on the offender. The greatest influences on sentencing decision-making are the seriousness of the crime and the offender's criminal history.

Sport Management: What is it?

We will address various defining characteristics of sport management in order to provide a foundational understanding of the field. We will discuss terms including sport, management, and sport management. First, sport has broadly been defined as (1) "institutionalized competitive activity that involves physical skill and specialized facilities or equipment and is conducted according to an accepted set of rules to determine a winner" (Woods, 2007, p. 7); (2) "any activity, experience, or business enterprise focused on fitness, recreation, athletics ..." (Pitts, Fielding, & Miller, 1994, p. 18); and (3) "all forms of physical activity which, through casual (informal) or organised [sic] participation, aim at expressing or improving physical fitness and mental well-being, forming social relationships or obtaining results in competition at all levels" (The Council of Europe, 2001, p. 1).

Parks, Quarterman, and Thibault (2007) describe sport as being a social institution. This institution is a distinctive social activity that is commonly the foundation of one's social identity (Coakley, 2006). As such, it is a social institution of almost unbelievable magnitude and influence. "The sheer power of sport mandates that people who wish to manage it acquire a sound understanding of its historical, psychological, sociological, cultural, and philosophical dimensions" (Parks, Quarterman, & Thibault, 2007, p. 14).

Eitzen (2006) details how sport is able to mirror society and the human experience. Being that sport mirrors society, managers of sport are able to appreciate its business aspects, such as general management issues and marketing considerations, as well as the social and cultural implications of sport.

The sport industry is a dynamic economic force comprised of various industry settings. In an effort to identify the nature and scope of the sport industry, VanderZwaag (1998) documented sixteen settings in which sport occurs:

1. School and college sports programs;
2. Professional sport;
3. Amateur sport organizations [i.e., USOC; USA Basketball; etc.];
4. Private club sport;
5. Other commercialized sport establishments [i.e., bowling alleys; public golf courses];
6. Arenas, coliseums, civic centers, and stadiums;
7. Community recreation sport programs
8. Industrial sport programs;
9. Sport programs in social agencies [i.e., YMCAs; Jewish Community Centers];
10. Military sport programs;
11. Sport marketing and consulting firms;
12. Developmental programs for sport [i.e., Women's Sport Foundation, Special Olympics, etc.];
13. Corporate sponsors [i.e., Chick-Fil-A Bowl; Bausch & Lomb Tennis Championship];
14. The sporting goods industry;
15. The sport news media [i.e., print and broadcast media]; and
16. Academic programs in sport management (pp. 4–6).

"The contemporary sport industry is complex and has unique legal, business, and management practices" (Masteralexis, Barr, & Hums, 2004, p. 1). Estimated at $213 billion, the sport industry "is one of the largest and fastest growing industries in the United States" ("Advertise with us—The sports industry," 2008, n.p.) and is "far more than twice the size of the U.S. auto industry and seven times the size of the movie industry" (n.p.).

By the nature of its name, "sport management" divulges the management nature of the field. Management is identified Chelladurai (2001) as being the "process of achieving organizational goals with and through other people within the constraints of limited resources" (p. 94). Management is characterized by incorporating management aspects including planning, organizing, directing, and monitoring (Jordan & Kent, 2005).

Pitts and Stotlar (2002), defined sport management as "all people, activities, businesses, and organizations involved in producing, facilitating, promoting, or organizing any product that is sport, fitness, and recreation related" (p. 4). Sport management is a multi-faceted field in academia. For the purposes of this chapter, sport management will be used as the default term used to indicate any program representing the various university-level academic programs premeditated to prepare students to take on positions within (and associated with) the sport industry.

Sport management is encapsulated in various academic units and even can be classified by a variety of names. Other academic disciplines or sub disciplines that pertain to sport may be associated with this. The focus of this section will address the notion of the academic discipline of "sport management."

Sport management and its related fields of study have been called by a number of terms; its proper name is debatable (for example, *sport management vs. sports management* or *sport management vs. sport administration*). Often, the distinctions between names are purely semantic and for the purposes of this chapter will not be discussed further. Beyond that, differences can be blamed on other considerations, including program focus or other departmental program associations and nomenclature considerations (i.e., sport and fitness management, sport and recreation management, etc.) or historical tie-ins (i.e., "that is the name we have always used—so why change it"). Additionally, there are related fields such as sport sociology, sport communication, and beyond.

How It Began

The history of the field of sport management can be traced back a half of a century. In 1957, Walter O'Malley—then president and chief stockholder of the Brooklyn Dodgers—predicted the growth potential for organized sport. Anticipating this growth and understanding the need for appropriately trained managers, he wrote a letter to Dr. James Mason inquiring as to where individuals could go to get appropriate academic training for jobs associated with the sport industry. This inquiry spawned the first academic program in sport management, a master's-level program at Ohio University founded in 1966 (Parkhouse & Pitts, 2005). Though a Baseball Administration program at Florida Southern College predated Ohio University's program, the latter is predominately recognized as the precedent setting program (Park, Quarterman, & Thibault, 2007).

Where It Is Now

Sport management has grown tremendously over the last 40 years as an academic discipline (Weese, 2002). Since the implementation of the first sport management program in 1966, approximately 300 new programs have been created. In the last half century, academic programs have exploded both domestically and globally. Undergraduate and graduate programs can be found worldwide. As of March 2009, the North American Society for Sport Management website lists 291 recognized Sport Management programs in the U.S. (260), Canada (12), Europe (17), Australia (8), New Zealand (4), Africa (3), and India (1) (Sport Management Programs, n.d.). Additionally, it should be noted that there are other programs that are have not been included in the NASSM list.

Who Manages Sport

Various professional organizations play a hand in providing structure, resources, and academic programs (such as conferences, etc.), and academic review and accreditation in the academic discipline of sport management. Among the organizations that provide such resources for sport management and the related sub-discipline areas (i.e., legal aspects of sport; sport marketing; and peripheral fields of study), are: North American Society for Sport Management (NASSM); the Commission on Sport Management Accreditation (COSMA); American Alliance for Health, Physical Education, Recreation, and Dance (AAHPERD) and the associated national association, the National Association for Sport and Physical Education (NASPE); Sport Marketing Association (SMA); Sport and Recreation Law Association (SRLA); and the North American Society for the Sociology of Sport (NASSS). Additionally, state organizations such as the Florida Alliance for Health, Physical Education, Recreation, Dance, and Sport (FAHPERDS) contribute to furthering sport management. There are other organizations on other continents, such as the European Association for Sport Management (EASM) and Sport Management Association of Australia & New Zealand (SMAANZ), which help to shape sport management.

Before linking sport management to criminal justice (and associated academic disciplines), the value of sport to society should first be addressed. For many, sport is quite important—the importance of sport goes far beyond TV dollars, rooting for your favorite team, or participating in community sport activities.

Sport is omnipresent and has commonly been referred to as a reflection of society. Eitzen (2006) proposes that sport is a microcosm of society because it shares the basic elements and expressions of issues abounding in life. Sport provides a looking glass for societal issues including, but not limited to sport's association with:

- Social values and socialization;
- Marketing and economic characteristics;
- Politics and governance;
- Diversity issues in sport (including gender, race, ethnicity and other characteristics of diversity);
- Globalization issues in sport;
- Media and communications;
- Sport and education; and
- Deviance and crime.

The Interface between Sport Management and Criminal Justice

The wide range of curricular areas engaged in the study of sport management present many prospects to collaborate with persons from other academic fields. An important collaborative area presented in this text is the interface between the academic fields of criminal justice and sport management. The "joining of forces" of these respective academic fields can present an underpinning for collaborative efforts including sport law (legal aspects of sport), socio-cultural issues, and other content areas. The primary focus of this work is to explore the interface between criminal justice and sport management regarding criminal behavior in sport.

Relevance to this Book

In drawing a relationship between the academic field of criminal justice (and associated fields) and sport, it seemed natural to develop a text that identified the connection between sport and criminal behavior. There are various issues of deviant and criminal behavior that exist in relation to the intersection of various criminal justice and sport management concepts. This book aims to address problematic areas associated with criminal behavior in sport, including:

- Alcohol and drug use (including illegal performance enhancement concerns);
- Violence in sport (i.e., within the context of sporting events; other associated aspects);
- Gambling in sport and the association of organized crime;
- Criminal fraud in port;
- Hazing in athletics;
- Criminal incidents by athletes on various level of sport (i.e., the concept of "Criminal Jocks");
- Homeland security/disaster preparedness in sport facilities; and
- Ticket scalping.

Number of Sport Management Programs, as listed by NASSM

[As of March 30, 2009]

Sport Management Programs: Africa [3]
- http://www.nassm.com/InfoAbout/SportMgmtPrograms/Africa

Sport Management Programs: India [1]
- http://www.nassm.com/InfoAbout/SportMgmtPrograms/India

Sport Management Programs: New Zealand [4]
- http://www.nassm.com/InfoAbout/SportMgmtPrograms/New_Zealand

Sport Management Programs: Australia [8]
- http://www.nassm.com/InfoAbout/SportMgmtPrograms/Australia

Sport Management Programs: Europe [17]
- http://www.nassm.com/InfoAbout/SportMgmtPrograms/Europe

Sport Management Programs: Canada [12]
- http://www.nassm.com/InfoAbout/SportMgmtPrograms/Canada

Sport Management Programs: United States [260]
- http://www.nassm.com/InfoAbout/SportMgmtPrograms/United_States

References

Advertise with us—The sports industry (2008). *SportsBusiness Journal*. Retrieved on October 11, 2008, from http://www.sportsbusinessjournal.com/index.cfm?fuseaction=page.feature&featureId=1492

Chelladurai, P. (2001). *Managing organizations for sport and physical activity*. Scottsdale, AZ: Holcomb Hathaway Publishers

Coakley, J.J. (2006). Sport in Society: Issues and Controversies (9th ed.). Boston: McGraw Hill.

Eitzen, D.S. (2006). *Fair and foul: Beyond the myths and paradoxes of sport* (3rd ed.). Lanham, MD: Rowman & Littlefield Publishing Group.

Falcone, D.N. (2005). *Dictionary of American criminal justice, criminology, & criminal law*. Upper Saddle River, NJ: Pearson Prentice Hall.

Fielding, L.W., Pitts, B.G., & Miller, L.K. (1991). Defining quality: Should educators in sport management programs be concerned about accreditation. *Journal of Sport Management, 5*(1), 1–17.

Fuller, J.R. (2006). *Criminal justice mainstream and crosscurrents*. Upper Saddle River, NJ: Pearson Prentice Hall.

Gaines, L.K. & Miller, R.L. (2008) *Criminal justice in action: The core*. Belmont, CA: Thomson Wadsworth.

Inciardi, J. A. (1999). *Criminal justice*. Orlando, FL: Harcourt Brace College Publishers.

Jordan, J.S., & Kent, A. (2005). Management and leadership in the sport industry. In A. Gillentine and R.B. Crow (Eds.). *Foundations of Sport Management* (pp. 35–54). Morgantown, WV: Fitness Information Technology.

Masteralexis, L.P., Barr, C.A., & Hums, M.A. (Eds.). (2004). *Principles and practice of sport management*, (2nd ed.). Sudbury, MA: Jones & Bartlett Publishers.

Neubauer, D.W. (2005). *America's courts and the criminal justice system*. Belmont, CA: Thomson Wadsworth.

Parkhouse, B.L., & Pitts, B.G. (2005). History of sport management. In B.L. Parkhouse (Ed.), *The Management of Sport: It's Foundation and Application* (4th ed.) (pp. 2–14). New York: McGraw-Hill.

Parks, J.B., Quarterman, J., & Thibault, L. (2007). Managing sport in the 21st century. In J.B. Parks, J. Quarterman, & L. Thibault,(Eds.). *Contemporary sport management* (3rd ed.). (pp. 5–26). Champaign, IL: Human Kinetics.

Pitts, B.G. (2001). Sport management at the millennium: A defining moment. *Journal of Sport Management, 15*(1), 1–9.

Pitts, B.G., Fielding, L.W., & Miller, L.K. (1994). Industry segmentation theory and the sport industry: Developing a sport industry segmentation model. *Sport Marketing Quarterly, 3*(1), 15–24.

Pitts, B.G., & Stotlar, D.K. (2002). *Fundamentals of sport marketing*. Morgantown, WV: Fitness Information Technology.

Schmalleger, F. (2009). *Criminal justice today*. Upper Saddle River, NJ: Pearson Prentice Hall.

Sport Management Programs (n.d.). Retrieved on March 30, 2009, from http://www.nassm.com/InfoAbout/SportMgmtPrograms

The Council of Europe (2001). The European Sports Charter (Revised). Retrieved on October 15, 2008, from http://sportdevelopment.org.uk/html/eucharter.html

VanderZwaag, H.J. (1998). *Policy development in sport management* (2nd ed.). Westport, CT: Praeger Publishing.

Weese, W.J. (2002). Opportunities and headaches: Dichotomous perspectives on the current and future hiring realities in the sport management academy. *Journal of Sport Management, 16*(1), 1–17.

Woods, R.B. (2007). *Social issues in sport.* Champaign, IL: Human Kinetics.

Worbleski, H.M. & Hess, K.M. (2003). *Introduction to law enforcement and criminal justice.* Belmont, CA: Thomson Wadsworth.

Part II

Drug Issues

2

Drug Issues in Sport: Steroid Performance-Enhancement

John Miller, Texas Tech University

Introduction

For many who compete in sports, pursuing success or excellence is an ideal to be admired. On a regular basis, the media depicts a present (Tiger Woods) or former (Michael Jordan) athlete as being a "winner" because they are great competitors. Winning, which is the ultimate form of success, is the most visible—and therefore may be considered the most important—goal in sports. As the old saying goes, winning isn't a sometimes thing, it is the only thing. While this quote was directed to professional athletes, it has permeated through other levels of sport competition, including interscholastic sports.

Situations exist in which the pursuit of sport excellence becomes so obsessive that a competitor loses sight of what is fair. This is not a new concept. Seventy years ago, Boje (1939) stated that the pursuit of breaking records as well as the desire to please a demanding public was becoming more important to athletes of the day than their own health. Because of this desire to achieve excellence or success, athletes have looked for avenues to gain an advantage or edge for many years. One way that has been available for athletes to create an advantage has been through the use of performance-enhancing drugs, such as anabolic steroids (Eichner, 1997; Silver, 2001).

Potential Physiological and Psychological Effects of Steroid Use

Testing for drugs has become commonplace at all levels of professional, Olympic, intercollegiate, and interscholastic athletics. Chief among the drugs currently being targeted by tests are anabolic steroids. Anabolic steroids are artificial forms of the male sex hormone that boost metabolism, increase protein production, and contribute to the growth of skeletal muscle (Miller, 2000; National Institute on Drug Abuse [NIDA], 2004).

Despite the fact that steroids can be used positively by the elderly or individuals who have undergone surgery, they can potentially cause irreparable physical and psychological harm in otherwise healthy individuals. Among the most serious physical damages that may occur due to anabolic steroid use include the enlargement of breast tissue in men, shrunken breasts in women, hypertension or heart disease due to the over-retention of fluid in the body, and liver damage (Adler, 2004; Heckman, 2003; Taylor, 2002; U.S. Department of Health & Human Services, 2003). Additionally, the results of a study of 16,000 private and public school students indicated that steroid users, after controlling for age, race/ethnicity, parental educational attainment, urbanicity, and recent exercise, were considerably were more likely to engage in other illicit drug, alcohol, and tobacco use, fighting, suicide attempts, sexual risk taking, vehicular risk taking, and pathogenic weight loss behavior (Miller, Barnes, Sabo, Melnick, & Farrell, 2002).

Research has also indicated that use of anabolic steroids may lead to psychiatric disorders in certain individuals (Malone, Dimeff, Lombardo, & Sample, 1995). Among the best-known psychological harm that may be incurred through steroid use is an increased aggression of the individual, which results in a state referred as steroid rage or "roid rage." The term "roid rage" describes steroid-induced spontaneous, highly aggressive, out-of-control behavior (Lubell, 1989). This is one of the most dangerous risky behaviors associated with steroids because it may put innocent people in danger. Kuipers (1998) indicated that while aggressiveness may be needed for athletic training, it may lead to violent behavior outside of the athletic realm. The violent behavior, Kuipers further asserted, has been equated with those who have taken anabolic steroids. Moreover, research has indicated that an individual with "roid rage" will exhibit such indicators as overconfidence, violence or paranoia (Fish, Goldberg & Spratt, 2004; Franks, 2004). However, staunch supporters against steroid use admit that "roid rage" occurs in less than one percent of steroid users (Yesalis & Cowart, 1998).

An investigation by Pope and Katz (1988) indicated that individuals who became abusers developed manic or depressive tendencies while using or withdrawing from steroids use. Moreover, steroid use may also be linked to experiences of euphoria or enthusiasm, irritability, hyperactivity, paranoia, and insomnia (Freinhar & Alvarez, 1985; Wilson, Prange, & Lara, 1974). Finally, a study by Kashkin and Kleber (1989) concluded that using steroids could be so addictive that they could thoroughly control and ultimately devastate the individuals' private life.

Steroids as a Gateway Drug

Anabolic steroids have many dangerous side effects: increased risk of cancer, infertility, premature cessation of growth, etc. One effect of steroid use that is rarely studied is the role steroids play as a gateway drug. A gateway drug is a drug that, in studies, shows a correlation between its use and the use of other drugs. Kanayama, Pope, Cohane, Hudson (2002) reported that anabolic steroid users displayed much higher rates of other illicit substance use, abuse, or dependence than non-users, with use of other illicit substances almost always preceding first use of steroids.

The use of steroids as a gateway drug seems especially prevalent in adolescents. According to a study by Rufant, Escobedo, and Heath (1995), adolescent steroid use has been associated with such dangerous actions such as drinking, use of other drugs, and tobacco smoking Another study found steroid users to have higher rates of STDs and were more likely to drink and drive or get into a fight than were their non-using peers. In addition, youth often share needles when using steroids, running the risk of contracting HIV or other diseases (Trenhaile, Choi, Proctor, & Work, 1998).

One reason for this dangerous behavior in adolescents could be the feeling of invincibility that comes with young age and steroid use. One study in the *Journal of Psychosomatic Research* lists increased confidence, surges in self-esteem, and a sense of invulnerability as psychological side effects of steroid use (Wroblewska, 1997). This sudden increase in self-esteem and feelings of invulnerability could lead children to take other drugs or be involved in risky behavior without considering the consequences or assuming that the negative effects won't happen to them. This could be especially dangerous because the majority of adolescents taking steroids are involved in sports or are at least somewhat athletic. These teenagers, because of their physical activity, are more likely to have higher levels of testosterone and be more competitive than their peers. These factors only add to the feelings of perceived invincibility and carelessness about the repercussions that the users already feel because of the steroid use.

Many steroid users also turn to other drugs to alleviate the negative effects that the steroids have on their bodies and minds. One of the most dangerous times for anabolic steroid users are the immediate weeks or months after they stop taking steroids (Gavin, 2005). During this time Gavin asserted that users are at risk of exhibiting irritability, paranoia, and severe depression, which may lead to suicidal thoughts or attempted suicide. Additionally, adolescents who use steroids may also be at greater risk for using other drugs, such as alcohol or cocaine (Gavin, 2005).

After stopping steroid use, many prescription drugs are used in large doses to counteract the irritability and depression that comes from the body's withdrawal (Gavin, 2005). Other drugs may be used to fill the void. As alcohol is a depressant, its use only increases the feelings of depression and anxiety. Stimulants such as cocaine and amphetamines are often used in an attempt to break-up these mounting layers of depression. The user then experiences greater feelings of irritability from the stimulants that may cause them to look for other ways to alleviate their suffering (Addiction Intervention Resources, 2007). Anabolic steroids are a gateway drug that can lead to a downward spiral of mounting drug use that is life altering and sometimes deadly for the user.

The theory of anabolic steroids becoming a gateway drug is slowly gaining support. Several studies are making strong arguments that steroids have a noticeable correlation with other drug use. This is a very serious issue that demands further research and could be very helpful in understanding some aspects of illicit drug use and further dangerous side effects of steroid use.

Steroid Use in the Olympic and Other Sports

Olympics

The use of performance-enhancing drugs in the Olympics is not a new trend. Documentation exists suggests some form of performance-enhancing drugs were used during the original Greek Olympic Games in 776 B.C. (Yesalis & Barhke, 2002). More recently, it was reported that the winner of the 1904 Olympic marathon received an injection of the performance-enhancing drug strychnine while the race was occurring (House of Commons, 2004). Francis (1990) reported that some German athletes may have taken anabolic steroids while preparing for the 1936 Olympic Games held in Berlin, Germany.

The first substantiated instance of steroid abuse in sport was at the World Weightlifting Championships in 1954, where the Soviets easily dominated many of the events. During these championships, the United States team physician questioned the Soviet team's doctor about anabolic androgenic steroids (AAS) (Voy, 1991). His Russian counterpart admitted that athletes were given testosterone injections while training for the championships (Fair, 1988). This confession marked the initial declaration of anabolic steroid use to increase athletic performance. However, since no policies or regulations existed regarding the use of such performance-enhancing drugs, the Soviet team incurred no penalties.

Looking to create another option for his team, Dr. John Zeigler, the U.S. team physician, developed a testosterone derivative, Dianabol, which became the most extensively used anabolic steroid ever (Yesalis, Courson, & Wright, 2000). Apparently, word spread about the physical effects of the drugs after early users experienced success, as athletes in such strength-related activities as field events and football started using steroids in the early 1960s (Yesalis, Courson, & Wright, 2000).

In 1968, the use of steroids as performance-enhancers was well known, but rarely addressed. For example, 1968 Mexico City Olympic decathlon winner, Bill Tomey, admitted that he had used them to increase his performance (Scott, 1971). A more startling revelation occurred at the 1971 Pan American games when heavyweight weightlifter, Ken Patera, stated that he wanted to meet the then-current world heavyweight weightlifting record-holder Vasily Alexeyev to "... see which are better, his steroids or mine" (Scott, 1971). The East Germans dominated nearly every worldwide sporting event from the late 1960s until the early 1980s, in part due to the recommendations of the East German chief medical officer to administer steroids to all East German athletes (Haley, 2003).

Professional Football

Steroid use in Olympic sports continued for the next 20 years as athletes such as Ben Johnson in the 1988 Seoul Olympics and Marion Jones in the 2000 Sydney Olympic Games admitted using steroids. However, Olympic athletes have not been alone in trying to develop an "edge." In 1963, Alvin Roy, the first strength coach employed by a professional football team, allegedly provided some San Diego Chargers with Dianabol (Gilbert, 1969). The prevalence of anabolic steroids apparently increased in the 1970s and 1980s as several notable players such as National Football League Hall of Fame member, Howie Long, once estimated that at least half of NFL linemen in the late 1980s used steroids (Zimmerman, 1986). This estimation was substantiated by the NFL drug advisor, who reported that the use of steroids was unbridled during the 1970s and 1980s (Miller, 1996). Ultimately, the death of Lyle Alzado due to complications brought on by steroid use throughout his career spotlighted the dangers of abuse (Kelley, 1991).

Professional Baseball

Professional baseball also has a history with performance-enhancing drugs. In 1998, a front office executive stated that use of anabolic steroids was rampant and thereby changing the nature of the game (Yesalis, Courson, & Wright, 2000). Kevin Towers, longtime general manager of the San Diego Padres, was more vehement in his assessment of steroid use in major league baseball. He perceived that steroids were more common in major league clubhouses than alcohol, tobacco, or any other substance (Yesalis, Courson, & Wright, 2000).

While the accomplishments of some athletes in other sports, such as cycling, gymnastics, and track and field, have been tainted by allegations of steroid use, properly addressing them would be beyond the scope of this chapter. The main theme of this part of the chapter is to provide a short synopsis of steroid use in sports. The next section of this chapter deals with an emerging area of steroid use in youth sports.

Steroid Use in Interscholastic Athletics

Recent media coverage has created a greater awareness of performance-enhancing drugs from the professional athlete's perspective but significantly less so at the amateur or youth levels (Miller & Wendt, 2007). Focusing on whether a professional athlete uses steroids is not a significant societal issue per se (Latiner, 2006). After all, professional athletes should be older and better informed, resulting in a greater capacity to understand the potential health risks related to steroid use and control those risks through their access to the best medical treatment available (Latiner, 2006). However, the prominence that is given to these athletes without any sanctions, legal or otherwise, sends the message that performance-enhancing drugs are accepted, if not essential, to achieve success. This perception was very evident to a young athlete who confessed to his father just prior to committing suicide:

> I'm on steroids, what do you think? Who do you think I am? I'm a baseball player, baseball players take steroids. How do you think Bonds hits all his home runs? How do you think all these guys do all this stuff? You think they do it from just working out normal? (Fainaru-Wada, 2004, p. A1).

Prevalence of High School Steroid Users

There have been a number of reports regarding the prevalence of high school students who have taken steroids. Silver (2001) estimated that 1 to 3 million U.S. athletes have taken steroids. Dr. Linn Goldberg, an expert on steroid abuse among adolescents stated:

> ... in 1993 there was about one user out of 45 kids in high school. That increased to one out of 16 in 2003. In 2005 it backed off a bit to about one out of 20 or so (Justice Talking, 2006).

A 2003 study conducted by the Blue Cross/Blue Shield Association suggested that more than 1 million adolescents between the ages of 12 and 17 had taken potentially dangerous performance-enhancing supplements and drugs (Speier, 2005). Even more striking was that all youths surveyed knew someone using performance-enhancing substances such as steroids (Blue Cross/Blue Shield, 2003). The Centers for Disease Control and Prevention (2004) indicated that illegal steroid use in ninth through twelfth grade students more than doubled from 2.7 percent in 1991 to 6.1 percent in 2003. A study conducted by the American College of Sports Medicine (2003) stated that more than one out of every ten students in the United States would have used steroids by 2010.

The use of steroids in interscholastic athletics was addressed in two recent studies. Miller and Wendt (2007) reported that interscholastic athletic directors in a northern Midwestern state believed that steroid use in interscholastic athletics was rampant throughout the United States. In a different study, 65 percent of athletic directors in three different states suspected that interscholastic athletes, in programs other than their own, had used or were using steroids (Miller, Wendt, & Kern, 2008). Finally, a majority of athletic directors in three different states agreed that testing for steroids should be conducted but the cost was too great (Miller, Wendt, & Seidler, 2008). Results from the same study indicated that nearly 70 percent of the respondents perceived that a combination of education and random drug testing would be the most effective means to reasonably prevent interscholastic athletes from using steroids. Although, these forecasts represent only four states and cannot be generalized to a greater population, they may denote the proverbial "tip of the iceberg" for steroid use in interscholastic sports.

Collins (2006) stated that the "war" on performance-enhancing drugs in sports have been conducted in two areas: drug testing by sport governing bodies and federal and state legislation. The next section will address drug-testing policies and penalties for notable sport organization such as the World Anti-Doping Agency (WADA) and the National Collegiate Athletic Association (NCAA).

World Anti-Doping Agency (WADA)

A majority of international federations introduced drug testing by the 1970s. However, the use of steroids was rampant, particularly in strength-related contests, due to the lack of adequate testing measures. A consistent way to analyze the presence of steroids was instituted in 1974, which was the same year the International Olympic Committee added steroids to its prohibited substance list. A large number of athletes were barred from strength-related events.

After the events of the 1998 Tour de France, sometimes referred to as the Tour of Doping, the International Olympic Committee (IOC) organized a world conference to consider options in the fight against doping in sport. This World Conference on Doping in Sport, produced the Lausanne Declaration on Doping in Sport, which fashioned an independent international anti-doping agency, aiming to have it ready for implementation by the 2000 Sydney Olympics. This independent organization became known as the World Anti-Doping Agency (WADA), the first and only international scientific research program that synchronized advanced detection methods of prohibited drugs in sport.

In 2003, all the members attending the World Conference on Doping adopted the Copenhagen Resolution. These members included the International Olympic Committee (IOC), the International Paralympic Committee (IPC), all Olympic sports, national Olympic and Paralympic committees, athletes, national anti-doping organizations, and international agencies to fight against doping in sport. The Copenhagen Resolution provided for the acceptance of the World Anti-Doping Code.

The World Anti-Doping Code (hereafter referred to as the Code) created the first formalized recognition of rules and responsibilities to counteract doping practices in sport where none may have previously existed. The Code set universal standards to determine whether a substance should be banned from use by considering two of the three following questions:

1. Did the substance enhance performance?
2. Did the substance pose a threat to the health of the athlete?
3. Did taking the substance violate the spirit of the sport?

On the occasions that it was determined that an athlete violated two of these three questions, the Code recognizes minimum and maximum standards. For a first offense, the sanction is two years in which the athlete can do everything but compete, while a second violation assesses a lifetime ban from competition.

Additionally, the Code also affords offenders the ability to decrease or increase the length of assessed penalties. Areas of consideration include the kind of anti-doping breach, the conditions of the individual case (level or absence of fault or negligence), the drug in case of the detection of a prohibited substance, and/or the recurrence of an anti-doping rule violation. In situations that reach litigation of a doping case, the Code employs WADA's right of appeal to the Court of Arbitration for Sport (CAS) on rulings by anti-doping organizations operating under the Code.

National Collegiate Athletic Association (NCAA) Drug Testing Program

The National Collegiate Athletic Association is the largest rule-enforcing agency in intercollegiate athletics. At the 1986 January National Collegiate Athletic Association convention, proposals 30 to 32 initiated a drug-testing program for intercollegiate athletic members. The program requires the collection of urine specimens from an athlete that are then sent to an approved laboratory for analysis. The analysis identifies performance-enhancing or potentially harmful substances. The NCAA recognizes such stimulants as amphetamines and cocaine, anabolic steroids, as well as other substances in banned drug classes (NCAA Drug Testing Program 2007–2008). According to the NCAA Bylaw 18.4.1.5:

> ... a student-athlete who is found to have utilized a substance on the list of banned drug classes, as a result of a drug test administered by the NCAA, shall be declared ineligible for further participation in postseason and regular-season competition during the time period ending one calendar year after the student-athlete's positive drug test (pp. 5–6).

Additionally, if the student-athlete tests positive out-of-season he or she would be charged with the loss of a minimum of one season of competition in the applicable sport. In an effort to offset performance-enhancing drug use, Congress intensified the penalties linked with steroid use beginning with the Anabolic Steroids Act of 1990 to the revised Anabolic Steroids Act of 2004.

Federal Steroid Legislation

Anabolic Steroids Control Act of 1990

The federal government has been aware of the harmful side effects of using steroids for non-medical reasons in young people for several years. In 1990, Congress passed the Anabolic Steroids Control Act (ASCA, 1990). The act positioned steroids on Schedule III of the Controlled Substances Act (the "CSA"). This positioning escalated the penalties for distributing steroids and for possessing steroids with the intent to distribute, as well as criminalizing simple possession of the drug. This act recognized 27 anabolic steroids as controlled substances in the following manner:

> The term "anabolic steroid" means any drug or hormonal substance, chemically and pharmacologically related to testosterone (other than estrogens, progestins, and corticosteroids) that promotes muscle growth, and includes—(i) boldenone, (ii) chlorotestosterone, (iii) clostebol, (iv) dehydrochlormethyltestosterone, (v) dihydrotestosterone, (vi) drostanolone, (vii) ethylestrenol, (viii) fluoxymesterone, (ix) formebulone, (x) mesterolone, (xi) methandienone, (xii) methandranone, (xiii) methandriol, (xiv) methandrostenolone, (xv) methenolone, (xvi) methyltestosterone, (xvii) mibolerone, (xviii) nandrolone, (xix) norethandrolone, (xx) oxandrolone, (xxi) oxymesterone, (xxii) oxymetholone, (xxiii) stanolone, (xxiv) stanozolol, (xxv) testolactone, (xxvi) testosterone, (xxvii) trenbolone, and (xxviii) any salt, ester, or isomer of a drug or substance described or listed in this paragraph, if that salt, ester, or isomer promotes muscle growth. (ASCA, codified at 21 U.S.C. § 812(c) (2000)).

The CSA separated drugs and other controlled substances into five schedules depending on (1) their potential for abuse; (2) their accepted medical uses within the United States; and (3) their potential for psychological or physical addiction (21 USC § 812 (1993)). As a Schedule III drug, the first conviction for the distribution or possession with the intent to distribute steroids allowed for a maximum sentence of five years imprisonment and/or a fine of not more than $250,000. Any successive convictions could carry potential sentences of up to ten years imprisonment and/or a fine of not more than $500,000 (21 USC § 812 (1993)).

In situations in which the receiver of the drug was under the age of 21, the CSA provided that the penalties for the first offense were doubled, with any infractions that followed resulting in the penalties being tripled. Simple possession of steroids could result in a sentence of not more than one-year imprisonment, a fine of at least $1,000, or both. It should be noted that before the act was adopted, the illegal distribution of steroids carried a punishment of not more than three years imprisonment or, if the recipient was a minor under eighteen years old, not more than six years imprisonment (Title II, 1988).

One of the functions of the Anabolic Steroids Control Act of 1990 was to " ... develop and support innovative demonstration programs designed to identify and deter the improper use or abuse of anabolic steroids by students, especially students in secondary schools." (ASCA, § 1906 (codified at 42 U.S.C. § 290aa-6 (2000)). This statement revealed that Congress understood that adolescents are potentially susceptible to the effects of steroid use. However, the House Energy and Commerce Committee chairman stated:

> Steroids have been linked to illness and death for years, particularly among athletes, and these newer, equally harmful substances are not covered by the Anabolic Steroids Control Act of 1990 (U.S. House of Representatives press release, 2004).

The Dietary Supplements Health and Education Act of 1994 (DSHEA)

The Food and Drug Administration (FDA) originally regulated dietary supplements as foods to ensure that they were safe and wholesome and that the labeling was truthful and not misleading. Congress passed and President Clinton signed into law the Dietary Supplements Health and Education Act of 1994 (DSHEA) to insure that consumers have current and accurate information about dietary supplements. The intent of Congress was to meet the concerns of consumers and manufacturers to help ensure that products were safe and appropriately labeled (O'Keefe, 2003).

Many in the dietary supplement industry used this loophole to promote their products, including products containing "steroid precursors" which were being promoted as a "safe" alternative to steroids. Since anabolic steroids are basically very similar in structure, a minute alteration of the molecular arrangement can create a new substance that possesses anabolic properties referred to as steroid precursors. A common steroid precursor is androstenedione or "andro," which is perhaps better known as the substance that former St. Louis baseball slugger Mark McGuire ingested during his career.

According to Powers (2002), the likelihood of negative side effects, such as decreased high-density lipoprotein cholesterol and increased estrogen concentrations, has been linked with precursor use. However, steroid precursors, which are drugs that metabolize into dangerous steroids when ingested, were not covered by ASCA of 1990. While supplements had to meet the requirements of some safety provisions, dietary ingredients used in dietary supplements were no longer subject to the pre-market safety evaluations required of other new food ingredients or for new uses of old food ingredients.

Through this loophole, DSHEA opened the floodgates for the manufacture, distribution, and exchange of steroid precursors (Iwata, 2004). As a result, an amendment was introduced in the Senate to spell out the expanded meaning of steroids and fund research and education regarding steroids and steroid precursors. In a tremendously lopsided result, the Senate voted to enact the Anabolic Steroid Control Act of 2004.

Anabolic Steroid Act of 2004

In the past ten years, the United States Congress heard testimony from major professional sports leagues, union and labor representatives, athletes, the NCAA, medical specialists and other experts. The Anabolic Steroid Act of 2004 was an attempt to "put some muscle" into the federal government's regulations outlawing steroid possession and use. The Anabolic Steroid Control Act of 2004 modified the existing federal anti-steroid statute by adding eighteen drugs to the controlled substances list, thus amplifying the scope of the federal government's regulation of steroids. It attempted to close the loophole created by the DSHEA. It reclassified these precursors from supplements to controlled substances.

Controlled substances are among the most highly regulated under federal law. The Act also required a review of the Federal Sentencing Guidelines for offenses involving steroids. Finally, the Act directed the Secretary of Health and Human Services to award grants to public and nonprofit private entities to carry out education programs in elementary and secondary schools to highlight the harmful effects of anabolic steroids. The amount appropriated to carry out this section is $15 million for each of fiscal years 2005 through 2010. Although custody and distribution of many known steroid derivatives have been criminalized, the success of the Anabolic Steroid Control Act of 2004 in preventing the flow of these harmful substances is vague.

Steroid Legislation Directed to Major Professional Team Sport

None of the previously mentioned pieces of federal legislation specifically addressed steroid use in sport. In part, the rationale was that the courts have traditionally avoided sport-related cases because it has been perceived that interscholastic, intercollegiate and professional sports leagues and associations possess bylaws and standards by which they should be able to legislate themselves. However, as more information about steroid use in professional sports has been revealed, the United States Congress and Senate have begun to institute means that may further curb steroid use. The next sections will identify how the federal government has introduced legislation specifying the means and punishments that face athletes who test positively for steroids.

Drug Free Sports Act and Clean Sports Act 2005

Senator John McCain, and Congressmen Tom Davis and Wendall Waxman announced the introduction of the Clean Sports Act of 2005 (H.R. 2565). In the same year, Representative Cliff Stearns introduced the Drug Free Sports Act (H.R. 1862). In both cases, the legislation was intended to fortify testing procedures and reinforce penalties specific for the use of performance-enhancing drugs in the four major American sports: Major League Baseball, the National Football League, the National Basketball Association and the National Hockey League. The minimum testing requirements for both bills would require every major professional league to institute policies and procedures for the express purpose of testing professional athletes for prohibited substances. Each test would be independently administered and be as stringent as the standards set by the World Anti-Doping Agency (Committee on Government Reform, 2005).

Other similarities of the bills include mandating professional sports leagues to test for the range of performance-enhancing drugs banned in Olympic competition. Secondly, both pieces of legislation would demand all athletes to be tested randomly throughout the year, both in-season and out-of-season, with no prior notification. Finally, the bills would recommend a study on college testing and procedures, and establish a commission on high school and college athletics (Committee on Government Reform, 2005).

While similar in nature, differences are apparent between the bills. For example, the punishment of an athlete testing positively, under the Clean Sports Act, would consist of a two year penalty for a first violation. If an athlete tested positively a second time, a lifetime ban would be enforced (Committee on Government Reform, 2005). Not meeting these criteria in a drug testing program would be treated as a violation of the Federal Trade Commission Act regarding unfair or deceptive practices, although leagues can make exceptions for legitimate medical explanations and therapeutic use. Finally, the refusal to test is also thought of as being a positive under the Clean Sports Act.

Conversely, the Drug Free Act would suspend an athlete from participation in the professional sports association for not less than half of the season for the first violation, a period not less that an entire season of play for a second violation, and permanent suspension from the professional association for further infringements (109th Congress, 2005). While there is some language in this bill regarding legitimate uses of the drug, the Federal Trade Commission offenses are not mentioned. Finally, there are no consequences highlighted if the individual refuses to participate in the testing procedure.

Concerns about the Drug Free Sports Act and Clean Sports Act

Although, previous federal legislation provided policies and penalties for those who used, distributed or abused steroids in the general public, legislation such as Drug Free Sports Act and Clean Sports Act targeted professional sports for the first time. The introduction and ultimate passage of these pieces were the result of senators and congressmen opining that administrators of the professional leagues have not moved quickly enough in adopting stiffer penalties for steroid use.

However, the passage of these bills raised concerns that have been voiced by members of the media and sport fans who ask where the line would be drawn regarding what Congress can and cannot regulate. To counteract overregulation, many individuals indicated that the professional leagues should be allowed to set drug testing and penalty procedures through a collective bargaining agreement.

During collective bargaining negotiations, representatives of the league and players union for each sport meet to set the rules for that sport, including rules about steroid penalties. For example, in the 2006 National Football League collective bargaining agreement, the drug and steroid policy stated:

> No Club may impose any discipline against a player, including but not limited to terminating the player's Player Contract, as a result of that Player's violation of the Policy on Anabolic Steroids and Related Substances or the NFL Policy and Program for Substances of Abuse, or for failing any drug test, provided, however, that the fact that a player has violated the Policy on Anabolic Steroids and Related Substances or the NFL Policy and Program

**Table 2.1 Comparing Steroid Policies in Various
Professional Sports and Olympics**

League or Association	1st test	2nd test	3rd test	4th test	5th test
Major League Baseball	50 games	100 games	*Lifetime ban		
Minor League Baseball	15 games	30 games	60 games	1 year	Lifetime ban
National Football League	4-game minimum	6-game minimum	1-year minimum	1-year minimum	1-year minimum
National Basketball Association	5 games	10 games	25 games	25 games	25 games
National Hockey League	No testing				
Olympics	2 years	Lifetime ban			

* —subject has the right to seek reinstatement after two years of suspension, with arbitral review of reinstatement decision. Source: ESPN.com news services

for Substances of Abuse, or has failed a drug test will not preclude the termination of his Player Contract if such termination is otherwise expressly permissible under this Agreement or the player's Player Contract (Collective Bargaining Agreement, p. 12).

The result of collective bargaining agreements may be viewed in Table 2.1 comparing the penalties for each of the professional sports leagues in North America and the Olympics, showing some of the discrepancies as of 2005. Of particular note is the National Hockey League, which is the only professional sport in North America that does not possess any policies to penalize players testing positive for performance-enhancing substances (Comparing the steroid policies, 2005).

Intercollegiate, professional, and Olympic sports possess specific programs and procedures which address steroid use. However, despite the previously discussed prevalence of steroid use among interscholastic athletes, a national unifying, regulation-enforcing interscholastic athletic organization does not presently exist. Although the National Federation of State High School Associations (NFHS) promotes position statements against steroid use in interscholastic sports, it does not possess the regulatory authority to require high schools to follow them. As such, several states have instituted legislation in an attempt to sway high school students away from using steroids.

State Steroid Legislation for Interscholastic Athletics

Previous literature has advanced the notion that society looks to protect its young people and deter drug use through drug testing policies (Martin, 1997). In response to testing athletes for steroids a Michigan legislator stated, "Is it a problem right now? I think we're naive to think that it's not, with the competitive nature of sports, especially among the kids who want to go on to the next level" (States consider high school steroid testing, 2005). It has been reported that 13 percent of high schools test for drugs nationally, but less than one-third of those schools test for steroids (National Federation of State High School Associations, 2003). Despite this traditional practice, some states (New Jersey, Florida and Texas) and counties (Polk County, Florida) have enacted legislation requiring interscholastic athletes to submit to steroid testing since 2005 (Moore, 2005).

New Jersey was the first state to implement drug testing for steroids on the high school level at an estimated cost of $100,000 (Lawlor, 2006). In December, 2005, acting Governor Richard Codey by Executive Order directed the New Jersey Department of Education to work with the New Jersey Interscholastic Athletic Association (NJSIAA)

> ... to develop and implement a program of random testing for steroids of teams and individuals qualifying for championship games to commence with the 2006–2007 school year (State of New Jersey, 2005).

Under the NJSIAA plan, the high school league randomly tested approximately 500 student athletes that qualified for state championship tournaments or competition, primarily in football, wrestling, baseball, track and field, swimming and diving, and lacrosse (NJSIAA Steroid FAQ, 2007). It is interesting that NJSIAA mandated that no student may participate in NJSIAA competition unless the student and their parent/guardian signed a random testing consent form. The consent form stipulated that if the student or the student's team qualified for a state tournament, the participant may be subject to testing for banned substances (NJSIAA Policy, 2007). If a student-athlete tests positive for steroid use, the penalty for such an offense is a one year suspension.

In 2007, the Florida State Legislature allocated $100,000 for testing and ordered the Florida High School Athletic Association (FHSAA) to facilitate a one year anabolic steroid testing program (2007–2008) for students in grades 9 through 12 who participate in boys' football, girls' flag football, girls' softball, boys' baseball, or boys' and girls' weightlifting (Florida Statutes, 2007). State Representative Marcelo Llorente, the bill's sponsor, said that those sports were chosen because they are sports where muscle mass most enhances performance (Kallestad, 2005).

Under the Florida plan each student-athlete who participated in the identified sports were required to sign a consent form (FHSAA Consent Form, 2007). It was estimated that 59,000 Florida high school students who participated in one of the three sports would be affected and be required to submit to random drug tests under the bill (Bender, 2007). If a student-athlete tested positive for steroids, a 90-day suspension penalty would be assessed.

Texas has perhaps the most ambitious plan. The state legislature allocated an estimated $3 million to implement high school steroid testing policies and procedures. As a result, the Texas University Interscholastic League (UIL), which governs interscholastic athletics, plans to test a minimum of 3 percent of the approximately 740,000 student athletes who participate in UIL athletic activities annually. To put this number into perspective, the three percent represents 22,000 high school students, which is more than those tested in the NCAA and Olympics combined in 2004 (International Herald Tribune, 2007).

Under the Texas program, each student and their parent/guardian agrees that as a prerequisite to participation in UIL athletic activities, they will, if selected, submit to steroid testing. As opposed to the three-month suspension that a Florida athlete who tests positive would have to serve, the consequences in Texas are more severe. For example, the punishment for the first time an athlete tests positive for steroids is a 30-day suspension. If that same student-athlete tests positive a second time, a one-year ban is assessed. Finally, a third time offender will be banned from any type of competition for the remainder of his/her career.

With all of the concern surrounding who might be taking steroids in interscholastic athletics, the concepts of reasonable suspicion and right to privacy must be discussed. Reasonable suspicion may be regarded as the degree of knowledge that would cause a reasonable person, under similar circumstances, to believe a student-athlete is involved in using or abusing a banned substance. A recent study indicated that a majority of interscholastic athletic directors suspected that student-athletes, in programs other than their own, of taking steroids (Miller, Wendt, & Kern, in press). In such cases an athletic director, athletic trainer, or coach may request a drug test. As a result, school officials need only have reasonable suspicion that a particular test will verify that a student-athlete has violated or is violating the law (Shulter, 1996; Yamaguchi, O'Malley, & Johnston, 2004; Zirkel, 2000).

Although reasonable suspicion may be present, the scope of the search must be such that the measures used are reasonably related to the purpose of the search and not excessively intrusive in light of the age and gender of the student and the nature of the suspected infraction for the search to be permissible. The *New Jersey v. T.L.O.* (1985) court stated:

> A school official may properly conduct a search of a student's person if the official has a reasonable suspicion that a crime has been or is in the process of being committed or reasonable cause to believe that the search is necessary to maintain school discipline or enforce school policies (*New Jersey v. T.L.O.*, p. 329, 1985).

In *Schaill v. Tippecanoe County School Corporation* (1988), the court held that the school's interest in protecting the health, safety, and integrity of the sport and school outweighed an athlete's diminished expectations of privacy. In *Schaill*, the school board chose to employ a random drug-testing program for all extracurricular participants, including interscholastic athletes and cheerleaders. The court judged the drug testing policy reasonable because it was commonly conducted in intercollegiate athletics and Olympic sports. Moreover, the students had previously consented to the testing procedure.

Drug testing of a student by a public school official is a search that must adhere to the stipulations of the Fourth Amendment that prohibits all unreasonable searches and seizures by state officers. Reasonableness is determined by balancing the governmental interest behind the search against the privacy intrusion of the search. Generally, courts have ruled that drug testing for athletic teams is allowed due to a diminished expectation of privacy of a student-athlete. For example, it is not uncommon for student-athletes to disrobe in front of others or use communal showers after a practice or game. Because these are normal practices, the courts have reported that those who choose to participate in interscholastic sports have a diminished expectation of privacy (Knapp, 1990).

The court in *Vernonia v. Acton* (1995) indicated that urine collection and testing compromised a search. To determine the constitutionality of searches, three steps are required. The first aspect to be considered is whether a search and seizure was conducted by a government entity. The second step needs to determine if the officials have the power to conduct the search. The third piece addresses whether the search was reasonable, depending upon the type of search.

In shaping the idea of reasonableness in searching high school students the Supreme Court stated that:

> The legality of a search of a student should depend simply on the reasonableness, under all the circumstances, of the search. Determining the reasonableness of any search involves a twofold inquiry: first, one must consider whether the action was justified at its inception, second, one must determine whether the search as actually conducted was reasonably related in scope to the circumstances which justified the interference in the first place. Under ordinary circumstances, a search of a student by a teacher or other school official will be justified at its inception when there are reasonable grounds for suspecting that the search will turn up evidence that the student has violated or is violating either the law or the rules of the school (*New Jersey v. T.L.O.*, 1985, p. 341).

While upholding the drug testing policy in Vernonia (1995), the Supreme Court balanced the school's interest in conducting the drug test against the privacy interest upon which the test intrudes. In the Court's opinion, safety risks were especially great in sports:

> ... it must not be lost sight of that this program is directed more narrowly to drug use by school athletes, where the risk of immediate physical harm to the drug user or those with whom he is playing his sport is particularly high. Apart from psychological effects, which include impairment of judgment, slow reaction time, and a lessening of the perception of pain, the particular drugs screened by the District's Policy have been demonstrated to pose substantial physical risks to athletes (p. 661).

Finally, the *Board of Education v. Earls* (2002) permitted urinalysis drug testing for all high school extracurricular participants. By doing so, the *Earls* decision expanded the scope identified in *Vernonia* by permitting a school district to test high school students with less of a foundation.

Conclusion

Sport at the most basic level depends on competition based on a level playing field and mutual respect. Yet, throughout history, many sport participants have used performance-enhancing drugs, such as steroids, to tilt the playing field to their favor. Apparently, not much has changed in recent times as reports have indicated that coaches, trainers, and even governments traditionally, have done little to curb the use of performance-enhancing drugs by athletes (Dubin, 1990; National Center on Addiction and Substance Abuse, 2000; Yesalis & Cowart, 1998). Even the Mitchell report (2007) stated that the trainer for a number of well-known professional baseball players knowingly injected them with steroids.

As Boje stated in 1939, a significant reason for the ingestion of performance-enhancing drugs may very well be the pressures associated with succeeding in the athletic arena. In today's society, the expectation to win is paramount in the minds of the fans, coaches, owners, as well as the athletes. Collins (2006) mentioned that the use of steroids in the sports realm may not be so much of a drug crisis as an ethical one:

> We need to ask the tough questions about what drives the "winning at all costs" attitude. To what extent has cheating become more acceptable in sports and in our society at large? To what extent does the failure of our public schools to teach morality play a part? To what extent are the economic factors and pressures success, inherent in the increasing commercialization of college sports, a culprit? Are cheating athletes so different in society who have lost their moral compass when faced with pressure or temptation? (p. 762).

Interestingly, it appears that, to a large extent, it is the health danger of taking steroids that mobilized several states to introduce legislation designed to curb steroid use in athletics. Conversely, the main point of concern in Olympic, professional, and intercollegiate athletics has been more of the ethical considerations that have been highlighted. Regardless, performance-enhancing drugs, at all levels of athletic competition, have become the new battlegrounds " . . . to redirect sport back to its competitive roots without the influence of unfair advantages and victory without honor" (McLaren, 2001, p. 380). Dick Pound, chairman of the World Anti-Doping Agency and former vice-president of the International Olympic Committee reported that any society or activity put together by a series of rules will tempt some members to cheat (Pound, 2004). According to the American Academy of Pediatrics (2005), steroid use in sports is not only a form of cheating; it is dangerous to an individual's health and safety. To that end, Congress, as well as some states, has enacted legislation that would exact penalties on athletes testing positively for steroids. However, previous studies have shown that assessing legal consequences does not impact a person taking performance-enhancing drugs, such as steroids (American Academy of Pediatrics, 2005).

So what needs to be done to most effectively attempt to curb the use of steroids in sport? A strongly supported answer may be educating athletes, especially young ones, about the potential physical, psychological, and practical ramifications of taking steroids. Several authors have stated that drug education programs that are particularly aimed at adolescent athletes possess a greater likelihood for behavioral change as well as being more cost-effective than increasing the number of drug testing programs (Bahrke & Yesalis; 2002; Miller, Wendt, & Seidler, 2008). A model such as the Adolescents Training and Learning to Avoid Steroids program (ATLAS), which uses the help of peers, family, coaches, media and sports figures to discourage the use of steroids (Goldberg, Elliot, Clarke, MacKinnon, Moe, Zoref, Green, Wolf, Gefferath, Miller, & Lapin, 1996), may be considered for more widespread use. It is hoped that the young athlete would be armed through proper educational processes with the knowledge to make well-informed choices.

References

Addiction Intervention Resources. (2007). Retrieved on January 6, 2008, from http://www.addictionintervention.com/addiction/steroids.asp

Adler J. (December 20, 2004). Toxic strength. *Newsweek*, 44–52.

American Academy of Pediatrics. (April, 2005). Use of performance-enhancing substances policy statement. *Pediatrics, 115*(4), pp. 1103–1106.

American College of Sports Medicine. (2003). *The use of anabolic-androgenic steroids in sports*. Retrieved December 5, 2007, from http://www.acsm.org/publications/newsreleases2004/steroids071404.htm

Anabolic Steroid Control Act of 2004. Retrieve on May 28, 2008, from http://www.theorator.com/bills108/hr3866.html

Anabolic Steroids Control Act of 1990, Pub. L. No. 101-647, 104 Stat. 4851, 4851–54 (1990) (codified as amended at 21 U.S.C. §§ 333, 333a, 801 nt., 802, 802 nt., 829 nt., 844 and 42 U.S.C. § 290aa-6 (2000)).

Are steroids worth the risk? (n.d.). Kidshealth.org. Retrieved on November 4, 2007, from http://kidshealth.org/teen/food_fitness/sports/steroids.html

Bahrke, M. S., & Yesalis, C. E. (November, 2002). The future of performance-enhancing substances in sport. The *Physician and Sportsmedicine, 30*(11), 51–53.

Blue Cross/Blue Shield. (2003). Blue Cross/Blue Shield says 1.1 million teens have used performance enhancing sports supplements and drugs. Retrieved on September 24, 2007, from http://www.supplementquality.com/news/ephedra _teens_BCBS.html

Board of Education v. Earls, 2002 U.S. LEXIS 4882.

Boje, O. (1939). Doping. Bulletin of the Health Organization of the League of Nations, 8, 439–469.

Centers for Disease Control and Prevention. (May 2004). National youth risk behavior survey: 1991–2003. Morbidity and Mortality Weekly Report. Retrieved on October 25, 2007, from http:www.cdc.gov/mmwr/PDF/SS/SS5302.pdf

Collective bargaining agreement between the NFL management council and the players association. (March, 2006). Retrieved on January 4, 2008, from http://www.nflpa.org/pdfs/Agents/CBA_Amended_2006.pdf

Collins, R. (Spring, 2006). Changing the game: The Congressional response to sports doping via the Anabolic Steroid Control Act. *New England Law Review, 40*, 753–763.

Committee on Government Reform (2005). Fact sheet bill comparison: The Clean Sports Act (H.R. 2565) and the Drug-Free Sports Act (H.R. 1862). Retrieved on January 12, 2008 from http://oversight.house.gov/documents/20050526103452-64714.pdf

Congressman Tom Davis News Release. Retrieved on December 21, 2007, from http://tomdavis.house.gov/cgidata/news/files/186.shtml

Dietary Supplement Health and Education Act of 1994, Public Law No. 103-417, Stat. 4325 (1994).

Dubin, C. (1990). *Commission of inquiry into the use of drugs and banned practices intended to increase athletic performance*. Ottawa, ON: Canadian Government Publishing Centre.

Eichner, R.E. (1997). Ergogenic aids: What athletes are using—and why. *The Physician and Sportsmedicine, 25*(4). Retrieved on September 10, 2008, from http://www.physsportsmed.com/issues/1997/04apr/eichner.htm

ESPN.com news services. *Comparing the steroid policies*. Retrieved on January 8, 2008, from http://sports.espn.go.com/mlb/news/story?id=1966196

Fainaru-Wada, M. (December 19, 2004). Dreams, steroids, death: A ballplayer's downfall. *San Francisco Chronicle*, A1.

Fair, J. (1988). Olympic weightlifting and the introduction of steroids: A statistical analysis of world championship results—1948–1972. *International Journal of the History of Sport, 5*, 96–114.

Fish, L., Goldberg, L., & Spratt, D. (2004). Anabolic steroids and young adults. *The Journal of Clinical Endocrinology & Metabolism, 89*(8). Retrieved on January 10, 2008, from http://jcem.endojournals.org/cgi/content/full/89/8/0

Florida High School Athletic Association. (2007). Consent of member school to participate in random testing of student-athletes in grades 9–12 for use of anabolic steroids. Retrieved on December 3, 2007, from http://www.fhsaa.org/compliance/steroid_testing/drug_school_consent_form.pdf

Florida Statutes. (2007). *1006.20 athletics in public K–12 schools*. Retrieved on December 3, 2007, from http://www.leg.state.fl.us/statutes/index.cfm?App_mode=Display_Statute&URL=Ch1006/ch1006.htm

Francis, C. (1990). *Speed trap*. New York: St. Martin's Press.

Franks, R.R. (Summer, 2004). Power hungry: Student athletes and their growing use of performance enhancement drugs. *NJO Journal*, pp. 14–17.

Freinhar, J.P., & Alvarez, W. (1985). Androgen-induced hypomania. *Journal of Clinical Psychiatry, 46*, 354.

Gavin, M.L. (2005). *Steroids*. Retrieved on January 5, 2008 from http://www.kidshealth.org/kid/exercise/safety/steroids.html

Gilbert, B. (June 23, 1969). Drugs in sport: Part 1. Problems in a turned-on world. *Sports Illustrated*, 64–72.

Goldberg, L., Elliot, D., Clarke, G.N., MacKinnon, D.P., Moe, E., Zoref, L., Green, C., Wolf, S.L., Greffath, E., Miller, D.J., & Lapin, A. (1996). Effects of a multidimensional anabolic steroid prevention intervention: The adolescents training and learning to avoid steroids (ATLAS) program. *Journal of the American Medical Association, 276*, 1555–1562.

Haley, J. (2003). Introduction. In J. Haley (Ed.) *Performance-enhancing drugs* (pp. 7–10). San Diego: Greenhaven.

Heckman, D. (2003). The evolution of drug testing of interscholastic athletes. *Villanova Sports & Entertainment Law Journal, 9*, 209–228.

House of Commons, Select Committee on Culture, Media and Sport. (2004). *Seventh Report of Session 2003–2004*, UK Parliament, HC 499-I.

International Herald Tribune. (2007). *Doping: China cracking down on the drug industry.* Retrieved on December 3, 2007, from http://www.iht.com/articles/2007/11/08/sports/DRUGS.php#end_main

Iwata, E. (December 21, 2004). Sales up as andro ban nears, *U.S.A. TODAY.* Retrieved on January 18, 2006 from http://www.usatoday.com/news/health/2004-12-21-andro-law-sales_x.htm

Justice Talking Radio Transcript. (August 21, 2006). *Does drug testing student athletes deter drug use?* Retrieved on November 1, 2007 from http://www.justicetalking.org/transcripts/060821_drugsstudents_transcript.pdf

Kallestad, B. (2005). *Steroid cleanup takes aim at teens.* Retrieved October 23, 2007, from http://www.washtimes.com/national/20050425-122712-5045r.htm

Kanayama, G., Pope, H.G., Jr., Cohane, G., & Hudson, J.I. (2003). Risk factors for anabolic androgenic steroid use among weightlifters: A case-control study. *Drug & Alcohol Dependence, 71,* 77–86.

Kashkin, K.B., & Kleber, H.D. (1989). Hooked on hormones? An anabolic steroid addiction hypothesis. *Journal of the American Medical Association, 262,* 3166–3170.

Kelley, S. (July 10, 1991). This chapter of Alzado's life is sad. *Seattle Times.*

Knapp, C. F. (1990). Drug-testing and the student-athlete: Meeting the constitutional challenge. *Iowa Law Review, 76,* 107–137.

Kuipers, H. (1998, March 7). Anabolic steroids: Side effects. *Encyclopedia of Sports Medicine and Science* [Online Serial]. Retrieved on November 5, 2007, from http://www.sportssci.org/steroids.html

Latiner, C. (Summer, 2006). Steroids and drug enhancement in sports: The real problem and the real solution. *DePaul Journal of Sports Law & Contemporary Problems, 3,* 192–219.

Lubell, A. (1989). Does steroid abuse cause — or excuse — violence? *The Physician and Sportsmedicine, 17*(2), 176–185.

Malone, D.A., Dimeff, R.J., Lombardo, J.A., and Sample, R. H., (1995). Psychiatric effects and psychoactive substance use in anabolic-androgenic steroid users. *Clinical Journal of Sport Medicine, 5*(1), 25–31.

Martin, J.C. (1997). Drug testing all students: The wrong answer to a difficult question. *Kansas Journal of Law and Public Policy, 6,* 123–140.

McLaren, R.M. (Spring, 2001). The court of arbitration for sport: An independent arena for the world's sports disputes. *Valparaiso University Law Review, 35,* 379–405.

Miller, A. (May 3, 1996). Reports of steroid use down, but abuse, not over, some say. *Atlanta Journal/Atlanta Constitution,* G4.

Miller, B.F. (2000). *Miller-Keane medical dictionary.* Philadelphia: WB Saunders Company.

Miller, J. & Wendt, J. (2007). Interscholastic athletic director's perceptions of steroid use: A state study. *Journal of Contemporary Athletics, 2*(3), 207–224.

Miller, J., Wendt, J.T., & Kern, S. (2008). Steroid use in interscholastic athletics: Is there reasonable suspicion? *Journal of Contemporary Athletics, 3*(2), 111–128.

Miller, J., Wendt, J.T., & Seidler, T. (April, 2008). Tackling steroid abuse in inter-scholastic athletics: Perceptions of athletic directors. *International Journal of Sport Management, 9*(2), 117–133.

Miller, K.E., Barnes, G.M., Sabo, D.F., Melnick, M.J., & Farrell, M.P. (Winter, 2002). Anabolic-androgenic steroid use and other adolescent problem behaviors: Rethinking the male athlete assumption. *Sociological Perspectives, 45*(4), 467–489.

Moore, D.L. (May, 2005). As steroid use doubles, a school fights back. How one high school is educating coaches and students is at the heart of a policy California might adopt this week, *U.S.A. Today*, 1A.

National Center on Addiction and Substance Abuse. (2000). *Winning at any cost: Doping in Olympic sports.* New York: National Center on Addiction and Substance Abuse.

National Institute on Drug Abuse. (2004). *Research report series—Anabolic steroid abuse 1.* Retrieved October 4, 2007 from http://www.nida.nih.gov/PDF/RRSteroi.pdf

NCAA Drug Testing Program 2007–2008. Retrieved on January 8, 2008, from http://209.85.173.104/search?q=cache:5rhJNCtKngIJ:www.ncaa.org/library/sports _sciences/drug_testing_program/2007-08/2007-08_drug_testing_program.pdf+ NCAA+Drug+Testing+Program+2007-2008&hl=en&ct=clnk&cd=2&gl=us

New Jersey State Interscholastic Athletic Association. (2007). *NYJSIAA steroid testing policy: Frequently asked questions.* Retrieved December 3, 2007, from http://www.njsiaa.org/NJSIAA/Steroid-FAQ.pdf

New Jersey v. T.L.O., 469 U.S. 325, 338 (1985).

O'Keeffe, M. (December 13, 2003). The straight dope: DSHEA opened door to scandals. *New York Daily News.* Retrieved on December 5, 2007, from http://pqasb.pqarchiver.com/nydailynews

Pope, H.G., & Katz, D.L. (1988). Affective and psychotic symptoms associated with anabolic steroid use. *American Journal of Psychiatry, 145*, 487.

Pope, H.G, Kouri, E.M, & Hudson, J.I. (2000). Effects of supraphysilogic doses of testosterone on mood and aggression in normal men: A randomized controlled trial. *Archways of General Pyschiatry, 57*(2), 133–140.

Pound, R. W. (2006). *Inside dope: How drugs are the biggest threat to sports, why you should care, and can be done about them* (Mississauga, Ontario [Canada]: John Wiley & Sons Canada, Ltd.

Powers, M. (2002, July–September). The safety and efficacy of anabolic steroid precursors: What is the scientific evidence? *Journal of Athletic Training, 37*(3), 300–305.

Rosenthal, K. (1998). *Steroids: Baseball darkest secrets.* MSNBC on the Internet.

Rufant, R.H., Escobedo, L.G., & Heath, G.W. (1995). Anabolic-steroid use, strength training, and multiple drug use among adolescents in the United States. Pediatrics, 96(1), 23–28.

Schaill v. Tippecanoe County School Corporation, 864 F.2d 1309 (7th Cir. 1988).

Scott, J. (October 17, 1971). It's not how you play the game, but what pill will you take. *New York Times Magazine.*

Silver, M. (2001). Use of ergogenic aids by athletes. *Journal of the American Academy of Orthopedic Surgery, 9,* 61–70.

Speier, B. (April 6, 2005). Senate health committee analysis — Steroids and performance-enhancing dietary supplements. Retrieved November 22, 2007, from http://info.sen.ca.gov/pub/bill/sen/sb_00010050/sb_37_cfa_ 20050404 _164929_sen_comm.html

State of New Jersey. (2005). *Executive order #72, acting Governor Richard J. Codey.* Retrieved December 3, 2007, from http://www.state.nj.us/infobank/ circular/eoc72.htm

States consider high school steroid testing. (2005). Retrieved September 21, 2007, from http://www.msnbc.msn.com/id/7628183/

Taylor, W.N. (2002). *Anabolic steroids and the athlete* (2nd ed.). Jefferson, NC: McFarland and Co.

Title II, § 2401, Pub L No 100-690, 102 Stat 4230 (1988), codified at 21 USC § 333(e) (1988).

Trenhaile, J., Choi, H.S., Proctor, T.B., & Work, P.B. (1998). The effect of ana-bolic steroid education in knowledge and attitudes of at-risk preadolescents. Journal of Alcohol & Drug Education, 43(2), 20–35.

U.S. Department of Health and Human Services. (October 28, 2003). *Statement on THG.* Retrieved on November 18, 2007, from http://www.fda.gov/bbs/ topics/NEWS/2003/NEW00967.html

Wilson, I.C., Prange, A.J., Jr., Lara, P.P. (January, 1974). Methyltestosterone with imipramine in men: Conversion of depression to paranoid reaction. *American Journal of Psychiatry, 131*(1), 21–24.

Wroblewska, A.M. (1997). Androgenic-anabolic steroids and body dysmorphia in young men. *Journal of Psychosomatic Research, 42*(3), 225–234.

Vernonia School District 47J v. Acton, 515 U.S. 646, 115 S. Ct. 2386, 132 L. Ed. 2d 564, 1995 U.S. LEXIS 4275, 63 U.S.L.W. 4653, 9 Fla. L. Weekly Fed. S 229, 95 Cal. Daily Op. Service 4846 (1995).

Voy, R. (1991). *Drugs, sport, and politics.* Champaign: Human Kinetics.

Yamaguchi, R., O'Malley, P.M., Johnston, L.D. (2004). Relationships between school drug searches and student substance use in U.S. schools. *Educational Evaluation and Policy Analysis, 26*(4), 329–341.

Yesalis, C.E., & Barhke, M.S. (2002). History of doping in sport. In M.S. Barhke and Yesalis, C.E. (Eds.), *Performance-enhancing substances in sport and exer-cise* (pp. 1–20). Champaign, IL: Human Kinetics.

Yesalis, C.E., Courson, S.P., & Wright, J.E. (2000). History of anabolic steroid use in sport and exercise. In C.E. Yesalis (Ed.)(2nd ed.), *Anabolic steroids in sport and exercise* (pp. 51–71). Champaign, IL: Human Kinetics.

Yesalis, C.E., & Cowart, V.S. (1998). *The steroids game.* Champaign, IL: Human Kinetics.

Zimmerman, P. (November 10, 1986). The agony must end. *Sports Illustrated,* 17–21

Zirkel, P. (2000). Suspicionless searches. *Principal, 79,* 57–61.

3

Alcohol Related Crime in Sport

Andy Gillentine, University of Miami

The acrid smell of smoke still lingered in the early morning hours. As the sun rose on Nov. 23, 2002, it cast an eerie light through the smoke from the smoldering fires. The flashing lights of scattered emergency vehicles added to the surreal surroundings. Among the overturned cars and burned out couches, a few people wandered aimlessly, some from shock and disbelief others out of curiosity. Water stood in the streets, residue from attempts to put out the purposely lit fires as well as to disburse the crowds. Amid the carnage you could hear an occasional shout, but not calling for help but one of celebration of the events that had sparked this war-like and chaotic scene ... Ohio State had beaten Michigan.

Introduction

The sport industry has grown at an often dizzying pace over the last quarter century. Sport economic experts have stated that the global economic impact of sport may be too great to accurately measure. In the United Stated alone, conservative estimates indicate that the sport industry generates in excess of $200 billion annually ("The Sport Industry," 2007). Through this economic impact, sport has established itself as a major force in the entertainment and leisure industries. As such, the consumption of the sport product and its ancillaries are now at all-time highs. Stadium and arena expansions and construction are frequent topics in the news media as sport organizations attempt to meet the increasing demand for their product(s). In continued efforts to expand potential revenue streams, the sport product has entwined itself in a variety of ancillary activities. While this rapid growth has spawned the growth of many new and exciting facets in the sport industry, it has not come without its drawbacks.

A consistent focal point of sport consumption has been its role as a catalyst for social gatherings. These gatherings occur in a variety of settings, from on-site formal gatherings to elaborate parties hosted both in private homes and in businesses. One consistent factor involved with the consumption of the sport product has been the consumption of alcohol.

Historical Relationship Between Alcohol and Sport Consumption

The relationship between alcohol consumption and sport can be documented throughout the history of mankind. Historical documents frequently describe the consumption of wine and other alcoholic beverages by spectators (and often participants) while in attendance at a sporting event (Collins & Vamplew, 2002). In the United States, the origins of this relationship can be found in the taverns that developed in the colonial period (1607–1776) and then flourished during the 19th century (Davies, 2007; Rader, 2004). The growth of taverns as a gathering place for relaxation and recreation coincided with the continued growth of a diverse cultural population base and the development of division of labor (industry) in the United States. As more amenities were available to inhabitants through sale and trade, Americans found themselves with increased amounts of leisure time. Many searched for diversions from their taxing daily work by frequenting taverns for entertainment and alcohol. Taverns were often located outside of the town or city limits to avoid the scrutiny of any disapproving members of the citizenry. These remote locations placed the taverns in areas surrounded by large plots of undeveloped land. The availability of this property lent itself to the establishment of contests that tavern owners could utilize as a means of attracting customers. While competitive card games and darts were played inside the tavern, outside events, particularly horseracing (and related gambling), grew around the taverns. The races and games were part of an emerging drinking culture, and soon the consumption of alcohol and sport became closely associated (Struna, 1996).

The growth of this relationship continued through the following century. During the 1800s, the consumption of alcohol and sport expanded from the common tavern to the exclusive Fishing and Yachting Clubs. This development added an air of acceptance to both the consumption of alcohol and sport as a "proper pastime" for those of higher economic and societal status (Peverely, 1866). It was also during the 19th century that America saw the growth of both professional boxing and the beginnings of professional baseball. Each of these sporting events further expanded the bond between alcohol and sport. Sport promoters quickly recognized these sports could be used as a means for selling large quantities of alcohol and, inversely, the availability of alcohol attracted more spectators to their events (Gorn, 1986; Rader, 2004). Additionally, these sports were also attractive to people of all socio-economic classes, which led to their rapid expansion and acceptance. As the sports became more of an accepted component of American culture, so did the related consumption of alcohol. Another factor related to both the consumption of alcohol and sport is the prevalence and acceptance of gambling as a part of the sporting experience.

The Prohibition Era (1920–1933)

The prohibition era unwittingly solidified the connection between alcohol consumption and sport through its ban of the manufacture and sale of alcoholic beverages. The impact of this legislation fostered the growth of an underworld that

took advantage of Americans desire to consume alcohol and to enjoy gaming activities. As in the colonial period, drinking establishments, know as speakeasies,
were established outside of the direct view of local authorities. The speakeasies
served as gathering spots for a variety of economic classes who shared the same
desire to consume alcohol. While many of these speakeasies offered games of
chance such as cards and dice, others resumed the age-old practice of gambling on
horse races to entice customers to spend more time and, consequently, more
money. A dramatic difference between the speakeasies and the taverns of colonial
times were the illegal implications of the activities. The 18th Amendment to the
U.S. Constitution, also known as the Volstead Act, made it illegal not only to sell
alcohol but also to manufacture it. This forced speakeasy operators and their consumers to adopt illegal practices to acquire alcohol. The bulk of illegal manufac-
turing, importing, and distribution of alcohol became the business of criminal organizations. The introduction of organized crime syndicates into this diverse
cultural and economic segment of the population created a sense of "acceptable
illegal behavior" by thousands of previously law-abiding citizens. The consumption of this illegal alcohol and the prevalence of its related behaviors became so
widespread that enforcement of the law became problematic. The inconsistencies
regarding the enforcement of the prohibition statutes contributed to a climate
that legitimizes inappropriate (and illegal) activities. Psychologists have often utilized Social Cognitive Theory in an attempt to explain how individuals who are
engaged in aberrant behavior justify their activities (Bandura, 1990; Bandura,
Barbaranelli, Caprara, & Pastorelli, 1996). Simply stated, this theory indicates
that once a person is comfortable with his or her actions, legal or illegal, it becomes easier for that person to justify in their minds other illegal (or unacceptable) behaviors. The application of this theory to the Prohibition Era in the
United States may provide the basis for the widespread acceptance for illegal alcohol consumption during this period. Further, it may also shed light on the levels of
tolerance to related occurrences, such as alcohol-related deviant behavior, alcohol
abuse and the acceptance of criminal behaviors related to the consumption (or
distribution) of alcohol.

The Prohibition Era coincided with the dramatic growth in the popularity and
the availability of sporting activities in the United States. This period is often referred to as the Golden Age of Sport and it exploded onto American culture as a
mega-popular form of entertainment for individuals in all socio-economic classes.
During this period, the relationship between sport, illegal alcohol and gambling
activities became further established. While the consumption of alcohol was illegal at publicly held athletic events, the consumption of illegal alcohol found its
way into the sporting events often through the pockets of spectators. The personal flask soon became the iconic symbol representing illegal alcohol consumption and sporting events. Through this method, spectators were able to consume
alcohol both before the event (an early form of tailgating) and during the event.
The acceptance of this illegal activity furthered the bond between alcohol consumption and sport as an appropriate mixture. Although the Prohibition Era
ended in 1933 with the passage of the 21st Amendment to the U.S. Constitution,
the willingness of the American public to "turn a blind eye" towards the consumption of alcohol and its associated behaviors seemed firmly entrenched.

An additional interesting outcome of the Prohibition Era was the inception of
what is today known as NASCAR. Stock car racing evolved from the need of

prohibition era bootleggers for fast vehicles to be used in the distribution of illegal alcohol. The cars utilized by bootleggers had to "outrun" law enforcement agents and make consistent deliveries. The penalty for losing that "race" was jail, loss of livelihood, and potentially injury or death (Yates, 2004). The drivers bragged amongst each other about who was the best driver and who had the fastest car. To settle these debates, bootleggers often raced on Sunday afternoons using the same car they used to deliver illegal alcohol. Inevitably, word of these races spread through the local communities and inhabitants gathered to watch these races. These events soon became extremely popular forms of entertainment, particularly in the Southeastern United States. Bootlegging continued following the repeal of Prohibition due to the high taxes placed on the sale and manufacture of whiskey. NASCAR today is one of the largest and most popular spectator sports in the world. The early relationship with alcohol is still visible through the sponsorship of the races and the race cars, as well as the ancillary events held in conjunction with the races. It is perhaps through this type of sponsorship that the relationship between sport and alcohol is most clearly evident to today's consumers.

The Rise of Sport Bars

The most recent incarnation of taverns and speakeasies is the sport-centered bar or restaurant, commonly referred to as the sports bar. These establishments advertise and promote drink specials designed to attract customers while co-mingling the focal point from solely the consumption of the athletic event to the act of consuming alcohol. Modern day sport bars are typically filled with multiple television sets that, through the advent of satellite television, allow for a multitude of sporting events to be seen on separate screens throughout the bar. This further broadens the economic capacity by allowing for multiple sports to be consumed, thus appealing to a larger base of potential customers (Rosenberg, 1992). One of the implications of this type of sport consumption can be the spreading of the "alcohol culture" that is associated with sport consumption. By attracting a variety of different customers for a large variety of sports, the association of alcohol and sport consumption may spread to sport consumers who normally would not have associated their particular sport with alcohol consumption. The acceptance of this model for sports consumption is frequently reinforced through popular print and electronic media by its "glorification" of the "Best Sports Bars" and related events (Williams, Perko, Belcher, Leaver-Dunn, Usdan, & Leeper 2006; "Big Shots," 2005). The potential for alcohol-related problems increases when sport consumption takes place in bars. A study conducted by Treno, Gruenewald, Remer, Johnson, and LeScala (2007), found a clear indication that individuals who exhibited problem behaviors showed a tendency to consume alcohol in bars, therefore involving other consumers and increasing the opportunity for violent behaviors. Related studies demonstrated increased levels of criminal behaviors in areas and neighborhoods in close proximity to drinking establishments ranging from alcohol-related noise and disturbances, vandalism, public intoxication, and disorderly conduct to assault (Kapner, 2003).

**Figure 3.1 Alcohol Advertising outside of Wrigley Field,
home of the Chicago Cubs**

Photo by Andy Gillentine.

Alcohol Sponsorship in Sport

The bond between alcohol and sport is also clearly evident through their economic partnership. From the previously discussed horse races sponsored by colonial taverns to the current "official beer sponsor" of the major professional sports, the two activities—alcohol and sport consumption—have mutually benefited from each other in capturing consumer dollars. Jimmy Roberts stated at the Executive Forum on Sports & Social Responsibility, "Alcohol is so deeply entrenched in the sports culture and, quite frankly, a lot of it is because of the large sponsorship presence that it brings to the game" ("Examining Sports' Interaction with the World," 2005). Research findings indicate that the alcohol industry invests over $500 million dollars in sport sponsorships and advertising annually (Lee, 2004; "Alcohol advertising and sports," 2007). This amount represents a 50 percent increase over expenditures on sport sponsorship and advertising during the previous years. The major investment in sport sponsorship and advertising is found at the professional sport levels. The *SportBusiness Journal* noted that over $330 million dollars were spent by the alcohol industry sponsoring professional sporting events, $218 million on professional football, $72 million on professional basketball, $19 million on professional baseball, and $19 million on professional hockey (Lee, 2004). These investments range from simple advertisements to complete event sponsorship.

Figure 3.2 Evidence of alcohol sponsorship at the Orange Bowl, former home of the University of Miami football team

Photo by Andy Gillentine.

While alcohol sponsorship is most commonly found in professional sport, it is also found at collegiate levels. During 2003, alcohol manufacturers invested over $50 million dollars in advertising on collegiate football and basketball (Lee, 2004). Frequently, company logos and slogans adorned the scoreboards of collegiate stadiums and arenas. For example, Miami's historic Orange Bowl, formerly the home of the University of Miami football team, proudly displayed the logos of their official sponsors Presidente Beer and Bacardi Rum (see associated Figures). Current television commercials strategically placed during collegiate football games display fans tailgating before games enjoying their favorite alcoholic beverage (beer). Despite the ending comment to "always drink responsibly" the message is clearly stated that alcohol and sport consumption are synonymous.

The growing influence of alcohol-related sponsorship and collegiate sport led to an uprising of concerned leaders and organizations prior to the final weekend of the 2003 NCAA basketball tournament. Before the tournament, concerned leaders lobbied for the ban of all alcohol-related commercials and sponsorships of the highly popular and successful NCAA basketball tournament. The NCAA responded to the outcry by disallowing any alcohol commercials from being shown during tournament games, although they were allowed to be shown during the pre- and post-game shows (Clarke, 2003). The NCAA regulates the type of alcohol advertised during their events to only those "malt beverages, beer and wine products that do not exceed six percent alcohol by volume ..." (NCAA, 2006). Such steps have not eased the tensions between those groups and individuals who desire to seek a complete severance of any alcohol related sponsorship of collegiate athletics. According to Dick Galiette, the former executive director of the National High School Coaches Association, "It [the advertising of alcohol during athletic events] undermines the purposes and ideals of higher education and promotes a mixed message to students about alcohol" (Prevention Campaign to NCAA, 2001).

Although the NCAA has taken the additional steps to limit the number of alcohol ads in game programs (no more than 14 percent of the total advertising content) and the total time dedicated to television alcohol related ads (no more that 60 seconds per hour), the relationship between alcohol and sport consumption

"The time has come to sever the tie between college sports and drinking—completely, absolutely and forever. Schools must consider voluntary guidelines that say 'No alcohol advertising on the premises of an intercollegiate athletics event, no bringing alcohol to the site of an event, no turning a blind eye to underage drinking at tailgate parties, and on campus, and no alcohol sponsorship of intercollegiate sporting events.'"

Donna Shalala (1998)

President of the University of Miami and former U.S. Secretary of Health and Human Services

still stirs controversy (Clarke, 2003). In 2003, the NCAA barred CBS from airing the controversial Miller Light Beer "Cat Fight" commercial during NCAA Final Four games. The banishment came in reaction to the continued push to ban all alcohol ads combined with new protests of the demeaning and sexist images portrayed in the commercial (NCAA is Asked to Ban alcohol Ads, 2005). Continued calls to end the ongoing relationship have come from the American Medical Association, the Center on Alcohol Marketing and Youth, the Center for Science in the Public Interest, and the Knight Foundation. Each of these organizations believes that the continued advertising of alcohol during collegiate athletic events promotes problem drinking patterns among college aged students.

Another demonstration of the alcohol industry's sponsorship of sporting activities can be seen in the purchasing of naming rights to events and stadiums, as well as through acquiring "official sponsor" status. Naming rights for events and facilities has become a necessary and often expected revenue component for the sport industry. The revenues generated from the exclusive naming rights of these facilities and events are often necessary for collegiate programs to break even and for professional organizations to survive (Lough, 2005). Studies indicated that naming rights from events and stadiums currently account for over $234 million; the alcohol industry accounted for $34 million of this amount (Lee, 2004). Professional baseball stadiums are the only facilities named for alcohol industries: Coors Field, home of the Colorado Rockies, is sponsored by Coors Brewing Company; the St. Louis Cardinals play in the new Busch stadium, sponsored by Anheuser Busch Brewing Company (which replaced the old Busch stadium); and the Milwaukee Brewers play in Miller Park, sponsored by Miller Brewing Company. While alcohol sponsors have not acquired naming rights for a large number of

Table 3.1

The current events featuring the name of alcohol companies include:

1. Budweiser Shootout—NASCAR
2. Corona Championship—LPGA
3. Crown Royal presents the Jim Stewart 400—NASCAR
4. Michelob Ultra Open—LPGA

*NASCAR has recently accepted a new sponsor for their complementary race series that was formerly know as the Busch Series (Anheuser Busch).

**Table 3.2 Alcohol Sponsored Secondary Naming Rights
of Professional Sport Venues**

NFL Stadiums			
Facility	Team	Sponsor	Branded Area
Jacksonville Municipal Stadium	Jacksonville Jaguars	Budweiser Crown Royal	Bud Zone (Sports Bar) Crown Royal Touchdown Club (Luxury Suites)
Edward Jones Dome	St. Louis Rams	Budweiser	Budweiser Brew House
Invesco Field at Mile High	Denver Broncos	Budweiser	Budweiser Champions Club
M&T Bank Stadium	Baltimore Ravens	Budweiser Miller Lite	Backyard Bash (Hospitality) Beer Garden Tents
Monster Park	San Francisco 49ers	Budweiser	Bud Light Goldmine (Entertainment)
Reliant Stadium	Houston Texans	Miller Lite	Miller Light Entrance
NBA & NHL Arenas			
Facility	Team	Sponsor	Branded Area
American Airlines Arena	Miami Heat	Dewar's	Dewar's 12 Lounge
US Airways Center	Phoenix Suns	Bud Light	Bud Light Paseo (Venue and Bar)
BankAtlantic Center	Florida Panthers	Patron Tequila	Patron Tequila Platinum Club
Nationwide Arena	Columbus Blue Jackets	Bud Light	Bud Light Arena Pub
Oracle Arena	Golden State Warriors	Smirnoff	The Plaza (Smirnoff) Club
Palace of Auburn Hills	Detroit Pistons	Jack Daniels Captain Morgan	Jack Daniels Old No. 7 Club Captains Quarters (Restaurant)
Phillips Arena	Atlanta Hawks	Absolute	Absolute Martini Bar
St. Pete Times Forum	Tampa Bay Lightning	Absolute	Absolute Experience Lounge
United Center	Chicago Bulls	Ketel One Jose Cuervo	Ketel One Club Jose Cuervo Cantina
Verizon Center	Washington Wizards	Johnny Walker Dewar's Crown Royal	Johnny Walker Coaches Club Dewar's 12 Clubhouse Crown Royal suite
Wachovia Center	Philadelphia 76ers	Bud Light	Bud Light Zone

Adapted from Goldfine & Sawyer (In Press). Facility Management in Gillentine, A. & Crow, B. (Eds.), Foundations of Sport Management (2nd ed). Morgantown, WV: Fitness Information Technology Publishing.

primary facilities, they have been successful in acquiring secondary naming rights in all sports.

While sponsors and consumers maintain the safe consumption of alcohol only adds to the consumers' enjoyment of sporting events, one must also carefully review the potential dangerous outcomes associated with alcohol consumption.

Negative Impact of Alcohol Consumption

The consumption of alcoholic beverages has ramifications to both the general public and individuals. While often defended as an individual's personal decision, the implication of that decision impacts countless others. Recent estimates indicate that alcohol-related incidences cost the U.S. population over $185 billion dollars each year (NIAA, 2008). This estimate takes into consideration loss of productivity, health care costs, prevention and treatment costs, criminal justice costs and losses due to crime (Herper, 2006). Crime reports indicate that alcohol-related crimes committed in the U.S. cost an estimated $108 million annually (Office of National Drug Control Policy, 2006). About 1 million violent crimes occur annually in which victims perceive the offender is under the influence of alcohol at the time of the offense (U.S. Dept of Justice, 2006). Specifically, research indicated that nearly 4 out of 10 violent crimes involved alcohol use, 4 out of 10 fatal automobile accidents were alcohol related, and about 4 out of 10 criminal offenders reported they were under the influence of alcohol at the time they committed the crime (Greenfield, 1996). Additionally 66 percent of domestic violence victims identified alcohol as a contributing factor, as did 20 percent of victims of violent assault. International research indicates similar incidences and governmental concerns over how to reduce this problem (Greenfield, 1996).

While overall alcohol related crime is a problem in society in general, it should also be investigated as a problem in and related to sport. Two specific questions must be explored related to this issue: (1) "Is alcohol abuse and its related criminal behavior worse among athletes?" and (2) "Is alcohol abuse and its related criminal behavior worse among sport fans?"

The question of whether alcohol abuse and its subsequent criminal behaviors are worse among athletes than the general public has been a point of debate for some time. In today's age of mass media communications, the image of today's athlete and his/her behavior is different from athletes of years past. While stories of Babe Ruth's drinking and anti-social behavior have been well chronicled, his behaviors most often were downplayed or covered-up by the adoring press of his era. This acceptance of alcohol abuse among athletes during the formative years of the sport industry can be readily documented through examination of many past stars. Among those stars of past years that exhibited questionable alcohol related behaviors are Jim Thorpe, Mickey Mantle, Ty Cobb, Grover Cleveland Alexander, and John L. Sullivan. The acceptance (and minimization) of the abuse of alcohol by these iconic sports figures has left a lasting impression on the athletes that followed them. As athletes aspire to achieve the athletic accomplishments of these former stars, they often also emulate their alcohol consumption patterns.

The abuse of alcohol and any subsequent behaviors by today's athletes are not ignored by a sympathetic press. The media outlets are constantly distributing stories detailing athletes' misbehaviors while under the influence of alcohol. The reported incidences range from the ludicrous, such as the display by Joe Namath in a drunken interview with ESPN's Suzy Kolber during the New York Jets football game, to the horrific, such as University of Kentucky football player Jason Watts, who was sentenced to 10 years in prison for the deaths of two young men who were passengers in his truck while he was driving drunk (Berkow, 1999). The in-

"I can't wait until the football team gets good, and we can show the Gators (University of Florida) and the 'Noles (Florida State University) that we can out party them and outplay them."

Unidentified College Student (Sperber, 2000, p. 169)

cidences have become so frequent that an Internet website has begun listing the athletes who have been arrested for driving under the influence, ranked by the blood alcohol level (www.BadJocks.com). Despite the abundance of popular media reports chronicling the drunken escapades of athletes, relatively little research exists examining the use of alcohol by athletes. In particular, there is a dearth of information regarding the use of alcohol by professional athletes.

In one of the few studies conducted specifically examining drug use by male professional athletes, Malone (1991) found that alcohol was clearly the regular drug of choice of professional athletes. Nearly 100 percent of the subjects ($n=248$) in the study indicated a lifetime use of alcohol and that 15 percent of the participants demonstrated alcohol consumption patterns that identified them as problem drinkers. When compared to peers in the general population, the study indicated a greater percentage of the athletes consumed alcohol on a regular basis. Alarmingly, approximately one-third of the athletes indicated they had one or more drinking sessions within the two weeks prior to completing the survey instrument in which they consumed five or more drinks in a row. This supported a previous study by Gallmeier (1988) that indicated heavy alcohol use was not an uncommon practice among professional athletes.

Collegiate Athletes

In contrast, significant research studies have been conducted investigating the alcohol consumption patterns and related behaviors among collegiate athletes. Murray Sperber, in his book *Beer and Circus* (2000), describes the problems associated with the "Animal House" drinking culture that has flourished on collegiate campuses. This culture is closely associated with the collegiate athletic programs sponsored by the universities.

While Sperber's attentions focus on the implications related to the academic standing of the university, it must be noted that student athletes have also become entangled in this web of alcohol abuse. Studies conducted over the last decade have consistently revealed that collegiate athletes demonstrate higher use and misuse of alcohol than non-athletes and are more likely to engage in binge drinking than non-athletes (Hildebrand, Johnson, & Bogle, 2001; Leichliter, Meilman, Presley, & Cashin, 1998; Nelson & Wechsler, 2001; Wechsler, Davenport, Dowdall, Grossman, & Zanakos, 1997). A study commissioned by the National Collegiate Athletic Association (2001) revealed that nearly 80 percent of collegiate athletes had used alcohol within the previous year. Based upon these findings, it is not surprising to find that collegiate athletes, when compared to non-athlete students, demonstrated significantly higher rates of alcohol related consequences

"Using alcohol may be part of the 'Work Hard, Play Hard' ethic the athletes follow ..."

Cheryl A. Pressley (Grace-Kobias, 1998 p. 1)

such as driving under the influence and/or riding with intoxicated drivers and unsafe sexual practices, which led to higher rates of contracting sexually transmitted diseases (Nattiv & Puffer, 1991). Additionally, collegiate athletes who consumed alcohol were more likely to commit acts of sexual violence than non-athletes (Fritner & Rubinson, 1993). It is important to also note that although male athletes demonstrate higher levels of alcohol consumption and misuse than female athletes, the gap between the genders has significantly narrowed (Wilson, Pritchard, & Schaffer, 2004).

It is important to note that alcohol-related criminal behavior is not always a singular act by an individual. Alcohol abuse has been frequently cited as the cause for team and group aberrant behavior (Neal, Sugarman, Hustad, Caska, & Carey, 2005) Incidences of member hazing, celebratory parties, and athlete recruitment have all been documented as having disastrous outcomes due to alcohol abuse. Examples of alleged alcohol related group criminal behavior are:

1. Duke Lacrosse Team — 2006;
   The University suspended the 2006 Lacrosse season and the coach was forced to resign after three players were charged with sexual assault (although later dismissed) following a team party that involved heavy consumption of alcohol.

2. California State University at Chico — 2006;
   University suspended the 2006 women's softball season following the hospitalization for alcohol poisoning of an under-age recruit for alcohol poisoning during her campus visit.

3. University of Colorado — 2004;
   Boulder, CO District Attorney Mary Keenan accused the athletic department of using sex and alcohol as recruiting tools. The head football coach was placed on administrative leave during the investigation.

[For additional examples see Chapter 10 on Hazing]

Sports Fans

The consumption of alcohol by fans attending a sporting event has become an accepted and often encouraged component of both collegiate and professional sports. This established consumption pattern has generated large revenue streams for sport organizations, but it has done so at a price. Team executives in the each of the professional sport leagues have consistently stated that the majority of crowd related problems were related to alcohol consumption and misuse (Steinbach, 2004; Ward, 2002). Despite regulatory attempts to curb these problems, al-

Table 3.3 Alcohol Related Problems Among Sport Fans

Binge Drinking	Accidents/injuries
Missed Work/School	Arguing with Others
Remorseful behavior	Vandalizing property
Operating an automobile after drinking	Problems with Police
Inability to keep up with work	Unplanned/unprotected sex

cohol related incidences at athletic events continue to be problematic. Richard Lapchick, founder of the Center for the Study of Sport in Society, noted, "Alcohol is almost always at the root of fan misbehavior. It's consistent with other aspects of life, where the potential for conflict is exponentially ratcheted up by alcohol" (O'Connor, 2003). Collegiate athletic events have not been spared the problems of alcohol consumption, despite the fact that few colleges and universities allow the sale of alcoholic beverages in their facilities. Research studies investigating the use and abuse of alcohol by fans offer alarming findings regarding sport fans and their consumption patterns.

A 2003 study of sport fans and alcohol consumption found that sports fans more frequently engaged in binge drinking (53 percent) and exhibited heavy drinking tendencies more than non-sports fans (Nelson & Weschler, 2003). Consequently, sports fans also reported more alcohol-related problems than their non-sport fan peers (see Table 3.3).

These problem drinking behaviors were also indicators of increased second-hand effects from alcohol consumption. A study of collegiate tailgaters found that 22 percent of fans who participated in pre- and post-game tailgating events were highly motivated by the opportunity to consume alcohol and that 11 percent had missed an athletic event due to tailgating (alcohol consumption) (Gillentine, 2003).

Tailgating, which most often is viewed as a safe and fun gathering of sport fans before and after an event, is also impacted by the consumption of alcohol and subsequent behaviors. From very humble beginnings, tailgating has developed into a social phenomenon that is an attractive component of sport consumption. Sport marketers often utilized the attractiveness of tailgating to increase ticket sales and to create the visual of an exciting sport environment of sport consumers (Gillentine, Miller, & Calhoun, 2008). These "parties in the parking lot" now involve thousands of individuals who frequently include alcohol consumption as part of their tailgating experience.

The consumption of alcohol over an extended period of time before the event increases the likelihood of the undesirable behaviors that are associated with alcohol consumption. Research indicates that alcohol consumption may increase an

"There's a strong connection between drinking and fan misbehavior. When you win, you're supposed to drink to celebrate, and when you lose you're supposed to cry in your beer."

Henry Wechsler (O'Connor, 2003 p. 2)

Figure 3.3 Tailgating at The Grove at the University of Mississippi

Photo by Andy Gillentine.

individual's tendencies towards violent behavior, especially when the alcohol consumption occurs in an emotionally charged atmosphere (Graham, Larocque, Yetman, Ross, & Guistra, 1980; Harford, Wechsler, & Muthen, 2003; Leonard, Quigley, & Collins, 2002). These findings are exemplified by recent incidents where significant injuries were attributed to drinking at tailgate parties (Gillentine & Miller, 2006; Romig, 2004). Sixty-six percent of over 400 senior-level sport industry executives who participated in a survey conducted by Turnkey Sports indicated that the biggest threat to the perceived safety of fans at major sporting events was alcohol abuse by unruly fans ("Turnkey Sports poll," 2006).

An investigation of the legal implications of tailgating indicated that sport organizations and local municipalities have reported tailgaters have been implicated in a number of policy and legal violations. Theses violations include violation of open container ordinances, public intoxication, underage drinking, public urination, lewd behavior, driving under the influence, destruction of public and private property, petty theft, grand theft, assault, manslaughter, and murder (Gillentine & Miller, 2006). Many similar violations are not reported or the law or policy in violation is not strictly enforced on "game day." Sport administrators cannot be surprised be the occurrence of such violations nor can they ignore the legal implications of them.

Perhaps the case that should serve as a benchmark for the need to acknowledge the problems associated with alcohol consumption and tailgating is *Bearman vs. Notre Dame* (1983). In this case, Bearman was leaving the football game at Notre Dame when she was injured by drunken tailgaters in the parking lot. The Bear-

Figure 3.4 Evidence of Wide Spread Alcohol Consumption at Tailgating Event

Note: Eyes blurred to conceal identity of individuals. Photo by Andy Gillentine.

mans sued Notre Dame for the injuries incurred. In this case, Notre Dame acknowledged that consumers who participated in tailgating activities may become intoxicated and pose a potential threat to themselves and others in the vicinity.

The consumption of alcohol at a tailgating event also played a significant role in the horrifying car wreck in 1999 that left 2-year-old Antonia Verni paralyzed from the neck down. In this case, Daniel Lanzaro was found to have a blood alcohol level of three times the legal limit. The results of the subsequent lawsuit awarded the Verni family one of the largest alcohol liability awards in the history of the United States ("Group: $135 million jury award," 2005) The attorney for the Verni's accused the NFL of creating a "culture of intoxication" and that "we're having a party, so park your car on our backyard, drink as much as you want, come into the stadium, get more wasted and then drive home" (Gottlieb, 2005).

The implications of widespread consumption of alcohol at athletic events become problematic through the associated behaviors. The aforementioned secondary effect of alcohol consumption at athletic events frequently includes verbal harassment of others, physical altercations, disorderly conduct, and drunk driving. In addition to these incidences, non-drinking attendees have expressed an overall reduction in their ability to enjoy a sporting event due to alcohol consumption. The lower level of satisfaction can dramatically impact the willingness of sport consumers in the decision to purchase event tickets and to participate in sport events.

An additional potential problem associated with the consumption of alcohol at athletic events is the possibility of large group mishaps. Incidences of "crowd mania" have occurred throughout sport history. Soccer riots have become all but common place in countries outside of the United States (Collins & Vamplew, 2002; Roadburg, 1980; Ward, 2002). While they are not always directly associated with the crowd's consumption of alcohol, alcohol consumption is often cited as a contributing factor.

Crowd disturbances in the United States are frequently exacerbated by the consumption of alcohol by attendees. Through both faulty promotions and poor alcohol sales management, attendees at sporting events have exhibited problematic behaviors at athletic events. In 2002, a drunken fan and his son attacked coach Tom Gamboa on the field during a baseball game. Later that same year, a fan assaulted umpire Laz Diaz during a game at U.S. Cellular Field in Chicago. The criminal behavior in both incidences was in part attributed to alcohol consumption by the attackers (O'Connor, 2003; Steinbach, 2004).

While these behaviors are most often exhibited by individual fans, they may result in large group disturbances, which can increase the potential for disastrous consequences. One example of crowd problems due to alcohol consumption is the infamous 1974 "10 Cent Beer Night" held at Cleveland's Municipal stadium during a professional baseball game between the Cleveland Indians and the Texas Rangers. In an attempt to generate increased ticket sales, fans in attendance were offered 10-cent, 8-ounce beers for the duration of the game. The promotion enticed over 25,000 people to attend the game that had been averaging roughly 8,000 fans per night. Previous on-field incidences had created an air of animosity between the two teams, which quickly spread to the alcohol consuming crowd. By the fourth inning, the behavior of the crowd had begun to deteriorate rapidly and order in the stands quickly disappeared. By the ninth inning, complete chaos had occurred as drunken fans were coming onto the field and throwing objects at the players. Players from both teams indicated they feared for their lives and grabbed bats and helmets to protect themselves from the fans. Realizing that order would not be regained, the umpire forfeited the game to the Rangers and called the game as both teams and umpires fled for safety (Robinson, 2008; Steinbach, 2004).

Celebratory Riots

Although individual criminal acts involving alcohol abuse that occur in relationship to a sporting event are disturbing, an even greater threat is that of a celebratory riot. A celebratory riot refers to a disturbance that includes a large numbers of individuals gathering in a common area that threatens public and personal safety and property. The term celebratory riot stemmed from a joint task force established by The Ohio State University and the city of Columbus, Ohio in 2003 to investigate the causes and possible solutions to such outbreaks. The task force described celebratory riots as " ... a large gathering of students who have consumed alcohol and who spontaneously engage in destructive, antisocial behavior" (The Ohio Sate University Report, 2003, p. 7). These celebratory riots typically are characterized as "chaotic, frightening, and dangerous for those present" and frequently involve multiple arrests and injuries (University of New Hampshire Student Summary, 2003). While celebratory riots may be associated with any event, they are most often associated with athletic events and collegiate campuses. There

Table 3.4 Intercollegiate Celebratory Riots Associated with Athletics

Colorado State University	1999
Clemson University	2002
Indiana University	2002
Iowa State University	2000
Kansas State University	1984
Michigan State University	1999, 2003
Ohio State University	1996, 1998, 2000, 2002, 2008
Purdue University	1999, 2001
University of Arizona	2001
University of Connecticut	2004
University of Colorado	1998
University of Maryland	2002, 2003
University of Massachusetts	2003
University of Minnesota	2002, 2003
University of Missouri	2003
University of New Hampshire	2002, 2003
University of West Virginia	2002
University of Wisconsin	2000

has been a dramatic increase in the number of celebratory riots on college campuses since 1990, as well as increases in the number of participants and levels of destruction (University of New Hampshire Student Summary, 2003; Van Slyke, 2005). In the report generated by The Ohio State University Task Force on Celebratory Riots (The Ohio State University Report, 2003), 20 universities responded by indicating that they had experienced at least one celebratory riot during the five-year period of 1997–2002. Further investigation indicates that 18 universities have encountered athletic related celebratory riots from 1984–2008 (see Table 3.4). While the impetus for these celebratory riots varies, they "almost always (are) associated with high volume alcohol consumption" (Van Slyke, 2005).

The prevalence of alcohol consumption and the inconsistencies in the enforcement of institutional policies and criminal law contribute to the establishment of an environment that accepts or legitimizes unacceptable (or illegal) behaviors. Failure to enforce violation of underage drinking laws, open container ordinances, and campus alcohol restrictions or bans facilitates the development of a culture accepting or ignoring the policies and/or laws. Unfortunately, these inconsistencies are consistent with the growth of alcohol related problems as discussed earlier in the chapter (i.e., Prohibition Era).

Alcohol consumption contributes to the likelihood of a celebratory riot by lowering participant inhibitions while also impairing their cognitive abilities. According to sport sociologist Merrill Melnick, "There is a thin line between ecstasy and anti-social behavior. It's like all the norms are suspended" (O'Toole, 2002, p. 3). Recognized as the most widely used and abused drug on college campuses, the role of alcohol consumption in celebratory riots cannot be overlooked. While alcohol consumption should not be solely blamed for the occurrences of celebratory riots, it must be noted that high-risk drinking clearly contributes to the occur-

Table 3.5 Characteristics of Celebrity Riots Associated with Athletic Events

- High volume of alcohol consumption
- Occur late at night
- Involves arson & destruction of property
- Typically young crowd of both genders
- Predominately Caucasian
- Resist police authority/intervention

---

rence of inappropriate and unacceptable behaviors (The Ohio State University Report, 2003). A review of the characteristics of a celebratory riot consistently indicates alcohol consumption/abuse as a primary component (see Table 3.5).

The financial impact of celebratory riots reverberates throughout the university and surrounding community. Damage and manpower cost estimates linked to these events range from a few thousand dollars to over a million dollars. These costs and other related expenses (i.e., medical, personal property, lost productivity, etc.) could have a direct impact on the university and surrounding community. This is especially true if the celebratory riot evolves into a ritualistic occurrence. In restrictive economic settings, these costs can place an unfair burden on the communities. The university and community may implement stricter and more prohibitive policies, guidelines and ordinances in response to these potential problems.

The sport consumer may also feel the economic impact of these celebratory riots. Consumers should not be surprised to see the costs of these events materialize in an increase in ticket prices, the most commonly manipulated revenue stream for collegiate athletics. An additional increase in parking fees and regulations may also occur as a result of compensating for costly celebratory riots. Municipalities and universities must also adjust and compensate their budgets due to increased security and law enforcement demands. These increased costs will be passed on to the sport consumer in the form of higher prices for ancillary products (i.e., parking, food purchases, merchandise, etc.) associated with the event.

Many universities have instituted stricter event attendance polices in hopes of minimizing the occurrence of celebratory riots. Through the implementation of no re-entry policies and requiring patrons to enter the event or leave the parking (and surrounding) areas, university and community officials hope to offset the impact of alcohol consumption as a contributing factor to celebratory riots. In some communities, tailgating is no longer allowed or is restricted to highly supervised areas. Universities have also adopted a zero-tolerance philosophy regarding student participation in such events. Sadly, the monetary impact of preparations for celebratory riots may have a direct effect of the level of student services the university is able to offer.

Consumers may also feel the impact of these occurrences through increases in auto and health insurance premiums. Premiums are adjusted by insurance companies to reflect the likelihood of loss. The frequent re-occurrence of celebratory riots could directly affect the premiums required by insurance companies. The impact of these increases could result in the movement of individuals and business out of the impacted areas and lead to the economic decline of an area. As businesses close and individual families move out of areas, local municipalities could see a loss in tax revenues generated through sales and property taxes.

Celebratory riots, while most often associated with collegiate settings, also occur in conjunction with professional sporting events. While alcohol consumption is viewed as a contributing factor in all sport-related riots, it is not considered a primary cause of celebratory riots occurring in conjunction with professional sporting events. In contrast to the study and examination of collegiate celebratory riots, limited research has been conducted regarding the causes of professional sport riots. The limited research conducted indicates that although alcohol consumption is generally involved, a greater emphasis is placed on the sociological factors affecting fan behavior and the influence of "band-wagoning" by criminal elements (Russell, 2004; Young, 2002).

The dearth of research available may be reflective of the rapid escalation of the occurrence of these events. Although sport riots have been documented throughout history, the impact and regularity of these events in North America has exploded over the last three decades. The suddenness of these events and the disruptive nature to large populations may have encouraged an emphasis on implementing measures to thwart their occurrence rather than examine the underlying causes (Ward, 2002). Incidences of large-scale destruction and property loss have been recorded in relationship to major North American professional sporting events in Boston, Chicago, Denver, Detroit, Los Angeles, Vancouver and Montreal (see Table 3.6). In additional to the large scale costs and damages incurred as a result of these events, these incidences have a heavy toll in terms of the individuals involved. Hundreds of people are arrested and jailed in response to their involvement in these events, placing a huge burden on the infrastructure of the city/county/state/province in which they occur. Many individuals are also physically injured and often fatalities have resulted from these riotous events. The riot following the Boston Red Sox World Series victory in 2004 resulted in the accidental death of a young woman who was hit in the eye by a pepper-spray bullet fired by police officers attempting to disburse the crowd (Arndorfer, 2005). Following the Boston Celtic's NBA championship in 2008, a 22-year-old died after being arrested by local authorities for his involvement in the post event mayhem (Sweet, Szaniszio, Van Slack & Fargen, 2008).

In order to stem the occurrence of these celebratory riots, sport organization and municipalities have been forced to develop strategies that minimize their likelihood and impact. Formal reports and investigations have been developed by the Ohio State University, the University of New Hampshire, and Iowa State University. These reports offer an interesting insight, not only into the celebratory riots themselves, but also into the procedures and actions to deter them in the future. Among the common threads offered in the reports is the implementation of training programs for event and facility staff as well as campus and local police forces. These training programs are recommended to prepare officials for dealing with the individuals involved both before any occurrence and at the onset. In addition to these training recommendations, the reports also suggested educating all potential parties (fans, students, merchants, law enforcement, etc.) regarding the impact of these occurrences. For those venues that serve alcohol, the model developed through the TEAM (Techniques for Effective Alcohol Management) program is recommended. The TEAM program is:

... an alliance of professional and collegiate sports, entertainment facilities, concessionaires, stadium service providers, the beer industry, broadcasters,

Table 3.6 Professional Sport Riots in North America

Year	City	Sport
1955	Montreal	NHL
1968	Detroit	MLB
1971	Pittsburg	MLB
1983	Toronto	CFL
1984	Detroit	MLB
1985	San Francisco	NFL
1986	Hamilton	CFL
1968	Montreal	NHL
1989	Detroit	NBA
1990	Detroit	NBA
1991	Chicago	NBA
1992	Chicago	NBA
1993	Chicago	NBA
1993	Montreal	NHL
1993	Dallas	NFL
1994	Vancouver	NHL
1994	Dallas	NFL
1996	Denver	NHL
1996	Chicago	NBA
1997	Chicago	NBA
1998	Denver	NFL
1999	Denver	NFL
2000	Los Angeles	NBA
2001	Denver	NHL
2003	Oakland	NFL
2004	Boston	NFL
2004	Boston	MLB
2006	Pittsburg	NFL
2008	Montreal	NHL
2008	Boston	NBA

governmental traffic safety experts, and others working together to promote responsible drinking and positive fan behavior at sports and entertainment facilities. In addition to stadium employee training in effective alcohol management, TEAM offers fan education materials designed to remind sports fans to consume alcohol responsibly and use designated drivers (TEAM Coalition, 2008).

Recommendations for changes regarding security at athletic events focuses on the consistent enforcement of existing laws and regulations. Security personnel must strictly enforce bans on bringing alcohol into sport facilities. Disruptive fans must be immediately removed and potentially banned from future attendance. It is also important that security measures include the recruitment of fans to help identify inappropriate behavior and abusive fans. Security can also minimize the potential problem by ensuring quick exit routes from the stadium and maintaining parking lots.

The role of the media in the minimization of these events can be enhanced through the amount and types of exposure occurrences are given. While the media should report news of events to the public, it must be careful not to glorify the event and thus encourage future participation. It is important that the media emphasizes the law enforcement presence to discourage aberrant behavior. Electronic media, such as text messages and emails, can be effective ways to ensure the safe atmosphere is maintained and emphasized.

Sport organizations and the local communities should carefully analyze the impact on alcohol sponsorship as a catalyst for such behaviors. The aforementioned policies of the NCAA may need to be revisited and applied more liberally to all collegiate events. Additionally, universities need to carefully evaluate their acceptance of alcohol sponsorships. Local communities and merchants must also evaluate the potential impact of alcohol sponsorships and/or drink specials on creating a potentially hostile environment. It is necessary to control the distribution of alcohol in areas vulnerable to celebratory riots. Strict enforcement of drinking ages and open container laws must be maintained.

The professional sport leagues also need to analyze their widespread use of alcohol sponsorships in relationship to alcohol consumption. If in fact a "culture of intoxication" is being promoted, the liability of the host organization increases (Miller & Gillentine, 2006). Further the sport organizations must realize that they are at risk of losing their next generation of fans if they fail to provide an environment conducive to its development.

Recommendations

In general, while the bond between alcohol consumption and sport is strong, they do not have to be considered equal components of the sport experience. Sport can exist without encouraging or condoning the unbridled consumption of alcohol. Sport organizations should feel obliged to create and maintain environments that minimize the influence of alcohol consumption. It is also the obligation of sport consumers to keep the consumption of sport and the consumption of alcohol as separate activities. The current sporting culture has caused many fans to co-mingle the two activities and confuse the identification of the core activity, the sporting event. Fans must also be encouraged to speak out regarding the development of undesirable environments due to the consumption of alcohol. Fans should not be expected to tolerate the aforementioned secondary effects of alcohol consumption. Even more importantly, the children of fans should not be forced to tolerate the associated undesirable behaviors caused by alcohol consumption.

Lastly, it is important for athletes to recognize their vulnerability to the effects of alcohol consumption. The athlete must also recognize the potential for problems when they attend events outside of the athletic event in which fans will be consuming alcohol. The chance for personal harm and confrontation may be increased for the athlete if he or she finds themselves in an alcohol influenced environment.

Alcohol consumption in the United States has had a dramatic impact on the sport industry. Through its presence in the growth of the popularity of sport, its relationship has become strong. The relationship with alcohol has not developed without the impact of alcohol's much publicized negative effects. The negative impact of alcohol consumption has impacted fans, players and communities. It has frequently been accepted as an excuse for not only undesirable behavior, but also for criminal behavior. The sport industry can no longer afford to accept alcohol consumption as a problem that must be tolerated. Sport organizations of all types, from Little League to professional leagues, need to take a firm stand on controlling the influence of alcohol on sport.

Case Study: Barrett Robbins

To most athletes, participation in the National Football League's 2003 Super Bowl would represent the culmination of a lifelong dream. The opportunity to display your talents on arguably the biggest stage in all of professional sports would be inspiring. For most athletes, the days before this event would be focused on last minute game preparations along side interviews with the media. No matter what the outcome of the game, a participant in this event life would be changed forever. For Barrett Robbins, the impact of the week of the Super Bowl was not the week player's dream of. Instead it was an opportunity lost due to alcohol abuse.

While his team, the Oakland Raiders, was playing in Super Bowl XXXVII, Robbins was in a San Diego hospital under what a family member described as a suicide watch. Two days prior to the Super Bowl, Barrett had a gone on a drinking binge which took him to bars from San Diego, CA to Tijuana, Mexico ("Timeline of events surrounding Barret Robbins," 2003). During this binge, his whereabouts were unknown to the Raiders organization and his family. Robbins reappeared minutes before the team's final meeting, but he was obviously disoriented and physically impaired. He was ordered out of the team hotel by the Raiders organization and informed he would not participate in the Super Bowl. Robbins' wife and agent checked him into a San Diego hospital where he remained until doctors were able to stabilize his condition.

Robbins suffers from bipolar disorder, which can be controlled through medication. Rather than continue his medication routine, Robbins' dependency on alcohol exacerbated the problem. Research studies estimated that 60 percent of individuals suffering from bipolar disorder abuse alcohol and other drugs.

Robbins' issues with alcohol were not hidden from the Raiders organization prior to the Super Bowl. Reports indicate his abuse of alcohol began in high school and that he drank alcohol at home with his parents' consent (Sacaceno, 2002). His drinking patterns continued during his college days at Texas Christian University, where he also allegedly began to abuse other drugs. Despite a record of bizarre behavior, Robbins' continued to play and received awards for his aggressive behavior.

Robbins was selected in the second round of the 1995 NFL Draft by the Raiders. His size and aggressive play soon made an impact on the Raiders. In 1998, he was ejected from a game for kicking Baltimore Ravens linebacker Ray Lewis in the head. In addition to his reputation on the field, Robbins was also developing a reputation off the field for his alcohol consumption. Although he was now abusing other drugs, family members acknowledged his main problem was alcohol (Sacaceno, 2002).

After his embarrassment at Super Bowl XXXVII, Robbins spent a month in the Betty Ford clinic following his release from the San Diego hospital. Although doctors recommended he spend more time at the rehabilitation clinic, Robbins refused. Within six weeks after his departure, Robbins was drinking again. Despite the debacle at the Super Bowl and his refusal to adhere to doctor's advice, the Raiders allowed Robbins to return to the team. He was eventually dismissed permanently from the team when he tested positive for steroid use.

During the following year, Robbins was accused of assaulting a security guard and charged with drunk and disorderly conduct. Although he agreed to once again enter a rehabilitation treatment center, Robbins instead headed for hedonistic South Beach in Miami, Florida. After two days of heavy drinking, Robbins was found by Miami police, hiding in a women's restroom of a closed office building. Three policemen, who were responding to a reported burglary, tried to remove Robbins from the premises when he suddenly became violent. The massive Robbins reportedly threw two of the officers against the wall and attempted to reach for one of the officer's weapon. A third officer shot Robbins twice, who despite being critically wounded, continued to mock and curse the officers (Nobles, 2005). Robbins was charged (2005) and convicted (2006) of attempted murder and battery, but only received a sentence of five years probation under the agreement that he avoid alcohol and continue prescribed treatment for his bipolar disorder ("Robbins gets 5 years," 2006). In September of 2007, the Florida State Attorney's office sought to extradite Robbins from his home in Texas for violation of his probation.

The sad story of Barrett Robbins resonates many of the issues discussed in this chapter regarding the consumption of alcohol and sport. It is important for professionals associated with the sport industry to challenge themselves to answer the questions generated through this case study:

1. Was Robbins' alcohol abuse tolerated because of his performance on the athletic field?
2. How should any of the sport organizations mentioned in this study have reacted differently?
3. Were the laws and policies of the municipalities adhered to or was special consideration offered because of athletic status?
4. What were the underlying causes of this alcohol abuse?
5. What is the social responsibility of the sport organization in such a situation?
6. What other issues should be discussed regarding this case study?

References

Alcohol advertising and sports (2007). Media Awareness Network. Retrieved June 26, 2008, from http://www.media-awareness.ca/english/resources/ educational/teaching_backgrounders/alcohol/alcohol_ads_and_sports.cfm

Arndorfer, B. (2005). Alcohol and sports: A deadly combination. *Gainesville Sun*. Retrieved July 5, 2008, from http://www.gainesville.com/article/2005 1102/LOCAL/51101046

Bandura, A. (1990). Selective activation and disengagement of moral control. *Journal of Social Issues, 46*, 27–46.

Bandura, A., Barbaranelli, C., Caprara, G., & Pastorelli, C. (1996). Mechanisms of moral disengagement in the exercise of moral agency. *Journal of Personality and Social Psychology, 71*, 364–374.

Bearman v. University of Notre Dame, 453 N.E.2d 1196 (Ind. Ct. App. 1983).

Berkow, I. (1999, August 25). College football; Alcohol abuse ends 2 lives and wrecks another. *New York Times*. Retrieved June 26, 2008, from http://query.nytimes.com/gst/fullpage.html?res=9C07E3D61E3AF936A15757 C0A96F958260&scp=1&sq=Alcohol+abuse+ends+2+lives+and+wrecks+anot her.+&st=nyt

Big shots: The perfect 10 college sports bars. (2005, February 10). *SIonCampus.com* (Sports Illustrated on Campus). Retrieved on June 25, 2008, from http://sportsillustrated.cnn.com/2005/sioncampus/02/09/big_shot0210/

Clarke, L. (2003, April 5). A beer Commercial is stopped cold. *Washington Post*, p. D1.

Collins, T., & Vamplew, W. (2002). *Mud, sweat and beers: A cultural history of sport and alcohol*. Oxford, UK: Berg.

Davies, R. (2007). *Sports in American life—A history*. Malden, MA: Blackwell Publishing.

Examining sports' interaction with the world. (2005, October 23). *SportsBusiness Journal*. Retrieved June 20, 2008, from http://www.sportsbusinessjournal.com/article/47536

Fritner, M., & Rubinson, L. (1993). Acquaintance rape: The influence of alcohol, fraternity membership, and sports team membership. *Journal of Sex Education Therapy, 19*, 272–284.

Gallmeier, C. (1988). Juicing, burning and tooting: Observing drug use among professional hockey Players. *Arena Review 12*(1), 1–12.

Gillentine, A. (2003). *Factors associated with participation in pre-game activities*. Paper presented at the meeting of the Southern District American Alliance Health, Physical Education, Recreation, & Dance. Savannah, GA.

Gillentine, A., & Miller, J. (2006). The legal implications of tailgating. *International Journal of Sport Management, 7*(1) 102–111.

Gillentine, A., Miller, J., & Calhoun, A. (2008). Negligent marketing. What all sport marketers should know. *Journal of Contemporary Athletics, 3*(2), 208–236.

Gorn, E.J. (1986). *The manly art: Bare knuckle prize fighting in America*. Ithaca, NY: Cornell University Press.

Gottlieb, H. (2005). Jury duns stadium beer vendor $105 million for injuries caused by drunken fan. *New Jersey Law Journal*. Retrieved on September 10, 2008, from http://www.freerepublic.com/focus/f-news/1326439/posts

Grace-Kabas, L. (1998). Survey of college drinking patterns show athletes drink more than non-athlete students, but fraternities hold the record. Retrieved June 26, 2008, from http://www.news.cornell.edu/releases/June98/athletes. drinking.lgk.html

Graham, K., Larocque, L., Yetman, R., Ross, T.J., & Guistra, E. (1980). Aggression and barroom environments. *Journal of Studies on Alcohol, 41,* 277–292.

Greenfield, L. (1998). An analysis of National Crime Data on the Prevalence of Alcohol Involvement in Crime. U.S. Department of Justice. Washington, D.C.

Group: $135 million jury award a warning to vendors and teams. (2005). CourtTV.com. Retrieved June 20, 2008, from http://www.courttv.com/news/2005/0121/aramark_ap.html

Harford, T.C., Wechsler, H., & Muthen, B.O. (2003). Alcohol-related aggression and drinking at off-campus parties and bars: A national study of current drinkers in college. *Journal of Studies on Alcohol, 64*(5), 704–711.

Herper, M. (2006). Cutting alcohol's cost. *Forbes.* Retrieved June 26, 2008, from http://www.forbes.com/2006/08/22/health-drinking-problems_cx_mh_nightlife06_0822costs_print.html

Hildebrand, K., Johnson, D., & Bogle, K. (2001). Comparison of patterns of alcohol use between high school and college athletes and non-athletes. *College Student Journal, 35,* 358–365.

Kapner, D. (2003). Alcohol and Other Drugs on Campus—The Scope of the Problem. The Higher Education Center for Alcohol and Other Drug Abuse and Violence Prevention. U.S. Department of Education, Washington, D.C.

Lee, J. (2004, August 30). Colleges Struggle with where to draw the line on Sponsorships. *SportsBusiness Journal,* 32.

Leichliter, J.S., Meilman, P.W., Presley, C.A., & Cashin, J.R. (1998). Alcohol use and related consequences among students with varying levels of involvement in college athletics. *Journal of American College Health, 46,* 257–267.

Leonard, K.E., Quigley, B.M., & Collins, R.L. (2002). Physical aggression in the lives of young adults: Prevalence, location, and severity among college and community samples. *Journal of Interpersonal Violence, 17,* 533–550.

Lough, N. (2005). Sponsorship and Sales in the Sport Industry. In A. Gillentine & B. Crow (Eds.), *Foundations of sport management.* (pp. 99–108). Morgantown, WV: Fitness Information Technology Publishing.

Malone, D. (1991). The nature and extent of drugs and alcohol use within a professional sport league. Ph.D. Dissertation. University of Pittsburg. Dissertations Abstracts International 52:2823A.

Miller, J., & Gillentine, A. (2006). An analysis of tailgating policies at Division I Universities. Journal of the Legal Aspects of Sport, 16(2), 197–215.

National Collegiate Athletic Association. (2001). NCAA study of substance use habits of college student athletes. Retrieved on June 26, 2008, from http://www.ncaa.org/library/research/substance_use_habits/2001/substance_use_habits.pdf

National Collegiate Athletic Association. (2006). NCAA study of substance use habits of college student-athletes. Retrieved on June 26, 2008, from http://www.ncaa.org/library/research/substance_use_habits/2006/2006_substance_use_report.pdf

National Institute on Alcohol Abuse and Alcoholism (2008) Five Year Strategic Plan. Retrieved January 21, 2008, from http://pubs.niaaa.nih.gov/publications/StrategicPlan/NIAAASTRATEGICPLAN.htm

Nattiv, A., & Puffer, J. (1991). Lifestyles and health risks of collegiate athletes and non-athletes. *Journal of Drug Education, 21,* 585–590.

NCAA asked to ban alcohol ads (2005, April 28). *St. Petersburg Times,* p. 7C.

Neal, D., Sugarman, D. Hustad, J., Caska, C., & Carey, K. (2005). It's all fun and games … or is it? Collegiate sporting events and celebratory drinking. *Journal of Studies on Alcohol, 66,* 291–294.

Nelson, T.F., & Wechsler, H. (2001). Alcohol and college athletes. *Medicine & Science in Sports & Exercise, 33*(1), 43–47.

Nelson, T.F., & Wechsler, H. (2003). Alcohol and collegiate sports fans. *Addictive Behaviors, 28*(1), 1–11.

Nobles, C. (2003). Former Raider is charged with attempted murder. *New York Times.* Retrieved Dec 15, 2007, from http://www.nytimes.com/2005/01/20/sports/football/20robbins.html

O'Connor, I. (2003, April 17.). Alcohol puts a damper on fun and games. *USA Today.* Retrieved August 8, 2007, from http://www.usatoday.com/sports/columnist/oconnor/2003-04-17-ian_x.htm

Office of National Drug Control Policy (2006). The Economic Costs of Drug Abuse in the United States 1992–2002. Retrieved January 21, 2008, from http://www.whitehousedrugpolicy.gov/publications/economic_costs/

The Ohio State University Task Force on Preventing Celebrator Riots-Final Report (2003). Retrieved on June 25, 2008, from http://www.popcenter.org/problems/student_riots/PDFs/OhioState_2003pdf.pdf

O'Toole, T. (2002, April 9) 'Celebratory Riots' creating crisis on campus. *USA Today.* Retrieved January 13, 2008, from http://www.usatoday.com.sports/other/2002-04-09-fan-violence.htm

Peverely, C. (1866). *The book of American pastimes.* New York: Author.

Prevention campaign to NCAA: End beer promotion during basketball championships. (2001 March 30). Booze News Updating advocates on alcohol prevention policies. 1–3.

Rader, B. (2004) American sports: From the Age of Folk Games to the Age of Televised Sports (5th Edition). Upper Saddle Creek, NJ: Pearson Prentice Hall.

Roadburg, A. (1980). Factors precipitating fan violence: A new comparison of professional soccer in Britain and North America. *British Journal of Sociology. 31,* 265–276.

Robbins gets five years probation for brawl with police. (2006) ESPN.com. Retrieved December 15, 2007, from http://sports.espn.go.com/nfl/news/story?id=2556553

Robinson, J. (2008). 10-Cent Beer Night. Retrieved June 25, 2008, from http://www.baseballlibrary.com/baseballlibrary/features/flashbacks/06_04_1974.stm

Romig, J. (2004, June 26). Niles man sentenced in hit-and-run death. *South Bend Tribune (Indiana)*, p. 4A.

Rosenberg, M. (1992, June 7). A new spring refrain: Take me out to the sports Bar. *New York Times*. Retrieved on June 25, 2008, from http://query.nytimes.com/gst/fullpage.html?res=9E0CE2DE133CF934A35755C0A964958260

Russell, G. (2004). Sport riots: A social-psychological review. *Aggression and Violent Behavior, 9*, 353–378.

Saraceno, J. (2005). A troubled Life on the line. *USA Today*. Retrieved on June 25, 2008, from http://usatoday.com/sports/football/nfl/2005-02-02-robbins-cover_x.htm

Shalala, D. (1998, January). The role of Athletics in Higher Education. 92nd Annual Meeting of the National Collegiate Athletic Association. Atlanta, GA.

Sperber, M. (2000). *Beer and circus: How big-time college sports is crippling undergraduate education*. New York: Henry Holt & Co.

The sport industry (2007). *SportBusiness Journal*. Retrieved June 20, 2008, from http://www.sportsbusinessjournal.com/index.cfm?fuseaction=page.feature&featureId=43

Steinbach, P. (2004, September). Drinking games. *Athletic Business*, 60–68.

Struna, N. (1996). *People of prowess: Sports leisure and labor in early Anglo-America*. Urbana, IL: University of Illinois Press.

Sweet, L., Szaniszio, M., Van Slack, J., & Fargen, J. (2008). Student Suffers cardiac arrest. *Boston Herald*. Retrieved July 5, 2008, from http://news.bostonherald.com/news/regional/general/view.bg?articleid=1101810

TEAM Coalition (2008). Retrieved June 25, 2008, from http://www.TEAM COALITION.org

Timeline of events surrounding Barret Robbins. (2003). ESPN.com. Retrieved on June 26, 2008, from http://espn.go.com/nfl/s/2003/0129/1500577.html

Treno, A., Gruenwald, P., Remer, L., Johnson, F., & LeScala, E. (2007). Examining multi-level relationships between bars, hostility and aggression: Social selection and social influence. *Addiction 103*, 66–77.

Turnkey Sports poll (2006, March 6). *SportsBusiness Journal*. Retrieved on June 20, 2008, from http://www.sportsbusinessjournal.com/article/49730

U.S. Department of Justice (2006). Student Party Riots. Retrieved June 26, 2008 from http://www.cops.usdoj.gov/pdf/Student_Party.pdf

University of New Hampshire Student Summary (2003). Retrieved June 26, 2008, from http://www.unh.edu/studentsummit/summary.html

Van Slyke, J. (2005). An analysis of issues related to celebratory riots at higher education institutions. Educations Law Consortium. Education Law & Policy Forum (Volume 1). Retrieved: June 26, 2008 from http://www.educationlawconsortium.org/forum/2005/papers/VanSlyke2005.pdf

Ward, R. (2002). Fan violence social problem or moral panic? *Aggression and Violent Behavior, 7*(5), 453–475.

Wechsler, H., Davenport, A.E., Dowdall, G.W., Grossman, S.J., & Zanakos, S.I. (1997). Binge drinking, tobacco, and illicit drug use and involvement in college athletics: A survey of students at 140 American colleges. *Journal of American College Health, 45*, 195–200.

Williams, R., Perko, M., Belcher, D., Leaver-Dunn, D., Usdan, S., & Leeper, J. (2006). Use of Social Ecology Model to address Alcohol Use among college athletes. *American Journal of Health Studies, 21*(4), 228–237.

Wilson, G., Pritchard, M., & Schaffer, J. (2004). Athletic status and drinking behavior in college students: The influence of gender and coping styles. *Journal of American College Health, 52*, 269–273.

Yates, B. (2004). *NASCAR off the record*. St. Paul, MN: MBI Publishing.

Young, K. (2002). Standards Deviations: An update on the North American sports crowd disorder. *Sociology of Sport Journal, 19*, 237–275.

Part III

Violence

4

Violence in Sport: Psychological Considerations and Implications

John W. Clark, Troy University
Phil Bridgmon, University of North Alabama

Introduction

Each year in the United States, millions of fans flock to stadiums throughout the country to watch their favorite teams and players. One sport that draws these fans is baseball. Professional baseball (particularly Major League Baseball) is often referred as the national pastime. According to Ozanian and Badenhausen (2008), attendance records show that baseball is more popular than ever. In 2007, baseball broke its attendance record for a fourth straight year as 79.5 million fans hit the turnstiles. The New York Yankees led the majors in attendance, with a record 4.3 million attending games. Major League Baseball team revenue in 2007 was $5.5 billion.

Another example of the popularity of professional sport is professional football (particularly National Football League). According to Badenhausen, Ozanian & Settimi (2008), the NFL has 19 teams worth over one billion dollars. The total paid attendance for the 2007 season was an average of 67,738 fans per game ("NFL sets regular-season paid attendance record," 2008). This increase to 17,341,012 tops last year's all-time mark of 17,340,879. Not surprisingly, professional basketball is in on the action as well, as the National Basketball Association (NBA) set attendance records during the 2006–2007 season, with 21,841,480 fans observing their favorite teams ("NBA sets all-time attendance records," 2007).

Do collegiate sports draw the same attention as popular professional sports? The answer is yes. According to Johnson (2008), NCAA football set a new attendance record during the 2007 season, with over 48,751,861 fans observing their favorite teams. The greatest indicator demonstrating the popularity of collegiate football is the new agreement between ESPN (Entertainment and Sports Programming Network) and the SEC (Southeastern Conference). According to Kramer (2008), ESPN will pay the Southeastern Conference an amazing $2.25 billion over the next 15 years for the conference's TV rights. This will allow the network all the SEC content that CBS does not broadcast.

While revenue and fan attendance is at an all time high, should we be concerned about the consequences of attending these events? Obviously, individuals view and attend sporting events to be entertained. However, is part of the entertainment the violence? A reasonable person could assume that people go to Talladega or Daytona for the crashes. Furthermore, people go to boxing matches to watch ten or twelve rounds rather than a knock out. Individuals go to hockey games to watch someone hit a puck into a net, not players fighting. On the surface, this violence seems innocuous. However, our youth are watching and listening. These children are visualizing themselves on those tracks, rings and arenas. Given this, are there psychological considerations and implications of attending these sporting events? Yes! The purpose of this chapter is three-fold. Part I examines violence in sports and provides examples of professional sports figures engaged in inappropriate behavior both on and off-the-field. Part II examines real world cases in which participants in amateur and youth league sports display inappropriate behavior. One must remember the apple does not fall from the tree. So if John Q observes his favorite baseball player fighting on the field then why can't he fight? Part III examines the psychological dynamics or process of the inappropriate behavior of both professional and amateur athletes. Ultimately, suggesting the behavior of athletes is positively reinforced by society.

Part I: Professional Sports

Violence in sports is as American as apple pie. According to Terry and Jackson (1985), "sports violence can be defined as behavior which causes harm, occurs outside of the rules of the sport, and is unrelated to the competitive objectives of the sport" (p. 2). It is important to note that players and fans have largely accepted this behavior. According to Lance (2005), many players and fans are more inclined to experience violence in sports as pleasurable and exciting. Therefore, violence continues to be a crucial social issue in modern sports since these sports are structured to promote tension instead of relieving it" (p. 213).

Importantly, with the growth in media outlets like cable and the internet, sports fans can consume sports news and information 24 hours per day, seven days per week. Not all of the air time is consumed with sports violence via replays of games and sports statistics. Much of the chatter on sports programs involves the personal lives of the players, including their hunting trips, vacations, honeymoons, children's activities, and off-field problems. The most sensational stories involve players' off-the-field antics, rather than their abilities on the field. Brett Favre's public breakup with the Green Bay Packers in the summer of 2008 was a virtual soap opera. Sports lives become our own lives, and as such the behavior of professional and amateur athletes is an important component of society to analyze.

It would be easy to say that modern professional athletes are rowdier than their early-to-mid-twentieth century counterparts, but we doubt that. Documentaries and biographies of past professional sports stars reveals they are engaged in womanizing, adultery, alcoholism, racism, cheating, and issues involving violence, including crimes such as assaults, DUI, and domestic violence. We certainly are not loudly proclaiming that we have discovered gambling going on in the casino, but what we hope to do is create a sense of the types of behaviors that are widely known and consumed by society. We do not intend to disparage or hold all professional athletes to these examples, but these well known cases illustrate how the stereotype of professional athletes develops and how their behaviors serve as role models for younger adults and children, particularly at impressionable ages.

O.J. Simpson

Perhaps no other athlete in professional sports personifies the caricature of professional athletes engaging in questionable behavior than O.J. Simpson. A former Hiesman Trophy winner at USC and Hall of Fame running back with Buffalo Bills and San Francisco 49ers, Simpson has been arrested on charges ranging from theft of cable services to the murder of his wife, Nicole Brown Simpson. On the latter charge, Simpson was also sued for the wrongful death of Ron Goldman, an acquaintance of Nicole Brown Simpson, who was murdered while with her in the summer of 1994. More recently, Simpson was convicted of actions over disputed sports memorabilia. Simpson was found guilty of storming the hotel room of a sports collectibles dealer with his entourage, holding the room hostage and threatening physical harm. Simpson's friends were armed, although Simpson claimed he was unaware of their firearms. Between the murders of Nicole Brown Simpson and Ron Goldman, which Simpson was charged with, and his latest clash with the law, Simpson was tried on charges of assault of a motorist in a road rage case (Handlin, 2001) and theft of DirecTV ("OJ Simpson fined for stealing cable," 2005).

Simpson's legal troubles are somewhat rare for professional athletes. His range of charges, from stealing cable TV to murder, typically does not plague a single individual. However, his success in defending himself is typical of professional athletes. In many of his legal cases, he has been able to sustain a defense; and while most professional athletes can defend themselves from criminal charges, civil wrongs typically catch up with them due to less stringent rules of evidence. In Simpson's cases, however, we are left to wonder how one individual can constantly be in either civil or criminal court. A reasonable person could question whether Simpson's tumultuous existence is exacerbated by his celebrity standing. Unfortunately, there are many professional athletes who seem to have chronic problems staying on the correct side of the law.

Adam Jones

Adam "Pacman" Jones was a first round draft pick for the Tennessee Titans in 2005. Trouble and sorrow have always seemed to follow him. It is believed that no male of his generation lived past 21 years of age. His father was gunned down, and his family fully expected him to die a violent death (Cunningham, 2008). This tragic thought foreshadows his legal issues. While in college, for instance, he beat a fellow West Virginia University classmate with a pool cue, for which he was placed on probation. This assault was only minor compared to Jones' first major run in with the law. In February of 2007, Jones and his associates were enjoying themselves at the Minxx Gentlemen's Club in Las Vegas when an apparent misunderstanding over $80,000 of Jones' money, which was being used to shower strippers, was gathered up and taken by the strip show's promoter. Jones and his entourage met the promoter, Chris Mitchell, outside the club in what led to a shooting that left three people wounded and a body guard paralyzed for life ("Police: Pacman's cash display," 2007). This episode was the third such incident in which Jones found his fortune turning sour outside a strip club, including one that led to charges on public intoxication and disorderly conduct.

In May 2007, the NFL suspended Jones for what was thought to be the Minxx incident, but "nine other off-field incidents where the police interviewed Jones don't help (they involved marijuana, public intoxication, assault, felony vandalism, and obstructing the police)" (Cunningham, 2008, n.p.). After the suspension, Jones took up a number of professions, including wrestling and song writing. He also fought his troubles in court where he plead guilty to some cases and others were dismissed. After being acquired by the Dallas Cowboys, Jones was reinstated to play for the 2008 season ("NFL reinstates Cowboys' 'Pacman' Jones," 2008). In the late evening hours of October 8, 2008, Jones was involved in an altercation with an off-duty officer serving as his team-provided bodyguard at a Dallas night spot (Mortensen, 2008). Such actions, in light of his previous transgressions, put his professional playing future in further jeopardy.

Michael Irvin

Another notorious offender, Michael Irvin, is also associated with the Dallas Cowboys. His off-field legal problems follow an impressively long timeline:

- **March 4, 1996:** In Irving Texas, police respond to complaints of a loud party at a motel. Police find marijuana and cocaine along with drug paraphernalia in the room where Irvin and three others are staying.
- **April 1, 1996:** Grand jury indicts Irvin and two others on misdemeanor possession of marijuana. Irvin also is charged with felony possession of at least 4 grams of cocaine.
- **July 15, 1996:** Irvin pleads no contest to second-degree felony cocaine possession in exchange for four years' deferred probation, $10,000 fine, and dismissal of misdemeanor marijuana possession charges against him. The deferred probation means if he stays out of trouble, the charge is cleared from his record.
- **Oct. 10, 1999:** Irvin suffers a neck injury that leaves him temporarily paralyzed on the turf of Veterans Field in Philadelphia.
- **July 6, 2000:** A Dallas judge ends Irvin's probation 9 days early.
- **July 10, 2000:** Irvin announces his retirement from the Cowboys and his new job as a commentator for Fox Sports Net.
- **Aug. 9, 2000:** Irvin arrested in a North Dallas apartment complex on a charge of misdemeanor possession of marijuana.
- **Aug. 11, 2000:** Members of a drug task force say they won't pursue marijuana charges against Irvin following his arrest in the North Dallas apartment complex.
- **June 21, 2001:** A Denton County grand jury indicts Irvin on a felony charge of possessing less than a gram of cocaine stemming from the August 9 arrest ("Irvin arrested on charge of cocaine possession," 2001, n.p.).

Irvin's issues are widely known and were an issue within his professional life. Primarily, these multiple off-the-field antics were part of public debate concerning his candidacy for the Pro Football Hall of Fame, although he was eventually inducted in the 2007 class (Michael Irvin, n.d.). Many observers on the television and talk radio circuit questioned whether his personal life should be considered in determining his Hall of Fame eligibility. The above chronology demonstrates a lengthy involvement in substance abuse. Further, Irvin's drug use ultimately led to his arrest and subsequent involvement in the criminal justice system. Research demonstrates there is a positive correlation between arrest and drug or alcohol abuse.

Pete Rose

Unlike O.J. Simpson and Michael Irvin, Pete Rose epitomizes the price an athlete can pay when his personal transgressions interfere with his professional accolades. Rose is currently banned from Major League Baseball for betting on the team he was managing, the Cincinnati Reds. As the sports all-time leader in hits, he is still a very popular figure in the sport, even though his ban makes him ineligible for the Baseball Hall of Fame.

What makes the Pete Rose story noteworthy for our analysis is that Rose denied any wrongdoing for almost a decade before admitting to betting on baseball, betting on his team, as well as other professional sports (Rose & Hill, 2004). His admission of a gambling problem simultaneously shook the confidence of his fans and gave Major League Baseball fresh evidence to justify his ban. By claiming he was addicted to gambling, Rose began the initial steps to possibly gaining readmission to baseball and eligibility in the Hall of Fame. Rose's issue with gambling began as a youngster—his neighborhood in Cincinnati was known as the place to go to explore booze, card games, and prostitutes (Rose & Hill, 2004). Though Rose's legal troubles were not directly related to violence, there is a definite connection to criminal behavior.

Latrell Sprewell

NBA and former University of Alabama basketball star Latrell Sprewell is probably best known for choking his coach, P.J. Carlesimo, during practice. Due to this incident, Sprewell's contract worth $32 million at the time was voided, and he was kicked off the team. This incident was not the first for Sprewell, who routinely fostered a bad boy image by exchanging vulgarities with fans and referees. His punishments included fines for both transgressions (Puma, 2004). Sprewell also captures the essence of many professional athletes when he claimed in 2004 that he could not accept a mere $21 million contract because he had a "family to feed" (Beck, 2004).

Sprewell's belligerent style is typical of bullying athletes who are aggressive toward fans, coaches, teammates, and even their own family. Many of his antics are no doubt associated with his feelings of entitlement. He once refused to talk to the media at the onset of a season. Rumors suggested his behavior was to antagonize his coach. Nevertheless, Sprewell's giving fans the finger and making an obscene reference towards a female fan are indicative of the inappropriate behaviors most fans witness. Incidentally, this era of NBA basketball took on a disproportionate amount of bad press for the on and off court behaviors of its players and led to a dress code for players (Dress code reaction, 2006). Clearly the league believed the antics of Sprewell and others were taking a toll on their image.

Part II: Amateur Sports

With the way professional athletes are glamorized in media, it is not surprising that the pressures of athletic superiority have filtered past colleges and into high schools and youth leagues around the United States. No one has to look further than Music Television's (MTV) popular documentary of big-time high school football at Hoover High School to see that high schools are now as pressurized and commercialized as colleges. Hoover's success and "system" became the subject of MTV's show *Two-A-Days*, which ran for two seasons. Hoover High School is in a wealthy school district south of Birmingham, Alabama. Until the recent fall from grace of its well-known coach Rush Propst for maintaining a secret family, Hoover was routinely featured on ESPN and several other regional telecasts. This type of interest in youth sports has allowed them to quickly become as commercially successful as some of their counterparts at the college and professional ranks. This success is not without consequences, including misplaced priorities and violence.

Lynn Jamieson, a professor and chair of Indiana University-Bloomington's Department of Recreation, Park and Tourism Studies, contends that this disturbing trend leads indirectly to violence and aggression due to the tremendous pressures associated with making youth competitive in athletics ("Violence in youth sports," n.d.). "I know a woman who worked two full-time jobs so her child could compete with a traveling team," (n.p.) said Jamieson, whose research interests include sports violence. "When your life revolves around the sport and competition, the stress and frustration can manifest itself in the player and parents" (n.p.). Professor Jamieson also contends that verbal abuse can be worse than physical abuse when it comes from coaches, parents or other players. It also can accelerate physical violence. Disturbingly, the examples of youth coach, parent, and player violence are numerous.

The National Association of Sports Officials (NASO), an organization with 18,000 members, routinely receives reports of incidents involving youth sports violence. The organization contends that it does not keep up with official numbers involving youth sports violence, and the examples it is aware of are just the tip of the iceberg ("Poor sporting behavior incidents," n.d.). Listed below are a few examples reported on the NASO website:

- New Jersey (Soccer) — Referee James Clay, a 50-year-old with seven years of officiating experience, was slugged in the head and neck after ejecting a Clayton High School player with 12:47 left in a scoreless game. The player, who had received a yellow card earlier in the game for incidental cursing, was given a red-yellow card for taunting about 15 minutes after the first incident. A red-yellow results in immediate ejection. The player, whose name cannot be released because he is younger than 18, was arrested and charged with aggravated assault. He was released to the custody of his parents (n.p.).

- Hawaii (Soccer) — Referee Kaleo Benz was pushed to the ground by a high school player on February 12 [2003] following a state quarterfinal game between Pearl City and Baldwin high schools. Benz had issued a yellow card to the player involved earlier in the contest. Benz was not injured as a result of the attack, but he did file a criminal assault complaint against the player. The Hawaii High School Athletic Association (HHSAA) and the Maui Interscholastic League (MIL) did its own investigation and handed out penalties. The HHSAA executive board ruled on April 10 [2003] that Baldwin boys' soccer coach Fred Guzman was banned for five years from coaching at the state tournament, Saffery is banned from participation in any state sports event and the team is on "conduct probation" for a year, which means they can compete but will be monitored closely. The MIL principals unanimously voted to support the actions taken by the HHSAA executive board. According to the executive director of HHSAA there was "overwhelming evidence" of other acts of poor sportsmanship by the Baldwin team during the season ... (n.p.).
- Tennessee (Baseball) — Umpire John Garland, of Nashville, [Tennessee], pointed out a couple of unsafe bats to a Little League coach during a youth game and ended up being the victim of violence a day later. Garland said that Coach Jason Swafford approached him and his 17-year-old son, Brian, who is also an umpire, in the parking lot after a game the next night. Swafford allegedly pushed, shoved, and punched John Garland in the neck when he turned his back to walk away. He also struck Brian Garland, who had pointed out the same bats in Swafford's game that night as his father did a day earlier (n.p.).
- Texas (Swimming) — A man was arrested after shoving the referee into a swimming pool during a morning swim meet among children in San Antonio. Benjamin Mora was not injured in the incident that centered around his disqualification of the parent's 8-year-old child (n.p.).
- Wisconsin (Baseball) — A 62-year-old volunteer baseball umpire is punched in the face several times by a coach who was angry over a noncall in an 11- and 12-year-old baseball game. The coach follows the umpire into the equipment room [and attacks] him (n.p.).

These examples are quite disturbing, but are becoming commonplace on evening news and cable sports channels. Amateur and youth sports include troubling levels of violence and inappropriate behaviors such as cheating and even assault. For example, Tonya Harding ordered an attack on Nancy Kerrigan during a figure skating competition — Harding's husband whacked Kerrigan in the knee in order to keep her from competing against his wife (Buckley, 1994). Of course, we also have examples of doping in Olympic sports and allegations of using ineligible players. Sports at all levels foster an extreme competitive desire for fame and triumph that routinely manifests itself into violence against teammates, coaches, referees, and fans.

Part III: Psychological Implications

The behavior of professional athletes on and off-the-field leaves an impression on individuals in our society. As we demonstrated, sports are saturated in our society 24 hours a day and seven days a week. Whether we like it or not, when professional athletes "act up" there are consequences to those who view them as role models. Without a doubt, children are watching. Parts I and II of this chapter demonstrated how professional, amateur and youth league participants display unacceptable behavior. Ultimately, why do these individuals feel they can exhibit deviant and criminal behavior? At the same time, what are the psychological implications of their behavior? Moreover, who really suffers? Is it the individual player, the fans or society as a whole? Obviously, these questions are difficult to answer; however, there exist several psychological theories which may assist us learning how and why these athletes behave as they do.

Social Learning Theory

According to Aronson, Wilson, and Akert (1999), Social Learning Theory holds that individuals learn social behavior by observing or modeling and then imitating others. One of the most well known studies of social learning was conducted by Albert Bandura in the early 1960s. Here, Bandura had an adult hit, kick, and yell at a plastic air-filled doll known as Bobo. Once struck, this plastic doll would bounce back up. It is important to note that both adults and children were involved in the study. However, according to Aronson, Wilson, and Akert (1999):

> In these experiments, the children imitated the aggressive models and treated the doll in an abusive manner. Children in a control group condition, who did not see the aggressive adult in action, almost never unleashed any aggression against the hapless doll. Moreover, the children who watched the aggressive adult used identical action and identical aggressive words as the adult (pp. 471–472).

Modeling Continued

As mentioned, an important component within social learning theory is modeling. For example, back in the 1970s, the professional baseball team Cincinnati Reds had a player named Joe Morgan. Whenever Morgan would bat his arm would twitch violently back and forth while awaiting the pitch. During this time, children across America modeled their batting stance after Joe Morgan. Another example is Pete Rose. Rose, also a Cincinnati Red, was notorious for sliding into a base head first. In fact, during the 1970 all-star game, Rose essentially ended catcher Ray Fosse's career by running him over at home plate. What was the reaction? Players around the country were running into home plate attempting to replicate Rose. However, for a model to observe or learn and then imitate a given behavior, there must be rewards and punishments. Rewards are something that is either tangible or intangible. Rewards can also vary from individual to individual. For example, a child who hits a game winning home run is likely to be the beneficiary of praise from coaches, friends, family and peers. A hockey player who gets into a fight with an opposing team's player often receives praise from parents, fans, coaches and peers. In contrast to rewards are punishments. When Boston Red Sox first baseman, Bill Buckner, committed an error at first base during the 1986 World Series, he was met with ridicule, degradation, and death threats. In professional sports, we often see punishments in the form of fines from the organization. According to the Dougherty (2008), Nick Barnett of the Packers was recently fined $132,647 for violating the NFL's personal conduct policy. According to ESPN ("NFL Personal Conduct Policy," 2007), the policy holds that:

> Engaging in violent and/or criminal activity is unacceptable and constitutes conduct detrimental to the integrity of and public confidence in the National Football League. Such conduct alienates the fans on whom the success of the League depends and has negative and sometimes tragic consequences for both the victim and the perpetrator. The League is committed to promoting and encouraging lawful conduct and to providing a safe and professional workplace for its employees (n.p.).

Aggression

Aggressive action is defined as "intentional behavior aimed at causing either physical or psychological pain" (Aronson, Wilson, & Akert 1999, p. 457). At what age do individuals begin to display aggressive behavior? Consider the following example by Feldman (2000):

> Four-year-old Duane could not contain his anger and frustration any more. Although he usually was mild mannered, when Eshu began to tease him about the split in his pants and kept it up for several minutes, Duane finally snapped. Rushing over to Eshu, Duane pushed him to the ground and began to hit him with his small, closed fists. Because he was so distraught, Duane's punches were not terribly effective, but they were severe enough to hurt Eshu and bring him to tears before the preschool teachers could intervene (p. 281).

As the above example demonstrates, the potential for violence is present during the preschool years. Children often use aggression to obtain some goal (i.e., obtain a toy or a desired seat). While aggression tends to subside in most children, there are many who continue to display aggression in later years. According to Feldman (2000), aggression is a stable characteristic where "the most aggressive preschool-age children tend to be the most aggressive children during the school-age years" (p. 282). Incidentally, the school-age years are when children begin participating in sports. Ultimately, we (our society) are sending incongruent messages to children. For example, consider this hypothetical. We have an aggressive child who is being punished for aggressive acts by parents and teachers. The child begins to play hockey or football, which are dominated by aggressive acts. The child is now receiving mixed messages from parents, teachers and coaches. One group suggests it is ok to hit, kick, and punch, whereas the other forbids this behavior.

Parts I and II demonstrated unacceptable behavior of individual athletes—however, is it possible that these individuals do not know how to act? The majority of society understands right from wrong. At the same time, citizens understand that when violence is displayed and crimes committed, consequences will follow. However, an argument can be made that many athletes do not understand nor did they learn the parameters. For many athletes, violence on-the-field translates to violence off-the-field. According to one athlete, how can the people that cheer me on-the-field, turn around and hate me off-the-field?

Entitlement

Another important psychological construct is entitlement. According to Schwartz and Tylka (2008) "entitlement is defined as an individual's attitude about what he or she has the right to expect from others" (p. 68). There are two forms of entitlement. The first is self-reliance. Without question, this form is necessary for an individual's well-being. In contrast to this is narcissistic entitlement or self-promotion. According to Schwartz and Tylka (2008), narcissistic entitlement or self-promotion "is characterized by an exaggerated idea of one's own rights without regard for the rights of others, resulting in self-centered and demanding behavior" (p. 69). Arguably, there are many athletes in professional, amateur and youth leagues that exhibit entitlement issues. Whether we like this or not, our society treats athletes differently. One could argue there is a conditioning process that occurs over time. For example, we have all heard about the star high school quarterback who was challenged academically. Nonetheless, the quarterback somehow makes the grades and is ultimately playing collegiate football. However, the same benefits that were afforded at the high school level no longer exist. Ultimately, you have a collegiate football player who believes he is entitled to preferential treatment. This sense of entitlement is based on years of previous treatment. In sum, this is the only frame of reference the individual has.

Conclusion

Sports stars and sports competition both have privileged status in the United States. Professional athletes at the pinnacle of their sports are given star treatment and idolized by adoring fans. They do serve as examples of success and fame, if not role models. This prominent place occupied by sports celebrities creates a desire among their amateur counterparts to be equally successful. As such, college and youth sports are placing strong emphases on winning and success. This led to speculation about why violence and cheating have permeated supposedly-innocent youth activities. The importance of sports necessitates that we pay attention to the violence it causes. Psychologically speaking, there are severe implications that follow America's love for violence in sports. As demonstrated, children from a very early age learn behavior from their role models and ultimately are rewarded for aggressive acts. The elementary discussion on social learning, modeling and aggression signifies a cycle that is forever present.

References

Aronson, E., Wilson, T., & Akert, R. (1999). *Social psychology* (3rd ed.) New York: Longman.

Badenhausen, K., Ozanian, M.K., & Settimi, C. (2008). The richest game: Special report. Forbes.com. Retrieved on September 8, 2008, from http://www.forbes.com/2008/09/10/nfl-team-valuations-biz-sports-nfl08_cz_kb_mo_cs_0910intro.html

Beck, H. (2004, December 29). Kinder, gentler Sprewell expected at the Garden. *New York Times*. Retrieved on October 3, 2008, from http://www.nytimes.com/2004/12/29/sports/basketball/29knicks.html

Buckley, S. (1994, February 2, 1994). Gilloly pleads guilty, says Harding approved plot. *Washington Post*, p. A1

Cunningham, S. (2008). *Esquire*. Retrieved on October 6, 2008, from http://www.esquire.com/features/history-of-pacman-jones

Dougherty, P. (2008). Notebook: Aim is for KGB to rush Romo. *Green Bay Press Gazette*. Retrieved on October 6, 2008, from http://www.greenbaypress gazette.com/apps/pbcs.dll/article?AID=/20080919/PKR01/809200401/1989/GPG02

Dress code reaction. (2006). NBA.com. Retrieved on October 3, 2008, from http://www.nba.com/news/dresscodereaction_051019.html

Feldman, R. (2000). *Development across the life span* (2nd ed.) Upper Saddle River, NJ: Prentice-Hall.

Handlin, S. (2001, October 21). Court TV News. Retrieved on October 6, 2008, from http://www.courttv.com/trials/ojroadrage/102201-pm_ctv.html

Irvin arrested on charge of cocaine possession. (2001). ESPN.com. Retrieved on October 3, 2008, from http://espn.go.com/nfl/news/2001/0618/1215598.html

Johnson, G. (2008). Football attendance Soars Again. *NCAA News*. Retrieved on February 8, 2008, from http://www.ncaa.org/wps/ncaa?ContentID=4232

Kramer, S. (2008). ESPN will pay $2.25 billion for some SEC rights; Live streaming included. Forbes.com. Retrieved on August 25, 2008, from www.forbes.com/2008/08/25/espn-southeastern-confeence.html

Lance, L. (2005). Violence in sport: A theoretical note. *Sociological Spectrum*, 25, 213–214.

Michael Irvin (n.d.) Pro Football Hall of Fame. Retrieved on October 3, 2008, from http://www.profootballhof.com/hof/member.jsp?player_id=246

Mortensen, C. (2008). Source: Cowboys determine Pacman scuffle didn't break rules. ESPN.com. Retrieved on October 9, 2008, from http://sports.espn.go.com/nfl/news/story?id=3634226.

NBA sets all-time attendance records. (2007). NBA.com. Retrieved on October 3, 2008, from http://www.nba.com/news/attendance_070419.html

NFL Personal Conduct Policy. (2007) ESPN.com. Retrieved on October 4, 2008, from http://sports.espn.go.com/nfl/news/story?id=2798214

NFL reinstates Cowboys' 'Pacman' Jones. (2008). *USA Today*. Retrieved on October 3, 2008, from http://www.usatoday.com/sports/football/nfl/cowboys/2008-08-28-pacman-reinstated_N.htm

NFL sets regular-season paid attendance record. (2008). NFL.com. Retrieved on October 6, 2008, from http://www.nfl.com/news/story?id=09000d5d805b5d53&template=without-video&confirm=true

OJ Simpson fined for stealing cable (2005, July 28). News.com.au. Retrieved October 3, 2008, from http://www.news.com.au/story/0,10117,16074238-1702,00.html

Ozanian, M.K., & Badenhausen, K. (2008). The business of baseball: Special report. Forbes.com. Retrieved October2, 2008, from www.forbes.com/2008/04/16/baseball-team-values.html

Police: Pacman's cash display sparked Vegas melee. (2007). ESPN.com. Retrieved on October 3, 2008, from http://sports.espn.go.com/nfl/news/story?id=2775250

Poor sporting behavior incidents reported to National Association of Sports Officials (n.d.). National Association of Sports Officials. Retrieved on October 3, 2008, from http://www.naso.org/sportsmanship/badsports.html

Puma, M. (2004). The 'choke' artist. ESPN Classic. Retrieved on October 3, 2008, from http://espn.go.com/classic/s/add_sprewell_latrell.html

Rose, P., & Hill, R. (2004). *My prison without bars*. Emmaus, PA: Rodale Publishing.

Schwartz, J., & Tylka, T. (2008). Exploring entitlement as a moderator and mediator of the relationship between masculine gender role conflict and men's body esteem. *Psychology of Men and Masculinity*, 9(2), 67–81.

Violence in youth sports—a bottom-line issue (n.d.). Retrieved on October 3, 2008, from http://newsinfo.iu.edu/web/page/normal/4727.html

5

Violent Acts within the Context of the Game: On-Field Occurrences and Prosecution

Barbara Osborne, University of North Carolina at Chapel Hill

Introduction

The frequency and severity of violent acts in sport are increasing—not just in collision sports such as football and ice hockey, but in seemingly every sport at every level of play, including professional, amateur, recreational, collegiate, high school, and youth. Athletes are expected to give "100 percent" to perform their best, and sport would not be as fun to play or watch if everyone was being very careful not to touch anyone else. A hard check is desired in hockey, a jolting tackle is revered in football, an intentional foul is strategy in basketball, and a collision at the plate is common and expected in baseball. All of these acts can cause serious injury. Is it possible to determine what is acceptable contact that falls within the normal scope and course of the game, and contact that is so aggressive or violent that it is unrelated to the game?

Imagine the following scenarios:

- In an NFL playoff game, a defensive tackle viciously hits the quarterback, taking him out at the knees, just as he is passing the ball. Media coverage for the week prior to the game continuously questioned the quarterback's readiness to play given recent knee injuries. The quarterback suffers severe ligament damage and is carried off the field in a stretcher (Lassiter, 2007).
- In a recreational basketball league game at a community gym, opposing players collide as they leap for a rebound. The player with the ball intentionally swings his elbows wide as he pulls the ball down. An opponent is elbowed in the head, falls to the floor unconscious, and later dies from his injury (Lau, 2000).
- In a college baseball game, the pitcher wants to send a message to a batter standing in the on-deck circle timing pitches. The pitcher nails the

on-deck batter with a 90-mph fast ball, fracturing his eye socket and permanently disabling him (Floyd, 2000).

In all three of these situations, an athlete is seriously injured by an opposing player in a situation that typically occurs during the course of play in that particular sport. Although most American sports fans do not want to see athletes seriously injured or die, many would matter-of-factly accept that these tragedies happen as a part of the risk of participating in sport. Others might lament that as athletes grow bigger, stronger, and faster, injuries are more frequent and severe. Still others might suggest that a societal emphasis on success in athletics fosters increasing levels of violence in order to win.

American society values sport, so from a public policy perspective, there is a need to promote free and vigorous participation in athletics (Harary, 2002; Lassiter, 2007). While some might believe that competitive contact sports are inherently violent, others believe that violence is encouraged because high levels of aggression actually enhance the entertainment value of sport (Lassiter). If this is true, then it is in the best interest of American society to effect policy that reduces violent acts in sport that create unreasonable risk of serious injury (Harary).

Every sport has rules that establish a "level playing field," as well as rules that protect the safety of participants. When an athlete violates the rules, officials make the call to penalize the athlete in a number of ways. The athlete may be sent out of the game for a period of time, as in hockey, or permanently expelled from the game, as in a red card situation in soccer. The athlete may accumulate a certain number of fouls before they are sent out of the game, such as five fouls in basketball or two yellow cards in soccer. The athlete's team may also be penalized by awarding yards to the opponent in football, providing a direct kick or penalty kick in soccer, or free throws in basketball. This system of penalties and awards provides incentive for athletes to conduct themselves in a sportsmanlike manner and play within the rules. When an athlete flagrantly violates a rule or displays an obvious lack of sportsmanship, the league or governing body may step in and impose additional punishment, such as suspending future participation in multiple games, levying fines, or expelling the player from the league.

While some believe that events that occur during the course of the game are best handled by those responsible for the conduct of the game—coaches, officials, and leagues—others believe that some acts of aggression are so heinous that they should be punished in the same way that all members of society are punished when they commit an act of violence. In the United States, if one person intentionally injures another or behaves so recklessly that no regard is given as to whether those actions will harm others, public policy dictates that the injured person is compensated by the person who caused the injury. In civil law, a battery is defined as intentionally touching another with intent to harm without the other's consent (Garner, 2004). The person that is found to have committed a civil battery is generally required to pay damages associated with the harm that he caused—in essence, to restore the injured party.

Sometimes an action is so terrible that it is considered to be offensive to society in general. In these situations, public policy demands that society be represented by a prosecutor, and the perpetrator be punished through the criminal justice system. In the United States, criminal law is based on society's need to be free from harmful conduct. Criminal behavior and punishment are defined by the laws of each state and the federal government (for federal crimes). Unlike civil law where the goal is to compensate the wronged party, the broad aim of criminal law is to prevent injury to the health, safety, morals, and welfare of the public in general.

Does criminal prosecution of intentional acts of violence on the athletics fields serve the goals of the criminal justice system? Do athletes who exercise excessive aggression within the context of play pose a threat to society in general? Cultural spillover theory argues that the more society encourages or legitimizes violent behavior in sports, the greater the likelihood that illegitimate acts of violence will spill over into other social settings (Oh, 2006, p. 322). Social culture in the United States encourages competition and rewards intense effort and aggressiveness. Young athletes learn these lessons early in their sporting careers and understand this to be accepted behavior (Barry, Fox, & Jones, 2005). Consistent with cultural spillover theory, the lessons young athletes learn on the playing fields carry over into the normal social settings of their everyday lives, escalating incidents of violent behavior in society. Similarly, the theory that athletes are role models indicates that sports fans, both young and old, will emulate the actions of their sports heroes on and off the playing field, whether those acts are legal or illegal (Barry, Fox, & Jones, 2005)

Those that lead sport organizations argue that the game penalties assessed by coaches, officials, and the leagues effectively establish acceptable standards of aggressive play for young athletes, thus teaching that uncontrolled acts of violence are unacceptable on the playing fields or in society. However, others believe that the penalty scheme for rules infractions is wholly inadequate to address intentional acts of violence that cause serious injury in a game (Lassiter, 2007; Oh, 2006). One reason is that coaches and leagues have a conflict of interest relative to punishing athletes for their aggressive acts on the fields, as those actions generally further the team objective of winning. At the professional level, punishing star athletes for their violent acts may be counter productive, as fans want to see athletes compete vigorously and even viciously. A recent fight in a Women's National Basketball Association (WNBA) game between the Detroit Shock and the Los Angeles Sparks raised interest and viewership in the league ("WNBA suspends," 2008). Those managing professional sport understand that violence sells; fighting may even be one of the reasons that fans attend various sporting events. Suspending athletes for violent acts could ultimately hurt professional sports in the bottom line (Barry, Fox, & Jones, 2005).

The appropriate forum for meting punishment for aggressive and violent acts on the playing field during the course of play has been widely debated by legal scholars (Clarke, 2000; Harary, 2002; Lassiter, 2007; Marder, 2004; Oh, 2006; Schoenfelder, 2001). Barry, Fox, and Jones (2005) surveyed a national sample of 1,000 trial court judges asking their opinions about violence in professional sports. Almost two-thirds (64 percent) of the judges who responded considered sports violence to be a serious problem. Almost all (93 percent) of the respondents indicated that they believe professional athletes do not consent to intentional acts of violence during the course of a game that go beyond the scope of the rules. However, 60 percent of the judges who participated agreed that it is difficult to distinguish between tolerable and intolerable levels of violence in sports. Nevertheless, the study found that 77 percent of judges felt that intentional acts of excessive violence within sports should be criminally prosecuted.

Although judges seem to believe that athletes should be criminally prosecuted, prosecutors hesitate to file charges against athletes for acts of violence during the course of play. One reason may be that prosecutors do not view athletes as "real criminals" and fear negative public relations for prosecuting a sports hero when there are so many other "real" violent crimes occurring in our society. Similarly, the victim of the athlete's violent actions usually does not want to file criminal charges against a fellow athlete, leaving the prosecution without a complainant. In each of the real situations described at the beginning of this chapter, no criminal charges were filed, even though the victims in each case were severely injured.

A recent incident at a professional hockey game illustrates the struggle for prosecutors in determining whether to press criminal charges against an athlete for a "crime" committed during the course of play. On March 8, 2007, New York Islanders winger Chris Simon slammed the shaft of his stick across the face of New York Rangers forward Ryan Hollweg (Anderson, 2007). Those viewing the act described it as a crude act of violence, labeled the stick a weapon, and screamed for punishment. Simon was suspended by the NHL for 25 games—the remainder of the regular season and any playoff games in 2007, and any additional games necessary in 2008 to reach 25. The length of the suspension was a record for the NHL (Anderson, 2007). Almost two weeks after the incident, the Nassau Country District Attorney announced that they would not prosecute Simon (Dellapina, 2007). The decision was made after thorough investigation of the act, assessment of the injury, the willingness of the victim to support a criminal prosecution, and the safety of the residents of Nassau County (Dellapina). Chris Hollweg declined to press charges, perhaps because he only required a few stitches in his chin (Anderson).

Another highly publicized incident created a public outcry that criminal charges should be filed. On October 15, 2006, the University of Miami was playing a NCAA Division I football game against Florida International University. With approximately nine minutes left in the third quarter, James Bryant incurred a 15 yard penalty for taunting after he caught a five yard touchdown pass, bringing the score to 13–0 in favor of Miami. As Miami scored the extra point, FIU player Chris Smith knocked down Miami holder Matt Perelli and punched him. Subsequently, approximately 100 players from both teams were involved in a brawl; media clips showed Miami players swinging helmets like weapons, stomping on FIU players that were on the ground, and an FIU player on crutches on the sidelines wielding his crutch like a weapon. There were no arrests ("Miami, FIU have," 2006).

Defining "Criminal Acts"

In order to access whether acts of violence occurring on the field of play should be criminally prosecuted, it is necessary to understand the criminal justice system and the various crimes that may (or may not) be committed. In criminal law each state may uniquely define its criminal code, while the federal government determines actions that are federal crimes. The Model Penal Code is a scholarly attempt to compile a comprehensive and coherent body of criminal law. Although it is not a source of law, the Model Penal Code does provide a resource for study of the criminal law, regardless of jurisdiction.

Using actual cases to illustrate the legal concepts, the required elements of the crimes will be defined as well as the most common defenses. Relative to the significant number of people who participate in sport, there are very few cases that are criminally prosecuted. The very first case in the United States was a boxing case, *People v. Fitzsimmons* (1895), however most legal analysis begins with Canadian ice hockey cases from the 20th century. Although Canadian cases do not establish precedent within the United States legal system, they do have influential value and provide insight into the development of the law in this area. Both Canadian and United States cases will be discussed in this chapter.

Elements of a Crime

The prosecutor bears the burden of providing beyond a reasonable doubt two essential elements that define a crime: *actus reas* (an unlawful action) and *mens rea* (an evil intention). In order to prove *actus reas*, the athlete must commit a voluntary, conscious act (Model Penal Code § 2.01). A hard tackle, throwing a ball, or grabbing a rebound are all lawful actions that occur everyday in sports. Similarly, using an enforcer whose role is to provide a physical presence on the team, and to protect the star athletes through retaliatory fouls, is common (Oh, 2006). Sending a message with a brush-back pitch, or even intentionally hitting a batter who slid into base with his cleats high, are ordinary occurrences accepted within the rules of the game. Even ritualized fighting in hockey or bench clearing brawls in baseball—acts of violence that do not occur during the regular course of play—are accepted by players, coaches, and fans as actions within the culture of the sport. However, the nature of an extremely aggressive or excessively violent action within the course of the game may transform that act into one that is unlawful (Lassiter, 2007).

The second element that must be proved to establish a crime is that the athlete had a guilty mind—*mens rea*. Within the definition of a crime, there is an associated mentality. The four criminal states of mind are: intentionally or purposely, knowingly, recklessly, and grossly or negligently.

Establishing intent is extremely problematic in a sport setting. As intent can only truly be known to the person who commits the act, it is through the accomplishment of the physical act that mens rea is established. A person acts intentionally, or purposely, if there is an act of the will and the action was not an accident (Garner, 2004). This mental state is required for specific intent crimes, meaning that the conscious objective of the athlete is to cause the specific harm that resulted. It is rare for an athlete to admit intent to purposely harm an opponent. In his 1980 book, *They Call Me Assassin*, former Oakland Raiders safety Jack Tatum bragged: "I never make a tackle just to bring someone down. I want to punish the man I'm going after. I like to believe my best hits border on felonious assault." In 1978, Tatum cleanly tackled New England Patriots wide receiver Darryl Stingley, paralyzing Stingley below the waist. Would Tatum's words satisfy the requirement of evil intention? Or do those words simply articulate a desired and acceptable standard of motivation on the playing field?

In the case of *Regina v. Francis* (1989), Allan Francis, an adult playing in a recreational, no checking hockey league was found guilty of assault causing bodily harm for knocking an opponent unconscious with a cross check to the back of the neck (p. 6). There was testimony that Francis had warned the victim on several occasions that "he was going to get him" (p. 5). Francis also skated over to the victim prior to a face-off just before the attack and threatened "keep your head up, I'm going to get you!" (p. 5). These words would seem to indicate that Francis acted intentionally or purposefully, but the court declined to address his mental state, instead opting for the simple knowing intent standard.

A person acts knowingly when he or she has conscious understanding that harm is likely to occur as a result of the action (Garner, 2004). It is assumed that a person intends the natural and ordinary consequences of his actions (*People v. Fitzsimmons*, 1895). The "knowingly" mental state is one of general intent; the athlete must be aware that his conduct may cause a harmful result. In *Regina v Francis* (1989), a case stemming from an incident in an adult recreational hockey league, Judge James Harper consolidates decisions from previous Canadian cases and suggests that the appropriate mental intent required in sports related cases should be "merely the intent to apply force to the person of another in such a manner that bodily harm could probably result, and the offence is complete whether or not actual bodily harm in fact ensues" (p. 84).

Marty McSorley, a defenseman for the Boston Bruins, testified at his trial that he never intended to harm Donald Brashear of the Vancouver Canucks ("Very major penalty," 2000). McSorley was charged with assault with a deadly weapon for a two-fisted swinging slash to the head of Brashear with only 3 seconds remaining in an NHL game. Judge William Kitchen believed that McSorley's actions showed that he intended to strike Brashear. The judge stated McSorley: "slashed for the head. A child, swinging as at a tee-ball, would not miss. A housekeeper swinging a carpet-beater would not miss. An NHL player would never, ever miss" ("Very major penalty," 2000).

An athlete demonstrates the recklessly mental state when he consciously disregards a substantial and unjustified risk that harm will result from his actions (Garner, 2004). With this mental state, there is no intent to cause harm, but the athlete is culpable for his actions because he is aware that harm is likely to result from his actions and yet, he ignores that risk (*People v. Hall*, 2000). In *People v. Hall*, the court focused on the mental state of recklessness and broke it down to the particular elements: consciousness, substantial risk, and unjustified risk. An athlete consciously ignores a risk when he is aware of the risk and chooses to act in spite of it. Unless the defendant was to admit this awareness, it is inferred because of the athlete's training, knowledge and prior experiences. Whether a risk is substantial is determined by assessing the likelihood that harm will occur as well as the magnitude of the harm. A risk may be substantial when the magnitude of the harm is potentially great even if the chance that harm may occur is unlikely. On the other hand, even if there is high probability that risk will occur, if the harm that is likely is only very minor, that would not be characterized as a substantial risk. Finally, if a risk is unjustifiable is determined by assessing the nature and purpose of the actor's conduct relative to how substantial the risk is. If there is a socially valid purpose for the action, then it may be justified.

The mental state for acting negligently or grossly is carelessness resulting in bodily harm, thoughtless disregard for the consequences of one's actions, or heedless indifference to the rights and safety of others (Garner, 2004). If a player commits an act of gross carelessness, or acts in a way that indicates no forethought regarding the consequences of those actions, the prosecution needs to establish that the player engaged in a gross deviation from the reasonable level of care that an ordinarily prudent athlete would exhibit in the same or similar circumstance (*People v. Fitzsimmons*, 1895; *People v. Hall*, 2000). The distinction between the mental states of recklessly and negligently/grossly is that criminal negligence is a failure to perceive of the consequential risk of one's actions (*People v. Hall*, 2000).

Historically, the simple act of playing a game negated criminal intent for an athlete's actions within that game. Under English Rule, if the conduct occurred within the rules of the game, it was assumed that a player operating in a setting in which violence is customary and approved was not acting with malice or criminal intent, but was merely following established practices of the sport (*Regina v. Bradshaw*, 1878). In *Regina v. LeClerc* (1991), the issue on appeal was whether the trial judge erred in his interpretation of the mens rea requirement by requiring proof of a specific intent to cause serious injury. In this case, the defendant, LeClerc, injured an opponent in a non-contact industrial league semi-final play-off game by viciously cross-checking him with his gloves and stick in the upper part of the back. The victim slammed head first into the boards and fell to the ice, his fourth and fifth cervical vertebrae fractured causing permanent paralysis. LeClerc maintained that he did not intentionally injure the victim, but pushed him from behind to move him off the puck, and that it was the speed of the victim falling into the boards that caused the injuries. Under Canadian law, the mens rea for an assault is the intent to apply force to another, either directly or indirectly. Because the judge in the trial court included an instruction that elevated the mens rea to that of specific intent to cause serious injury to another, the appellate court held that the trial court erred. However, the appellate court ruled that the faulty instruction did not impact the final outcome of the case: LeClerc was acquitted, as the physical contact was an instinctive reflex within normal play that lacked malicious intent to inflict bodily harm.

If a player's action is deemed to be an involuntary reflex, mens rea is negated. According to the Model Penal Code, § 2.01(2)(a), a reflex is not a voluntary act (2001). If a player can prove that the act causing harm was a bodily movement that was otherwise not a product of the effort or will of the athlete, but unconscious or habitual, criminal intent is also negated (Model Penal Code, § 2.01(2)(d), 2001). Athletes are trained by repeating movements over and over until they become reflexive. In *Regina v. Green* (1970), the court found that the accused player's actions were instinctive within the context of a game that is played a high speed with people who are "keenly on edge" (p. 142).

Assault

An athlete who commits a particularly egregious or violent act within the course of play is most likely to be charged with assault. Within criminal law, assault may be an attempt to cause harm, but also includes actually causing bodily injury, which is defined as a battery within the civil law. The Model Penal Code § 2.11.1 divides criminal assault into two categories: simple or aggravated. A person is guilty of simple assault if he attempts to cause, or purposely, knowingly, or recklessly causes bodily injury to another; or negligently causes bodily injury to another with a deadly weapon; or physically attempts to put someone in fear of imminent serious bodily injury. A simple assault is a misdemeanor, unless it is committed during a physical altercation that was entered into by mutual consent of both parties, making it a petty misdemeanor. An aggravated assault is an attempt to cause serious bodily injury to another, or purposely, knowingly, or recklessly causing bodily injury under circumstances indicating extreme indifference to the value of human life. A person is also guilty of aggravated assault if she attempts to injure, or purposely or knowingly physically injures another person with a deadly weapon (Model Penal Code § 2.11.2). Aggravated assault may be either a second or third degree felony, depending on the circumstances.

Gino Guidugli, the starting quarterback for the University of Cincinnati football team, was convicted of misdemeanor assault for punching an opponent during a fight that broke out in an intramural basketball game on campus (*State v. Guidugli*, 2004). The fight started when one of Guidugli's teammates protested a foul and then exchanged heated words with an opponent. When the opposing player grabbed the teammate by the shirt, both benches emptied and there was a lot of pushing and shoving. Guidugli testified that he was trying to pull players apart when he saw a punch coming and reacted by punching Levi Harris in the eye in self-defense. Conflicting testimony indicated that Guidugli was the aggressor, winding up before punching Harris. The trial court rejected Guidugli's claim of self-defense, concluding that his actions were retaliatory. Although the appellate court questioned the necessity of criminal prosecution for an injury as trivial as a black eye, they found no reversible legal error and Guidugli's conviction was upheld.

High school soccer star Dwight Angelini was convicted of felony assault with a deadly weapon for kicking an opponent in the head during a soccer game (Schoenfelder, 2001). The deadly weapon was his foot. The victim suffered severe head trauma. Angelini was immediately ejected from the game, removed from the high school soccer team, and suspended from school for two days (Schoenfelder). Similarly, at a youth hockey game in Gurnee, Illinois, an unnamed 15-year-old player was charged with aggravated battery and use of a deadly weapon (his hockey stick). Testimony conflicted as to whether the offensive act, a cross check, occurred before, at, or just after the buzzer signaling the end of the game. The contact forced the victim, also 15 years old, into the boards, leaving him paralyzed (Isaacson, 2000).

Reckless Endangerment

Although recklessly causing injury is included in the Model Penal Code definition of assault, recklessly endangering another person may be a separate crime. Under the Model Penal Code, a person commits a misdemeanor if he recklessly engages in conduct which places or may place another person in danger of death or serious bodily injury (§ 211.2).

Homicide

If an athlete's actions within the context of a game cause the death of an opponent, the athlete could be charged with homicide. Under the Model Penal Code, homicide is defined as purposely, knowingly, recklessly, or negligently causing the death of a human being (§ 210.1(1)). Homicide may be murder, manslaughter, or negligent homicide (§ 210.1(2)). There are no recorded cases of athletes being charged with murder for actions within the context of the game. According to the Model Penal Code, manslaughter is recklessly causing the death of a human being (§ 210.3(a)). In *People v. Fitzsimmons* (1895), a professional boxer was charged with manslaughter in the first degree, as it was then defined in the New York Penal Code, for the death of his opponent in a sparring exhibition. Fitzsimmons and his sparring partner, Riordan, participated in one of many boxing matches scheduled at the Grand Opera House in Syracuse, New York, on November 16, 1894. Within the first minute of the fight, Fitzsimmons hit Riordan on the side of the head and chin with a blow that was described as fairly light. After being hit, Riordan apparently struggled to maintain balance, slumped to the mat, and was removed unconscious from the ring by stretcher. He died five hours later; the autopsy revealed several blood clots and a laceration in the brain. The prosecution charged that participation in the fight was a misdemeanor under New York law, and that manslaughter in the first degree is committed when a person causes the death of another while engaged in a misdemeanor, regardless of whether there was intent to cause death (*People v. Fitzsimmons*, 1895, p. 1106). The jury apparently did not believe that the prosecution satisfied the burden of proving the elements of the various homicides beyond a reasonable doubt, as Fitzsimmons was acquitted.

A more recent case, *People v. Hall* (2000), provides an example of a reckless manslaughter prosecution of an athlete in an individual, non-contact sport in a recreational context. Under Colorado law, the charge of reckless manslaughter requires that a person consciously disregard a substantial and unjustifiable risk that causes the death of another person. In this case, Nathan Hall was a former ski racer, trained in skier safety, who worked as a ski lift operator at a resort. When his shift ended, Hall skied straight down a steep and bumpy mountain, arms out to his sides, totally out of control and being thrown from mogul to mogul. He was skiing so fast that he became airborne after bouncing off a mogul and was unable to avoid hitting another skier who was traversing down the slope. Hall's ski hit the victim just above the ear at the thickest part of the skull, and the collision was so forceful that the victim died from a fractured skull and severe brain injuries. The trial court dismissed the case initially finding that a skier would not have been able to consciously disregard a substantial risk of death, because skiing ordinarily carries a very low risk of death. The higher court reversed and remanded the decision, finding that Hall's excessive speed, lack of control, and improper technique significantly increased both the likelihood that a collision would occur and the extent of the injuries that might result from such a collision, including the possibility of death. While this case does not ultimately address whether Hall was guilty of reckless manslaughter, it does define the legal requirements that a court must examine to determine whether the crime of reckless manslaughter occurred in a sport setting. The court must inquire into the specific facts of each case to determine beyond a reasonable doubt whether the athlete consciously disregarded a substantial and unjustifiable risk of death based on the likelihood of the risk, the potential magnitude of the harm, and the nature and purpose of the actor's conduct" (p. 224).

Negligent homicide occurs when an athlete commits an act negligently that causes the death of another (Model Penal Code § 210.4). The four elements of negligence—duty, breach, causation, and damage—must be proven. The athlete's act must grossly deviate from the action that a reasonably prudent player would take under the same or similar circumstance, to satisfy the greater criminal law threshold. In the case of *People v. Hall*, described in the previous paragraph, the prosecutor requested that, with respect to the manslaughter count, the court also consider the lesser charge of negligent manslaughter, if it was found that Hall did not act with conscious disregard for the safety of others, but merely failed to perceive the risk that occurred as a result of his actions.

Defenses

In criminal law, the prosecutor has the burden of proving beyond a reasonable doubt that the defendant committed the crime. Then, the defendant has the opportunity to launch a defense. The most common defenses used in the sports context are consent and self-defense.

Self-defense

The first contemporary case that addressed the issue of an athlete's criminal liability for actions within the context of the game is the Canadian case of *Regina v. Maki* (1970). On September 21, 1969, the Boston Bruins and St. Louis Blues were playing a NHL exhibition game at the Ottawa Civic Centre in Ottawa, Canada. A little over halfway into the first period, Ted Green of the Bruins shoved Wayne Maki of the Blues in the face with his glove. Maki was slightly dazed and the two players separated, but came together again in front of the Boston net. Green swung at Maki with his stick, striking him on the shoulders and neck. Maki then sliced at Green, his stick glancing off of Green's stick before it struck him in the head causing a skull fracture. Green required five hours of surgery to remove skull fragments from his brain. Maki was charged with assault causing bodily harm and claimed self-defense (*Regina v. Maki*, 1970).

Self-defense may be used as justification for a criminal act when the person who is not the aggressor in an encounter uses a reasonable amount of force against his adversary when he reasonably believes that he is in immediate danger of unlawful bodily harm and that the use of such force is necessary to avoid this danger (Model Penal Code § 3.04(1)). Applying self defense is generally problematic for participants in sport for several reasons. First, the amount of force used is limited to that which is reasonably necessary. Most unlawful behavior in sports contexts involves contact and then escalating levels of retaliation. In *Regina v. Maki*, evidence indicated that the near fatal blow to Green's head may have been the result of escalating levels of contact beginning with an incidental rules infraction. Another problem is timing: the participant/defendant must have had an honest belief that the danger of serious bodily harm was imminent. Athletes often retaliate after the danger has passed, although in this case, the entire incident lasted between five and ten seconds. Third, self-defense is not a viable defense if the defendant was the initial aggressor in the incident, and in this case Green had been the aggressor up until Maki's blow to the head. Finally, some states allow self-defense only if the defendant had no reasonable means of retreat. In most situations, a player can stop the confrontation by retreating; however Maki testified that he expected Green to come after him if he had turned away (*Regina v. Maki*, 1970).

In *Regina v. Maki*, the judge considered several facts as important in deciding to dismiss the assault charges. First, he found no evidence that Maki had intent to harm Green, which is essential in a criminal trial. Maki testified that he was not angry at Green and swung in desperation only to protect himself. Although the force used by Green far exceeded the force exerted by Maki earlier in the game, the court found that the amount of force Green applied was not excessive given the context of a hockey game. There was significant evidence that Green was the initial aggressor, thus possibly provoking the attack. The judge ultimately held that self-defense was an appropriate justification.

Because this was a case of first impression for the Canadian courts, the judge felt compelled to address an alternative defense presented by the accused, that of consent. Although dicta has no precedent value, Judge Carter opened the door for further prosecution of athletes for violent actions within the course of the game and laid out a foundation for application of consent as a future defense in those cases:

> In cases where life and limb are exposed to no serious danger in the common course of things, I think that consent is a defence [sic] to a charge of assault, even when considerable force is used, as, for instance, in cases of wrestling, single-stick, sparring with gloves, football, and the like; but in all cases the question whether consent does or does not take from the application of force to another its illegal character, is a question of degree depending upon circumstances (*Regina v. Maki*, 1970, p. 167).

He further stated that players assume the risks and hazards of the sport when they step onto the field or rink, which would be an appropriate use of consent as a defense. However, Judge Carter refused to draw a bright line distinguishing activity that is defensible by consent and that which is criminal, deferring to a totality of the circumstances approach that would examine the specific facts of each case instead (*Regina v. Maki*, 1970).

Consent

Consent is defined as a voluntary agreement to another's proposition (Garner, 2004). Consent is express when there is verbal or written agreement. Consent is implied, or agreement is inferred, when the surrounding circumstances would lead a reasonable person to believe that consent is given (Model Penal Code § 2.11, 2001). Whereas consent is often used as a defense in civil cases of assault or battery, it has not normally been considered a viable defense to criminal charges because crimes are wrongs committed against society. The public has an interest in the personal safety of its citizens, and it is the public that is injured when the safety of any individual is threatened (*People v. Fitzsimmons*, 1895). Therefore, it would be against public policy for a person to consent to become a victim of a crime. However, in the sports context, consent is the defense that has been used most often and most successfully by athletes accused of an assault while competing in a sporting event. The Model Penal Code (2001) expressly describes the use of consent as a defense to criminal charges arising from actions within the context of a sporting event. When conduct is charged as a criminal offense because it either causes or threatens bodily injury, consent to the conduct or to the infliction of the injury is a defense if the bodily injury is a reasonably foreseeable hazard of joint participation in a lawful athletic contest or competitive sport or other concerted activity not forbidden by law (Model Penal Code § 211 (2)(b)).

The first contemporary sports related case that successfully used consent as a defense was *Regina v. Green* (1970). Ironically, Ted Green, the victim in the *Regina v. Maki* case, was also charged with assault for his actions during that altercation. The facts as presented in *Green* differ slightly from those presented previously in *Maki*. The situation was instigated by a skirmish along the boards behind the Boston net whereby Green struck Maki in the face with his glove (p. 138). The officials testified and the judge found as a fact that Maki speared Green during the scuffle along the boards. The players came off the boards with their sticks raised high, and Green testified that after he had been speared in the testicles by Maki, he struck Maki with a chopping motion on the shoulder. Maki then retaliated with the blow to Green's head that fractured his skull. Judge Fitzpatrick acknowledged in his decision that "players who enter the hockey arena consent to a great number of assaults on their person" particularly because of the vigorous and competitive level that is played in the NHL (p. 140). The initiating action, Green striking Maki in the face with his glove, was characterized as the type of contact that happens often in hockey and is one of the types of risk that a player assumes. However, the judge described the Maki spearing Green in the groin and Maki slashing Green in the head as "serious, grievous assaults …" (p. 141). He did not find that Green had criminal intent to harm, but merely chopped Maki on the shoulder as a warning to desist within the furious activity along the boards (p. 142). Although Green is acquitted because his conduct was typical of that which a player would normally consent to by participating in a NHL game, the judge also holds that Green's actions were instinctive and in self-defense, relying also on the traditionally accepted defenses at that time.

The application of consent as a defense for actions occurring within the context of the game continues to develop in *Regina v. Watson* (1975), another hockey case, but at a non-professional level, involving 18-year-old athletes. The victim, David Lundrigan, was a forward wing playing for Bay Ridges, while the defendant, Robert Watson, was a defenseman playing for Ajax. Lundrigan and Watson were jostling in the slot in front of the Ajax goal. During the contact, there was testimony that Lundrigan struck Watson on the shoulder with his stick (p. 152). The puck was cleared to the other end and Lundrigan took off after it, while Watson dropped his stick and gloves and skated after Lundrigan. When Lundrigan spotted Watson, he also dropped his stick and gloves in anticipation of a fight. Watson put an armlock around Lundrigan's throat and both players fell to the ice. Watson continued to squeeze Lundrigan until his eyes bulged, fluid came out of his mouth, his legs kicked and quivered until he eventually lost consciousness and a referee separated them (p. 153). Lundrigan suffered an injury to his eye and a sore throat. Watson was charged with assault causing bodily harm.

All of the common defenses were raised—self-defense, lack of intent because the act was reflexive, and consent, both express and implied—but none were effective as Watson was found guilty. The basis of the self-defense argument was that Lundrigan provoked Watson by striking him on the shoulder with his stick while they were jostling for position in the slot. The judge found that Lundrigan's contact with Watson was the type that would be typically consented to by players in a hockey game, and was therefore not an unlawful assault that would have invoked self-defense. Further, there was both linear and temporal distance between Lundrigan's contact with Watson, and Watson's subsequent attack on Lundrigan. The initial contact occurred in front of the Ajax net, while the fight occurred at the opposite end of the rink. It was not necessary for Watson to repel Lundrigan's contact, as Lundrigan had already skated away to the other end of the rink. Watson testified that he was not provoked by Lundrigan's contact, further negating the idea that the initial contact was an unlawful assault. Further, the court found that the amount of force applied by Watson was overly violent and excessive, and therefore disproportionate to the contact initiated by Lundrigan. Finally, the court concluded that by his actions of dropping his gloves and skating after Lundrigan, Watson intended to apply force to Lundrigan, negating self-defense as a viable justification.

There were three potential acts by Lundrigan that could have implied consent: his mere participation in the game, his contact with Watson while they were in the slot, and dropping his stick and gloves when he saw Watson coming after him. The court quoted the judgment in *Regina v. Maki* (1970) that players accept the risks and hazards of the sport, but that no athletes would "be presumed to accept malicious, unprovoked or overly violent attack" (p. 156). Defense counsel argued that the rules of the game tolerate or encourage fighting, which was rejected by the court because the rules discourage fighting by punishing players with various penalties for such conduct. While recognizing that fights certainly do occasionally occur in ice hockey as a result of fast, vigorous competition with a significant degree of body contact between players, the court did not concede that players would consent to fights of unlimited violence. Nor would the court accept that any contact during the course of play would constitute consent for retaliatory actions, as that would turn hockey into a game that was far too hazardous or dangerous to play. Lundrigan's act that would most seemingly appear to indicate consent to fight, dropping his stick and gloves, was summarily dismissed by the court as merely a "reflexive action of a gentlemanly player recognizing that he was about to be attacked" (p. 158). In holding that Watson was guilty of assault causing bodily harm, the court finally concluded that the consent defense was immaterial as "no person can license another to commit a crime" (p. 158).

The scope of consent is further delineated in the case of *Regina v. St. Croix* (1979), a case of assault during an informal neighborhood hockey game played at a community outdoor rink. In this case, the players expressly agreed to the rules: no goaltenders, the puck is not to be lifted off the ice. The players were not wearing protective equipment. A brief wrestling match occurred early in the game, but play resumed after other players intervened. About 15 minutes later, the defendant, Richard St. Croix, accused the complainant, James Shaule, of pushing him into the net after a goal was scored. St. Croix started pushing Shaule with his stick, holding it horizontally across his chest. Shaule told St. Croix to put his stick down and turned away to resume play. When Shaule looked back, St. Croix knocked out four of Shaule's teeth with his stick by cross checking Shaule in the mouth. In his decision, the judge explained that the consent defense is limited both qualitatively and quantitatively. The quality of the consent is limited to normal risks and types of contact that are foreseeable in a game, while the quantity is limited to a foreseeable amount of contact. The judge held that St. Croix's conduct was beyond any foreseeably consented to act for a neighborhood game, as it was not an act of self-defense or an instinctive reaction in the course of play. St. Croix was found guilty of assault causing bodily harm.

Under the reasonable foreseeability test, it is accepted that players consent to applications of force that are reasonably incidental to the specific sport as well as to the particular class of play within various levels of that sport (*Regina v. Mayer*, 1985). Determining which acts of violence are reasonably foreseeable is difficult (*Regina v. Green*, 1971). One method is to determine whether the conduct is a customary aspect of the game. In boxing, for example, it is reasonably foreseeable that an opponent would be knocked unconscious, as the objective of boxing is to render an opponent unconscious. Similar conduct, swinging a fist at an opponent's face or head, would not be reasonably foreseeable within the context of the game in sports such as basketball or soccer. Even in ice hockey, where it is fairly common for fights to break out, a junior league player who swung at another player from behind and sucker punched him, was convicted of assault because such conduct was such a deviation from the normal conduct of hockey players it could not be reasonably associated with the game (*Regina v. Mayer*, 1985).

Defining consent was the focus of Jason Shelley's appeal of his conviction for second degree assault for punching an opponent in the face and breaking his jaw in three places, during the course of a pick-up basketball game on a college campus (*State v. Shelley*, 1997). The trial court had applied a "rules of the game" instruction to the jury, stating that the victim cannot consent to conduct not within the rules of a given sport (*State v. Shelley*, 1997, p. 30). The "rules of the game" test represents an extremely narrow approach to the issue of consent to contact experienced within the context of a game. Under this approach, every foul could be a potential crime, because by its very definition, a foul is something that is not allowed within the rules of the game. Also, strict reliance on all rules of the game would be unreasonable, as some rules are designed to promote player safety while others make the game more interesting. For example, under the rules of the game test, a player who injured another during a play in which he was offside would exceed the scope of the injured player's consent because of a rule prohibiting a football player from crossing the line of scrimmage before the ball is hiked (Restatement (2nd) of Torts, § 50 cmt. b, 2008).

The appellate court in *State v. Shelley* (1997) rejected the rules of the game test and adopted the reasonable foreseeability test from the Model Penal Code. The court held that "a defendant is entitled to argue that another player may legally consent to conduct that causes or threatens bodily harm if the conduct and the harm are reasonably foreseeable hazards of joint participation in a lawful, athletic contest or competitive sport ..." (*State v. Shelley*, 1997, p. 34). However, when considering the nature of the game, the participants' expectations, the location where the game was played and the rules of the game, Shelley's conviction was upheld because the magnitude and dangerousness of his behavior exceeded that which would be reasonably foreseeable in the game (p. 33).

Use of consent as a defense is also limited to actions within the course of the game; players do not consent to injuries caused by intentional acts that are not part of the game. Acts of violence that occur prior to the game, after the game has ended, or during a stoppage of play are generally not considered "a part of the game" and are more closely scrutinized to determine whether that conduct was "within the bounds of fair play and incidental to the sport" (*Regina v. Henderson*, 1976). In *People v. Freer* (1976), one of the first cases in the United States addressing the issue of criminal liability for actions by players within the course of an athletics contest, the court parsed out the various actions of the players to determine which were considered within the course of the game and which were not part of the game. Defendant Freer was carrying the ball in a youth football game. While he was tackling Freer, there was testimony that the complainant punched Freer in the throat. Both players fell to the ground and were covered by others in a pile up. The complainant was still lying on the ground when Freer got up and punched him in the eye, causing a laceration that required plastic surgery. The court held that any contact by the complainant to Freer's throat occurred during a tackle which is the type of contact that is reasonably foreseeable within the context of a football game. However, the pile up determined the end of the play, and Freer's action of getting up and intentionally punching the complainant was outside of the scope of the consent defense. Freer was convicted of assault in the third degree.

Similarly, in *State v. Floyd* (1990), violent acts that occurred during a time when play had stopped were not within the scope of the consent defense. The setting in this case was a four-on-four recreational summer league championship basketball game. Play was described as rough but not dirty. The referee stopped play to report a foul, two players exchanged words and one shoved the other. The referee called a technical foul and the players began to brawl. The defendant, William Floyd, had been on the bench during the play and when the initial altercation occurred on the court, but joined in the fracas. The defendant hit several players, some whom had been on the court and some whom had been on the sidelines. Floyd seriously injured two opponents, knocking one unconscious and breaking the nose of another. The defense argued consent, but the court found that there was no nexus between the defendant's actions and playing the game of basketball—particularly when play had ceased and the defendant was not on the court and engaged in play at the time of the acts. Floyd was convicted of two counts of assault causing bodily injury.

Appropriate Punishment

Justification for criminal punishment generally falls within three public policy purposes. There is no consensus that punishment of athletes for violent actions within the course of the game falls within these rationale. The first justification is a prevention theory—punishment will keep a criminal from becoming a repeat offender. The court in *Regina v. Green* articulated the unlikely application of this theory in a sport setting: "It is very difficult in my opinion for a player who is playing hockey with all the force, vigour [sic] and strength at his command, who is engaged in the rough and tumble of the game, very often in a rough situation in the corner of the rink, suddenly to stop and say, 'I must not do that. I must not follow up on this because maybe it is an assault; maybe I am committing an assault' " (p. 446).

The second public policy purpose is deterrence—punishing bad conduct deters others from committing crimes lest they suffer the same fate. Deterrence is apparently the message the court in *Regina v. Ciccarelli* (1988).

" ... it is time now that a message has to go forth from the courts that un-provoked violence, whether in a hockey game or for that matter under any other circumstances, is not tolerated in our society.... The sentence that I impose has to leave no doubt in anyone's mind that if violence in sports con-tinues, the days of discharges have passed and the perpetrators can expect punitive measures including jail sentences." (pp. 45, 46).

The third purpose for criminal punishment is based on an education theory—publicity surrounding a criminal trial and the sentence imposed serves to educate the public as to the nature of right and wrong. Sport violence is apparently news-worthy, as newspaper, television and other media sources replay it, discuss it, and imprint it on the public conscious (Yasser, McGurdy, Goplerud & Weston, 2003). Increased awareness of sport-related criminal acts may support education theory, but it also contributes to the cultural spillover theory discussed at the beginning of this chapter.

Many of the criminal cases that have gone to trial have been dismissed or re-sulted in an acquittal. Those athletes who have either been convicted or pled guilty generally faced stiffer punishment from the various leagues than they have from the courts, as indicated in Table 5.1. The McSorley case provides an excel-lent example. The NHL suspended McSorley for the remainder of the season, a total of 23 games. The Vancouver court that convicted McSorley gave him 18 months probation and ordered him not to play in any game against Donald Bras-hear ("Very major penalty," 2004). The data would seem to support those who believe that sport-related incidents are best handled by those who manage sport, rather than in the criminal justice system. The lone exception would be the *State v. Limon* (2000) case; in that situation the court was required under mandatory sentencing rules for repeat offenders to issue a five year sentence.

Other Possible Crimes

It is the athlete who is ultimately responsible for his or her actions on the field. However, if athletes are to be subjected to criminal punishment, shouldn't those who teach, train, encourage or direct the athlete to engage in violent acts also be held criminally accountable? Although there is no precedent to support this infer-ence, charges of solicitation, conspiracy, or accomplice liability could be levied in theory.

Under the Model Penal Code § 5.02(1), a person is guilty of solicitation to commit a crime if he commands, encourages, or requests another person to en-gage in an action that would constitute a crime, or an attempt to commit a crime. There has been at least one conviction for criminal solicitation of an athlete to commit an assault in the United States. At a Little League baseball game in Penn-sylvania, a 10-year-old pitcher was given a $2 bribe by a police officer to hit a batter with a fastball (Nack & Munson, 2000). The officer was convicted of so-licitation to commit simple assault as well as for corruption of a minor (Nack & Munson, 2000).

Although it is almost inconceivable to believe that a police officer would bribe a child to intentionally throw a ball at a batter, it is common and accepted in

Table 5.1 Comparison of Charges, League Punishment, and Criminal Sentences

Case	Charge/Disposition	Sport	League punishment	Sentence
People v. Fitzsimmons (1895)	Manslaughter in the first degree; Not guilty	Boxing	n/a	
Regina v. Maki (1970)	Assault causing bodily harm; Dismissed	Hockey	13 games (NHL)	
Regina v. Green (1970)	Assault; Acquitted	Hockey	13 games (NHL)	
Regina v. Watson (1975)	Assault causing bodily harm; Guilty	Hockey	Suspended for 6 games by his team	Process of appearing in court must have been agony; absolute discharge.
State v. Forbes (1975)	Aggravated assault with a dangerous weapon; Mistrial	Hockey	10 games (NHL)	
Regina v. Maloney (1976)	Assault causing bodily harm; Acquitted		Unknown	
People v. Freer (1976)	Assault in the third degree; Guilty	Football	Unknown—youth football game	Youthful offender sentencing
Regina v. St. Croix (1979)	Assault causing bodily harm; Guilty	Hockey	n/a—neighborhood game	Discharge conditioned upon paying victim $259 within 6 months.
Regina v. Mayer (1985)	Assault; Guilty	Hockey	Suspended for 25 games by the league (Junior A)	6 month conditional discharge; no criminal record
Regina v. Ciccarelli (1988)	Assault; Guilty	Hockey	10 games (NHL)	1 day in jail plus $1,000 fine
Regina v. Francis (1989)	Assault causing bodily harm; Guilty	Hockey	Match penalty, otherwise unknown	1 day in jail plus $300 fine or 30 days in jail.
Regina v. Paul (1989)	Assault causing bodily harm; Guilty	Hockey	Match penalty, otherwise unknown (adult recreational league)	Sentence not reported
State v. Floyd (1990)	Two counts of assault causing bodily injury; Guilty	Basketball	Unknown (YMCA adult recreation league)	Two years; remanded for resentencing
Regina v. Leclerc (1991)	Aggravated assault; Acquitted	Hockey	Match penalty; otherwise unknown (adult recreational league)	
State v. Shelley (1997)	Second degree assault; Guilty	Basketball	n/a—pick-up game	Sentence not reported
People v. Schacker (1998)	Assault in the third degree; Dismissed	Hockey	Unknown (recreational game)	
Jason MacIntyre (1998) (Yates & Gillespie, 2002).	Third degree assault; Pled guilty	Hockey	Permanently banned from West Coast Hockey League	2 years probation; anger management counseling; $500 fine
Jesse Boulerice (1998) (Farmer, 2000).	Assault; Pled no contest to aggravated assault	Hockey	1 year suspension from Ontario Hockey League	90 day probation; record expunged
Chris Fox (1998) (Freeman, 1998).	Assault; Pled guilty	Hockey	Unknown (summer league)	3 years probation; 200 hours community service; $1200 court costs & fines

Table 5.1 Comparison of Charges, League Punishment, and Criminal Sentences, *continued*

Case	Charge/Disposition	Sport	League punishment	Sentence
People v. Hall (2000)	Reckless manslaughter; convicted of criminally negligent homicide	Recreational downhill skiing	n/a	Sentence not reported
Marty McSorley (2000) (CNNSI.com, 2000)	Assault with a deadly weapon; Guilty	Hockey	1 year suspension from NHL	18 months probation; conditional discharge
State v. Limon (2000)	Aggravated assault with serious bodily injury; pled nolo contendre	Basketball	Unknown	5 years in prison
Regina v. Bertuzzi (2004)	Assault causing bodily harm; Pled guilty	Hockey	NHL suspension for remainder of season (13 games) plus playoffs	Conditional discharge with probation for one year and 80 hours of community service; victim surcharge of $500
State v. Guidugli (2004)	Misdemeanor assault; Guilty	Basketball	Unknown (college intramural game)	180 day suspended jail sentence; 60 days of home incarceration; 1 year of probation; anger management counseling; court costs and $100 fine

sport for coaches to encourage athletes to be aggressive and intimidate their opponents. On February 22, 2005, Temple University men's basketball coach John Chaney sent 6'8", 250 pound Nehemiah Ingram into a game against St. Joseph University to "send a message" ("Chaney sent player," 2005). Ingram, swinging his arms and elbows hard, committed his allotted five fouls in only four minutes. One of the fouls, a hard elbow to St. Joseph forward John Bryant while he was in mid-air attempting a lay up, knocked Bryant to the floor, breaking his right arm. During the post-game news conference Coach Chaney admitted to sending in a "goon" to make a physical impression because he was frustrated by what he perceived to be illegal screens ("Chaney sent player," 2005). Coach Chaney's admitted instruction and Ingram's subsequent action appear to satisfy the elements of criminal solicitation; however, no criminal charges were filed.

Conspiracy is an agreement between two or more persons to accomplish some criminal or unlawful purpose, or to accomplish a lawful purpose by unlawful means (Model Penal Code § 5.03(1), 2001). Under a conspiracy theory, an agreement between coaches and players to physically intimidate or injure an opponent could be prosecuted. Solicitation to commit a crime is an included element of criminal conspiracy (Model Penal Code § 5.03(1)(a) and (b)), the key difference between the two being that crime of solicitation is complete when the instruction is given, even if the athlete refuses to act on it, while the crime of conspiracy is complete upon the agreement of two or more parties. Theoretically, a charge of conspiracy could also be included for the agreement between Coach Chaney and his "goon" to commit assault.

Accomplice liability is a common law doctrine that certain persons who aid and abet a crime are liable for the same punishment as the principal. Under the

Model Penal Code, a person is an accomplice if he solicits another to commit an offense, aids, agrees or attempts to aid in the planning or commission of the act, or fails to prevent commission of the offense if he has a legal duty to do so (§ 2.06(3)(a)(i)–(iii), 2002). In a case where the athlete was convicted of a crime such as assault, the coach could be subject to the same punishment as an accomplice. The facts of *State v. Limon* (2000) provide some insight into the potential for the coach's liability as an accomplice. Tony Limon was a popular student and star basketball player at San Antonio High School. In a game against East Central High, Limon fractured an opponent's nose and gave him a concussion. According to witnesses, basketball coach Gary Durbon was overheard after the injury telling Limon, "It's about time someone drew some blood" (*State v. Limon*, 2000). Even with no evidence that Coach Durbon instructed or solicited Limon to injure his opponent, an argument could still be made for accomplice liability for his failure to control the violent actions of his player.

Although coaches have not yet been charged nor convicted of solicitation, conspiracy, or accomplice liability, civil lawsuits have raised the issue of accountability of owners, associations, and leagues for allowing and/or encouraging aggressive and violent play (*Sullivan v. Quiceno*, 2007; *McKichan v. St. Louis Hockey Club*, 1998). The victim in the *State v. Limon* case included both coach Durbon and the South San Antonio School District in his civil lawsuit for medical expenses (Clarke, 2000). While holding coaches and management responsible for criminally aggressive conduct by their athletes might reduce the overt encouragement of violent acts on the playing fields, it would also likely change the face of athletics competition.

Conclusion

The world of sports is a place where athletes are glorified for their physical aggression. Athletes are socialized to win at all costs, and acts of violence that would be criminal in the "real world" are standard in the sports world (Clarke, 2000). Given the double standard and the revered place of competitive sport in our culture, it may seem inconsistent to prosecute athletes for acts of aggression on the playing fields that are not only encouraged but also exalted. However, as violence on the playing fields increases both in intensity and quantity, concerns for the impact of this behavior on society have been raised. The courts have drawn a line between reasonably foreseeable acts of aggression within the context of play that are consented to by the athlete by participating in the game, and those acts of violence that far exceed in severity the level of injury an athlete could consent to or are entirely retaliatory in nature (*State v. Guidugli*, 2004). A distinction has also been made between those acts that occur within the course of play and those that occur during times when play has stopped. Prosecutors, once hesitant to file charges, are now bringing charges more frequently against male and female athletes in all levels of sport — professional, amateur, collegiate, scholastic, and recreational. Athletes are being convicted of criminal charges, plead guilty more often, and are receiving stiffer sentences. It appears that athletes in the United States have come to the point where they do, in fact, have to ask themselves whether the action they embark upon is an assault.

References

Anderson, D. (2007, March 12). A player's eruption draws appropriate fire. *The New York Times*, p. D10.

Barry, M.P., Fox, R.L., & Jones, C. (2005). Judicial Opinion on the Criminality of Sports Violence in the United States, *Seton Hall Journal of Sports & Entertainment Law*, 15, 1–24.

Chaney sent player in to foul. (2005, February 28). ESPN.com Retrieved on July 31, 2008, at http://sports.espn.go.com/ncb/news/story?id=1999665

Clarke, C.A. (2000) Law and Order on the Courts: The Application of Criminal Liability for Intentional Fouls during Sporting Events, *Arizona State Law Journal*, 32, 1149–1193.

Dellapina, J. (2007, March 20). DA won't try to try Simon. *Daily News*, p. 71.

Farmer, T. (2000, February 23). Hockey; Experts: It was assault, McSorley crossed line in attack *The Boston Herald*, p. 106.

Floyd, Jennifer, Line Blurs between Tough Play, Violence; Courts Step in when Games get too Rough, *Milwaukee Journal Sentinel*, Oct. 22, 2000, at 11C.

Freeman, R. (1998, July 20). Fox receives three years probation for '97 assault. *The Michigan Daily*. Retrieved on July 31, 2008, from http://www.pub.umich.edu/daily/1998/jul/07-20-98/news/news5.html

Garner, B.A. (2004). Black's law dictionary (8th ed.). St. Paul, MN: Thomson West

Harary, C. (2002) Aggressive Play or Criminal Assault? An In Depth Look at Sports Violence and Criminal Liability, *Columbia Journal Of Law & the Arts*, 25, 197–217.

Isaacson, M. Court's Harshest Sentence: Facing up to Raw Emotions, *Chicago Tribune*, Oct. 29, 2000, at p. 3.

Lassiter, C. (2007) Lex Sportiva: Thoughts Towards a Criminal Law of Competitive Contact Sport, *St. John's Journal of Legal Commentary*, 22, 35–98.

Lau, A. Playing Rough: Evidence Mounts that sportsmanship is turning into violence in amateur athletics, *The San Diego Union-Tribune*, Aug. 14, 2000, at B1.

Marder, J. (2004) Should the Criminal Courts Adjudicate On-Ice NHL Incidents?, *Sports Law Journal*, 11, 17–35.

McKichan v. St. Louis Hockey Club, 967, S.W.2d 209 (App. Ct. Ed. Mo. 1998).

Miami, FIU have 31 suspended for role in brawl. (2006, October 16). ESPN.com Retrieved on July 31, 2008, at http://sports.espn.go.com/ncf/news/story?id=2627372

Model Penal Code (2001) St. Paul, MN: Thompson West.

Nack, W. & Munson, L. (July 24, 2000). Out of Control; The rising tide of violence and verbal abuse by adults at youth sports events reached its terrible peak this month when one hockey father killed another. *Sports Illustrated*, 86.

Oh, T. (2006) From Hockey Gloves to Handcuffs: The Need for Criminal Sanctions in Professional Ice Hockey, *Hastings Communications & Entertainment Law Journal*, 28, 309–331.

People v. Fitzsimmons, 34 N.Y.S. 1102 (1895).

People v. Freer, 86 Misc. 2d 280 (1976).

People v. Hall, 999 P.2d 207 (2000); upheld 59 P.3d 289 (Colo. Ct. App. 2002).

People v. Schacker, 670 N.Y.S.2d 308 (1998).

Regina v. Bertuzzi, 2004 BCPC 472 (British Columbia Provincial Ct, 2004).

Regina v. Bradshaw, 14 Cox C.C. 83 (1878).

Regina v. Ciccarelli, 5 W.C.B. (2d) 310 (Ont. Prov. Ct., 1988).

Regina v. Francis, 8 W.C.B. (2d) 166 (New Brunswick Prov. Ct., 1989).

Regina v. Green, 16 D.L.R. (3d) 137 (Prov. Ct., 1970).

Regina v. Leclerc, 67 C.C.C. (3d) 563 (Ontario Court of Appeal, 1991).

Regina v. Maki, 14 D.L.R. (3d) 164 (Prov. Ct., 1970).

Regina v. Mayer, 41 Man. R. (2d) 73 (Manitoba Provincial Court, 1985).

Regina v. Paul, 7 W.C.B. (2d) 207 (Manitoba Prov. Ct., 1989).

Regina v. St. Croix, 47 C.C.C. (2d) 122 (County Court, 1979).

Regina v. Watson, 26 C.C.C. (2d) 150 (Prov. Ct., 1975).

Restatement (Second) of Torts (2008). American Law Institute.

Schoenfelder, C. (2001) Timeout! Prosecuting Juveniles for Sports-Related Violence and the Effect on Youth Contact Sports, *Journal of Juvenile Law*, 22, 139–158.

State v. Floyd, 466 N.W.2d 919 (Iowa Ct. App. 1990).

State v. Guidugli, 157 Ohio App. 3d 383 (2004).

State v. Limon, No. 1999-CR-2892 (144th Jud. Dist. Ct., Bexar Co. Tex 2000); appeal dismissed 2001 Tex App. LEXIS 2305 (Tex. App. San Anton. 2001).

State v. Shelley, 85 Wn. App. 24 (1997).

Sullivan v. Quiceno, No. CV054003173S Super. Ct. Conn., New Haven Dist. (2007).

Tatum, J. & Kushner, B. (1980). *They Call Me Assassin*. New York: Avon Books.

Very major penalty McSorley found guilty of assault, avoids jail time. (2000, October 7). CNNSI.com. Retrieved on August 5, 2008, at http://sportsillustrated.cnn.com/hockey/nhl/news/2000/10/06/mcsorley_assault_ap

WNBA suspends 10 players, Mahorn for brawl. (2008). Retrieved on July 31, 2008, from http://nbcsports.msnbc.com/id/25806412/

Yasser, R., McCurdy, J.R., Goplerud, C.P., & Weston, M.A. (2003). Sports Law, Cases and Materials (5th Edition). Anderson Publishing Co.: Cincinnati, OH. p. 635

Yates, J. & Gillespie, W. (2002) The problem of sports violence and the criminal prosecution solution. *Cornell Journal of Law and Public Policy* 12(1), 145.

Part IV

Gambling, Fraud, and Misappropriation

6

Gambling and Organized Crime

Stephen L. Mallory, University of Mississippi

Because sentence against a bad work has not been executed speedily, that is
why the heart of the sons of men has become fully set in them to do bad.
— *Ecclesiastes 8:11*

Introduction to Organized Crime

The public's perception of organized crime may well be one that is based upon
material and movies presented by the media that are not always accurate. When
the term "organized crime" is discussed, many think of the Italian mafia or La
Costa Nostra (LCN) that operates in the United States and other countries. However, the term organized crime covers a large number of traditional and emerging
groups that are becoming transnational, dynamic, and complex organizations
that operate large enterprises generating profits that are greater than that of most
major corporations. Despite the enormous amount of publications and information regarding organized crime, there remains considerable debate on its definition and which groups should be classified as belonging to organized crime.

Most experts agree that the threat of organized crime continues to be a significant challenge for governments, law enforcement, and humanity worldwide. Violence, corruption, and penetration of markets are hallmarks of organized crime.
Drug trafficking, human trafficking, weapons trafficking, and illegal gambling are
among the activities that have produced major profits for organized crime groups.
Gambling has been a long-standing activity for many organized crime groups and
sport betting initiatives are the major profit producer of bookmaking operations.
Sport betting is defined as the activity of predicting sport results by making a
wager on the outcome of a sporting event. The tolerance of sport betting and lack
of law enforcement priority to enforce laws against illegal gambling has resulted
in gambling and sport betting being a relatively low-risk enterprise for organized
crime. Charles Hynes, Brooklyn district attorney, stated that illegal sport betting
is a very serious problem for our society and is not a victimless crime, but rather a
cash cow for organized crime (Jacobs & Moynihan, 2006). The advances in technology and the globalization phenomena have also contributed to creating an enterprise that is very attractive to organized crime groups.

This chapter will address the question of the definition of organized crime and its structure, which varies from group to group. We will briefly discuss the history of organized crime to allow the reader a better understanding of who the players are, how they operate, and how they continue to survive despite concentrated efforts by governments and law enforcement. The reader will be introduced to the processes and procedures of organized crime's illegal gambling operations and how they have impacted sport programs and the sport industry. The chapter will conclude with current efforts against illegal sport betting and a view of the future of this enterprise.

As our world becomes one that is commonly characterized as global (borderless), technology-driven, paperless, and cashless, organized crime will likely remain a part of our environment that will need to be addressed by governments, businesses (including the sports industry), and the individuals who are part of theses entities. Workers and citizens alike will need to be educated and informed in regards to organized crime and its associated activities. By knowing the true nature of organized crime and the impact on our world, citizens and businesses can become more active and supportive in the efforts to address the dynamic and dangerous phenomena of organized crime, and not be involved or supportive of activity that contributes to the continuation and growth of these criminal enterprises.

Defining Organized Crime

Defining organized crime is difficult and requires a synthesis of definitions from law enforcement, academia, and the law. The Omnibus Crime Control and Safe Street Act of 1968 defines organized crime as the unlawful activities of the members of highly organized, disciplined association engaged in supplying illegal goods and services including but not limited to, gambling, prostitution, loan-sharking, narcotics, labor racketeering, and other activities of members of organizations. Common characteristics found in organized crime groups include conspiracy of a continuing enterprise that is formed around social, ethnic, or legal or illegal business relationships or around a product, frequent use of violence, intimidation and threats to achieve goals, planned criminal activity for profit, and the corruption of governments, businesses, and law enforcement to achieve profits while avoiding arrest and prosecution (Albanese, Das, and Verma, 2003). Transnational organized crime is often based in one state while committing crimes in several countries (Shelly, 1995). Other characteristics of organized crime include: non-ideological motive, organized hierarchy, restricted membership, governed by a set of rules and codes of secrecy, engaged in long term planning, and developed job specialization and a division of labor (Mallory, 2007).

Organized crime groups are becoming more transnational and international and frequently invest their profits in legal enterprises that are eventually controlled by the organized crime members. These groups are more likely to be diversified or engaged in many illicit practices or businesses which allow them to become the most powerful criminal groups in existence. This amalgamation may be based on geography, product, service, or ethnicity. The two key elements that ensure the continued existence of organized crime are the theme of corruption and the public's demand for elicit goods and services. With these driving forces, along with the desire for greed and power, organized crime groups will continue to take advantage of financial systems and open market societies (such as that of the United States). Organized crime is defined by both its members and activities. In 1969, Donald Cressey, a consultant to the 1967 President's Commission Task Force on Organized Crime, wrote that the positions of corruptor, corrupted, and enforcer were essential to the activities of organized crime. The conclusion from the examination of past research and law enforcement experience is that organized crime would cease to exist without public support and corruption.

There are a variety of terms that have been used to describe organized crime groups. The "outfit" and "the family" are used to refer to American Italian organized crime in Chicago and New York. The American Italian organized crime or La Cosa Nostra consisted of up to 28 families/groups that were located in major cities throughout the United States: in locations such as New Orleans, Detroit, Chicago, New York, Kansas City, Las Angles, and etc. The term "cartel" is used to describe the Colombian and Mexican groups that operate major drug networks. Gangs, clans, triads, and syndicates are additional terms that are synonymous with organized crime.

The Federal Bureau of Investigation (FBI) considers organized crime a priority for its investigations. La Cosa Nostra (LCN), major national gangs (such as MS13, Bloods, Crips, Black Gangster Disciples), outlaw motorcycle gangs (including the Hell's Angels, Bandidos, Pagans, Outlaws), the drug cartels of Mexico and South America, Russian mafia, and Asian organized crime groups (including the Japanese Yakuza, and Chinese triads and tongs) are among those targeted by the FBI for criminal activity. Most of these groups have engaged in illegal gambling activity in some form. These groups are involved in criminal conspiracies that are international and/or transnational, allowing the groups to develop into structured and disciplined organizations that are diversified in their criminal and legitimate business operations. These organizations are both efficient and effective, and have survived increasing law enforcement efforts for decades while expanding their operations.

Emerging Transnational Nature of Organized Crime

The most significant change in organized crime in this century is that many groups are now collaborating in a manner that makes them more dangerous and effective in the delivery of their goods and services. In addition to networking, the groups are extremely dynamic in responding to changing markets and advances in technology. The involvement and corruption of businesses, law enforcement officials, politicians, and a willing public that continues to demand the goods and services of organized crime has allowed these groups to become more global and powerful.

Transnational organized crime involves the planning and execution of illicit business ventures by groups or networks of individuals working in more than a single country. These criminal groups weaken economies and financial systems by the extensive use of violence and corruption and are a threat to the stability of nations worldwide. These groups are often headed by a powerful leader and involve hierarchies. The Russian mafia, La Cosa Nostra, and the Yakuza are considered by most experts to be transnational organized crime, and each of these groups have been and continue to be involved in illegal gambling operations (Albanese, 2004; Finckenauer & Voronin, 2001).

In 2008, a 170-page indictment in the United States resulted in the arrest of dozens of LCN members on numerous charges, including loansharking and book-making. Operation "Old Bridge" focused on New York and the Sicilian Mafia in Palermo, which were operating a trans-Atlantic operation that mended ties between U.S. and Italian clans such as the Gambino and Inzerillo crime families. Among those arrested was Salvator Lo Piccolo who was attempting to become the next "boss of bosses," and Gambino boss John D'Amico. This case is a clear indication of the continued transnational nature of LCN (Hays, 2008).

The United States Attorney in the Southern District of New York on June 16, 2006 announced the sentencing of four members of a violent Albanian racketeering enterprise. The organization referred to as the Corporation was operating in clubs in Queens and the Bronx in competition with the Lucchese and Gambino LCN families. Alex Rudaj, the reputed leader of the Albanian organized crime, was sentenced to 27 years in prison and was described as extremely violent in seizing control of illegal gambling in LCN strongholds. The organization operated bookmaking operations that rivaled that of LCN.

The International Criminal Police Organization, Interpol, coordinated activities with law enforcement from a number of Asian countries including Malaysia, Singapore, Thailand, Vietnam, and China, that resulted in the arrest of 423 individuals for their involvement in an illegal soccer betting operation. This operation was also linked to other offenses such as corruption, money laundering, and prostitution. Interpol estimated that the gambling 262 dens had $680 million in illegal sport bets from around the world. The law enforcement operation was done in advance of the impending 2008 Olympic Games in Beijing, China, to target the sport betting operations of organized crime (Garner, 2007).

The trend of organized crime expanding their activities in more than one country is made possible by these groups forming alliances or networking, in much the same way that a legitimate business expands into a new country. These groups cooperate across ethnic or racial heritage lines. LCN, Russian mafia, Mexican and Colombian drug cartels, and Asian groups have formed alliances to achieve goals related to their criminal activity. Many of these alliances are those of convenience that are formed to increase the efficiency and effectiveness of the criminal operations. Furthermore, many experts are concerned about the link between traditional criminal activity of organized crime groups and terrorists as the criminal activities of these groups are yet another means of potentially funding terrorist groups (Mutschke, 2000).

Gangs, such as MS13 or outlaw bikers, have increased their reach and number of members in more than one country. In the United States alone, the U.S. Department of Justice estimated that there were over 30,000 gangs with 800,000 members that are a concern for 2,500 communities/cities (Mallory, 2007). These gangs have members and groups in many countries and have the potential to expand their operations into other countries. The growth and expansion of these gangs and alliances with other organized crime groups is becoming the new face of organized crime.

The growth of internet gambling operations, including sport books, are contributing to the growth and expansion of organized crime activity. Most of the entities pay no U.S. taxes and the chance of winning is about 1 in 10. Internet gambling is one of fastest growing illegal businesses on the internet. Gambling provides organized criminals with everything they desire—anonymity, large cash flow, the ability to control the odds, and a very small chance of getting arrested and prosecuted. The number of sites and banks or card issuers that support internet gambling is growing, even though internet gambling is illegal for U.S. citizens (Americas Watchdog Reports, 2007). This type of operation certainly contributes to the ability of organized crime to become more transnational.

The phenomenon of transnational organized crime is organized crime's response to advances in technology, transportation, global communication systems, dynamic global markets, and financial entities that allow money to change hands rapidly and anonymously. Organized crime can now deliver their illegal services and goods to anybody, anywhere, at anytime, and with a diminished chance of being connected to the criminal activity. However, the phenomenon of organized crime remains a local crime problem, requires corruption, and responds to the demands of the public.

A Brief History of Organized Crime and Gambling in the United States

The histories of organized crime and gambling in the United States have been and continue to be intertwined. Gambling, both legal and illegal, has a history dating back to colonists placing lottery bets in Jamestown, Virginia. Organized crime has been involved in a variety of gambling activities including organizing card and dice games, lotteries/numbers/policy betting, casino gambling and "skimming" operations (stealing part of the gross before taxes are reported or paid), poker and gambling machines, dog and horse racing wagering, and slot machines. Loansharking (usury) is often associated with the illegal gambling operations. However, bookmaking, more specifically sports betting, is a major profit producer for organized crime. Sport and gambling have existed and continue to exist in a dangerous dichotomy. In the early years, sport gambling focused on boxing and horse racing. The rise of the team sport of baseball is said to have been successful due to gambling. Football and then basketball have now become favorite sports that attract wagers (Ordine, 2007). Organized crime's involvement in gambling is well documented and the connection between organized crime and the gambling industry continues to make the headlines. Eleven different organized crime families have participated in labor unions and casino service providers in Atlantic City in the 1980s (Irwin & Richey, 1986). The Associated Press (1998) reported that in 1998, the Detroit Mafia had attempted to gain a secret interest in three Nevada Casinos.

In December, 2007, members of the Lucchese crime family were involved in a $2.2 billion illegal betting operation in New Jersey, which included bets on professional and college sports. The Lucchese crime family was working with gang members of the 9 Tre Gangsters, a subset of the Blood street gang (Santi, 2007).

This case illustrates that sport betting has become a cash cow for organized crime, with some organizations grossing more than $45 million annually. Over $230 billion is bet on sport each year in the United States. The arrests in this operation included members from the Gambino crime family and Fukanese crime organizations (Rivero, 2006).

Organized crime began in the United States in the era of colonial piracy (attacking shipping and stealing valuable goods). Like sport betting today, the colonists accepted piracy because it provided services and goods the public demanded. The pirates ingratiated themselves with the colonists and government officials much the same way as today's organized crime members do with their operations. The trend of American organized crime was established in early colonial America by the cooperation of the pirates with the public and the corruption of governments and businesses (Browning & Gerassi, 1980; Mallory, 2007).

Dunstan (1997) described this era at the first wave of the history of gambling in the United States. He writes that two groups, the English and the Puritans, had different views of gambling. The Puritan colonies outlawed all gambling, including dice, cards, and gambling tables, while the other English colonies viewed gambling as a harmless diversion. In this era, lotteries, wagering on horse racing, and taverns and roadhouses with dice and card games were common. Another development was the Mississippi Valley organized enterprise of river boat gambling. The South had an open view of gaming—New Orleans was known as the capital for gambling. The period around 1860 represented the end of the glory days of riverboat gamblers. Lottery scandals, the Civil War, and groups opposing gambling led to most states banning lotteries by 1840 and the war interrupted almost all river travel. This first wave, 1600s to the mid 1800s, ended with only horse racing surviving.

The next era in the history of organized crime was the rise of the "robber barons." A number of American businessmen began to monopolize the American economy using both violence and corruption. These powerful businessmen used the law, police, and their political influence to gain control of the American economy. During this era, these ruthless businessmen were referred to as "robber barons." Sutherland and Cressey (1960) among others considered the large number of violations by these powerful corporations as a type of organized crime.

The second wave of gambling history was from the mid 1800s to early 1900s (Dunstan 1997). This era included the expansion of the Western frontier, with miners and the gold rush in places such as San Francisco replacing New Orleans as the center for gambling in the United States. From 1849 to 1855, California patrons, including women, blacks, and Chinese immigrants, gambled in establishments licensed by the state and cities. The first slot machine was invented in San Francisco in 1895.

Lotteries made a comeback—the Louisiana Lottery was approved and then prohibited. Nevada legalized and then banned gaming. By 1910, almost all forms of gambling were prohibited in the U.S.—Arizona and New Mexico had to outlaw casinos to gain statehood. As a result, gambling was forced underground and operated as a black market.

The political machines (symbiotic relationships between politicians, gangsters, and businessmen formed to protect illegal operations and keep corrupt people in office) such as Tammany Hall in New York, the Ed Crump machine of Memphis, and the Pendergast machine in Kansas City became the power in growing major cities in the United States. The massive immigration of ethnic groups like the Irish established a block vote along ethnic lines and founded the corrupt political machines. Immigrant groups, including the Jews, Italians, and the Irish, gained control of cities by means of alliances between the politicians, gangs, and gamblers. Characters like William March "Boss" Tweed in New York and Mike McDonald of Chicago, who controlled gambling in their cities, became allied with the politicians and gangs, creating yet another form of organized crime. Cities were wide open to gambling and vice, which was protected by the politicians and the corrupt police they employed. These organizations were the beginning of the criminal organizations such as LCN (Browing & Gerassi, 1980; Peterson, 1952). In Chicago, Mont Tennes, who succeeded McDonald, syndicated gambling. Tennes gained control of the wire service, which transmitted results of horse races. James Colosimo, Johnny Torrio, and Al Capone all contributed to the growth of organized crime in Chicago. The Chicago today outfit is structured in crews that are controlled by bosses, who oversee the activities of the crewmembers. A specialty crew who answer to the Outfit hierarchy run the major gambling operations.

Each city where organized crime exists has its own story. New York had their Tammany Hall, which allied with gangs such as the Dead Rabbits, Five Points, and the East Side Gang, lead by Monk Eastman. Arnold Rothstein, a Jewish criminal, was a major contributor to the organization of crime in New York. He is often referred to as the "Godfather" or the "Brain" of early organized crime in New York. His contributions included specialization, a structured hierarchy and creating a model of bureaucracy for the criminal groups. He became famous for his involvement in fixing the 1919 World Series, known as the "Black Sox Scandal," one of the first indications of the involvement of organized crime in sport. The World Series was between the Cincinnati Reds and the Chicago White Sox. Although the players were never convicted of a crime, Federal Judge Kenesaw Landis, the first commissioner of baseball, banned eight players, including standout "Shoeless" Joe Jackson of the White Sox, from baseball for life. Eliot Asinof wrote a book *Eight Men Out* about the scandal, which later became a movie by the same name.

Prohibition is often credited with creating organized crime in America. However, drug trafficking, gambling, and vice have all contributed to the growth and continuity of organized crime. Men such as Meyer Lansky, Benjamin "Bugsy" Siegel, Charles "Lucky" Luciano, Carlo Gambino, Joseph Profaci, Joseph Colombo, Joseph Bonanno, and Thomas Lucchese became names synonymous with organized crime in New York. However, Carlos Marcello of New Orleans, along with numerous others, contributed to the establishment of organized crime across America (Abadinsky, 2003).

The third wave of gambling history was from 1930s to present (Dunstan 1997). This area was characterized by the rise of LCN, Benjamin "Bugsy" Siegel's move to the west coast, and his and LCN's role in expanding gaming and book-making operations. These mobsters financed many casinos, including the Las Vegas Flamingo. During this era, Nevada legalized most forms of gambling in the state. Nevada legalized casino gambling in 1931 and New Jersey did so in 1978.

As of 1999, citizens in all but two states, Hawaii and Utah, were able to place bets in some legal form including casino gambling, lotteries, bingo, parimutuel wagering, river boat casinos, and video gambling. Today, the Internet has created a new method of gambling. Websites now offer both casino and sport book gambling from offshore locations. The Internet has made illegal gambling an international issue (Forshey & Olson, 2000).

The history of the growth of organized crime and gambling can also be found in the reports by several commissions that attempted to define and study organized crime and its activities. The Chicago Crime Commission conducted one of the first inquiries in 1915 and noted that certain traits of criminal groups were different from other forms of criminal activity. This included aspects such as special traditions and practices, etc. In 1929, the Wickersham Commission examined the impact of prohibition on criminal activity and concluded that more study of organized crime was needed. The Kefauver Crime Committee, chaired by Estes Kefauver in 1950, was the first congressional investigation into organized crime in the United States. This body concluded that crime was syndicated in many cities and that corruption allowed the syndicates to flourish. The committee found extensive interstate contact between gamblers and LCN. In 1956, the Mc-Clellan Committee heard the testimony of Joseph Valachi, who was a soldier in the Genovese Family of New York. Valachi described the structure of LCN and the commission that governed the organization.

President Lyndon Johnson established the President's Commission on Law Enforcement and Administration of Justice. This committee recognized the threat that organized crime presented to the national security. They concluded that LCN dominated crime and was pervasive due to public corruption.

In 1968, Congress passed the first comprehensive organized crime bill, the Omnibus Crime Control and Safe Streets Act. This bill defined organized crime and included gambling as a major activity of organized crime. A Task Force on Organized Crime was established and found that 24 criminal groups were operating in major cities across the United States, known as LCN.

In 1970, the Organized Crime Control Act was passed containing the RICO (Racketeer and Corrupt Organizations) statue. This statue makes it a crime to acquire, receive income from, or operate an enterprise through a pattern of racketeering, thus allowing prosecutors to prosecute patterns of criminal acts committed by direct and indirect participants in criminal enterprises. This task force also concluded that gambling was a major source of income for organized crime. The Regan administration created the President's Commission on Organized Crime by executive order in 1983. This committee recognized that other groups that could be classified as organized crime were emerging. These groups included the drug cartels, which produced the greatest income of organized crime. These committees and task forces document the growth and expansion of organized crime in the United States and serve as a reminder that organized crime is difficult to study and more difficult to control.

Other organizations, including the Yakuza, whose origins include Bakuto (traditional gamblers), the triads, tongs, and Asian gangs, have a long tradition of involvement in gambling. These groups, often referred to as nontraditional organized crime, have also made their presence known in illegal gambling in the United States. Today's headlines are ripe with stories of illegal sport betting and gambling operated by both traditional and nontraditional organized crime, or with both types operating together in an alliance.

The history of organized crime and gambling in the United States is difficult to document due to a lack of accurate or reliable sources and the large number of groups that have emerged that can be classified as organized crime. Each city, region, and group has their stories of how organized crime developed and expanded into the national threat it is today.

The Process and Procedures of Organized Crime Gambling Operations

Gambling attracts people who are drawn to the potential for instant wealth. Gambling is associated with other crimes, such as loan sharking, that often involved violence and extreme intimidation to collect. Gambling can also create debts which some bettors cannot pay. Credit is often extended when the bettor cannot pay his losses. This continues and allows organized crime to eventually take over or control these businesses due to the gambling debt of its owners. The business is then used to benefit to the criminal organization. As discussed previously, gambling includes a large number of games of chance that can be profit makers for the criminal organizations. Although organized crime operates in an assortment of illegal gambling operations, its primary income comes from the numbers game and bookmaking. It is estimated by some experts that over $40 billion a year is generated by organized crime's illegal gambling operations. This estimate varies considerably among law enforcement and experts in the field, but the income from gambling is considerable.

The bookmaking accounting process or forwarding the bettor's wagers to the operation has many methods, but the process at the office level has changed little over the years. Wagers are still recorded under the bettor's account designation, which can be the bettors' name, nickname, or a series of organized codes. Winning and losing wagers are totaled to determine the "bottom figure." A bottom sheet is a list of accounts and bottom figures for an operation. The bookmakers often pay winners and collect from losers once per week, frequently on Tuesdays to allow for betting on Monday night football games. Sport lines or point spreads are developed by an "oddsmaker" who attempts to create wagering conditions that will attract an equal amount of wagering on both sides of a sport contest. The oddsmakers take into account anticipated wagering volume, home team advantage, weather, player injuries, past performance, and other statistical data. As these conditions change the line may be changed. It is essential that a bookmaker has current line information in order to avoid wagers at a line which he cannot layoff. Bookmakers may furnish customers with a preprinted schedule called a line sheet, used to record opening lines and any line changes. Each team on the line sheet has an identifying number, known as the rotation number, that is derived in Las Vegas. These sheets make it convenient to furnish changes in the line to customers. The bookmaking operation typically includes the following individuals:

- **Bookmaker** or head of the operation.
- **Half Book** or partner, who receives half of the profits and is responsible for half the debts.
- **Quarter Book** or partner, who gets 25 percent the profits or responsible for 25 percent of the debts.
- **Line Source** or oddsmaker, who may have knowledge of the operation.

- **Layoff Source** or a bookmaking operation in which the bookmaker places his own wagers or rebetting the money received in his operation (laying off).
- **Agents** or writers, who accept wagers from customers and receive a commission (normally 10 percent).
- **Office workers** or salaried employees, who accept phoned or faxed wagers, chart wagers, and perform other task to support the operation,
- **Financiers** or bankers, who provide financing for the operation.

The operation can also include runners, collection agents, computer experts, and others. In the past, a bettor would have to deliver their wager by hand to a known agent of the illegal operation. These agents were usually bar tenders, door men, or other service occupations that interacted with the general public. With the use of telephones, agents began to accept wagers over the telephone. The large bookmaking operations would set up "offices" where salaried employees would work the telephones. Bettors did not know the location of the offices. "Pickup men" would deliver the "works" (wagering records) to the bookmaker. Online bettors can now email their wagers or place wagers on gambling websites. Modern technology allows the bookmakers to stay current on lines and run a very effective and efficient operation. Although technology has changed the bookmaking operation in many ways, the structure and accounting process has changed very little. The technology has made the illegal operations more difficult to investigate. Bookmakers have progressed with technology and will continue to do so (Forshey & Olson, 2000).

However, identifying the structure of an illegal operation remains a priority of law enforcement. Information about the structure is often presented to juries to demonstrate the methods of operation, profits generated by the illegal operation, positions of the members of the operation, and the size of the operation. Structures vary with geography and the size of the operation. Different criminal organizations may vary in structure (LCN versus Russian organizations and etc.).

A numbers operation employs writers to take bets in a variety of locations, including bars or businesses and on the street. They are paid a commission of 25 percent. The writers pay the winners and collect from the losers. Pickup men collect the bets from writers and are paid a commission of 5–10 percent. The bets are then taken to a bank and are totaled and recorded. Large operations may use a layoff bank that covers large betting action in the event the local banker (a person or persons who finance or put up the money for the operation) cannot cover the bets. Some operations employ thousands of writers and take thousands a day in bets. The criminal organization operating the numbers betting retains between 40–50 percent of the money for its salaries and expenses.

The layoff bank is likely a service that is provided by organized crime groups. The writers and local banks may not be members of an organized crime groups, but often are required to use services such as layoff banks and enforcers fro their operations who are organized crime members (Abadinsky, 2003; Boyd, 1975; Potter &, Lyman, 2004; Mallory, 2007).

Sport betting has replaced horse racing as the primary business of bookmakers. The wagering process begins with the bettor placing their wager with a bookmaker. A bookmaker or "bookie" is not difficult to find, even in small towns. A wager or bet can be done on a person-to-person basis, directly or indirectly by means of a cell phone or telephone, on the internet or web mail, or through a middleman. The bookmaker is a broker who, for a fee known as vigorish (or "vig," "juice," or cut) percent (usually 10 percent), takes the wagers. The goal is for a balance among bets that results in the payoffs made to winning bettors paid from losing bettors' money, with some money left over for the bookmaker. If wagers on each side of a contest are the exact same with the same line, the bookmaker is guaranteed to win the 10 percent vigorish charged to losing wagers, as achieving what is called a "balanced book." Middlemen, who are not concerned with a balance, may be bartenders, waitresses, cab drivers, etc., who funnel bets to a bookmaker in return for a percentage. Other terms used include "handbook" (a person who accepts horse race wagers), "writer" (persons who accept numbers wages), and a "sub-book" or "runner" (accepts sports wagers for percentage of the net profit).

In the 1970s, a number of devices and procedures were used to conceal the true location of the bookmaker or the telephone he used. "Backstrap," "cheesebox," and use of third parties were common. The backstrap was an extension wire that enabled the bookie to move the phone to a new location. The cheesebox was an electronic device that allowed incoming calls on one line, which was known to bettors to be transferred as outgoing calls on a second line that was know only to the bookmaker. The bookmaker may use a service that answers calls of the bettors who have a code where they can be reached. The bookmaker collects the messages from the service and calls the bettor who can then place a bet.

Third parties are also used by the bookies. They are paid to record wagers placed by bettors that are retrieved by the bookmaker. Tools of the modern bookmaker include laptop computers, answering machines/devices, pagers, facsimile machines, forwarding services, satellite telephones, mobile telephones, cassette recorders, wire rooms with banks of telephones, and even the old-fashioned betting slips or paper records for documentation. Gambling operators use "flash paper," which is ignited easily and burns rapidly, or rice paper, which dissolves quickly in water thus destroying evidence of illegal gambling.

The bookmaker has wager notations or records that identify the bettor by name or code and the amount of the bet. Wager records may be in the form of tally sheets, which contain the summary of all wagers accepted on a given team, horse, or number. These records and account records that contain amounts to be paid to bettors or collected from them are evidence that a person is a bookmaker. With modern technology, these records may be stored electronically on cell phones or computers that can be easily destroyed in the event of a raid or arrest of the bookmaker.

Sport wagering caters primarily to the affluent and is the king of bookmaking. The sport bookmaker acts as a broker, bringing together money from both sides of a sport contest in hope of a balance where the loser's money will be more than sufficient to cover payments to winners. To achieve a balance or equality between teams, a handicapping process occurs. Handicapping is done by subtracting from the favorite's score or adding to the underdog's score for wagering purposes. For example, if the New England Patriots are considered one touchdown stronger than the Indianapolis Colts, the handicap (called the line, points, spot or spread) would be "New England 7." A bettor choosing New England would give seven points (i.e., New England -7) and would win his wager only if New England won by eight points or more. A bettor choosing Indianapolis (Indianapolis +7) would win his wager only if Indianapolis won the game or lost it by less than seven points. If the difference in the final score was seven points in favor of New England, the wager would be void or termed a "push," "tie," or "even," and no money would change hands. Ties can be avoided by quoting the line in half points. Handicapping in baseball is done by varying the amount of money which a bettor must put up to win a wager (risk $7.50 to win $5.00 on a team).

Sports wagers are most often done on credit. If a bettor bet $10,000 on a team and won, he collects $10,000. If a bettor bet $10,000 and lost, he would pay the bookie $11,000 which includes the "vigorish" of ten percent or $1,000 profit for the bookmaker. The goal of the bookmaker is to achieve a profit regardless of the game's outcome and is known as a "balanced book." Most bookmakers have excellent financial resources and can withstand losses or balance his book by other means. This can be done by line changes. If bettors believe that one team is more than a touchdown or score stronger than the other team, the bookmaker can move the line from 7 to 7 ½. The desired effect would be that more money is accepted on the stronger team to achieve balance.

Another method to withstanding short-term losses by bookmakers is the use of a layoff. The bookmaker may be a local who does not have enough capital. He calls another bookmaker, placing wagers with him. Bookmakers who specialize in handling layoff action are often organized crime members. Lines may be classified as nonwagering lines and published in newspapers. This line represents the difference in strength between teams. A wager line is intended to attract equal amounts of money bet on each team. The bookmaker may obtain his line from a legitimate service or may obtain it by networking with other bookmakers. Some games or contest are not accepted for wagers. The bookmaker will furnish his best customers with a printed schedule of the lines. This schedule is called a "sheet."

Wager terms used frequently include the following:

- **Quarter** or a $25 wager
- **Half** or a $50 wager
- **50 cents** or a $50 wager
- **Dollar** or a $100 wager
- **Yard** or a $100 wager
- **Nickel** or a $500 wager
- **Dime** or a $1,000 wager

There are several types of wagers. A *straight action* is a wager on a single team and is the most common type of bet. *Middling* involves a bettor wagering on both sides of a contest at different lines in hopes of winning both contests. Middling occurs when the bookmaker has moved the line. Proposition bets are wagers made on specific outcomes of a match or contest. An example of this would be betting whether a quarterback in a football game will pass for a set amount (i.e., total yardage) or a baseball player will get more hits than another player on a separate team. *Run line* or *goal line* bets offer a fixed point spread that offers a higher payout for the favorite and a lower one for the underdog.

Wikipedia offers a discussion on sports betting including types of bets, bookmaking, betting scandals, and sports betting forums (Sports Betting, 2007). A parlay is a single wager on two or more teams, all of which must win for the bettor to collect. Parlay wagers increase the payoff. A "buy" wager is the same as a conventional wager, except that the bettor buys an extra half point in the bettors' favor at the cost of increased juice (typically 20 percent instead of 10 percent). Round-robins are wager on three or more teams by taking all possible two-team parlays. Teaser is a parlay wager in which the bettor obtains a favorable point spread, but the bookmaker will pay less in the event the bettor wins. Over and under are wagers where the bettor chooses a contest and not an individual team (wagering that the sum of the scores of each team will be over or under a specific figure). Parlay cards may be distributed by individuals or organizations as well as bars or restaurants, etc. The cards have a number of contests or games and the player selects a minimum of three or four, indicating his choices by circling the appropriate numbers on the bottom and tear-off portion of the card. All teams must win for a card to be a winner. In the event of a tie, the bettor loses. Writers of parlay card operations receive a commission on the gross amount of money received for parlay card wagers instead of only receiving commission on losing wagers. The payoff amount is determined by the number of teams chosen. There is no juice involved. Bookmakers make a profit based solely on the odds of winning. The "ties lose" feature gives the operation a 50–50 chance or better of making a profit. True odds and payoff rates for a typical card are as follows:

Teams	True Odds	Payoff Rate
3	7 to 1	5 for 1
4	15 to 1	10 for 1
5	31 to 1	15 for 1
6	63 to 1	25 for 1
7	127 to 1	40 for 1
8	255 to 1	60 for 1
9	511 to 1	90 for 1
10	1023 to 1	150 for 1

In football and basketball, *handicapping* is done by adding points to the underdog or subtracting points from the favorite. In baseball, a *money line* is used in handicapping. A money line involves varying the amount of money that a better must wager in order to win a specified amount. If the team is favored, a twenty-cent line might be quoted as "braver 6½–7½", or "braves 7½." In this scenario, a bettor must wager $7.50 to win $5.00.

A *pitcher line* is a wager that will only take place if the specified pitcher starts the game. A *run line* is same as a point spread in football or basketball. Run lines can be used along with money line. For example, on a run line of Mets 30 -2, to wager on the Mets, the bettor would lay $130 and give up two runs to win $100.

A *flat line* is a wager where the favorite and underdog wager 11 to 10, or 6 to win 5, but there is no goal difference added or subtracted for each team's score. Hockey wagering can involve money lines along with puck lines. Over and under wagers are frequently made in hockey wagering.

Auto racing is a popular sport that also attracts wagering. Sportbooks post money lines for a driver's probability of wining a race. Wagers called "head-to-head" or "matchup" give odds that a particular driver will beat another driver (Forshey & Olson, 2000).

On average, the bookmaker will collect eight dollars and pay out only five dollars (a profit of three dollars) out of every eight dollars bet. Sports betting profit is usually 3–5 percent of the gross, while the profit is 40 percent or more in number wagering. The bettors' chance of winning in numbers is often as little as 1,000 to one. However, numbers operation requires more people to operate and more administration expenses. The backers of numbers wagering usually make a profit of between 7–8 percent. Organized crime is frequently the financial backer of interstate numbers operations (Boyd, 1975).

Perhaps today online gambling is becoming the new method of making large profits without being identified for organized crime. Legal sport betting in Nevada on athletic events during a 12-month period that ended in June 2007 was a reported $2.48 billion. However, the majority of sport wagering is done through illegal bookmakers or over the Internet. A report by the National Gambling Impact Study Commission estimated that illegal sport betting ranged from $80 to $380 billion annually (Ordine, 2007).

Although online gambling is illegal, there are a number of companies providing the service, such as virtual casinos, gaming rooms, off-track betting parlors, etc. It is illegal to place cyber bets on sporting events or in virtual card games. Additionally, it is illegal to transfer money electronically for gambling and to wager in offshore internet casinos, even if you live in the United States. It is also illegal for a business to run gambling websites and to solicit online bets. Illegal bookmaking operations are constantly evolving in order to increase efficiency for the operation, attract bettors, and provide security from law enforcement. The Internet, as well as toll-free telephone service, has allowed bookmakers to conduct their operations from offshore, offering both anonymity and safety from U.S. law enforcement. The bookmaker can purchase a casino license from a nation such as Antigua and operate out of the reach of the U.S. legal system. Another advantage of internet gambling operations is the volume of wagers that can be accepted.

Although internet gambling operations offer a variety of gambling opportunities, sport wagering is the most common type offered. The four forms of sport wagering include straight sport wagering, "fantasy" sport wagering that allow bettors to choose athletes for a fantasy team and accumulate points based on the athletes' performance during a season, pari-mutuel sport wagering, and sport brokering operations that arrange wagers between bettors and charge a commission. Most internet sites offer no credit wagering where the bettor is required to establish an account with the operation before they can bet. Other operations partner with another betting operation and offer credit to established customers (Forshey & Olson, 2000).

The FBI is currently investigating more than a dozen online gambling operations. A federal grand jury in St. Louis returned a 22-count indictment against 11 individuals and four companies for illegal online gaming and related activities. One company, BetonSports, pled guilty to racketeering charges (Hanaway, 2006; The St. Louis Division: A Brief History, 2008). The company was taking bets on professional and college football and basketball, as well as other amateur sporting events and contests. In such instances, bettors established with bookies could place their wagers in three ways: (1) online at one of 60 internet sites by using a username and password, (2) calling in the bet to the central office in Costa Rica, or (3) calling a bookie or "sheetholder" (bookie; person taking wages).

There were 44 search warrants executed in 30 locations based on evidence obtained by electronic intercepts during the investigation of gambling in the New York area. Guns, steroid-filled syringes, marijuana, computers, printers, and $1 million in cash were seized and 18 operators and bookies arrested. The indication is that gambling operations are part of diverse illegal criminal operations (Associated Press, 2007).

Online betting is similar to using betting stores or casinos with the added value of convenience. Registration is required to open an account with the online bookie. There are hundreds of online bookmakers, like Bet365.com, Sportingbet.com, and numerous others. The bettor transfers money to an online sportsbook account. This can be done by credit card or debit card, or by money transfer services and bank transfer options. There is usually a minimum deposit required where winnings can be transferred to or withdrawn anytime. The types of bets offered include straight bets, parleys, teasers, over and under, and money line wagers. There are "exotic bets," where the correct score and other specific events or outcomes can be wagered on by the bettor. The demand is very high for this type of gambling. The web site Sportingbet.com offers a glossary of terms associated with online gambling (Lobo, 2002).

One of the first arrests of a major online betting operation was the arrest of professional poker player James Giordano. The operation was a billion-dollar-a-year scheme that rivaled casino sports betting. With thousands of customers in the United States, the ring had 2,000 bookies. The bettors were assigned a secret code to track their wagers and results on a restricted Web site. The 27 people arrested placed millions in shell corporations/fronts for illegal operations and banks accounts in Central America, the Caribbean, Switzerland, Hong Kong and other locations. The charges included enterprise corruption, money laundering, and promoting gambling. One of those arrested was former scout for the Washington Nations, Frank Falzarano (Associated Press (2006).

In another notable bust, Queens district attorney Richard Brown announced the arrest of 17 in a gambling operation. Two of the men arrested were identified as soldiers from the Genovese and Bonanno LCN crime families of New York. The gambling operation took bets out of bars in Queens and did business with an Internet gambling site in Costa Rica (Rashbaum & Ramirez, 2005).

Another operation reported by the United States Attorney's office generated $200,000 a year in gambling and was tied to the Genovese family. They operated at the wholesale produce market at Hunts Point in the Bronx and were open to anyone who stopped by the market. These operations are an indication that traditional organized crime continues to operate using modern technology and well as the traditional method of placing bets.

Many organized crime groups with strong hierarchies, including LCN, practice profit sharing with management or bosses. Soldiers, who make a profit in operations such as bookmaking, share the profit with the caporegime, underboss, and boss of the family; money flows up through the hierarchy. Bookmakers and gamblers who are not LCN members (independents) often pay tribute to LCN families to operate in their geographic areas. If a bookmaker refuses to pay, LCN will use violence or intimidation and corruption to gain compliance. Corrupt police officers will raid the bookmaker and give them a message from LCN to pay or continue to be raided. Other organized groups do not practice profit sharing. These include many of the street gangs and some of the outlaw biker groups.

Profits from gambling operations are used to bridge the gap between the underworld and the upper world by means of corruption. Profits are also used to pay enforcers who may commit crimes, such as assault and murder, to ensure the wishes of the bosses are being carried out. The members of groups such as LCN have significant contacts that can help with control and communications with police, businessmen, union leaders, and government officials. These reciprocal relationships or strategic contacts can be in the form of political or support in areas such as regulation of an industry (Abadinsky, 2003).

Any profit from any of the activities of organized crime is used to make the group more powerful, which leads to the expansion of all of their criminal activity. Most people who gamble on sports or smoke a "little dope" have never thought about their actions supporting the growth and expansion of organized crime.

Infiltration of Sports Programs by Organized Crime

Because sports bookmaking is a multi-billion dollar industry in North America, it is a target for organized crime and has become a major profit producer for these criminal organizations. Large scale operations can generate in excess of $4–5 million over a 90-day period. These organizations are diversified in their operations and often are involved in drug distribution, murder for hire, major frauds and thefts along with their bookmaking operations. Both professional and college sports and individuals who participate in these sports become targets for the corruption of the sport.

Following the 1919 World Series scandal orchestrated by mob boss Arnold Rothstein when eight members of the Chicago White Sox were given lifetime suspensions, there have been numerous incidents where betting on sport has caused a problem for individuals and teams. Perhaps one of the most notable cases is that of professional baseball player Pete Rose. Rose admitting to betting on sporting events, but there remains no evidence of him betting on games in which he played. There is also no evidence of a connection to organized crime, but, as with any gambler, the possibility is always present that organized crime would try to take advantage of a situation such as this one.

A more recent case involving a National Basketball Association referee Timothy Donaghy demonstrates the connection of sports betting to organized crime. Donaghy, a 13-year veteran with the National Basketball Association (NBA), pled guilty to participating in an illegal sports betting scheme that included betting on games in which he officiated. He also provided his coconspirators with insider/nonpublic information and betting recommendations on NBA games (Federal Bureau of Investigation New York Division, 2007). There is evidence that this information was used by organized crime members in their bookmaking operations. The investigation of this case is continuing under the direction of the FBI.

Another case resulted in the arrest of 23 people operating an illegal sports betting ring that had ties to LCN and six casinos. The operation took bets on college and professional football and basketball in the poker room of the Borgata Hotel Casino and Spa in Atlantic City, New Jersey. Andrew Micali, the accused leader of the operation, is an associate of Philadelphia mob boss Joseph "Skinny Joey" Merino. The operation had two wire rooms in Philadelphia that tallied bets and calculated winnings and payouts. Money laundering was a major part of the operation, which included taking cash, converting it to chips, "washing" (making them appear to be for legal gambling operations) the chips by betting, and then turning the chips in for cash. Losing bettors were forced to take out loans from the operators at loan rates of 50 percent interest. Casino employees charged in operation included dealers, supervisors, and a bartender (Parry, 2007). This case is an indication of the LCN's continued interest in both casinos and sports betting.

A scandal in 1996 that involved Boston College students and football players had ties to an organized crime syndicate that the Massachusetts Middlesex County District Attorney would not identify. Thirteen Boston College football players were suspended for betting on college and professional football and major league baseball games. The investigation revealed that students were used as bookmakers. It was reported that the ring ordered a severe beating for a student bookmaker who was behind in payments on bets ("Organized Crime Tied to Betting Scandal," 1997).

There are a number of cases that did not have an overt connection to organized crime, but somewhere up the line there is a good probability that organized benefited from many of these scandals. These criminal organizations have the means to obtain information about any game fixing or scandal that can be used to benefit their organizations.

Other sports gambling scandals include the case of Arizona State basketball players Stevin "Headache" Smith and Isaac Burton Jr., who pled guilty in 1997 to conspiracy to commit sports bribery in a point shaving scheme that fixed four Sun Devils games. This 1994 investigation by the FBI revealed the scheme benefited LCN figures and other individuals in four games. The players had amassed $32,000 in gambling debts with campus bookies. Recruited to fix games in exchange for wiping out gambling debts, the players were paid additional monies up to $25,000 per game to fix games. Three different LCN groups were involved in the operation: Chicago LCN, New York LCN, and New Jersey LCN. An additional group of campus bookies not affiliated with LCN were also involved in the scheme.

In 1998, Northwestern football player Brain Ballarine plead guilty to running a betting operation at Northwestern and the University of Colorado. In this case, basketball players Dion Lee and Dewey Williams tried to fix games in 1995. For further examples, a search on the internet will result in a history of sports gambling scandals.

Although there is no evidence of betting on hockey by this gambling ring, former Philadelphia Flyer hockey star Richard Tocchet and a New Jersey State Police trooper, James Harney, ran an illegal sports betting operation that handled $1.7 million in bets on college and professional football and basketball and the Super Bowl in a 40-day period. The ring had ties to the LCN and involved several professional hockey players. The charges included promoting gambling, money laundering and conspiracy with a possible 10-year sentence for Tocchet and a 20-year sentence for Harney if convicted. Harney pled guilty and was sentenced to only five years because of his cooperation in the case. Tocchet, now a Phoenix Coyotes' assistant coach, plead guilty to charges of conspiracy to promote gambling and promoting gambling, and as a first offender is not predicted to get jail time. The LCN ties were the Bruno-Scarfo crime family in South Jersey and Philadelphia. They were believed to have been in operation for five years (Holly, 2007; Moroz, 2006; Nelson, 2007).

It should be noted that LCN and other organized crime groups operate gaming houses, own and operate video gaming and lottery machines, and are involve in internet gambling (the fastest growing illegal business on the internet) in addition to operating bookmaking networks. Assets and monies derived from their illegal gambling operations support other legal and illegal operations such as drug trafficking and money laundering, which have a nexus to murder, assault, loan sharking, and corruption. These criminal organizations are the essence of enterprise crime and the criminal infiltration and corruption of governments and financial institutions.

The FBI offers advice and gives presentations to college athletes concerning the dangers of sports gambling. The National Collegiate Athletic Association (NCAA) has a zero tolerance policy on sports gambling by its athletes. If an athlete is caught betting on just one game, their career as a college athlete is over. The agency tells players that betting opens the door to more serious involvement with organized crime. If an athlete loses big and owes the campus bookie money and cannot pay, the bookie may offer the athlete another method to satisfy the debt. The bookie may not be a member of organized crime, but probably pays up the line to one. The inside information an athlete can provide on who starts, who is injured, and etc. can be extremely valuable to organized crime; who sets the line, places bets, and sells this information to other bookies. They may have the player shave points or play below their potential to change the final score. The criminals then bet against the line using this insider information or influence. The big problem comes with the realization by the athlete that the mob now owns them and continues to make demands using blackmail to ensure the athlete's continued participation in the illegal scheme ("Don't bet on it: Advice to athletes on sports gambling," 2006).

The Impact of Organized Illegal Gambling

Some experts believe that gambling has had at least some positive impact on society. Gambling is a large employer of people and in some lower economic areas is a major employer providing income. They argue that smaller business in some urban areas cannot compete with business chains or larger business organizations. Gambling and bookmaking allow these businesses to stay in business (Potter & Lyman, 2004; Silberman, 1978). However, there are problems with this argument, such as addiction, loss of tax revenue, corruption, and revenue for investment or support of other organized crime activity. After river boat casinos were in operation in such states as Mississippi, addiction did become a problem for some people who began gambling.

Michael Franzese, a former caporegime (captain) in the Columbo organized crime family, now gives presentations on how organized crime infiltrates a sport program and the impact of this activity. He gives examples of how devastating the effect is on an athlete's career and a university's image. According to Franzese, organized crime members love to gamble and bet as much as $400,000 to $1 million on a game. Franzese was recruited by the FBI to work with professional sports teams and college athletes at the end of his 10-year prison term for racketeering. Franzese believes that everyone in bookmaking is connected by some means to organized crime. Athletes, their friends and family, and acquaintances are seen as commodities by bookmakers and are part of the business for them, according to Franzese. These athletes are not always the high-profile players. Gamblers hang out where athletes hang out, looking for a target or inside information to help place successful bets (Elgass, 1998). Additional information pertaining to Michael Franzese can be found in Appendix 2 "Organized Crime and Sports Wagering: Insider Perspectives with Mike Franzese" located at the end of the book.

Gambling has always been a major activity of organized crime and sports betting is today's cash cow for these criminal organizations. Most operations include betting on a wide variety of sporting events including, football, baseball, basketball, soccer, hockey, tennis, boxing, dog racing, NASCAR, and horseracing. Today, internet gambling places any program at risk of involvement with organized crime. The $3.3 billion online gambling operation that resulted in a Miami, Florida couple pleading guilty to enterprise corruption and a violation of New York State's Organized Crime Control Act is typical. The operation handled more that $3 billion in online bets on a variety of sports over a two year period (Hopkins, 2007).

Other sports are concerned about the integrity of their sport. The United States Open/U.S. Tennis Association hires security firms to monitor gambling activity and to insure that the Open doesn't have a gambling scandal. Security investigated suspicious betting activity on a match involving Nikolay Davydenko. Davydenko has agreed to talk to officials, but denies any involvement in betting or violations of the policy. The Open's gambling policy prohibits participation in or aiding and abetting, directly or indirectly, on any form of gambling or betting involving tennis (Fendrich, 2007).

Sport betting remains a prevalent activity that is so widespread that it is possible for anyone to become vulnerable to the chance of making large amounts of money by illegal means. However, the winners are always the bookies and organized crime. The FBI does not consider gambling a victimless crime. A father and son were indicted for conducting an illegal gambling business and using facilities in interstate commerce to carry on unlawful activity. Bets were accepted by telephone out of an office in Nashville, Tennessee. Point spreads were obtained via an internet web site maintained by a Nevada-based company. Michael P. Williamson (aka "Big Mike") and his son Michael W. Williamson (aka "Little Mike") were also charged with conspiracy to conduct an illegal gambling operation. The FBI reported that three other participants plead guilty in the case to conducting an illegal gambling operation and are awaiting sentencing (Federal Bureau of Investigation-Memphis Field Division, 2007).

In addition to father and son cases, there are numerous cases that involve the destruction of lives. In a 1995, case over 32 locations including affluent New York neighborhoods in Yonkers, Mount Vernon, and the Bronx, people were arrested along with organized crime bookmakers operating 12 gambling telephone banks. One of those arrested was a second-grade schoolteacher, who took bets on football games using cellular telephones that would forward calls to avoid a trace or detection (Berger, 1995). These cases are similar to the prohibition era when many people who had never been involved in criminal activity became part of illegal alcohol operations. Illegal drug operations present yet another means of involving large numbers of people in criminal activity either by using the product or engaging in transportation, money laundering, and distribution of the illegal substance.

The widespread activity of sport betting has prompted some states and individuals to consider legalizing it. Federal law restricts legalized sport betting to Delaware, Montana, Nevada, and Oregon. These states and individuals question why millions of dollars should go to Las Vegas, offshore casinos and the mob. Others argue that legal betting on sport would create a climate of suspicion about any controversial play in a game.

The NFL and NBA have both opposed legalized sport betting in New Jersey, but New Jersey State Senator Raymond Lesniak stated that sports organizations have not enforced illegal use of steroids and thug behavior among players, which is worse than betting on the sport. There is a movement to legalize sports betting in New Jersey. The legalization issue has been around for years, including debates over legalization of drugs and alcohol. Alcohol is now legal, but is the leading substance of addition in the U.S. today. It seems that no matter what is legal or not legal, organized crime continues to find illegal services and goods that are not provided by governments and these provide enormous profits for these criminal organizations.

Illegal gambling, while appearing to be a minor activity for organized crime such as LCN, is the foundation upon which most other illicit activities are supported. Illegal sport betting provides capital for these criminal organizations to invest in more legitimate and illegitimate enterprises, thus making these organizations more powerful and influential. Sport betting is related to such crimes as loan sharking, money laundering, corruption, and even murder. The Canadian Security Services has identified illegal gambling as one of three transnational crimes that are a growing risk to national security. Monies and assets derived from illegal sport betting are not taxed, and millions of dollars are lost due to this activity. Organized crime has corrupted all the businesses, individuals, and events it has touched, and will continue to corrupt the sport industry and the people who work or play in the industry. With billions bet illegally around the nation every year on amateur and professional sport, the impact of organized crime is substantial. With the growth of illegal online gaming and related activities, this impact is likely to become more critical to national security and the business community.

Current Responses to Organize Crime by Law Enforcement and Sports

Conspiracy (two or more engaged in criminal enterprise organized much like legal business) is much of the how of organized crime. Conspiracy is the agreement of two or more people to commit an illegal act or the agreement of two or more people to engage in a legal act by illegal means. The charge of conspiracy, along with money laundering and RICO (Racketeer and Corrupt Organization Statue, 18 U.S.C. 1961–1965), are among the most common statues that are used to convict members of organized crime. The 1986 Money Laundering Act (18 U.S.C. 1956 and 18 U.S.C. 1957) made it a federal crime to launder money, which includes money from illegal gambling operations. *Money laundering* is defined as the activities designed to conceal the existence, nature, and final disposition of funds gained through illicit activities which includes income from illegal sports betting operations. The Financial Crimes Enforcement Network (FinCEN) divides money laundering into three stages: placement into a financial system, layering through a series of financial transactions, and integration of funds into an organization in a manner that they appear to be derived from legitimate income (putting money in a business, hiding its existent, and recovering the money to spend as it appears to be derived from legal enterprises). Gambling is also a predicate offense under the RICO Act. RICO allows for prosecution of a pattern of crimes that are committed by an organization or enterprise rather than proving conspiracy or that a person committed a specific crime. RICO makes it a crime to receive income from a pattern of racketeering through the collection of an unlawful debt which would include income from a sports betting operation. As presented in the many cases cited in this chapter, the arrest of bookmaking operations more often than not included a violation of RICO, which carries mandatory punishment of 20 years in prison, a substantial fine, and allows for the seizure and forfeiture of assets acquired by an organization in violation of RICO.

Bookmaking evidence includes the detailed business records that are required by the operation. Records are obtained by means of search warrants, trash pickup or runs by law enforcement, undercover recordings and electronic intercepts. The bookmaking operation will have one or more "offices" or central location that accepts wagers. These can be residences, businesses, rented apartments, other settings that provide the bookmaker with communication facilities and security. Office locations, which are not known by the bettor, may contain several telephone lines with advanced features, fax machines, and computers. Shredding machines, flash paper or soluble paper are often found at office locations. Evidence of a bookmaking operation includes audio recordings, wagering records, accounting records, and supporting paraphernalia. Recording can be from court authorized wire intercepts, undercover devices, or from the bookmaker's own recording devices that are used to record bets. Records can include answering machine tapes, fax and email, and written documents. Bottom sheets contain balances for different wagering accounts, and pay and collect sheets track amount collected or paid to accounts. Paraphernalia include line sheets, salary information for employees, or rule sheets that state specific rules for wagering, such as payout amounts, times wagers accepted and maximum wagering amounts. Internet gambling evidence includes accounting records, customer records, advertising records, and corporation records. Customer records include pay and collect sheets, records of initial deposits, and customer information. Advertising records are brochures, rule sheets, line sheets, and company information. Corporate records have the structure and operation of the business, diagrams, financial statements, and shareholder letters. Internet operations and their partners have bottom sheets and accounting records (Forshey & Olson, 2000).

Organizations such as the NCAA, the NBA, and NFL have zero tolerance policy when it comes to sport gambling by its athletes. These organizations are partners with law enforcement when it comes to identifying, prosecuting, and preventing organized crime and their members form infiltrating sports. Agents from the FBI make annual presentations to college athletes about the danger of sport gambling and the vulnerability of athletes to outside influences such as organized crime. From 1919 until today, the sports gambling scandals have continued and must be addressed with a cooperative effort between the sport industry, their organizations and law enforcement. This effort appears to have been at least somewhat effective.

Conclusions, Predictions, and Recommendations

Illegal gambling has been and continues to be a major profitable activity of organized crime. With reports that estimate illegal sports wagering to range from $80 to $380 billion annually, it is a problem that needs to be addressed by both the sport industry and law enforcement. It appears that no sport is exempt from the infiltration or attempted infiltration of organized crime. These scandals have a devastating effect on the sport industry and the people who make up the industry.

Former mob captain Michael Franzese stated that everyone that engages in illegal bookmaking is somehow, in some way linked to organized crime. Not unlike illegal drug trafficking, effectively addressing illegal sports gambling will require education and support of the public, the sport industry and players, prevention, and effective law enforcement to meet the challenge presented by organized crime's involvement in sport.

Although total elimination of illegal sport betting may not be possible, these strategies can make a difference. Again, online gambling, the fastest growing illegal business on the internet is an addictive from of gambling that will become more than a $20 billion illegal industry dominated by organized crime. Millions of Americans gamble on sport and millions gamble online every day. Neither federal nor state government receives tax revenue or benefit from illegal gambling, nor does online gambling create any job in the United States. However, organized crime does benefit from the enormous income from online illegal gambling and sports betting. In the future, illegal Internet gambling operations will likely receive a larger share of the illegal gambling market as organized crime becomes more entrenched in these operations.

Albini (1971) described the patron-client relationship of organized crime over 30 years ago. There is no better example than illegal sport betting to demonstrate the mutual support of organized crime by corrupt politicians, government officials, law enforcement, business owners, and a willing public. Conspiracy and corruption remain the means of organized crime activity and growth. As long as the demand by the public and profits are there, organized crime will continue to provide the illegal services and goods. The public must be made aware that participating in illegal sport gambling is supporting organized crime and all the illegal activities in which these criminal organizations engage. Greed and power remain the driving forces behind the activity of illegal sport betting. For these reasons, organized crime will likely continue to survive the way it has for centuries, and the sport industry will continue to be a victim of these criminal organizations.

It's easy to get people's attention; what counts is getting their interest.
—A. Philip Randolph (1889–1979)

References

Abdinsky, H. (2003). *Organized crime* (7th ed.). Belmont, CA: Wadsworth/ Thompson Learning.

Albanese, J.S., Das, D.K., & Verma, A. (2003). *Organized crime: World perspectives*. Upper Saddle River, NJ: Prentice Hall.

Albanese, J.S. (2004). Organized crime in our times. Cincinnati, OH: LexisNexis Anderson Publishing.

Albini, J.L. (1971). *The American mafia: Genesis of a legend.* New York: Appleton-Century-Crofts.

Americas Watchdog Reports (2007). Americas Watchdog Reports on the Involvement of U.S. Banks and Major U.S. Credit Card Issuers in Internet Gambling. Retrieved on October 8, 2008, from http://prweb.com/releases/2007/8/prweb549001.htm

Associated Press (1998, March 3). Skimming Scheme Overheard, FBI Agent Testifies at Detroit Trial," *Las Vegas Sun,* p. 6B.

Associated Press (2006). 27 arrested in first online gambling bust since Bush signed law banning Internet wagering. Fox News. Accessed October 8, 2008, from http://www.foxnews.com/story/0,2933,229677,00.html

Associated Press (2007). New York officers bust $2 million-a-week Internet sports betting operation. Fox News. Accessed October 8, 2008, from http://www.foxnews.com/story/0,2933,270521,00.html

Berger, J. (1995). Police Sweep Shuts Down Sports Gambling Rings. *New York Times.* Retrieved on October 8, 2008, from http://query.nytimes.com/gst/full page.html?res=9C00E7DB1E39F937A35751C1A963958260&scp=1&sq=Police+Sweep+Shuts+Down+Sports+Gambling+Rings&st=nyt

Boyd, K. (1975). *Gambling technology.* Washington, D.C.: FBI Laboratory.

Browning, F., & Gerassi, J. (1980). *The American way of crime.* New York: G.P. Puttnam's and Sons.

DeMarco, J.V. (2001). Gambling Against Enforcement—Internet Sports Books and the Wire Wager Act. Retrieved on October 8, 2008, from http://www.usdoj.gov/criminal/cybercrime/usamarch2001_5.htm

Don't bet on it: Advice to athletes on sports gambling (2006). Federal Bureau of Investigation Headline Archives. Retrieved on October 8, 2008, from http://www.fbi.gov/page2/nov06/gambling110606.htm

Dunstan, R. (1997). History of Gambling in the United States. Retrieved on October 8, 2008, from http://www.library.ca.gov/CRB/97/03/Chapt2.html

Elgass, J. (1998). Former mob captain gives tough lesson on sports gambling. *The University Record.* Retrieved on October 8, 2008, from http://www.umich.edu/~urecord/9899/Nov02_98/12.htm

Federal Bureau of Investigation-Memphis Field Division (2007). Goodlettsville Father and Son Indicted on Charges Relating to Operation of Illegal Nashville Based Gambling Business. Retrieved on October 8, 2008, from http://memphis.fbi.gov/dojpressrel/pressrel07/me090507.htm

Federal Bureau of Investigation New York Division (2007). National Basketball Association referee pleads guilty to participating in an illegal sports betting scheme involving NBA games. Retrieved on October 8, 2008, from http://newyork.fbi.gov/dojpressrel/pressrel07/sportsbetting081507.htm

Fendrich, H. (2007). Davydenko to Talk to Investigators. Fox News. Retrieved on October 8, 2008, from http://www.foxnews.com/printer_friendly_wires/2007Aug27/0,4675,TENUSOpenDavydenko,00.html

Finckenauer, J., & Voronin, Y. (2001). The Threat of Russian Organized Crime. Washington DC: U.S. Department of Justice, National Institute of Justice, NCJ 187085.

Forshey, J , & Olson, D. (2000). *Illicit Gambling*. FBI Laboratory Technical Supplement. Federal Bureau of Investigation Racketeering Records Analysis Unit.

Garner, J. (2007). Interpol Arrests Hundreds in Asian Sports Betting Sting: More than 400 Arrested for Betting on Soccer. Retrieved on October 8, 2008, from http://www.associatedcontent.com/article/457984/.html

Hanaway, C. (2006). Eleven individuals and four corporations indicted on racketeering, conspiracy and fraud charges. Federal Bureau of Investigation-St. Louis. Retrieved on October 18, 2008, from http://stlouis.fbi.gov/dojpressrel/pressrel06/racketeering071706.htm

Hays, T. (2008). Dozens sought in mob raids in US, Italy. Fox News. Retrieved on February 11, 2008, from http://www.foxnews.com/printer_friendly_wires/2008Feb07/0,4675,ItalyUSMafia,00.html

Hopkins, J. (2007). Miami couple pleads guilty in $3.3 billion online gambling operation. 777 Gaming News. Accessed October 8, 2008, from http://news.777.com/2007-03/couple-guilty-in-online-gambling-operation

Irwin, V., & Richey, W. (1986, August 28). Holding the mob at bay? *Christian Science Monitor*, 18.

Jacobs, A., & Moynihan, C. (2006). 10 are accused of running sports gambling operations. *New York Times*. Retrieved on October 8, 2008, from http://www.nytimes.com/2006/03/27/nyregion/27bookies.html

Lobo, A. (2002). A fan's guide to online betting on the soccer World Cup. Rediff.com. Retrieved on January 1, 2008, from http://www.rediff.com/search/2002/may/28bet.htm

Mallory, S. (2007). *Understanding organized crime*. Sudbury, MA: Jones and Bartlett Publishers.

Moroz, J. (2006). Ex-Flyer Tocchet and New Jersey trooper charged in illegal sports betting ring. Officer.com. Retrieved on October 8, 2008, from http://www.officer.com/publication/printer.jsp?id=28486

Mutschke, R. (2000). The Threat Posed by the Convergence of Organized Crime Drugs Trafficking and Terrorism. Retrieved on January 14, 2008, from http://www.globalsecurity.org/security/library/congress/2000_h/001213-mutschke.htm

Nelson, G. (2007). Former hockey star pleads guilty to gambling charges. 777 Gaming News. Retrieved on October 8, 2008, from http://news.777.com/2007-05/hockey-star-pleads-guilty-to-gambling-charges

Omnibus Crime Control and Safe Streets Act of 1968. (18 U.S.C. 2510–2520). Washington, D.C.: U.S. Department of Justice. Accessed October 19, 2008, from http://www.usdoj.gov/crt/split/42usc3789d.htm

Online gambling: Don't roll the dice. (2007). Federal Bureau of Investigation Retrieved on October 8, 2008, from http://www.fbi.gov/page2/june07/gambling060607.htm

Ordine, B. (2007). Gambling, sports have long link: Gambling, games have long history. *Baltimore Sun*. Retrieved on January 1, 2008, from http://www.baltimore sun.com/sports/basketball/balsp.gambling30oct30,0,7764651,full.col ...

Organized Crime Control Act of 1970. (18 U.S.C. 1956, 1957). Retrieved on January, 14, 2008, from http://trac.syr.edu/laws/18USC1956.html and http://trac.syr.edu/laws/18USC1957.html

Organized Crime Tied to Betting Scandal. (1997). *New York Times* Retrieved on January 6, 2008, from http://query.nytimes.com/gst/fullpage.html?res=9507E2 DF153BF93BA25752C0A961958260&scp=1&sq=organized+crime+tied+to+ betting+scandal&st=nyt

Parry, W. (2007). Alleged Sports Betting Ring Busted at Borgata. 6ABC.com. Retrieved on October 8, 2008, from http://abclocal.go.com/wpvi/story?section= local&id=5761177

Peterson, V.F. (1952). *Barbarians in our midst: A history of Chicago crime and politics*. Boston: Little, Brown and Company.

Potter, W., & Lyman, M. (2004). *Organized crime* (3rd ed.). Upper Saddle River, New Jersey: Prentice Hall.

President's Commission on Law Enforcement and Administration of Justice (1967). *The Challenge of Crime in a Free Society*. Washington, D.C.: U.S. Government Printing Office.

Racketeer Influenced and Corrupt Organizations Act (RICO). (1970). (18 U.S.C. 1961–1965). Retrieved on December 4, 2006, from http://usinfo.state.gov/ usa/infousa/laws/majorlaw/rico/rico.htm

Rashbaum, W. ,& Ramirez, A. (2005). Metro briefing | New York: Queens: 17 accused in gambling ring. *New York Times*. Retrieved on October 8, 2008, from http://query.nytimes.com/gst/fullpage.html?res=9406E0DB1F3FF936 A35757C0A9639C8B63&scp=1&sq=17+accused+in+gambling+ring&st=nyt

Rivero, T. (2006). City-wide sports gambling sting nets 10 arrests: WCBStv.com. Organizations grossed more than $45 million annually. Retrieved on October 8, 2008, from http://wcbstv.com/topstories/Gambling.DA.Hynes.2.234201.html

Santi, A.D. (2007, December 18). Reputed mob ring busted in New Jersey. *International Business Times*. Retrieved on October 19, 2008, from http://www.ibtimes.com/articles/20071218/reputed-mob-ring-busted-in-new-jersey.htm

Shelly, L.I. (1995). Transnational organized crime. *Journal of International Affairs,* 48(2), 485.

Silberman, C.E. (1978). *Criminal violence, criminal justice*. New York: Random House.

Sports Betting. (2007). Wikipedia. Retrieved on October 8, 2008, from http://en.wikipedia.org/wiki/Sports_betting

The St. Louis Division: A Brief History. (2008). Federal Bureau of Investigation-St. Louis Field Division. Retrieved on October 19, 2008, from http://stlouis.fbi.gov/history.htm

Sutherland, E., & Cressey D. (1960). *Principles of criminology* (6th ed.). New York: Lippincott.

United States Attorney Southern District of New York (2006). Four Leaders of Violent Albanian Racketeering Enterprise Sentenced to Between 22 and 27 Years in Prison and Ordered to Forfeit $5,755,000 and Four Properties to the Government. Retrieved on October 8, 2008, from http://www.usdoj.gov/usao/ nys/pressreleases/June06/rudajsentencingpr.pdf

Uniting and Strengthening America by Providing Appropriate Tools to Intercept and Obstruct Terrorism Act (USA Patriot Act) of 2001. Washington, DC: Electronic Privacy Information Center. Retrieved on October 19, 2008, from http://www.epic.org/privacy/terrorism/hr3162.html [link is no longer active]

Unlawful Internet Gambling Enforcement Act of 2006. Retrieved on January 1, 2008, from http://www.techlawjournal.com/cong109/bills/house/gambling/ 20060929.asp

7

Fraud in Non-profit Sport: A Case Study of the Sport Sun State Soccer Association

Jeffrey E. Michelman, University of North Florida
Jason W. Lee, University of North Florida
Bobby E. Waldrup, University of North Florida[1]

Introduction

This case is based on actual events, but elements have been fictionalized to illustrate particular issues of organizational governance and risk management (financial and otherwise), as well concepts of organizational control, and criminal susceptibility in a non-profit sport organization. All names and places have been changed in order to mask the identity of both the organization and individuals involved.

Sun State Soccer Association (SSSA) is a non-profit soccer organization located in the metropolitan Orlando, Florida area. The nature of SSSA's philosophy of governance and its operating style were not conducive to an effectively controlled environment, allowing an opportunity for fraud. The lack of order, regulation, and record keeping, coupled with procedural shortcomings, laid a foundation for a number of abuses. Trust and belief were placed in the officials within this non-profit sport organization, and this trust, combined with a practice of allowing a single individual the responsibility of handling all checks and cash that came in through organization, left it at risk for financial fraud.

Although SSSA was supposed to have security policies established through its bylaws, the management board's lack of organizational oversight allowed problems to occur. As one individual sought to gather information needed for a grant application, he quickly realized there were various obstacles in his path: copies of organizational policy and financial records were unavailable. After enlisting the help of a local accounting professor, the financial records

1. This case was developed with the help of Oscar Harvin, John Watler, Katie Stratton, and Carolyn Russell, graduate students in the Coggin College of Business at UNF.

were finally obtained from the financial institution that held the organization's account. Many red flags appeared in the financial reports, including various unaccounted expenses and checks that were both issued and endorsed by the organization's treasurer. Such policies show a lack of appropriate "checks and balances" resulting from a system where policies were merely perfunctory, unenforced, or not properly obeyed.

Management practices and procedures did not require proper safeguards to monitor individual officer activities. The treasurer's ability to keep control of the funds entering and exiting the organization laid the foundation for the trouble identified in the following case.

Understanding Non-profits

In order to gain a full appreciation for the information presented in the case, it is important for readers to have a foundational understanding of what a non-profit organization is. In general, a non-profit organization is organized for purposes of social welfare, civic improvement, pleasure or recreation, or for any purpose except profit (Section 149.1(1), Income Tax Act of Canada, 2008). Non-profit organizations are quite prevalent in today's society. The motivation and makeup of such organizations can vary.

The fundamental distinction between non-profits and a traditional for-profit organization is one of purpose: rather than existing to earn a profit, a non-profit's success is measured primarily by how well it renders a service (Anthony, 1977). Official non-profit organizations can vary in regards to involvement, membership (though not all non-profits actually have members), and leadership. In regards to leadership, boards, such as leadership boards, management boards, boards of directors, boards of trustees, etc, lead non-profits. Examples of non-profit entities include most educational institutions, religious organizations, and notable charitable organizations such as: the American Red Cross, Goodwill Industries, Habitat for Humanity, Salvation Army, and United Way.

In addition to the aforementioned examples, non-profit sport organizations compose a significant number of sport agencies. Among the notable sport non-profit organizations are the Amateur Athletics Union (AAU), Boys and Girls Clubs, Jewish Community Centers (JCC), Little League Baseball, National Collegiate Athletic Association (NCAA), the United States Olympic Committee (USOC), and Young Men's Christian Association (YMCA), to name some of the more visible of such organizations. Beyond the large-scale aforementioned examples, there are a tremendous number of non-profit sport organizations residing in locales throughout the country (and beyond for that matter). Examples of such organizations can include soccer associations, golf and country clubs, lacrosse leagues, basketball leagues, wrestling clubs, etc.

Non-profit sport organizations are a significant provider of sport activities for participants of all ages. The awareness and public perception of these sport organizations are important. Building and maintaining a trustworthy image can have a significant impact in reaching key goals and objectives, including establishing relations with potential participants, benefactors, and other key stakeholder, all of which aides in the process of effectively running these organizations. In this case, various safeguards and effective governance controls were overlooked leading to ethical breaches and criminal actions. The results of these actions allowed the organization to be defrauded and great efforts were taken to see that this abhorrent behavior remained hidden. Significant issues, shortcomings, and further related actions are identified, laying the foundation for further examination and evaluation by readers (either individually or in group settings).

Non-Profits and Youth Sports

From 1996 to 2006, the number of non-profits in the U.S. increased from 1,084,939 to 1,478,194 (NCCS, 2008). This 36.2 percent increase is even more significant when public charities are examined. This group went from 535,930 in 1996 to 904,313 in 1996, which was a 68.7 percent increase. In 2006, there were 56,778 recreation, sports, leisure, and athletics organizations, with over $11 billion in gross receipts and over $21 billion in total assets. Not all of these organizations served youth, but it is easy to see the importance of this sector (NCCS, 2007).

Non-profit organizations take a variety of forms. The most common organizational structure for a youth sports organization is to organize as a non-profit tax exempt organization under section 501(c)(3) of the Internal Revenue Code. Such entities must be organized and operated for the tax exempt purpose and none of its earnings may inure to any of its members or other constituents (Internal Revenue Code, 2008). Members of this group of organizations are often referred to as charitable organizations, since contributions to this type of organization are tax-exempt. Organizations failing to operate for the benefit of its members or allowing employees or outsiders to inure benefits may be subject to excise taxes applicable to both the organization and those individuals involved (Fremont-Smith, 2004).

Challenges Presented

For many, the term non-profit is a misnomer, as people commonly think that such organizations have little to no funding and operate off of an almost nonexistent budget. While that may be true for some organizations, many organizations are anything but. Some of the most notable sport providers are non-profit organizations. Whether it is a large international organization or a local lacrosse league, there are various issues of which such organizations need to be mindful. Among these are proper governance aspects; these can include measures ensuring that the proper actions are taken to maintain non-profit status.

Beyond that, there are various other actions that need to be taken to ensure the ongoing success of the organization. There is a need to ensure that the organization is geared to protect itself from potential risks. While all risks cannot be removed, effective management practices can help to equip organizations for troubles that emerge.

Among the particular risk areas that could confront such organizations include the risk of financial misdealings. Such misdealings include runaway costs, improper fund usage, fraud, and theft. The case presented here identifies issues and occurrences that opened the door for theft and fraudulent behavior in one non-profit. Failing to obey provisions deterring unfortunate occurrences can negatively impact the financial bottom line, as well as create trust issues and image concerns.

The case presented in this chapter illustrates issues associated with a non-profit soccer association. Details of this association, including governance issues, financial protocols, and aspects associated with unethical and illegal behaviors, as well as mismanagement, will be detailed in Part I and II.

Fraud in Non-profit: A Case Study of the Sport Sun State Soccer Association

Part I

It was January 2007 and Matt Jackson looked at the pictures of his sons wearing their soccer uniforms. Both boys were good athletes and excelled in various sports, especially soccer. During his association with Sun State Soccer, Matt had met many great people involved with the association, but serious problems had emerged over the previous six years, and he wondered if it was worth it to continue his membership on Sun State's board of directors.

The Sun State Soccer Association (SSSA) operated in much the same fashion as other community youth sports organization throughout the country. Operated by parent volunteers for the enjoyment and athletic skill development of youth participants, its sports facilities were located in a local neighborhood in suburban Winter Park, Florida, in the outskirts of Orlando. Based solely on appearances, the association was dominated by individuals with good morals, ethical values, and good intentions. Matt moved his family to the Orlando area because of the great opportunities it offered, because he viewed the area as somewhat of a "cow town," where locals were not as well educated or informed about matters of business as his friends from his hometown in New Jersey.

He was also confident in his business acumen and believed his actions saved SSSA from financial devastation. In May 2001, almost immediately upon moving to the area, Matt's children became involved with the SSSA. After becoming frustrated with how his children were being coached, Matt volunteered to serve as an assistant coach and eventually became a head soccer coach. In 2002, he was approached by some of the board members of the association and was invited to join the board. He accepted the nomination because the position would allow him to schedule his sons' matches at times that would be convenient for his family.

Matt's career as an inside representative for several wholesale distributors progressed well. He had an associate degree in business and had taken several accounting classes. As a professional sales representative, he learned to read his customers and felt very confident in his ability to judge the character of those he interacted with.

Matt believed he had much to offer SSSA. He viewed his contributions to SSSA as very positive because without him, the association would be financially ruined, but, with every step he took forward, he felt the board had pushed him two steps back. They just did not understand (or want to understand) the business aspect and *politics* of running a successful non-profit organization. Matt remembered with a slow boiling anger the many incidents of both fraudulent and unethical behavior that occurred while he was involved with the association. SSSA operated

Table 7.1 What are Robert's Rules of Order?

Robert's Rules of Order:

[p]rovides common rules and procedures for deliberation and debate in order to place the whole membership on the same footing and speaking the same language. The conduct of ALL business is controlled by the general will of the whole membership—the right of the deliberate majority to decide. Complementary is the right of at least a strong minority to require the majority to be deliberate—to act according to its considered judgment after a full and fair "working through" of the issues involved. Robert's Rules provides for constructive and democratic meetings, to help, not hinder, the business of the assembly. Under no circumstances should "undue strictness" be allowed to intimidate members or limit full participation.

The fundamental right of deliberative assemblies require all questions to be thoroughly discussed before taking action! (Kennedy, 1997, n.p.).

[Excerpt from www.robertsrules.org]

with no concept of business skills or management, and the opportunity for growing the organization into a major sports league in the area had almost been squandered.

Serving on the Board

During his first term on the board, Matt went along with the flow and worked hard to understand the nuances of how the association operated, as well as the operation of the board members. He was surprised to learn that the board used neither Robert's Rules nor any other such meeting rules.

This struck Matt as being odd, though he did not ask as about it because he felt that it would be best to get to know the board better before questioning their policies and procedural operations. Although there were written by-laws, they existed only for the purpose of attaining and maintaining its 501(c)(3) non-profit status with the IRS.

While everyone knew there were by-laws that limited board membership and officer terms, and required general election of board members by the association membership (parents or guardians held one vote per registered youth), no one really worried about following the by-laws to the letter. Additionally, enticing members to volunteer was difficult at best. Offices were occupied through self-selection, general agreement of the board, and until voluntary resignation despite term limits in their by-laws (see Table 7.3).

During Matt's tenure on the board, Paul Simmons served as board president, Sandy Wilson held the office of vice-president, and Pam Fields was the treasurer. Matt would later learn that these individuals had held their offices for five years prior to Matt joining the board. Initially, Matt felt that the fact these individuals

Table 7.2   501(c) Taxable Status

How does the IRS categorize an organization as a tax-exempt non-profit?

To be tax-exempt under section 501(c)(3) of the Internal Revenue Code, an organization must be organized and operated exclusively for exempt purposes set forth in section 501(c)(3), and none of its earnings may inure to any private shareholder or individual. In addition, it may not be an action organization, i.e., it may not attempt to influence legislation as a substantial part of its activities and it may not participate in any campaign activity for or against political candidates.

Organizations described in section 501(c)(3) are commonly referred to as charitable organizations. Organizations described in section 501(c)(3), other than testing for public safety organizations, are eligible to receive tax-deductible contributions in accordance with Code section 170.

The organization must not be organized or operated for the benefit of private interests, and no part of a section 501(c)(3) organization's net earnings may inure to the benefit of any private shareholder or individual. If the organization engages in an excess benefit transaction with a person having substantial influence over the organization, an excise tax may be imposed on the person and any organization managers agreeing to the transaction.

Section 501(c)(3) organizations are restricted in how much political and legislative (lobbying) activities they may conduct. For a detailed discussion, see Political and Lobbying Activities. For more information about lobbying activities by charities, see the article Lobbying Issues … (Exemption Requirements, n.d., n.p.).

Excerpt from Internal Revenue Code section 501(c)(3) [Available at: http://www.irs.gov/charities/charitable/article/0,,id=96099,00.html]

Readers may also want to refer to Application for Recognition of Exemption under Section 501(c)(3) of the Internal Revenue Code (2006). [Available at www.irs.gov/pub/irs-pdf/f1023.pdf]

had served for so many consecutive terms was a positive indicator of the solid commitment and integrity of the organization. Matt's involvement with the board allowed him to know Pam Fields. Pam's daughter played on a field next to Matt's youngest son. Pam took pride in her appearance and Matt enjoyed the opportunity to flirt with her on occasion. She seemed to enjoy the attention from the male members of the board. Although happily married, Matt saw nothing wrong with an occasional flirt outside of his wife's view.

Matt felt he had a decent relationship with the other members of the board and by his second term, he felt he understood how the board operated. As he entered his new board term, he decided to become more active as a board member. He was aware that a new development was going in near Lake Shore, and that part of the development deal included deeding forty acres of land to the city for a public park. He thought the location would be great for soccer fields, since the number of teams had outgrown the local high school playing field. He brought the board the idea of pursuing use of the land for the association soccer teams, along

Table 7.3 Organizational Structure of SSSA

EXECUTIVE OFFICERS
  (1) President
  (2) Vice President
  (3) Treasurer
  (4) Secretary

BOARD OF DIRECTORS
  (1) Chairman of Sports Events
  (2) Chairman of Registration
  (3) Commissioner of Coaches
  (4) Advance Director of Soccer
  (5) Chairman of Special Events
  (6) Chairman of Facilities
  (7) Chairman of Fund Raising
  (8) Chairman of Referees
  (9) Chairman of the Booster Club
  (10) Chairman of Sports Programs

with putting in a grant application for state funding to further develop the fields, including a building for the association.

Matt spent a good deal of time talking and planning with Paul, the board president, about the opportunity to grow the association. Paul seemed interested, but Matt knew that Paul did not have the expertise to pursue this goal. Over a beer one evening after the district championships, Matt convinced Paul to allow him to pursue exclusive rights to use the park at Lake Shore and the necessary grants to fund the project. Matt was thrilled and saw this as a special assignment from the board president.

At the December 2001 board meeting, Matt requested time to speak and present his plan as an informational item. When the time to speak arrived, he proudly dispersed copies of his business plan, which included lobbying for the exclusive use of the Lake Shore park land, as well as applying for a $100,000 city grant and a $450,000 state grant.

During his presentation, Matt did not notice the puzzled looks of the board members and the heated whispers. When finished giving his spiel, he looked to Paul, believing that he had impressed the board with the business plan and presentation. In reality, Matt's presentation was greeted with a lukewarm response at best. He simply thought the members did not quite understand, since they were not business people, and chided himself for using "business" terminology words throughout in his presentation.

After the meeting, Matt proudly approached the association treasurer, Pam, and the vice-president, Sandy. He chatted with them briefly about the upcoming state tournament. Sandy turned to talk with the association registrar, leaving Matt and Pam alone. Matt could not help but think that there was just something about Pam, and although he knew they were both happily married, he just felt sparks fly between them. Furthermore, while working on the business plan, it oc-

curred to him that the grant application process might provide just the right opportunity to spend more time with Pam. So, with this in mind, he asked, "What
did you think of my business plan for the association?" She responded, "Well, it
seems like you put a lot of work into it." He smiled and leaned forward, "You
have no idea how hard I worked on it. I am hoping now that it has been presented
to the board, that we will proceed forward. And I'm hoping that you will help me
put together financial statements for the application." She hesitated, and then
said, "Sure, no problem." Then Pam's husband walked up, spoke to Pam, and reminded her of the time. She bid Matt goodnight, and said that she looked forward
to hearing more from him regarding the project.

By May 2002, Matt completed the grant applications, except for the financial
statements and the description of the financial controls of the organization. He
did not know what financial controls were involved, but assumed Pam would. He
pressed Pam privately for help on the financials, and though they scheduled many
times to meet, Pam inevitably canceled at the last minute. In the meantime, the
gossip mill was churning with the news that Paul had separated from his wife because of his affair with Pam, which Matt highly doubted. Eventually, Paul con-
fided to Matt that he had been drinking too much, and had showed up to his job
in no condition to work, and was subsequently fired. Paul also explained that his
separation from his wife was due to his job loss and drinking. Regardless, this additional drama seemed to be occupying everyone's time, except for Matt—he had
a goal to accomplish and Pam was holding things up.

At the June 2002 board meeting, a very frustrated Matt requested that the
board either compel Pam to help him on the financials, or give him the books so
he could take care of the matter himself. Other board members responded negatively to what he perceived to be a reasonable request, and the meeting very
quickly turned heated and tempers flared. Matt was taken aback by the board's
resistance to requiring Pam to assist him with the financial information and description of the financial controls needed for the grant application. Matt looked
at Pam to see her response, and she appeared lost in thought. It seemed as though
the other members had been meeting behind his back and decided to gang up on
him. This was confusing, as it never occurred to Matt that anyone on the board
disagreed with the business plan he presented six months prior, and not a word
had been mentioned since. Matt had taken this as a silent approval and proceeded
forward with Paul's support. Paul called the meeting back to order and requested
that Matt give Pam the application information so that she could review it. Sandy
suggested that perhaps Matt should compile the financial information himself
since it was "his little project." To Matt's relief, Pam spoke up and promised to
meet with him and work on the financials before the next board meeting.

Pam kept their arranged meeting, and brought the completed financial sections
of the grant application. Matt's pride was still hurt from statements made at the
board meeting the week before. "Pam, I can't believe the board turned on me like
they did," he said. "Well, Matt, you did come on pretty strong, and it does seem
like you are really the only one pushing the issue of growing the organization and
getting these grants."

Matt was surprised, and it was becoming obvious that she and the others did
not know that he was acting on Paul's direction. Pam looked shocked when he
told her that he and Paul had been discussing this project for nearly a year, and
that he was simply helping Paul. It was obvious that Pam doubted what she was

being told and there were clearly trust deficiencies. He quickly wondered if the financial information she included on the grant application was accurate. Matt felt that something was not right, and wondered to himself if Pam changed the financial information to sabotage his efforts. Rather than confront her head-on, he decided to take the easy way out. "Pam, I'd like to look at the books just to confirm these numbers. I may have to answer questions about the application, and if I understand how you got these numbers, then I can answer them and won't have to bother you." Pam looked visibly shaken and became quite defensive, "You don't trust me? I am twelve hours short of a bachelor's degree in accounting and have managed my own businesses. I have been keeping these books since 1997, and no one has ever questioned my bookkeeping." He tried to assure her that he did not doubt her bookkeeping, but she was packing up to leave and would not engage in any further discussion. Matt knew that he needed to talk to Paul about this situation.

The Business of the Business Plan

Over a beer later that evening, Matt detailed what had transpired during his meeting with Pam earlier that day. Matt told Paul he was concerned that there might be additional board members involved that had convinced Pam to complete the financial application in such a way that it would result in the association losing the grant opportunity. He told Paul that it seemed like no one but the two of them seemed to have any vision for the organization.

Paul told him he would think things over and look for the best way deal with Pam. In the meantime, he asked Matt to make sure the rest of the grant application was in order. He also reminded Matt that Pam was under a great deal of financial stress in her personal life and did not mean any harm. Paul insisted he had complete faith in Pam's ability. Matt, dissatisfied, pressed the issue of seeing the books for himself. Matt knew that Paul had called a special meeting of the executive board, which included Sandy and Pam. The rest of the board was informed that the purpose of the executive meeting was to consider the status of Matt's business plan and related grant applications. Matt trusted Paul, and believed that Paul was trying to ensure Matt's access to the organization's books with no further resistance from Pam or the other board members. Matt was very excited about moving forward with his project. He made great contacts during the process that would certainly help not only the organization, but also his bid for a city council seat. Running for political office had always been a goal for Matt, and his participation in the soccer association fueled his desire to be elected to a public office.

Matt called Paul a couple of days after the executive board meeting for an update. Paul assured Matt that the business plan was on course, and that all relevant financial statements and a description of the financial controls would be reviewed by the board in time for the grant application.

At the August 2002 board meeting, Paul opened the meeting with two agenda items. The first issue involved a minor revision to the 2001 tax return. There were no questions about why there was a revision and Paul did not volunteer any information beyond the existence of the revision and the re-filing. Matt was too excited about the second agenda item to have the first agenda item take up any more time. The second agenda item was his business plan. He was looking forward to having the entire board review the books of the organization, thus giving him assurance that there was no sabotage in the works. Pam began shuffling papers and Matt waited for his copy of the financials and other related information. When she began to give an oral review of his application, there were no written financial statements. Matt was so angry he could hardly breathe. His heart was pounding. He looked at Paul, but Paul was concentrating on Pam's presentation.

The board thought it all sounded interesting but deferred action until the following month. As Matt drove home after the board meeting, he was beyond livid. He had expected hard copies of the financial reports, along with a written description of the organization's financial controls. Apparently, no one, including Paul, realized the seriousness of these grants, as time was passing quickly and the deadline for submitting the application was looming. Matt would have to seriously consider how to complete the work.

Several weeks passed and Matt was still frustrated. He felt betrayed by Paul, who had not pushed Pam to bring hard copies of data to back up the financial information she had provided. He thought about perhaps enlisting an outside resource to help him finish the application, since no one on the inside seemed to care. Eventually, the grant deadline came and passed. Fortunately, no one applied for the grant, and the opportunity was reissued for fall 2003, which was almost one year to the day that Matt had hit the dead-end with Pam, Paul, and the board. This time, he vowed, the opportunity would not be missed.

In April of 2003, Matt and his wife, Laura, went out to dinner with some friends. One of Laura's friends was married to an accounting professor, Dr. Bateman, who taught accounting at Orlando International University. Maybe it was the bottle of wine before dinner, but Matt saw this social encounter as an opportunity to ask the professor to help with the grant application. Matt asked Dr. Bateman about his experience in the area of responding to non-profit grants. He talked extensively about his grant writing and it seemed to Matt that Dr. Bateman was just the expert needed for his cause. The professor listened with great eagerness to Matt's description of what was needed for the grant for the soccer association. He was very interested in helping Matt because such effort would look great on his resume. This would be a major project, and might even get the professor in the running for Dean of the Business School. Dr. Bateman immediately offered to help Matt and the board. Matt was thrilled with this offer. How could the board refuse? It was getting late, and Laura was ready to go. Matt asked for the professor's business card and promised to call him to set up a time to go over the grant application.

Matt could not wait for the next board meeting. He called Paul in advance to request additional time to address the board and to let Paul know about Dr. Bateman's offer to help with the grant application. Paul seemed pleased about Dr. Bateman's offer to volunteer his time to help with the grant application. Matt made it a point to ask Paul to request Pam bring all of the organization's financial records and related documents with her to the next board meeting. The next board meeting would not be until after the new year, so Pam would have plenty of time to gather all of the necessary paperwork. It was an unexpectedly cool early fall evening in 2003, when the board convened. Matt could hardly contain himself. This time, the grant would not be lost, he was sure of it. After opening the meeting, Paul turned the floor over to Matt. He opened with the vision for the betterment of the association and told them that the grant opportunity was available again.

He talked about what the grant and the subsequent growth of the organization would bring to the community and its youth participants. Matt carefully stated that a weakness in the last grant application was the inability to complete the financial section of the application. Matt stressed the importance of the financial statements. He had since learned from Dr. Bateman that information about the financial controls and how the organization protected its assets from fraud, misappropriation, and theft was critical. Matt reminded the board about the importance of being able to describe how well the board protected cash and accounted for assets. Then, he broached the idea to invite Dr. Bateman to help put together the grant application. Matt went over all of Dr. Bateman's credentials, and emphasized the number of grants the professor had been awarded. He looked over to Pam expecting to see her roll her eyes or exhibit some other dramatic behavior. Pam seemed very collected and was waiting for the discussion to stop before she began to speak.

Once Pam decided to speak, she said:

Matt, I am sorry that you feel additional accounting expertise is required to address your needs for the grant proposal. I have made myself available to review all the financials on your little project and you now insist on outside consultation. If you and the board believe that the services I have provided to this association for the last eight years have been insufficient, I will gladly step aside and your so-called experts can fill my position.

After this retort, the room was silent. Matt was briefly shocked at Pam's response, but the shock quickly turned into his excitement. It was fine with him if she wanted to turn the books over—at least then he could get what he needed for the grant application. Then he noticed that the other board members were now standing and attempting to console Pam.

Paul spoke up and said, "Pam, your services are invaluable to the association and I am sure that Matt was not implying that you cannot handle responding to the grant application." Pam seemed to sigh with appreciation. Matt had not meant to hurt her feelings, but it was apparent that he had. Pam looked straight and Matt and said, quietly, "Thank you, Paul, for your vote of confidence." The meeting ended before Matt had a chance to complete his presentation, and he left disappointed and disheartened.

The next day, Matt called Dr. Bateman and set up a lunch meeting for the following week. Matt was not sure how to proceed, but he knew that the responsibility was his, since the board did not appear to understand the importance of the grant and application process. Dr. Bateman was waiting for him at the table, but Matt was still unsure how to engage the professor's help without the association's support. Fortunately, the professor never asked if the board had approved his involvement, and Matt figured that since the board did not actually disapprove, no mention was necessary either way.

He reviewed the grant application with Dr. Bateman. The professor seemed to have a grasp of what was needed. He asked for the financial records so that they could complete the financial portion of the application. He also asked Matt to provide any copies of organizational procedures, board minutes, and board by-laws that outlined the procedures that would detail the association's financial controls. Matt had no idea how he would get the information, but he assured the professor that the documents would be provided within the next few weeks.

Later in the week, Matt called Paul and told him that he would not bother the board any more about the grant application. He even apologized to Paul for upsetting Pam. He told Paul that Dr. Bateman had agreed to help with the grant, but Matt needed some basic information. Matt had figured how to get the necessary financial control descriptive information, but needed Paul's help as the board president to get financial records. Matt needed Paul to call Mid-State Bank and request copies of the bank statements for the last four years. Dr. Bateman had told Matt that it was best to create financial statements using the bank statements to assure accuracy. Matt liked this approach, because it meant he would not have to bother Pam. Since the grant required proof of the income as stated on the application, the professor stated that it made sense to work from bank statements, rather than from the association's books. Paul agreed to make the call. As Paul was requesting the bank records, Paul gathered copies of the association's by-laws, board meeting minutes, and other documents he thought would help describe the financial controls of the organization.

Two weeks passed and the statements were expected any day. The night was a bit foggy, as Matt was walking toward the association building where the board met for their monthly meetings. Suddenly, Pam materialized out of the fog. Pam said, "I just picked up two years worth of reprinted bank statements in the mail from Paul's desk. I do not know what you are up to, but if you are trying to give my job to your professor friend, you can think again." She continued:

> I know that you and Paul requested these statements; it's in the letter the bank wrote when they sent the statements. But, let me tell you, Paul is not your friend. He is playing both of us and not being honest with either one of us. Why don't you ask him about his honesty.... in fact, ask him about the $5,000 check he wrote himself, and how that would look in an audit.

Pam did not wait for a response or even an acknowledgement she just walked away.

Matt waited until after the meeting to talk to Paul: "Pam intercepted the bank statements. She is very angry. She made mention that in those statements I will find that you wrote a check to yourself for $5,000." Matt held his breath and waited for Paul to deny Pam's accusation. Paul was silent for a moment and then said, "We will just request the statements again and this time have them mailed to my house."

Matt waited for Paul to deny Pam's allegations. Paul made no acknowledgement of the $5,000. Matt point blank asked Paul about Pam's allegation. Paul said, "I will not dignify that question with a response." He simply walked away. Matt wondered on the drive home about Paul and Pam, the allegations, and could not figure out why Paul had not denied the allegations outright. "Could they be true?" he asked himself. He also wondered to himself, "If so, then why would he help me to get the statements knowing I would find out?" He further worried about the rumors that he had heard about Pam and Paul, but had dismissed. Paul had become his friend, but the issue of the $5,000 check made him look at Paul in a different light.

Part I Questions/Discussion Items

1. Discuss the organization of the board, motivations for why people choose to serve on a board, and how board organization is particularly important in a non-profit organization with no staff.
2. How are members of a board selected and how are they retained?
3. What is the responsibility of people who serve on a non-profit board of directors?
4. Is sexual misconduct/harassment an issue in the case and, if so, how does it impact on board member roles and responsibilities?
5. What is fraud, and is this something that board members should be concerned about?
6. What actions, or lack thereof, by the SSSA leadership created an organizational atmosphere that was conducive to fraudulent behavior?
7. What is a policy and procedures manual, and why is it important?
8. What is Matt's responsibility when he believes that something is wrong?

Fraud in Non-profit: A Case Study of the Sport Sun State Soccer Association

Part II

Paul requested that the bank reprint the bank statements. Within a few days, the bank called, and Paul picked them up and delivered them straight to Matt so that he could complete the grant proposal. Matt called Dr. Bateman and apologized for the delay in gathering the information. They scheduled a meeting for the following Monday to review the bank statements together. Matt was pleased that Dr. Bateman seemed eager to begin the application process. They met over lunch and Matt delivered the overstuffed envelope of bank statements to the professor.

"I will be ready for the first review in two weeks," Dr. Bateman informed Matt. "While I'm working on the bank statements, if you will gather the board minutes and other related documentation, then I can work on the description of the financial controls while you review the statements," the professor said.

The next two weeks inched by in what seemed like an eternity. Matt anxiously awaited the opportunity to submit his grant application. He had already addressed the large white envelope in preparation to mail it in. He thought that this packaging would stand out from of all the other applicants who would probably use standard manila envelopes to submit the application. The application had been two years in the works and he hoped that this would mark the beginning of a long career in public service.

The professor called after one week and said his analysis was already complete. Matt was pleasantly surprised at the timely response. Dr. Bateman joked about the graduate students he had asked to help compile the data. "These overachievers had this finished in two days. Nevertheless I have a few concerns about what I am seeing in these financials. Why don't we meet this weekend and go over this stuff?" Matt hung up the phone, curious about what Dr. Bateman could possibly have found. Matt figured it was simply the $5,000 check Paul wrote to himself, but he could not help but wonder if there was more. How would the professor's concerns affect his grant application? Matt could hardly wait for the weekend.

The meeting was very structured. Dr. Bateman had created financial statements from what he extracted from the bank documents. The professor informed him:

> I also created a top ten cash payments list, which details the ten highest dollar amounts spent out of the account. This is where it gets interesting. Sun State Soccer Association had revenues of around $500,000 and expenses of nearly $450,000. At first glance, one would assume this to be the case being a non-profit; all of the revenues collected should be used for the betterment of the association. SSSA paid "FSA" $120,000 over the last two years. There had been $50,000 spent at the office supply store and $75,000 spent at some store called "FM" over the last two years.

All of these locations were expected to receive funds from the association, but Matt was having trouble with the amounts — these were just too high. The professor asked Matt to elaborate on the relationship with FSA. "FSA is the Florida Soccer Association; we pay quarterly fees to be under their guidance. They are the governing body of youth soccer associations in Florida," Matt told him.

The professor interrupted. "Quarterly fees? Is your association on an installment plan? I see checks clearing about every two weeks for random amounts. Here are the copies of the canceled checks," he said. The professor's next question took Matt by surprise, "Is Pam Fields on the board at FSA as well as SSSA?" "No," Matt replied, "She barely has time for our association, much less another board. Why do you ask?" The professor responded, "If you look, 90 percent of the FSA checks are signed by Pam and endorsed on the back by her, as well. Actually, there were additional charges that seem odd, which were paid for with checks signed by Pam," Dr. Bateman stated.

The professor then proceeded to read through a list of vendors,

> ... Sephora, Massage Mansion, QVC, Banana Republic, Bed, Bath & Beyond, and Verizon Wireless. I believe these are personal expenses paid for by the association on behalf of Ms. Fields. I was also reading in the bylaws where two signatures are required for any checks over $100; however, Pam Fields alone has signed all of these checks.

He paused, and said, "I think the grant application is going to have to take the back burner for the moment. We may have discovered an embezzlement issue that requires immediate attention." Matt was completely blown away, as Dr. Bateman recommended that Matt contact Brady Magee, a district attorney who happened to be a close friend. As Dr. Bateman handed Matt a small piece of paper, he said:

> Brady will be able to help you uncover what is going on and help protect you and the other board members from any association with this potential criminal activity. We will need to complete the analysis of what are valid charges associated with SSSA and what we believe is fraudulent activity. Here is his phone number ... I will finish compiling the financial statements from the bank statement and get them to you to take to Brady.

Two weeks and $238,694.13 in questionable charges later, Matt was ready to talk to Brady. He had an envelope with canceled checks written and endorsed by Pam over the last two years that appeared to be an inappropriate use of the association's funds. Brady started by saying that, while Dr. Bateman had already outlined the basis of the case, Matt would need to fill in further details and the board would have to file a formal complaint against Pam—it all seemed so formal, and so serious.

Matt answered all of Brady's questions to the best of his ability. Brady asked Matt if anyone else on the board was involved with the thefts. Matt thought about Paul; he did not want to lie, but he did not want to get Paul in trouble. He decided that the check Paul had written to himself must have been alright as otherwise Paul would not have helped him get the bank statements. He thought about Pam's warning, but decided she was just trying to cover her own actions.

Two hours went by, and the two gentlemen went back and forth. Brady was playing the devil's advocate by trying to justify the expenses for the association's use, while Matt insisted that the funds in question had not been spent in accordance with the associations' intents or rules, nor had the board voted on or approved of the expenditures.

Matt was getting frustrated and at one point he told Brady, "I'm not lying, this money can't be spent this way." He had come to feel as though he was the criminal and Brady was defending Pam. Brady quickly assured Matt that what Pam had done was completely illegal. He explained that the point of the interview was to assure that there was a case that would stick. It was then that Matt realized that the discovery of Pam's thefts was to his credit. He thought about what a great public service he had done for the association.

At the close of the interview, Brady informed Matt that the evidence was strong enough to warrant a formal investigation by the state, and told Matt that the relevant law enforcement agencies would be notified. Brady very clearly informed Matt not to communicate with the other board members because the extent of the theft and who had knowledge of it was unclear. Brady said he would schedule a meeting for Matt to make a formal statement for the case file.

The big day had finally come; Matt, Pam, and Paul were scheduled to give depositions. Brady and Matt walked into the police station, followed by Paul and Pam a few moments later. They all had their respective attorneys at their side for what was guaranteed to be an interesting day. All three were sequestered to separate interrogation rooms. Each interview lasted around forty-five minutes, except for Pam's. Two hours had passed and she still had not come out of the 10' × 13' concrete block room. She and her attorney were in the middle of questioning from the investigator. So far it had been established that Pam had opened a checking account for her business, FSA, to create a way to provide compensation for the consulting services she was providing as treasurer to SSSA. The $5,000 compensation Paul allocated for himself was also confirmed and formal charges were being filed.

Pam was insisting that Paul advised her to open a business account under FSA and had hired her as a consultant to keep the books. She was unable to explain the checks to various vendors and the continuation of the consulting fees Pam had accrued over the past two years without board approval. There was currently over $100,000 in Pam's FSA account. Pam was also unable to quantify the charges that she had incurred for her benefit with the association's funds.

Part II Questions/Discussion Items

1. Discuss the role of regulatory agencies in ensuring that organization like SSSA adhere to behaviors consistent with their mission and fiduciary responsibilities.
2. Why are people like Matt generally reluctant to report this type of behavior to authorities?
3. Could Matt have reported this to anyone besides the State Attorney?
4. For further information pertaining to the result of the criminal actions, including the penalties given to the wrongdoers, refer to the Conclusion.

Conclusion

Sun State Soccer continues to exist, although membership is down somewhat due the arrest of the two board members in 2004. Shortly after the arrest and conviction of these two board members, Matt Jackson became concerned that board members had begun to receive benefits from coaching, running the concessions, and working with hotels. Matt expressed concern to the board and suggested that a consultant be hired to evaluate the organization's internal controls, given the recent cases of fraud. Matt was rebuffed by the other board members and shortly thereafter was voted off the board after he missed two meetings.

Pam Fields plead guilty to stealing between $66,000 and $82,000 from Sun State Soccer Association. She was sentenced to ten years probation under the agreement that she repay the entire amount by the end of her probation. Paul Simmons was sentenced to five years probation under the agreement that he pay back the $5,000.

References

Application for Recognition of Exemption under Section 501(c)(3) of the Internal Revenue Code (2006). Retrieved on September 22, 2008, from www.irs.gov/pub/irs-pdf/f1023.pdf

Anthony, R.N. (1977), Can nonprofit organizations be well managed? in D. Borst and P.J. Montana (eds.), *Managing Nonprofit Organizations*, New York: AMACOM.

Exemption Requirements (n.d.) Internal Revenue Code section 501(c)(3). Retrieved on September 21, 2008, from http://www.irs.gov/charities/charitable/article/0,,id=96099,00.html

Fremont-Smith, M. (2004) *Governing nonprofit organizations*. Cambridge, MA: Harvard University Press.

Kennedy, B. (1997). Roberts Rules of Order. Retrieved on September 21, 2008, from http://www.robertsrules.org/

NCCS (2006). National Center for Charitable Statistics, Number of Nonprofit Organizations in the United States, 1996–2006. Retrieved on September 22, 2008, from http://nccsdataweb.urban.org/PubApps/profile1.php?state=US

NCCS (2007). Number of Non-501(c)(3) Exempt Organizations in the United States, 2006. Retrieved on October 1, 2008, from http://nccsdataweb.urban.org/PubApps/profileDrillDown.php?state=US&rpt=CO

Section 149.1(1), Income Tax Act of Canada (2008).

Additional Resources

Agsten, M. (2004) Governance and Nonprofit Corporations: Requirements and Expectations in a Post-Sarbanes-Oxley World. Retrieved on September 21, 2008, from www.wiggin.com/pubs/alerts_abstract.asp?ID=1542541142004

Albrecht, S., Albrecht, C., Albrecht, C., & Zimbleman, M. (2008). *Fraud examination*. Cincinnati, OH: Thomson/SouthWestern.

Carver, J., & Carver M. (1996). *Basic principles of policy governance*. Hoboken, NJ: Jossey Bass.

COSO (2004). Enterprise Risk Management—Integrated Framework Executive Summary. Retrieved on April 7, 2009 from http://www.coso.org/Publications/ERM/COSO_ERM_ExecutiveSummary.pdf

Cuomo, A. (January 2005). Internal Controls and Financial Accountability for Not-for-Profit Boards. Retrieved on September 22, 2008, from http://www.oag.state.ny.us/bureaus/charities/pdfs/internal_controls.pdf.

Everson, M.W. (2004). Written Statement of Commissioner of Internal Revenue before the Commissioner of Internal Revenue before the Committee on Finance, United States Senate Hearing on Charitable Giving Problems and Best Practices. Retrieved on September 21, 2008, from http://finance.senate.gov/hearings/testimony/2004test/062204metest.pdf

Hempel, J., & Borrus, A. (2004, June 21). How the nonprofits need cleaning up. *Business Week* [online]. Retrieved on September 21, 2008, from http://www.businessweek.com/magazine/content/04_25/b3888085_mz021.htm

Jackson, P., & Fogarty, T. (2005). *Sarbanes-Oxley for non profits*. Hoboken, NJ: John Wiley & Sons.

McDermott, Will & Emory, Best Practices: Nonprofit Corporate Governance (2004). Retrieved on September 21, 2008, www.mwe.com/info/news/wp0604a.pdf

McNeal, A., & Michelman, J. (2006). The CPAs' role in fighting fraud in nonprofit organizations. *CPA Journal 76*(1), 60–63.

Moerschbaecher, L. (2004, October 28). Nonprofit Integrity Act comes to California: Will nation follow? Planned Giving Design Center. Planned Giving Design Center, Retrieved on September 22, 2008, from http://www.pgdc.com/pgdc/article/2004/10/nonprofit-integrity-act-comes

NPCC (2006). Sarbanes-Oxley for Nonprofits, The Nonprofit Coordinating Committee of New York (NPCC). Retrieved on September 22, 2008, from http://www.npccny.org/info/gti10.htm)

Panel on the Nonprofit Sector. (2005, June). Strengthening Transparency, Governance, Accountability of Charitable Organizations: A Final Report to Congress and the Nonprofit Sector. Retrieved on September 22, 2008, from http://info.ethicspoint.com/files/PDF/resources/Panel_Final_Report.pdf

The Institute of Internal Auditors (2005). Putting COSO theory into practice. *Tone at the Top*. Retrieved on September 22, 2008, from http://www.theiia.org/download.cfm?file=42122

The Sarbanes-Oxley Act and Implications for Nonprofit Organizations, published by Board Source and Independent Sector (2006). Retrieved on September 22, 2008, from http://www.independentsector.org/PDFs/sarbanesoxley.pdf

Thompson & Thompson Corporation (2008). IRS Conflicts of Interest Policy. Retrieved on September 22, 2008, http://www.t-tlaw.com/np-11.htm

Wells, J. (1997). *Occupational fraud and abuse*. Dexter, MI: Obsidian Publishing Co.

Wolf, T. (1999). *Managing a nonprofit in the 21st Century*. New York: Simon and Schuster.

Zack, G. (2003). *Fraud and abuse in nonprofit organizations*. Hoboken, NJ: John Wiley & Sons.

8

Trademark Counterfeiting of Sport Merchandise and Criminal Law

John Grady, University of South Carolina
Annie Clement, University of New Mexico
Jeff Woishnis, University of South Carolina

"The secret of life is honesty and fair dealing. If you can fake that, you've got it made."
— *Groucho Marx*

Introduction

Trademarks and service marks play a significant role in the business of sport. Companies invest thousands of dollars in attaching their trademarked logos to sporting events and merchandise. These companies, in turn, acquire goodwill through brand equity, allowing the company to garner widespread recognition that portrays a positive image of the firm to the public (Jennings, n.d.). In sport, trademark law covers two distinct types of marks: trademarks and service marks. A trademark is "any work, name, symbol, or device, or any combination thereof, adopted and used by a manufacturer or merchant to identify his goods and distinguish them from those manufactured or sold by others" whereas a service mark is "a mark used in the sale or advertising of services to identify the service of one person (agency) and distinguish them from the services of others" (Lanham Act, 15 U.S.C. § 1051–1127). Trademarks cover goods; Nike is a trademark. Service marks cover services; Gold's Gym is a service mark. "A trademark serves many of the same functions for commercial entities that a signature does for an individual" (Goldstone & Toren, 1998, p. 4). A company's trademark serves as both an indicator of the source of the goods and an indicator of the quality of the merchandise. Think, for example, of how a customer perceives the quality of a Nike running shoe simply because it contains Nike's trademarked swoosh logo.

While "the need to recognize the value of intellectual property rights has become increasingly important and significant within the matrix of revenue generating opportunities open to the commercial world of sport" ("The business of football," 2007, p. 42), the rise in counterfeiting of sport merchandise poses a continuing threat to the financial viability of both sport organizations as well as officially licensed manufacturers of sport merchandise.

> Companies lose more than customers to counterfeiters; they lose credibility when the legitimate manufacturers and retail businesses that follow strict standards ensuring the durability and quality of their products are called into question. Misspelled names and shoddy workmanship are just two examples of the ways counterfeiters can damage consumers' perception of legitimate businesses ("Fake out," 2002, p. 1).

Called the economic crime of the twenty-first century (McDonoug, 2007), trademark counterfeiting is a problem that numerous industries, including the sport industry, must address vigilantly or else face the potential loss of tens of millions of dollars in revenue derived from the sale of authentic merchandise. A similar, yet sufficiently distinct, problem facing the sport industry is the sale of unlicensed goods. "Unlike counterfeits, which are made by unscrupulous companies to varying degrees of authenticity and quality, unlicensed goods are those made by licensed manufacturers under agreement with the original designer, but just not declared" (PricewaterhouseCoopers, 2007, p. 10).

This chapter describes the status of trademark law to enable the reader to recognize methods of control and/or elimination of the counterfeiting of sport products, particularly memorabilia, apparel, and equipment. The chapter first outlines the scope of the problem and details the steps the sport industry has taken thus far to combat this problem. The chapter then focuses on both civil and criminal laws that may be utilized as part of a comprehensive strategy to stop the sale of counterfeit sport merchandise. The chapter concludes with a case study of counterfeiting and the Olympics, including analysis of the relevant issues faced during the 2008 Summer Olympic Games in Beijing.

Counterfeiting is a serious national and international problem affecting many industries. The negative effects of counterfeiting and product piracy are felt worldwide and cost the U.S. economy billions of dollars every year (Paradise, 1999); "U.S. authorities seized $40 million of counterfeit sport merchandise in 2004" (Batagello, 2005). In addition to the loss of revenue to creative individuals and businesses for authentic work, there is also the loss to the nation in taxes and the harm to quality brands as a result of inferior products. Another loss is to local businesses retailing authentic merchandise. Authentic products, in this context, refer to items covered by registered trademarks. The United States Customs Services estimated that in the ten years prior to 2002, over 750,000 United States jobs were lost to counterfeit products ("Fake out," 2002). Some also believe that the revenue from counterfeit sales may play a role in financing gang activity and terrorism.

The Status of Counterfeiting in Sport

Fake sport products exist as memorabilia, apparel, and equipment. The geographic boundaries of counterfeiting are limitless. This can include products carrying American logos made and sold in various countries, products carrying American logos made in various countries of the world and sold only in the

United States, and products carrying American logos made and sold in the United States. Sport apparel carrying counterfeit logos are often manufactured a short distance from the legitimate business owner of the mark. Counterfeiting in sport is not isolated to the United States and, in fact, transgresses national borders. Mexico is the NFL's second largest market for merchandise sales and viewership (Millan Gonzalez, 2008). Many of the items bearing NFL and MLB logos sold in Mexico are counterfeit. In fact, according to a European Commission Report, nearly 60 percent of all textile and clothing products sold in Mexico are counterfeit. Given these statistics, protecting license holders is one of the NFL's top priorities. In 2006, Mexican companies licensed by the NFL made nearly $18 million in sales of league-approved items.

The scope of counterfeiting in sport is not limited to apparel. Companies in the markets for sport products and memorabilia also must deal with problems related to counterfeiting. In 2006, Spalding executive Robert Zucker reported that while sales of as many as six million basketballs with the Spalding logo were expected in China, only one million would be authentic products (Freebairn, 2006). Similarly, experts estimated that 50 percent to 90 percent of sport and celebrity memorabilia is counterfeit. Many forged autographs have been subjected to a process suggesting they are genuine. Among the sports memorabilia often sold are jerseys, shoes, bats, balls, signed papers, photographs, posters, and trading cards.

One of the largest sport industries forced to deal with fake products is golf. Grant Clark, writing for the *International Herald Tribune* in 2005, may have best described the problem through his title, "Fake golf clubs are 'nightmare,' counterfeiting from China leave buyers and makers frustrated" (n.p.). Golf products are covered by the three major areas of intellectual property: copyright, patent and trademark, and face counterfeit situations in all three. Trademarks are used to protect a company's name, club title and the unique styling of the logo. These characteristics are registered under the element of trade dress, which applies to how the product is "packaged" (Jorgense, 2006). Many of the illegal golf clubs are manufactured outside the United States and sold both in the country of manufacture and in the United States.

Industry Response

What is being done in the United States to deal with these problems? The Federal Bureau of Investigation (FBI), the Internal Revenue Service (IRS) and the Department of Homeland Security (DHS) have joined forces in an effort to reduce the counterfeiting of all products, including sport memorabilia, apparel and equipment. Border patrols also play a role in confiscating counterfeit products. In addition, the sport industry has responded by creating its own agency to assist in the identification and seizure of counterfeit sport products. The Coalition to Advance the Protection of Sports Logos (CAPS), an alliance formed by the Collegiate Licensing Company (CLC), Major League Baseball Properties, NBA Properties, NFL Properties, and NHL Enterprises, works in conjunction with local law enforcement agencies to seize counterfeit property.

Bruce Siegal, general counsel for the Collegiate Licensing Company, has been successful in seizing over nine million pieces of counterfeit merchandise featuring logos of various sports leagues and teams, colleges and universities (CAPS, 2007). CAPS provides the following guidelines to members to use in licensing products:

1. Officially licensed CAPS-member products are distinguished by a sticker, hangtag, or sewn-in label identifying the apparel as "genuine" or "official."
2. Each CAPS member has developed a unique trademark hologram that is affixed to licensed regular season and/or post-season merchandise. All collegiate championship products should also bear the NCAA hologram.
3. The licensee's identification should be sewn in or screened onto the product or printed on the interior or exterior label of all licensed products.
4. Beware of ripped tags or irregular markings on apparel. Those who violate the trademark rights of the CAPS members are notorious for producing unauthorized products on irregular or imperfect apparel. Apparel manufacturers often denote such irregularities by clipping or ripping the sewn-in neck tag or label. The CAPS members' licensees are not allowed to produce products on irregular merchandise (CAPS, 2007).

In 2001, CAPS "participated in 136 collective enforcement actions in 12 states, which led to 531 arrests and seizures of more than 250,000 items of product" ("Fake out," 2002). During the 2002 Rose Bowl, CAPS confiscated over 5,000 products and located a production facility in South Central Los Angeles that was producing merchandise for professional leagues ("Fake out," 2002). In 2005, nearly 300,000 pieces of counterfeit merchandise featuring logos of various professional sports leagues and teams, colleges, and universities valued at over $60 million were seized ("NHL and Mighty Ducks issue warning to fans," 2006). Not surprisingly, the sale of counterfeit sport apparel usually spikes around the time of a championship in a professional sport or during a collegiate championship game. The NBA and CAPS issued warnings to Cleveland Cavaliers fans as the teams advanced to the NBA Eastern Conference Finals to be aware of counterfeit merchandise ("NBA issues warning to Cavalier fans," 2007).

On the criminal enforcement front, a successful resolution was obtained in connection with a 2006 Final Four Seizure. During CLC's 2006 Final Four enforcement in Indianapolis, two individuals were arrested and cited for violating Indiana's counterfeiting statute. They were selling unlicensed t-shirts bearing the marks of the NCAA and the participating teams, the University of Florida and UCLA. The CLC legal staff worked closely with the local prosecutor's office during the months leading up to the trial. One defendant pled guilty to forgery (a Class C felony, which mandates longer periods of confinement and larger financial penalties), while the other defendant was found guilty of the same offense. Each defendant will serve a suspended sentence (meaning no actual time spent incarcerated) with multi-year periods on probation.

Game-Day Enforcement

Perhaps one of the most effective ways to stop the sale of counterfeit merchandise is to utilize game-day enforcement measures. Collegiate institutions conduct trademark enforcement actions at game-day events throughout the year. CLC, on behalf of collegiate institutions, maintains an enforcement presence at regular-season games, conference championships, bowl games, and major NCAA championships. Relationships with law enforcement agencies are key to organizing successful seizure actions at these events and enforcing applicable state or federal trademark laws.

Bowl Games

The Tostitos Fiesta Bowl hosted the 2007 BCS National Championship Game. The University of Florida prevailed over Ohio State in a landslide victory, making UF the first team to hold both football and basketball National Championships at the same time. Following the National Championship game, CLC staff converged upon the state of Florida to support the National Champions merchandising program and to conduct compliance and infringement enforcement. Leading up to and on game-day, CLC's communications department set up media opportunities, leading to CLC staff participation in several television, newspaper, and radio interviews. This media exposure helped expand consumer awareness of trademark licensing requirements and the hologram required by CAPS guidelines.

NCAA Championships

During the NCAA Men's Basketball Championship, CLC staff worked in conjunction with law enforcement officials at each venue hosting the first and second rounds, the regional championships, the Men's Final Four, and the Women's Final Four. At the Men's Final Four in Atlanta, 19 vendors were cited for selling infringing merchandise, which led to the seizure of approximately 500 items. Vendors also were forced to surrender several hundred infringing t-shirts and ticket lanyards at the Women's Final Four.

Believing that educating consumers was another way to stop the spread of counterfeit goods, CLC's communications group lined up television interviews with the local television affiliates as well as with major national media outlets. Media coverage enhances consumer recognition of the importance of seeking out officially licensed products by explaining how to identify licensed products and to avoid fakes.

Laws Affecting Counterfeiting

In the United States, trademark counterfeiting is most frequently addressed using federal or state trademark laws, which are civil as opposed to criminal laws. Civil laws provide for money damages and also allow for injunctive relief, such as confiscating infringing goods, but do not provide criminal penalties, such as imprisonment. Historically speaking, criminal law has been utilized less often than civil law in the United States to control the problem of trademark counterfeiting. However, given the scope of the problem that currently exists and the financial impact on the marketplace, criminal law may eventually provide a more effective deterrent to stop those who engage in counterfeiting. This section provides an overview of the civil law protections found in the U.S. law covering trademarks, the Lanham Act, and explores the possibility for criminal law to be used to supplement current enforcement efforts.

Trademark Civil Law

The Lanham Act allows manufacturers, sellers, and producers of goods and services to prevent a competitor from:

1. using any counterfeit, copy or imitation of their trademarks (that has been registered with the U.S. Patent and Trademark Office), in connection with the sale of any goods or services in a way that is likely to cause confusion, mistake, or deception, (15 U.S.C. § 114[1]) or
2. using in commercial advertising any word, term, name, symbol, or device, or any false or misleading designation of origin or false or misleading description or representation of fact, which: is likely to cause confusion, mistake, or deception as to affiliation, connection, or association, or as to origin, sponsorship, or approval, of his or her goods, services, or commercial activities by another person, or (b) misrepresents the nature, characteristics, qualities, or geographic origin of his or her or another person's goods, services, or commercial activities (15 U.S.C. § 1125[a] [1]).

Trademark court decisions have occurred under both state and federal law; however, today most cases are decided using federal law. In order for an agency to gain a right to a trademark or a service mark in federal court, the mark must be registered by formal application, must have been in use for the previous two years, and a minimum amount of sales or services must have occurred. Failure to use the mark for a period of two years is considered abandonment and permits the mark to be taken by another person or agency.

Trademark Infringement

Violation of someone's trademark or service mark is called infringement. Infringement can occur when a person or agency uses the mark or a similar mark of another in advertising, in a title, or on a product. Also, when one submits an application for a mark, they may find that the mark is currently registered to another person or agency. On occasion, the new applicant may choose to contest the original owner's exclusive right to the mark. When the mark is owned by an obscure and unknown person or agency, a few courts have permitted two entities to retain ownership of a similar mark.

Considerable trademark litigation exists in amateur and professional sport. The majority of the infringement cases have been based on name confusion or trade dress.

Name Confusion

Name confusion in sport litigation has involved the Olympics, exercise and fitness centers and equipment, professional, collegiate and scholastic teams, and the sports of golf, yachting, cycling, and surfing (Clement, 2002). One of the first things a court will examine under word or name confusion is whether the word is generic. A generic word is one that is recognized by the public in general and can not be identified as belonging to one person or agency. For example, the courts were asked to rule on the word "Hog" for a motorcycle. The court ruled that the word "Hog" was generic and could not be owned by Harley Davidson (*Harley Davidson v. Grottanelli*, 1999). Another factor the courts will consider is whether the two names or words create real confusion to consumers. When such confusion exists, the courts will tend to rule for the original owner and will conduct no further examination of the confusion.

When the infringement is complex, the court will use the following eight factors, called the *Polaroid* factors, in making a decision (*Polaroid Corp. v. Polarad Electronics*, 1961).

1. Strength of the mark;
2. Similarities between marks used by the parties;
3. Proximity of the products;
4. Likelihood that plaintiff will "bridge the gap";
5. Actual confusion;
6. Defendant's good faith or intent;
7. Quality of defendant's services; and
8. Sophistication of purchaser.

In the case, *King of the Mountain Sports v. Chrysler Corporation* (1999) the courts made use of the above analysis. Chrysler Corporation decided to use the phrase "Jeep, King of the Mountain Downhill Series" on advertisements and clothing to promote their recently acquired ski race series. Unbeknownst to them, the phrase "King of the Mountain" was already registered by a clothing company producing camouflage patterned outdoor clothing and accessories. The clothing company sued Chrysler. In analyzing the similarities between the two trademarks, the court found that the marks were not similar; the logos were totally different in color and image. Under the intent to benefit from the reputation and goodwill of the original owner, the court determined that it was undisputed that Chrysler had no knowledge or intention of taking the clothing company's recognition. Both parties were allowed to maintain their respective marks.

Trade Dress

When the confusion of the mark or service is one of image rather than name or title, the court's analysis turns to specific features of the product such as "size, shape, color or color combination, texture, graphics or even sales techniques" (*Harland Co. v. Clarke Checks, Inc.*, 1983, p. 980). Often the problem in trade dress is that the public associates a certain product with its appearance and thus the product has a secondary meaning. For example, one commonly associates the golden arches with McDonalds, a phenomenon referred to in trademark law as distinctiveness.

Trademark Criminal Law

Collegiate institutions have continued to support efforts to enact or improve anti-counterfeiting laws in their states. CLC, the professional leagues, and other interested trademark owners and licensors have worked with organizations such as the International Anti-Counterfeiting Coalition, the International Trademark Association, and most recently the U.S. Chamber of Commerce, through a renewed effort to focus its resources on various intellectual property initiatives. These groups are seeking to enact state anti-counterfeiting laws modeled after the recently revised federal anti-counterfeiting law. The goal of the program is to upgrade state criminal penalties, provide mandated restitution awards, and strengthen and broaden forfeiture provisions. The question then becomes: can criminal law provide a more effective means to curb the infringement of trademarks which occurs through counterfeiting of sports merchandise?

When trademark infringement becomes trademark counterfeiting, violation of the law moves from a civil violation to a criminal offense. In trademark law, violations are satisfied by injunction or immediately stopping the action causing the violation. Fake materials are destroyed. Infringement or civil violations are satisfied through financial penalties. Such penalties are sufficient to make the injured party whole as if the infringement never occurred. When violations involve counterfeiting, criminal sanctions include all of the above in addition to a steeper fine, as well as a jail or prison sentence. An action in civil court is brought by an individual or agency against another individual or agency. An action in criminal court is brought by the state or the federal government against an individual or agency. Although state and federal criminal courts have, on occasion, heard trademark issues, the need for criminal penalties for trademark violations did not become apparent until the 1980s.

Trademark Counterfeiting Act of 1984

The Trademark Counterfeiting Act of 1984 was created to protect the public against the purchase and use of fake or undocumented products. Often an individual is not aware that such products are available for purchase and some who are aware that the products are not registered are unaware of the harm that can be caused when a product has faulty or defective parts. Congress's decision to criminalize trademark counterfeiting "created an appropriate means of deterring trademark infringement, ... preventing fraud, enforcing commercial honesty, punishing theft of property, and enhancing market reliability" (Goldstone & Toren, 1998, p. 10). A major reason for implementing criminal sanctions at the time was the fact that the Lanham Act did not provide punitive damages and, as a result, some businesses viewed civil penalties (i.e., monetary damages) for trademark infringement as merely the cost of doing business (Goldstone & Toren, 1998).

The Trademark Counterfeiting Act of 1984 provided that "whoever intentionally traffics or attempts to traffic in goods or services and knowingly uses a counterfeit mark on or in connection with such goods or services shall, if an individual, be fined or imprisoned" (18 U.S.C.A. § 2320(a) (1994). The following four elements must be established:

1. The defendant trafficked or attempted to traffic in goods or services;
2. that such trafficking, or the attempt to traffic was intentional;
3. that the defendant used a "counterfeit mark" on or in connection with such goods or services; and
4. that the defendant "knew" that the counterfeit mark was so used (18 U.S.C. 2320(a) (1994).

The key factors are that the defendant intends to traffic in marks and that he or she knows that the product is counterfeit. Courts have required only proof of general intent; thus, it is not necessary to show that the product was faulty or caused harm. The following discusses the elements in detail.

To traffic or attempt to traffic means to transport, transfer, or dispose of, to another, for something of value. This covers all activity from manufacture to final sale, including aiding or conspiring to traffic counterfeit products (Goldstone & Toren, 1998). The defendant's trafficking or attempt to traffic must be intentional. He or she does not have to intend to break the law, only to participate in trafficking the product. The third element is whether the defendant used a counterfeit mark on or in connection with goods or services. Here, the courts have to determine that the mark is counterfeit. Congress created a five part definition to determine a counterfeit mark. The mark must be spurious, not authentic or genuine. It must have been used in conjunction with trafficking goods or services. The counterfeit mark must be identical or substantially indistinguishable from the registered mark. The genuine mark must be registered and active. The use of the mark must be likely to cause confusion or to deceive the public. Finally, the defendant must knowingly use the counterfeit mark (Goldstone & Toren, 1998).

Defenses to the Trademark Counterfeiting Act of 1984

The primary defenses to the Trademark Counterfeiting Act of 1984 are "overrun" and "gray market goods." Overrun goods are products made by a manufacturer after the approved number of licensed products have been produced. Even though these "additional" products were not licensed, the manufacturer cannot be held to have committed counterfeiting. By contrast, gray market or parallel imports are "trademarked goods legitimately manufactured and sold overseas, typically at a much lower price than they are sold domestically, and then imported into the United States outside of the trademark owner's traditional distribution channels" (Goldstone & Toren, 1998, p. 42). In addition, all defenses listed under the Lanham Act can be included under criminal law. Among those are fraud by the mark's owner in obtaining the registration, abandonment of the mark, misrepresentation or unclean hands in the use of the mark, fair use or prior use, use of the trademark in violation of antitrust laws, and equitable defenses.

Penalties

The general federal criminal limitation period for non-capital crimes is five years. This statute carries a possible ten-year prison term or a fine of up to $2,000,000, or both, for the first time offender. A second conviction carries a prison term of twenty years and a fine of up to $5,000,000, or both. In 1996, Congress made trafficking in counterfeit goods or services a predicate offense under federal racketeering laws. A violation of these laws carries a maximum penalty that includes twenty years of imprisonment and a fine of up to twice the gross profits or other proceeds of the racketeering activity.

Since 1984, the following Acts or Amendments to the Trafficking in Counterfeit Goods and Service Statute (18 U.S.C.A. § 2320) have strengthened the law: Importation of Merchandise Bearing Counterfeit Marks; Anti-counterfeiting Consumer Protection Act of 1996; Protect American Goods and Services Act of 2005; Stop Counterfeiting in Manufactured Goods Act of 2006. Although each of these acts has further strengthened the federal counterfeiting statute, it is the Importation of Merchandise Bearing Counterfeit Marks and the 2006 Stop Counterfeiting in Manufactured Goods that have made the greatest contribution to today's law (18 U.S.C.A. § 2320).

Importation of Merchandise Bearing Counterfeit Marks

The United State Customs Service is authorized to seize goods containing infringing marks or names that are identical or substantially indistinguishable from registered marks (15 U.S.C. § 1124). The goods are destroyed by Homeland Security and the persons involved are subject to fines. A traveler is permitted to bring in a single item for their own use.

Penalties

Injunction or stopping the use of the mark is the primary penalty. All articles containing the infringed mark are to be destroyed as well as all means of making or documenting such marks. Treble damages (three times the actual damages) and attorney fees are also included. Statutory damages, rather than those suggested above, may be in the amount of less than $500 or more than $100,000 per counterfeit mark (15 U.S.C. § 1116–1118).

Stop Counterfeiting in Manufactured Goods Act of 2006

The Stop Counterfeiting in Manufactured Goods Act of 2006 eliminates what was termed the "component part" or "label loophole." Counterfeiting became big business as technology enabled counterfeiters to duplicate near perfect replicas of legitimate product labels. Counterfeiters began importing counterfeit labels and component parts separate from fully assembled counterfeit goods (McDonoug, 2007). The question the court's faced was whether labels and component parts were "goods" under the existing trademark law. Courts disagreed on the answer to this question. The 2006 amendment to the Trafficking in Counterfeit Goods or Services statute provided a definitive answer. The Act applies to:

> Whoever intentionally traffics or attempts to traffic in goods or services and knowingly uses a counterfeit mark on or in connection with such goods or services, or intentionally traffics or attempts to traffic in labels, patches, stickers, wrappers, badges, emblems, medallions, charms, boxes, containers, cans, cases, hangtags, documentation, or packaging of any type or nature, knowing that a counterfeit mark has been applied thereto, the use of which is likely to cause confusion, to cause mistake, or to deceive ... (18 § U.S.C.A. 2320[a]).

The amendment stops counterfeiters who separated and shipped products in component parts to later be re-assembled, thus bypassing the law. It also gives prosecutors new weapons to stop those who defraud consumers (McDonoug, 2007). The person convicted under the statute must pay restitution to the owner of the mark and revenue lost to the victim. In addition to any other fines, including those detailed in the 1984 legislation, the person must forfeit the property or assure the court that it has been destroyed. The Act states that the victim is allowed to submit a victim impact statement to be used by the court in resolving the dispute. The Act also authorizes an accounting of the trafficking activity to the Attorney General of the United States to present to the U.S. Congress. The report also identifies the role of Internet usage in trafficking products and services, and the role of the Customs Services in seizures. The Act covers copyright, trademark and patent.

Based on recent amendments and additions to the federal counterfeiting statute, criminal law appears to provide an alternative avenue to address the problems of sport merchandise counterfeiting and, given enhanced criminal penalties, may ultimately be more effective in deterring future counterfeiting in the sport industry.

Case Study: Counterfeiting and the Olympics

Some of the most high profile instances of counterfeiting in sport have occurred at the Olympic Games. This phenomenon is likely attributed to the fact that the Olympic emblem of five multi-colored, interlocking rings is one of the most recognizable symbols in the world (Wall, 2002). The International Olympic Committee (IOC) is primarily responsible for addressing the problems associated with counterfeit Olympic merchandise at the international level. The IOC is a non-profit organization that was established to protect and regulate all trademarks of the Olympic Games, including flags, symbols, anthem, and motto. In addition, each host city's organizing committee works alongside the IOC to help prevent and police all counterfeiting activity while that city hosts the Olympic Games.

Counterfeiting in the Olympic context occurs primarily through the sale of unlicensed goods, where a party without a license to use Olympic marks creates products such as clothing or memorabilia containing the Olympic marks or a confusingly similar mark (Batcha, 1998). The sale of unlicensed merchandise not only jeopardizes the relationships that the IOC and the National Olympic Committees (NOCs) have with officially licensed suppliers, but also contributes to a loss of substantial licensing revenues (Batcha, 1998). Revenues from officially licensed products totaled over $530 million in retail sales and $86 million in royalties during the 2004 Summer Games in Athens, with 4,000 licensed products on the market (International Olympic Committee, 2004). The vigilance in stopping the sale of unlicensed merchandise is necessary because the exclusive rights to use the words and symbols of the Olympics on merchandise are some of the Olympics' most valuable assets (Batcha, 1998).

"Given the crucial nexus between the protection of intellectual property rights and the financial success of the Games, as well as the profits the Games themselves generate for corporate sponsors, it is not surprising that the IOC places heavy emphasis on protecting Olympic intellectual property" (Donatuti, 2007, p. 209). Infringement of Olympic intellectual property occurs in several ways, including ambush marketing, counterfeiting, cybersquatting, and trademark infringement (Wall, 2002). During the recent history of the Olympic Games, a noticeable increase in counterfeit products has been prevalent at the host city level (Wall, 2002). To combat against the inferior products, organizations have been established to aid the IOC in the seizure of counterfeit merchandise.

In 2006, United States Customs agents and FBI agents worked with the Organizing Committee's Brand Protection organization within and around the Olympic venues to investigate unlawful activities, including counterfeiting (Wall, 2002). SLOC worked with the USOC to protect Olympic marks and images, investigating over 430 cases of Olympic intellectual property infringement (Wall, 2002). SLOC also utilized advertisements in trade and consumer publications to alert all citizens and tourists to the problems related to counterfeit merchandise. These advertisements also served to educate the public about licensing requirements to sell merchandise and helped raise awareness of potential for counterfeit goods (Wall, 2002). Additionally, SLOC distributed a video entitled "The Protection of Olympic and Paralympics Marks" to all media outlets and publicized legal actions imposed on offenders including the penalties for distributing counterfeit merchandise (Wall, 2002). SLOC also sought the support of local retailers to curb counterfeiting after an investigation revealed that half of the shops on Main Street in Park City, Utah visited by SLOC "mystery shoppers" appeared to be carrying unlicensed merchandise using Olympic-related marks (Wall, 2002). Along with raising public awareness, SLOC drastically increased enforcement at the Olympics to target counterfeit violators by establishing a "clean zone," which was used to prevent unlicensed businesses from selling goods (Wall, 2002). After the Salt Lake Games concluded, officials looked for areas to improve security in order to prevent future counterfeiting operations. By taking such measures, each successive Olympic Games has gained a greater base of knowledge, which can be used to more effectively control the problems related to counterfeiting.

Was Beijing Up to the Challenge?

In the summer of 2008, Beijing, China hosted the Summer Olympics. For many years, China has been one of the largest contributing countries to counterfeit merchandise, both within its own borders and internationally. Called the "pirating and counterfeiting capital of the world" (Mickleburgh, 2009, p. 1), China has been identified as the "world's major intellectual property infringement culprit" and is responsible for nearly two-thirds of the world's counterfeit goods (Priest, 2006, p. 797). These figures caused great concern for the IOC, the Beijing Organizing Committee (BOCOG), as well as the numerous officially licensed retailers who planned to sell their merchandise during the Games. As a result of concerns about China's historically weak protection of intellectual property, the IOC and BOGOC had to devise a plan which would sufficiently protect all Olympic trademarks and intellectual property in accord with the requirements for such protection for all host cities outlined in the Host City Contract. The Host City Contract requires protection of both the IOC's and BOCOG's respective trademarks (Wang, 2005). Soon after being awarded the Games, BOCOG took action to protect Olympic intellectual property by enacting local regulations (Misener, 2003), as well as national laws, to protect Olympic intellectual property rights (Mendel & Yijun, 2003).

In the past, government officials in China have passed laws that had minimal penalties and enforcement for violating intellectual property rights. In fact, before 1993, there was no enforcement of intellectual property rights by Chinese customs (Wang, 2005). The reason for the "hands off" approach to counterfeiting was due, in part, to the views of the Chinese people. China's economy benefits from having counterfeit merchandise, causing many people in China to be in favor of counterfeiting (Donatuti, 2007), a notion which is markedly different from the American perspective, in favor of vigorous intellectual property protection. The argument has been made that if the Chinese public were denied access to counterfeit products, they would be hurt economically, as the price of counterfeit products is exponentially less than the price of the original product (Chu, 2004). Donatuti (2007) effectively argued that "[a]lthough Olympic merchandise clearly does not constitute all of the potential merchandise to be counterfeited in China, if manufacturers do not understand why they should not produce counterfeited goods in general, they will likely seize upon the relatively substantial market for counterfeit Olympic goods" (p. 233).

Part of the problem China had with enforcing their laws can be blamed on local officials. Many local police tend not to enforce laws, as they do not want to stop something that benefits the economy. In 2003, about 75 percent of the United States counterfeit products originated in China (Priest, 2006, p. 798). In 2005, Chinese officials seized over 4.5 million counterfeit publications of books, music, and videos ("Beijing issues IPR Policy for Companies," 2006).

Given China's history in producing counterfeit goods, BOCOG and the IOC took several steps to prevent the distribution of counterfeit goods prior to and during the Bejing Games. BOCOG established a legal affairs department, the first such department in the history of Chinese sport, which worked to combat intellectual property infringement and protect the IOC's interests ("Beijing Moves to Assure Rights of IOC Patrons," 2002). In 2003, BOCOG's president addressed the importance of Olympic intellectual property protection as a critical component of hosting a successful Games and addressed specific efforts to protect the 2008 "Dancing Beijing" logo ("2008 Beijing Olympic Emblem Unveiled," 2003). Additionally, local authorities were used to inspect shops, printing companies, tourist locations, and various advertisements to minimize counterfeit merchandise ("2008 Beijing Olympic Emblem Unveiled," 2003). Similar to previous Olympic Games, intellectual property protection efforts were coordinated by BOCOG's Brand Protection Department. In addition, during the Beijing Games, Olympic licensed goods were sold only in licensed, certified stores, and all licensed products were to contain anti-counterfeiting labels using advanced anti-counterfeiting technology (Lei, 2004). The success of the anti-counterfeiting measures in place during the Beijing Olympics is uncertain as one reported noted:

> in an underpass by Tiananmen Square, for instance, peddlers are doing a landslide business hawking non-sanctioned Olympic flags for a paltry 16 cents. Cheap Olympic T-shirts are everywhere, and rare is the shop that isn't trying to tie into the Games (Mickleburgh, 2008, p. 1).

Despite best efforts, it is clear that China generally and BOCOG specifically faced many unique difficulties in their attempt to protect Olympic intellectual property.

Predicting the Future of Counterfeiting in the Sport Industry

With the increased sophistication of those engaged in counterfeiting today, coupled with the advent of new technology which allows counterfeiting to appear more rapidly and in many more markets than in the past, counterfeiting of fake products will undoubtedly increase. It has been suggested that counterfeiting will exist wherever a high profile sporting event is located. The coordination and strategies employed by counterfeiters suggests the sophistication with which they operate:

a. counterfeiters target market items with the highest demand;
b. many are sophisticated enough to operate on a seasonal basis just like retail stores;
c. most counterfeiters are highly versatile and operate across a myriad of industries; and
d. other advanced counterfeiters beguile the market by becoming specialists in specific labels and brands or particular fabrics like denim or fleece ("Fake out," 2002).

Continued growth in trafficking counterfeit products has occurred over the past decade and should be expected to continue into the future if no effort is made to strengthen the enforcement of trademark counterfeiting policies and related laws.

References

2008 Beijing Olympic Emblem Unveiled. (2003, August 3). Retrieved March 16, 2008, from http://www.china.org.cn/english/2003/Aug/71475.htm

Batagello, D. (2005, May 3). Counterfeit goods a growing threat. *Windsor Star.*

Batcha, E. (1998). Who are the real competitors in the Olympic Games? Dual Olympic battles: Trademark infringement and ambush marketing harm corporate sponsors — violations against the USOC and its Corporate sponsors, *Seton Hall Journal of Sport Law, 8,* 229–259.

Beijing Issues IPR Policy for Companies (2006, April 14). *China Daily.*

Beijing Moves to Assure Rights of IOC Patrons. (2002, January 14). *China Internet Info. Ctr.* Retrieved March 16, 2008, from http://www.china.org.cn/english/2002/Jan/25220.htm

The business of football (2007, May 21). *Time International* (European Edition), p. 42.

Clark, G. (2005, May 18). Fake golf clubs are 'nightmare', counterfeiting from China leave buyers and makers frustrated. *International Herald Tribune.* Retrieved March 20, 2008, from http://www.iht.com/articles/2005/05/17/bloomberg/sxgolf.php

Clement, A. (2002). Contemporary trademark law and sport. *Journal of Legal Aspects of Sport, 12,* 1–35.

Coalition to Advance the Protection of Sports Logos. Retrieved December 28, 2007, from http://www.capsinfo.com/content.cfm?capsnav=about

Donatuti, J. (2007). Can China Protect the Olympics, or Should the Olympics be Protected from China? *Journal of Intellectual Property Law, 15,* 203–237.

Fake out (2002, June 1). *Sporting Goods Business.* Retrieved December 10, 2007, from http://www.allbusiness.com/retail-trade/miscellaneous-retail-miscellaneous/4475469-1.html

Freebairn, W. (2006, June 15). Spalding tries to prevent basketball counterfeiting. *The Republican.* Retrieved March 19, 2008, from http://www.masslive.com/business/republican/index.ssf?/base/business-0/1150357408144680.xml&coll=1

Goldstone, D.J., & Toren, P.J. (1998). The criminalization of trademark counterfeiting. 31 *Conn. L. Rev.* 1. Change to *Connecticut Law Review, 31,* 1–76.

Harland Co. v. Clark Checks, Inc., 711 F. 2d 966 (11th Cir. 1983).

Harley Davidson v. Grottanelli, 164 F. 3d 806 (1999).

International Olympic Committee, Athens 2004 Marketing Report 96.

Jorgense, C.B. (2006). Golf club technology: Intellectual property and the counterfeiting epidemic. *Syracuse Science and Technology Reporter, 13,* 58.

King of the Mountain Sports v. Chrysler Corp., 185 F. 3d 1084 (10th Cir. 1999).

Lanham Act, 15 U.S.C. § 1051–1127.

Lei, L. Pilot stores for Olympic products to start. (2004, August 4). *China Daily*.

McDonoug, T.L. (2007). Piecing it all together: The Amendments to the Federal Trademark Counterfeiting Act prevents circumvention through component parts. *American Intellectual Property Association Law Journal, 35,* 69.

Mendel, F. & Yijun, C. (2003). Protecting Olympic intellectual property, 17 *China L. & Prac.* 33. Change to *China Law and Practice,* (*17*), 33.

Mickleburgh, R. (2008, August 15). Sticking to official brands—with duct tape. *The Globe and Mail.* Retrieved August 15, 2008, from http://www.theglobeandmail.com/servlet/story/RTGAM.200-80815.wolymduct15/BNStory/beijing2008/home

Millan Gonzalez, O. (2008, January 12). "Great sums" lost to bootleggers of American pro sports gear. *Union Tribune.* Retrieved March 19, 2008, from http://www.signonsandiego.com/news/mexico/tijuana/20080112-9999-1b12bootleg.html

Misener, L. (2003). Safeguarding the Olympic insignia: Protecting the commercial integrity of the Canadian Olympic Association. *Journal of Legal Aspects of Sport, 13,* 79–96.

NBA issues warning to Cavalier fans: Beware of counterfeit merchandise. (2007, May 23). *Business Wire.* Retrieved December 10, 2007, from http://www.allbusiness.com/services//business-services/4337007-lihtml

NHL and Mighty Ducks issue warning to fans: Beware of counterfeit merchandise: NHL will be on the lookout for counterfeiters at the Western Finals in Anaheim. (2006, May 22). *Business Wire.* Retrieved on September 19, 2007, from http://findarticles.com/p./articles/mi~mOEIN/is-2007-May-22/ai-n1674758/print

Paradise, P. (1999). *Trademark counterfeiting, product piracy, and the billion dollar threat to the U.S. economy.* Westport, Connecticut: Greenwood Publishing Group.

Polaroid Corp. v. Polarad Electronics Corp., 287 F. 2d 492 (2nd Cir. 1961).

PricewaterhouseCoopers (2007). Managing the risks of counterfeit products. Retrieved March 19, 2008, from http://www.pwc.co.uk/pdf/managing_the_risks_of_counterfeit_products.pdf?utr=1

Priest, E. (2006). The Future of music and film piracy in China. *Berkeley Technology Law Journal, 21,* 795–871.

United States Department of Justice, U.S. Attorney, Southern District of California. (2000, April 12). *Three year FBI and IRS investigation reveals nationwide black market dealing in hundreds of millions of dollars in counterfeit and celebrity memorabilia.* Retrieved December 10, 2007, from http://www.usdoj.gov/criminal/cybercrime/sports.htm

Wall, A. (2002). The game behind the Games. *Marquette Sports Law Review, 12,* 557–581

Wall, A. (2006). Intellectual property protection in China: Enforcing trademark rights. *Marquette Sports Law Review, 17,* 341–426.

Wang, S.H. (2005). Great Olympics, new China: Intellectual property enforcement steps up to the mark. *Loyola Los Angeles International and Comparative Law Review*, 27, 291–322.

Yeh, B.T. (2007, July, 27). *Intellectual property rights violations: Federal civil remedies and criminal penalties related to copyright, trademarks and patents.* CRS Reports to Congress, Order Code RL 34109, Congressional Research Service.

Part V

Athletes and Criminal Actions

9

Clearing the Haze: The Definition, Scope, and Legal Issues Related to Hazing in Athletics

Brian Crow, Slippery Rock University

Introduction

Hazing in athletics has received unprecedented media coverage in the 21st century. Sport-related hazing occurrences have attracted increased attention from parents, student-athletes, attorneys, coaches, administrators, and, perhaps most importantly, the media, since the early part of the 1990s. This increased exposure has placed a great deal of pressure on coaches, athletic administrators, and student-athletes to examine historical initiation practices and make adjustments within the context of legal and ethical issues. Historically, hazing incidents receiving the most publicity have been related to fraternity and sorority activities at colleges and universities (Trota and Johnson, 2004). The contents of this chapter will enable the reader to become more familiar with reasons for the increased scrutiny of hazing activities, make aspiring athletic administrators aware of the current state of hazing in athletics, encourage an understanding of why hazing occurs in sport, address legal issues related to sport hazing, and suggest some possible prevention techniques to reduce the incidence of hazing in athletics.

Is Hazing Real?

Perhaps some who are reading this text have never been exposed to hazing, or only believe it occurs in Greek organizations on campus. Most college students have heard the term "hazing," and envision scenes from the movies *National Lampoon's Animal House* or the more recent *Old School*. While these Hollywood productions place a comedic spin on hazing, there is a more serious and insidious side to these activities, which place student-athletes in harm's way with alarming frequency. Consider the following examples, chosen from dozens in the first eight years of the 21st Century.

1. Two Tallmadge (OH) High School football players were convicted of rape-related charges in a hazing incident that happened in fall 2007 in the locker room during football practice, police said. A seventeen year-old was found guilty in Summit County Juvenile Court of first-degree felony delinquency by rape and one count of hazing, a misdemeanor. A teammate, also seventeen, was found guilty of one count of hazing. The convicted will have to register as a sex offender for repeatedly stabbing the victim (his teammate) in the buttocks and sodomizing him with a plastic drinking straw (Meyer, 2008).

2. In 2008, a 16-year-old former high school football player in Utah was found guilty of forcible sexual abuse and attempted forcible sodomy. The judge in the case decided that these actions were more than "horse-play," as the defendants claimed (Reavy, 2008).

3. In 2003, rookie football players from Mepham High School on Long Island were sodomized by veteran teammates with broomsticks, golf balls, and other foreign objects while attending a football camp in Pennsylvania. The season was cancelled, coaches were fired, and many players still suffer the physical and emotional scars of that torturous week (Longman, 2004).

4. In August 2005, rookies on the Northwestern University's women's soccer team were forced to engage in underage drinking and other activities in violation of the school's anti-hazing policy, resulting in suspensions, probation, and community service (Athletic director's statement on hazing, 2006). A website that has since been removed showed pictures of the rookies in t-shirts and underwear, blindfolded and with their hands tied behind their backs. They also had words or pictures scribbled on their bodies and clothes, and were photographed drinking alcohol (Northwestern suspends women's soccer team, 2006).

5. "On September 17th, 2004, Lynn Gordon Bailey Jr. ("Gordie") was found dead at the Chi Psi Fraternity house at the University of Colorado at Boulder. On the evening of September 16th, Gordie and twenty-six other pledges dressed in coats and ties for "bid night," were taken blindfolded to the Arapaho Roosevelt National Forest where they were "encouraged" to drink four "handles" (1.75 liter bottles) of whiskey and six (1.5 liter) bottles of wine around a bonfire in 30 minutes. They were told, "no one is leaving here until these are gone." When the group returned to the Fraternity house, Gordie was visibly intoxicated and did not drink anymore. He was placed on a couch to "sleep it off" at approximately 11pm. His brothers proceeded to write on his body in another fraternity ritual. Gordie was left to "sleep it off" for 10 hours before he was found dead the next morning, face down on the floor. No one had called for help." [direct quote taken from Gordie's Story (n.d.), available at: http://www.gordie.org/Gordies-Story.aspx].

So, yes, hazing can and does happen with discouraging regularity in sport. Remember, these are just a handful of *reported* incidents. Hundreds, if not thousands, of hazing incidents go unreported each year for reasons addressed later in this chapter.

Keep in mind, too, that an athletic administrator or coach can ultimately be held responsible if hazing occurs on his or her team, as in an incident in Baltimore. In 2007, a high school coach in the Baltimore metropolitan area was released from his position due to a hazing incident. Both the incident and subsequent coaching change made local headlines, and months later there was even a follow-up article on the situation. Unfortunately, in follow-up interviews, the coach still didn't understand the significance of his actions, made excuses, and placed blame on the lack of administrative support.

> [I]t is the job of the athletic director to help facilitate education on the issue and to promote rational thought from the involved parties. Because athletic directors are on the front lines in dealing with these volatile situations, we have to be knowledgeable about all aspects of hazing and how to protect against it (Hoch, 2007, para. 2).

High school and college athletic directors, a position to which many aspire, must deal with this issue in a proactive manner, and understand the consequences of hazing incidents.

Ground-breaking study

In response to a major hazing incident on its campus in the late 1990s, officials at Alfred University commissioned a ground-breaking study on the prevalence of hazing in intercollegiate athletics. The results of that research, and a subsequent study on hazing in high schools, which showed that hazing was prevalent in schools across America, were the catalyst for the growth in hazing research in the first decade of the 21st Century (Hoover & Pollard, 1999).

Hazing Defined

Developing an all-encompassing definition of hazing can be quite difficult. Many singular definitions exist but must be understood together to fully appreciate the breadth and depth of hazing activities, punishment, and prevention. Hazing has been defined as "any activity expected of someone joining a group that humiliates, degrades, abuses, or endangers, regardless of the person's willingness to participate" (Hoover & Pollard, 1999, p. 6). This definition was used in a seminal research study of thousands of college student-athletes in 1998–1999, and is generally accepted to convey the broad meaning of hazing.

Karen Savoy of Mothers Against School Hazing (M.A.S.H.) adds that, "hazing is a broad term encompassing any action or activity which *does not contribute to the positive development of a person*; which inflicts or intends to cause physical or mental harm or anxieties; which may demean, degrade, or disgrace any person, regardless of location, intent or consent of participants. Hazing can also be defined as any action or situation that intentionally or unintentionally endangers a student for admission into or affiliation with any student organization" (What is Hazing, 2008).

Many anti-hazing advocates feel the underlined phrase above " ... does not contribute to the positive development of a person ..." is critical to accurately describing the harmful effects hazing has on an individual. However, because this terminology is purposefully vague, the definition is difficult to use in legal proceedings. In addition, some experts (D. Westol, personal communication, March 30, 2007) characterize the levels of hazing as "little h" hazing—that which satisfies the definitions above, but may or may not result in physical or emotional harm and "Big H" Hazing—that which produces measurable physical or emotional harm. The progression from little "h" to big "H" is often when serious injuries occur.

The Disconnect

The researchers mentioned above have, in academic terms, clearly defined hazing. The question to be asked, however, is if student-athletes and professional athletes agree. Further research (Allen & Madden, 2006) has shown that students admit to participating in activities that researchers classify as hazing, but students consider team-building, positive initiation, or just plain fun. If these constituents can't agree on what activities are hazing, how will student-athletes know if what they are doing, or have had done to them, is hazing? Additionally, how will sport administrators prepare anti-hazing messages for their coaches and athletes?

Hazing Behavior

In an ideal world, the moral compass of athletes would guide them away from hazing activities, but that is not always reliable. Young students, many of whom are naïve and impressionable, will often suspend their moral beliefs in order to be part of a team or organization. That is the insidious nature of hazing; it exploits one's basic desire to be part of a group. The group to which they aspire often engages in what Irving Janis (1997) termed "groupthink"—a phenomenon in which bad decisions (that may endanger others) are made by members of a cohesive group who temporarily suspend good judgment and moral reasoning because of pressure to belong. In easier terms, think of the housewife or businesswoman who normally abides by a strong moral code, but when in the middle of a group of rabid football fans behaving badly at a game, tosses that code aside and berates officials and opposing players along with her fellow fans.

Why Haze?

Hazing is widespread in today's college culture. Consider the following selected statistics:

- 55 percent of college students involved in clubs, teams, and organizations experience hazing.
- In more than half of hazing incidents, pictures were posted on a public web space.
- In 95 percent of cases where students identified their experience as hazing, campus officials were not notified.
- 54 percent of hazing activities in college athletics involved alcohol consumption and drinking games.
- 69 percent of students involved in campus activities were aware of hazing in student organizations.
- 47 percent of students entering college have experienced hazing.

Discussion Activity

1. Locate your university's anti-hazing regulation in the student-handbook. Do the activities described seem dangerous? What would you change?
2. Determine if your home state has an anti-hazing statute (go to www.stophazing.org).
3. Develop a chart comparing the following:
   a. The definitions or activities that are prohibited by these regulations and laws.
   b. The penalties—are they severe or strict enough?
4. Do these documents help you understand hazing, or do they make things more unclear?

Which of these activities should be considered hazing? Discuss your reasoning.

- Making rookies carry upperclassmen's bags
- Making underclassmen perform skits or sing songs
- Making underclassmen wear clothes of the opposite sex
- Making rookies drink excessive amounts of alcohol
- Shaving the heads of teammates

- 90 percent of students who have experienced hazing in college do not consider themselves to have been hazed (Allen & Madden, 2008, p. 2).

The reasons why hazing continues in athletic settings are varied and complex. Researchers in the past decade (Allen & Madden, 2006; 2008; Crow, 2001; Crow, Ammon, & Phillips, 2003; Rosner & Crow, 2002) have studied the seemingly illogical reasons why hazing persists, and the conclusions are clear. Student-athletes, and in many cases professional athletes, do not understand nor appreciate the dangers involved in hazing.

Why Does Hazing Occur?

Why do rookies or first-year players subject themselves to abuse to be part of a team or group within a team? Why do some veterans feel the need to haze? Why do upperclassmen not involved in hazing, the bystanders, not report the incidents or rush to protect the victims? The answers are complex, but can best be understood by examining three components of hazing (power, acceptance, and exploitation) that together may explain why some hazing occurs.

1) **Power**—the veterans or upperclassmen possess status and perceived power. This allows them to control who may or may not gain entrance into the upper echelon of the team. In addition, there is further stratification among teammates that solidifies this power structure; there are starters and reserve players, letter-winners and non letter-winners, and leaders and followers. Hazing is all about one group having power over another, and this power often is based on seniority.

2) **Acceptance**—hazing exploits the basic human desire to be part of a group. Consider the following excerpt from the NCAA's anti-hazing materials:

- Of the three components of hazing addressed above, to which have you been exposed?
- Should hazing victims who willingly consent to being hazed be able to recover damages?

Athletic Identity: This is often defined as an athlete's view of his- or herself, in terms of his or her role on the team and the expectations for his or her performance! The stronger the sense of one's athletic identity, the more importance he or she places on being accepted by the athletic environment he or she is attempting to join. Consequently, there is a greater risk of participation in hazing activities in a misguided attempt to reinforce acceptance by teammates (Wilfert, 2008, p. 16).

3) **Exploitation**—flows from acceptance. Exploitation is the act of victimizing someone for selfish purposes—in this case, that the perpetrator might garner that feeling of power and status. Most hazers were hazed themselves, and feel a strong need to continue the cycle (Lipkins, 2006). Perpetrators who were once victims to gain acceptance exploit those who come after to regain the control they lost when they were hazed.

Power, acceptance, and exploitation are three of the main components visible when analyzing why student-athletes are involved in hazing. For a more detailed look at the reasons why people haze, please visit www.insidehazing.com and www.stophazing.org.

Of course, alcohol consumption is a significant contributing factor to hazing activities (Allen & Madden, 2008), particularly in relation to hazing among female athletic teams (Hoover & Pollard, 1999). Twenty-six percent of those hazed in college were involved in drinking games, and 12 percent were required to drink large amounts of alcohol to the point of sickness. Even more shocking is that 54 percent of all hazing behavior among all student-athletes involved drinking games (Allen & Madden, 2008, p. 17). Alcohol consumption alone, however, does not explain why hazing occurs—it is merely a catalyst for poor decision-making.

Mixed Media Messages

Another often overlooked factor that may contribute to hazing in high school and college athletics is the irreverent manner in which members of local and national media cover, often in a humorous or light-hearted way, hazing that occurs in professional sport (Nuwer, 2008). It is these same media members who would vilify and castigate student-athletes involved in hazing, who make light of professional athletes doing the same. For instance, one can conduct a daily Internet search for "hazing," and discover stories about high school and college student-athletes being punished for hazing allegations and activities, alongside stories calling hazing by professional athletes a "tradition" that must be upheld.

Numerous examples of this egregious disregard for professional journalism exist, including a story from ABC News in which the hazing of New York Yankees rookies (pictures included) was covered tongue-in-cheek. "It was rookie hazing day for the New York Yankees, and this well-worn baseball tradition came with a theme: The Wizard of Oz" (Walker, 2007, para. 3). "I'd rather be here dressing up than anywhere else," pitcher Ian Kennedy said, stepping into the sparkling ruby red slippers as Dorothy. "It makes you feel like one of the guys" (para. 7).

The message from the media is that hazing is OK; it's just a little "fun between the guys." Impressionable student-athletes, who perhaps already idolize and try to emulate these professional sport figures on the field, will undoubtedly copy off-the-field behavior as well.

In perhaps the most incongruous example of media "approval" of hazing, a writer for MLB.com, the official site of Major League Baseball, wrote an article entitled "Rookies face hazy days of spring" (Footer, 2008). Following are a few quotes from the story, which also included a picture of a pitcher pushing an elk head around the field in a shopping cart:

- Most young players know their roles during Spring Training. The rules are simple. Don't talk too much. Keep your head down. Work hard. And when your veteran teammates pick on you, you must take it. And for good measure, it doesn't hurt to pretend you're enjoying it.
- And the Rockies' No. 1 draft pick in 2007, Casey Weathers, has quite a load to carry—literally. After having to push around a shopping cart containing an elk head on the first day of camp, he has had to haul a red carpet wherever he goes, because stars, of course, always walk red carpets.
- Wes Roemer, one of Arizona's two sandwich picks in 2007, has had a colorful spring as well. Upon finishing first in running drills by the pitchers, an unnamed player, or players, took Roemer's spikes and tennis shoes from his locker and spray-painted them gold. That was a nod to former United States Olympic sprinter Michael Johnson, who wore gold shoes while winning five gold medals in the 1992, 1996 and 2000 Olympics. "I thought that was good, and he took it very well," manager Bob Melvin said of the prank. "You see quite a bit of that in camp, **and I think that's good for morale**—it keeps things light. Where he's going to find his next pair of shoes, I'm not sure, but I'm sure they'll take care of him down the line."
- Most of today's rookies will soon jump to the other side of the clubhouse divide, serving as the instigators instead of the butt of the jokes. Because most of them escape the annual Spring Training rite of passage unscathed, **it is likely rookie hazing will never become a thing of the past**. Generation after generation, it's as commonplace as batting practice and bullpen sessions.

At the end of the story, in very small print, was this disclaimer: *"This story was not subject to the approval of Major League Baseball or its clubs."*

Discussion Questions

1. Are some forms of hazing harmless?
2. Do you think media coverage of professional sport hazing sends a mixed message to high school and college students?
3. Do you think the disclaimer in the above example from MLB should absolve the league from any responsibility or accountability?
4. What are some other external factors that influence your understanding and willingness to participate in hazing?

Legal Issues

As of this writing, there is no federal anti-hazing statute in the United States. There is, however, some form of hazing legislation in forty-four states (www.stophazing.org/laws.html). Most states have only hazing laws (see Table 9.1) that result in a misdemeanor charge, then add existing statutes governing manslaughter, kidnapping, providing alcohol to minors, and other crimes in hazing cases where a death or serious injury occurs (State Anti-Hazing Laws, n.d.). "More students are being prosecuted under state anti-hazing laws and more institutions are being held responsible for their care" (Crow & Rosner, 2002, p. 87), but there is very little uniformity in the creation of state laws and their prosecution.

Hazing and the Courts

Perpetrators of hazing can be held criminally and civilly liable for hazing and its associated activities (see examples throughout chapter), but what happens to coaches and administrators of teams involved in hazing? Oftentimes they face civil lawsuits, generally but not exclusively based on the lack of adequate and proper supervision (Rosner & Crow, 2002). Other types of negligence lawsuits can fall under the doctrine of in loco parentis (in place of the parents), which establishes a reasonable standard of care for school personnel responsible for the welfare of students (Rosner & Crow, 2002). In 1999, the University of Vermont paid $80,000 to Corey LaTulippe, a former goalie on the UVM hockey, in an out-of-court settlement resulting from a heinous act of hazing (Finley & Finley, 2006).

In 1999, the Nebraska Supreme Court found that officials at the University of Nebraska had a legal duty to protect a student who was severely injured while trying to escape a fraternity hazing incident, because the hazing was *foreseeable*. The main implication is that administrators and coaches must be aware if hazing has occurred in the past and is likely to occur in the future, and if so, they can be held accountable in some states (Crow & Rosner, 2002).

In 1998, during the last night at the New Orleans Saints training camp, each rookie was forced to wear a pillowcase over his head and run a gauntlet down a

- Should there be a federal anti-hazing statute?
- Why do you think six states do not currently have anti-hazing laws?

- Develop an anti-hazing policy for a professional sport league.
- Check out the resources listed at the end of the chapter. What type of information, if any, is missing to curb the increased number of hazing incidents?

---

dormitory hallway as veterans punched, kicked, and pushed them. Several veterans, however, filled pillowcases with coins, injuring three rookies enough to require hospital treatment. One player sued the Saints, six players, and an assistant coach; the suit was subsequently settled out-of-court for an undisclosed amount, while two of the alleged perpetrators were released from the team (Crow & Rosner, 2002). It is clear from the recent professional sport incidents previously mentioned that very few, if any, professional sport organizations monitor the hazing activities of their players.

The legal issues surrounding hazing are as complex as anti-hazing laws are inconsistent. Often, perpetrators are prosecuted for other criminal activities associated with the hazing incident, such as (1) providing alcohol to minors, (2) endangerment, and (3) kidnapping, among many others. Athletic administrators and coaches are wise to be judicious in providing as much anti-hazing material, including written materials, websites, speakers, meetings with team captain, and even meetings with parents, as possible. The most important step, however, is to reinforce that message with a zero-tolerance policy, backed up by strict penalties for both perpetrators and bystanders.

Summary

It should be clear after reading this chapter that hazing, in its various forms, is still a serious problem in amateur, interscholastic, intercollegiate, and professional sport. Although efforts have been made to curb this trend, there is still a long way to go before student-athletes and professional athletes fully understand the dangers associated with these activities. Although the majority of states have an anti-hazing law, the implementation and enforcement of such laws has not lead to any precedent-setting court findings. In addition, as coaches, administrators, parents, and athletes continue to accept the fallacy that hazing should be considered an accepted tradition, it will most likely continue to cause immeasurable harm and injury to student-athletes nationwide.

Table 9.1 State Anti-Hazing Laws

State	State hazing statute	Classification of crime	Is failure to notify a crime?	Anti-hazing policy required in schools?	Is consent a defense?	Type of school impacted
Alabama	16-1-23	Class C misdemeanor	Yes	No	Yes	Any school
Alaska	None					
Arizona	15-2301		No	Yes	No	Public
Arkansas	6-5-201	Class B misdemeanor	Yes	No	Yes	Any school
California	32050-1	Misdemeanor	No	No	Yes	Any school
Colorado	18-9-124	Class 3 misdemeanor	No	No	Yes	Any school
Connecticut	53-23(a)		No	No	No	Higher education
Delaware	9301-04	Class B misdemeanor	No	Yes	No	Each institution
Florida	240.326	First degree misdemeanor, Third degree felony	No	Yes	No	College/university where students receive state financial assistance
Georgia	16-5-61	High and aggravated misdemeanor	No	No	No	Any school
Hawaii	None					
Idaho	18-917	Misdemeanor	No	No	Yes	College or university setting
Illinois	720 ILCS 120	Class A misdemeanor, Class 4 felony	No	No	Yes	Any school
Indiana	IC 35-4-2-2	Class A or B misdemeanor, Class C or D felony	No	No	No	Not restricted to school settings; any person
Iowa	708.10	Serious or simple misdemeanor	No	No	No	Any school
Kansas	21-3434	Class B misdemeanor	No	No	Yes	Any social or fraternal organization—not limited to schools
Kentucky	164.375		No	Yes	Yes	State colleges & universities
Louisiana	1.959027778		No	No	Yes	Only fraternities in any educational institution receiving state funds
Maine	6653		No	Yes	Yes	Public school; post-secondary institution state incorporated or chartered
Maryland	27-268H	Misdemeanor	No	No	No	Any school, college, or university
Massachusetts	269-17		Yes	No	No	Any student or other person on public or private property
Michigan	750.411t	Misdemeanor or felony	No	No	No	Any school
Minnesota	127.465		No	No	Yes	Each school board; student or staff hazing
Mississippi	97-3-105	Misdemeanor	No	No	Yes	Not specific to schools; any organization
Missouri	578.365	Class A misdemeanor, Class C felony	No	Yes	No	Public or private college or university

Table 9.1 State Anti-Hazing Laws, *continued*

State	State hazing statute	Classification of crime	Is failure to notify a crime?	Anti-hazing policy required in schools?	Is consent a defense?	Type of school impacted
Montana	None					
Nebraska	28-311.06	Class II misdemeanor	No	No	Yes	Postsecondary educational institution
Nevada	200.605	Misdemeanor, Gross misdemeanor	No	No	No	High school, college, or university in the state
New Hampshire	631.7	Class B misdemeanor	Yes	No	No	Any school
New Jersey	2c:40-3	4th Degree crime	No	No	No	Any student or fraternal organization
New Mexico	None					
New York	120.16	Class A misdemeanor	No	No	Yes	Not specific to schools or students
North Carolina	9:14:35–38	Class 2 misdemeanor	Yes	No	Yes	Any school or college
North Dakota	12.1-17-08	Misdemeanor	No	No	No	Not limited to schools
Ohio	2307.44; 2903.31	Misdemeanor	No	No	No	Any school
Oklahoma	21-1190	Misdemeanor	No	No	No	Any school
Oregon	163.197	Misdemeanor	No	No	Yes	College or university
Pennsylvania	5352	3rd Degree misdemeanor	No	Yes	No	Institution of higher education-associate degree or higher
Rhode Island	11/21/2001	Misdemeanor	No	No	Yes	Any school
South Carolina	59-101-200	Misdemeanor	Yes	No	No	Institution of higher learning
South Dakota	None					
Tennessee	49-7-123		No	No	Yes	Higher education institution
Texas	37.152	Misdemeanor	Yes	Yes	No	Any school
Utah	76-5-107.5	Misdemeanor	No	Yes	No (under 21)	High school level
Vermont	76		No	Yes	No	All educational institutions
Virginia	18.2056	Class I misdemeanor	No	No	Yes	Any school
Washington	28B.10.901	Misdemeanor	Yes	No	No	Any school
West Virginia	18-2.33	Misdemeanor	No	Yes	No	Public Schools
Wisconsin	948.51	Class A misdemeanor, Class E felony	No	No	Yes	Any school
Wyoming	None					

This chart was originally created by Brian Crow for *Law for Recreation and Sport Managers* (2nd ed.) and updated for this text.

References

Allen, E., & Madden, M. (2006). Examining *and transforming campus hazing cultures*. Pilot study report. Retrieved September 12, 2007, from http://www.hazingstudy.org

Allen, E., & Madden, M. (2008). Hazing in view: college students at risk. Retrieved March 13, 2008, from http://www.hazingstudy.org/publications/hazing _in_view_web.pdf

Athletic director's statements on hazing. (2006). Retrieved February 7, 2008, from http://www.northwestern.edu/newscenter/stories/2006/05/soccer.html

Crow, B., Ammon, R., & Phillips, D. (January/February 2004). Anti-hazing strategies for coaches and administrators. *Strategies*, 26(2) 22–25.

Crow, R.B. (2001). In Cotten, Wolohan, & Wilde (Eds.), *Law for recreation and sport managers*. (pp. 251–260). Dubuque, IA: Kendall/Hunt Publishing.

Crow, R.B., & Rosner, S.R. (Winter, 2002). Institutional and organizational liability for hazing in intercollegiate and professional team sports. *St. John's Law Review* 76(1), 87–114.

Finley, L., & Finley, P. (2006). *The sport industry's war on athletes*. Westbury, CT: Praeger Press.

Footer. A. (March 3, 2008). Rookies face hazy days of spring. Retrieved March 4, 2008, from http://mlb.mlb.com/news/article.jsp?ymd=20080303&content_ id=2401889&vkey=spt2008news&fext=.jsp&c_id=mlb

Gordie's Story. (n.d.). The Gordie Foundation. Retrieved on September 14, 2008, from http://www.gordie.org/Gordies-Story.aspx

Hoch, D. (2007). Getting a handle on hazing. Retrieved March 14, 2008, from http://www.athleticmanagement.com/2007/08/getting_a_handle_on_hazing.html

Hoover, N. & Pollard, N. (1999). Hazing and Initiation Rites. Retrieved December 12, 2007, from http://www.alfred.edu/news/html/hazing_study.html

Longman, J. (September 29, 2004). Year after assaults, play begins but pain never ends. *New York Times*. Retrieved February 3, 2008 from http://www.nytimes.com/2004/09/29/sports/othersports/29mepham.html

Janis, I.L. (1997). Groupthink. In R.P. Vecchio (Ed.), *Leadership: Understanding the dynamics of power and influence in organizations*. (pp. 163–176). Notre Dame, IN: University of Notre Dame Press.

Meyer, E. (April 28, 2008). Tallmadge teen gets probation in hazing case. Retrieved March 15, 2008, from http://www.ohio.com/news/break_news/ 18342059.html.

Northwestern suspends women's soccer team (May 16, 2006). ESPN News Services. Retrieved February 7, 2008, from http://sports.espn.go.com/ncaa/ news/story?id=2446321

Nuwer, H. (2008). High school hazing page. Retrieved March 13, 2008, from http://hazing.hanknuwer.com/hs2.html

Reavy, P. (March 1, 2008). Ex-East high football player guilty in hazing incident. *The Deseret Morning News*. Retrieved March 8, 2008, from http://www.deseretnews.com/article/1,5143,695257857,00.html

Rosner, S. & Crow, B. (Summer 2002). Institutional liability for hazing in inter-scholastic sports. *Houston Law Review, 39*(2), 276–300

State Anti-Hazing Laws (n.d.). StopHazing.org. Retrieved on September 15, 2008, from http://www.stophazing.org/laws.html

Trota, B & Johnson, J. (2004). Introduction: A brief history of hazing. In J. Johnson and M. Holman (Eds.), *Making the team: Inside the world of sport initiations and hazing* (pp. x–xvi). Toronto: Canadian Scholars' Press.

Walker, B. (September 24, 2007). Yankees rookies dress up in Oz costumes. Retrieved September 26, 2007, from http://abcnews.go.com/Sports/wireStory?id=3645430.

What is Hazing (n.d.). MASH, Inc. Retrieved on September 14, 2008, from http://www.mashinc.org/resources-whatis.html

Wilfert, M. (2008). Building new traditions: hazing prevention in college athletics. Indianapolis, IN: National Collegiate Athletic Association.

Additional Resources

www.stophazing.org

www.hazingstudy.org

NCAA Hazing Prevention Handbook

www.hazingprevention.org

http://www.hazing.cornell.edu/

www.insidehazing.com

www.mash-inc.org

10

Criminal Jocks: Professional and Collegiate Incidents ... And Beyond

Kadence A. Otto, Western Carolina University[1]

Chapter Overview

This chapter provides an overview of criminal acts committed by college and professional athletes. Specifically, this chapter focuses on criminal incidents perpetrated by players in the National Football League (NFL), the National Basketball Association (NBA), Major League Baseball (MLB), the National Hockey League (NHL), professional boxing, the National Collegiate Athletic Association (NCAA). In addition to the predominant occurrence of criminal acts perpetrated by males, female incidents are also addressed. A description of each incident is given, including the actual punishment each athlete received for his or her crime. An analysis of motivations, causal links, and sociological factors that contribute to committing such acts are examined. Finally, this chapter provides a summary of the preventative programs that seek to reduce the number of criminal acts committed by athletes.

Introduction

Over the past decade there has been an increase in the number of reported incidents of criminal behavior committed by collegiate and professional athletes. Newspaper articles and television reports regarding athletes' involvement in criminal behavior have left people wondering whether there is a relationship between an athletes' participation in sport and crime. News reports concerning murder, rape, assault, battery, perjury, and substance abuse have filled the airwaves with direct links to athletes.

---

1. The author would like to thank Rachel Hils, graduate assistant at Western Carolina University, for her assistance with data collection.

Sociologists have noted that sport is a microcosm of society; namely, the behavior exhibited by athletes is reflective of the behavior exhibited by those in society in general (Coakley, 2007; Eitzen & Sage, 2003). As a result of the negative press professional and college athletes have received, people have called into question the commonly held belief that socializing children through sport aids in developing them into productive members of society.

This chapter addresses five specific questions: (1) what type of crimes athletes commit;[2] (2) what punishments athletes receive for their involvement in criminal activity; (3) why athletes commit crimes; (4) if African-American athletes are over-represented as perpetrators of criminal acts; and (5) what can be done to prevent such incidents from occurring?

Incidents of Criminal Behavior

Incidents of criminal behavior are listed historically by sport as follows: NFL, NBA, MLB, NHL, professional boxing, NCAA, and female athletes, regardless of sport.

Professional

NFL

In 1992, Lewis Billups, former defensive back for the Cincinnati Bengals, was accused of videotaping an incident in which he allegedly drugged and sexually assaulted a woman in an attempt to extort $20,000 in exchange for not sending the tape to her husband. Billups pleaded no contest to a reduced charge of criminal conspiracy and was sentenced to three years' probation. In 1994, Billups died in an automobile accident when he allegedly lost control of his car ("Cases Involving Athletes and Sexual Assault," 2004).

In 1994, Tim Barnett of the Kansas City Chiefs was accused of exposing himself to a 14-year-old hotel maid and groping her. As a result of the media attention surrounding the allegations against Barnett, the Chiefs released him. Barnett was convicted of second-degree sexual assault and was sentenced to three years in prison. After serving only one year in prison, Barnett was granted parole (Teitelbaum, 2005).

In 1995, Keith Henderson, former running back for the Minnesota Vikings, pleaded guilty to three counts of fourth-degree criminal sexual conduct. Henderson served six months in prison ("Cases Involving," 2004).

In 1997, Cornelius Bennett, former linebacker for the Atlanta Falcons, was accused of sexually assaulting a woman in a hotel room. Bennett pleaded guilty to a misdemeanor charge of sexual abuse and was sentenced to 60 days in jail, but only served 36 days. Bennett was also fined $1,000, was ordered to pay $617 of

---

2. For a complete overview of crime and the various types of crimes see Chapter 1.

the woman's hospital bills, perform 100 hours of community service, and undergo anger management and substance abuse counseling. Following this incident, the league did not fine Bennett, nor did the Falcons release him (Benedict & Yaeger, 1998).

Lamar Thomas, former receiver for the Miami Dolphins, served 10 days in jail in 1997 for beating his pregnant fiancée. The league did not discipline Thomas and the Dolphins offered him a new contract (Benedict, 1998a). In 2006, while employed as a television analyst for Comcast Sports SouthEast, Thomas was fired for the comments he made during the University of Miami verses Florida International football brawl. When the sideline-clearing brawl occurred, Thomas was quoted as saying,

> Now, that's what I am talking about. You come into our house, you should get your behind kicked. You don't come into the OB [Orange Bowl] playing that stuff ... you can't come over to our place talking noise like that. You'll get your butt beat. I was about to go down the elevator to get in that thing (Reynolds, 2006, p. 1).

In 1998, Dextor Clinkscale, an All-American defensive back at South Carolina State University and former Dallas Cowboy, was charged with second-degree criminal sexual conduct and providing alcohol to a minor. Clinkscale pleaded guilty to simple assault and providing alcohol to a minor. He was fined $400 ("Cases Involving," 2004).

In October 1998, Leonard Little, formerly with the St. Louis Rams, drove his SUV into Susan Gutweiler's car, killing her. Following this incident, the Rams put Little on paid leave. Little pleaded guilty to involuntary manslaughter. He served 90 days in jail, four years' probation and 1000 hours of community service. The NFL banned Little for the first eight regular season games costing him $125,000 of his salary (Benedict, 1998b).

In 1998, Jeff Benedict and Don Yaeger published *Pros and Cons: The Criminals Who Play in the NFL*. In their book, the authors reported that one out of five players in the NFL had been charged with a serious crime. An examination of a subset of 180 of the crimes revealed that 30 percent were charged with assault and/or battery, 22 percent were charged with DUI or DWI, 14 percent were sexual crimes, 9 percent were weapons charges, 9 percent theft, 8 percent drugs, 6 percent resisting arrest, and 2 percent murder and/or attempted murder (see Figure 10.1). Of those charged, 27 percent were convicted and/or pleaded guilty, 25 percent were dismissed, 14 percent were reported pending, 13 percent had the charges against them reduced, 11 percent were acquitted, and 10 percent pleaded no contest (see Figure 10.2).

Following the release of *Pros and Cons*, in 1999, Ray Carruth, a former receiver for the Carolina Panthers, was charged with first-degree murder. Carruth was charged with conspiring to kill Cherica Adams, his then pregnant girlfriend. The jury heard testimony that Carruth led Adams down a road in his own car, stopped his car (effectively blocking Adams' passage) when another car with three men pulled up alongside her and fired gunshots through her window.

Van Brett Watkins told jurors that Carruth paid him to kill Adams. Watkins pleaded guilty to second-degree murder, conspiracy to commit first-degree murder, attempting to kill an unborn child, and shooting into an occupied vehicle. He

Figure 10.1
Athletes' Criminal Charges

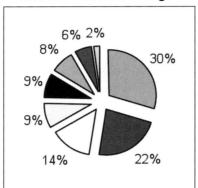

Figure 10.2
Legal Outcome of Crime Committed by Athletes

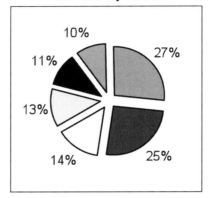

(Benedict & Yaeger, 1998; subset, n=180)

was sentenced to a minimum of 40 years and 5 months for the shooting of Cherica Adams. Watkins admitted in court that he fired the gun that killed Adams. Her son, who was delivered from her mortally wounded body, survived. Cherica's son was born 10 weeks premature and now suffers from cerebral palsy because he lacked oxygen during his birth.

Ray Carruth was acquitted of first-degree murder but was convicted of conspiracy to murder, shooting into an occupied vehicle, and attempting to kill an unborn child. He is currently serving a minimum prison sentence of 18 years and 11 months ("Gunman sentenced in Carruth case," 2001).

On Super Bowl weekend in January 2000, Ray Lewis, linebacker for the Baltimore Ravens and 2003 NFL defensive player of the year, and two other men were charged with murder in connection with the stabbing deaths of two men outside a nightclub. The charges against Lewis were eventually dropped. Lewis pleaded guilty to obstruction of justice and was placed probation for one year (Powell, 2004).

In February 2004, former Baltimore Ravens running back, Jamal Lewis, was indicted on federal drug charges (conspiring to possess cocaine with the intent to distribute and using a cell phone in the commission of the crime). Lewis pleaded guilty to using his cell phone to set up a drug deal. He spent four months in prison and was suspended by the NFL for two games ("NFL suspended Lewis for two games," 2005).

In 2004, Sean Taylor, a first-round draft pick of the Washington Redskins, was charged with aggravated assault with a firearm. Taylor pleaded no contest to misdemeanor battery and assault. Taylor was placed on 18 months' probation and was required to speak about the importance of education at ten Miami schools, as well as contribute $1,000 scholarships to each of the schools. As for the league, the NFL fined Taylor $71,764 (Pugmire, 2006). On November 27, 2007, Sean Taylor was shot to death in his home in Miami, Florida. Detectives are exploring whether Taylor's death might be connected to the previous incident that led to criminal charges against Taylor (Shipley & Whoriskey, 2007).

In November 2005, Tank Johnson, a former defensive lineman for the Chicago Bears, was sentenced to 18 months' probation after pleading guilty to a misdemeanor gun charge. In December 2006, police raided Johnson's Chicago home and found unregistered guns that resulted in a probation violation and his third arrest in 19 months. In his possession were a semiautomatic rifle, a loaded .45-caliber handgun, and 550 rounds of ammunition (Plaschke, 2007).

In January 2006, Cincinnati Bengals receiver Chris Henry pleaded guilty to a concealed weapon charge (Pugmire, 2006). In January 2007, Henry pleaded guilty to providing alcohol to minors (an incident which occurred at a hotel in the spring of 2006). Henry was sentenced to 90 days in jail, but was only required to serve two days.

In September 2006, while awaiting sentencing for providing alcohol to minors, Henry, along with teammates Odell Thurman (who was already serving a four-game suspension for violating the NFL's substance abuse policy) and Reggie McNeal, were stopped at a DUI checkpoint. Thurman, the driver of the vehicle, was charged with DUI. Following this incident, Henry was suspended for one game by head coach Marvin Lewis and two additional games by NFL commissioner Roger Goodell for violating the league's personal conduct policy. Goodell also suspended Henry for eight regular season games during the 2007 NFL football season,. In April 2008, following the dismissal of assault charges, the Bengals waived Henry. Following the NFL's reduction of Henry's open-ended suspension to just that of the first four games of the 2008 season, he signed a two-year contract with the Bengals (Curnutte, 2008).

On December 11, 2007, Michael Vick, former quarterback for the Atlanta Falcons, was sentenced to 23 months in federal prison for running a dog fighting operation ("Bad Newz Kennels"). At the time of his arrest, Michael Vick was one of the NFL's premier stars, having signed a 10-year, $130 million contract in 2004. Nevertheless, Michael Vick was instrumental in the promotion and funding, as well as the facilitation of killing a number of dogs. He admitted bankrolling the dog-fighting ring on his 15-acre property in rural Virginia. Further, he admitted providing money for bets on the fights but said he never shared in any winnings ("Apologetic Vick gets 23 month sentence on dog fighting," 2008).

Vick received a harsher sentence than the others in the federal conspiracy case because he lied about killing the pit bulls (dogs that did not perform up to expectations were killed by electrocution, hanging, drowning and other violent means). The horrific details concerning the brutal methods of killing the dogs prompted a public backlash. Animal-rights groups were enraged and used the case to call attention to the brutality of dog fighting. In addition to initially lying about his role in the killing of the dogs, Vick tested positive for marijuana use in violation of the terms set for his release. Along with the prison term, Vick was fined $5,000 and is required to serve three years' probation after his release ("Apologetic Vick," 2008). In August 2008, the NFL challenged a Minneapolis judge's ruling, which allows Vick to keep $16.25 million of a total of $20 million in bonus money (Myers, 2008).

In February 2008, former Tennessee Titan cornerback, Adam "Pacman" Jones accepted a plea deal in return for his testimony about a triple shooting at a Las Vegas strip club. Jones pleaded no contest to one charge of conspiracy to commit disorderly conduct, a gross misdemeanor, in return for a one-year probation sentence instead of serving a year in county jail. The Las Vegas police identified Jones as the person who incited a fight inside a club minutes before three people were shot outside. Jones was also required to attend anger management classes, complete 200 hours of community service within a year, and submit to random drug testing ("Lawyer say Pacman Jones to take deal," 2008).

Prior to Jones' most recent legal troubles, he was charged in February 2006 with one felony count of obstruction of a police officer and two misdemeanors after police accused him of throwing a punch and biting an officer's hand. For this incident, Jones was sentenced to three years of probation and required to pay a $500 fine. NFL commissioner Roger Goodell suspended Jones in April 2007 for the season for violating the NFL's personal conduct policy after having been arrested six times since he was drafted (Ritter, 2008). Not long after being suspended from the NFL, Jones signed a contract to appear as a professional wrestling personality with Total Nonstop Action Wrestling ("Pacman to make first TNA appearance Thursday," 2007).

NBA

In March of 1992, former Celtics guard Charles Smith was convicted of vehicular homicide and leaving the scene of a crime in a hit-and-run accident that ended the lives of two Boston University students. Smith was sentenced to four and a half years in prison. In 1995, Smith returned to the NBA, playing eight games with the Minnesota Timberwolves ("Smith, a former Celtic, gets a split verdict," 1992).

In 1993, Marcus Webb, a former Boston Celtics player, was accused of raping his 22-year-old girlfriend. He pleaded guilty to a reduced charge of indecent assault and was sentenced to 30 days in jail (Lipsyte, 1995).

In 1998, Anthony Mason of the Miami Heat was arrested on two counts of third-degree rape of two teenage girls. He pleaded guilty to two counts of endangering the welfare of children and was sentenced to 200 hours of community service ("Cases Involving," 2004).

Ken Wilburn, former NBA and ABA player and elementary school teacher, was accused of molesting six girls aged 11 to 15 over a six year period. In 1998, he was charged with 20 counts of aggravated sexual assault, sexual assault, endangering the welfare of a child and aggravated criminal sexual contact. He pleaded guilty to two counts of misconduct, was sentenced to eight years in prison and barred from teaching ("Cases Involving," 2004).

In November 2005, former NBA player, Johnny Newman was sentenced to 60 days in jail and fined $500 for assaulting his wife. Newman was convicted of domestic assault and battery. In the same year, Newman was named president of basketball operations and general manager of the Richmond Generals of the American Basketball Association. Newman, the University of Richmond's leading career scorer, was chosen in the second round of the NBA draft and played for seven teams in a 17 year career ("Ex-NBA player Newman guilty of domestic battery," 2005).

One of the worst brawls in the history of U.S. professional sports took place November 19, 2004 at The Palace of Auburn Hills, where the Indiana Pacers were playing the Detroit Pistons. The incident occurred when Pistons center Ben Wallace shoved Pacers guard Ron Artest following a hard foul. Once the players were separated, a fan threw a beverage into Artest's chest. Artest rushed into the stands after the fan who purportedly threw the drink. What ensued was a terrible display of players and fans fighting one another on national television. The NBA tried desperately to handle the matter in-house; they suspended Artest for the remainder of the season and disciplined his Pacer teammates (Stephen Jackson and Jermaine O'Neal were suspended for 30 and 15 games respectively) ("NBA player sentenced in brawl," 2005). Although the NBA perceived its punishments against the players to be extremely harsh, it was not enough to stop the fans involved from filing criminal charges against the athletes.

Ron Artest, Jermaine O'Neil, Stephen Jackson, David Harrison, and Anthony Johnson all pleaded no contest to misdemeanor assault and battery charges stemming from the brawl. In the fall of 2005, a judge sentenced the players to a year of probation, 50–100 hours of community service, anger management counseling and ordered each to pay a $250 fine ("NBA player sentenced in brawl," 2005).

A detailed analysis of the specific sentences that were handed down to each individual player revealed that Artest, who initiated the brawl by charging into the stands after the fan, was given the lightest sentence (50 hours of community service, a year of probation, and a $250 fine). Anthony Johnson received the harshest sentence (100 hours of community service, a year of probation, anger management counseling and a yearlong ban on alcohol use as well as required drug and alcohol testing) (McCarthy & Upton, 2006). Different judges applied their own standards regarding the actions of the athletes, which resulted in the differing sentences.

John Green, the fan who purportedly threw the cup at Artest, was convicted of misdemeanor assault and was sentenced to 30 days in jail, two years' probation and a $500 fine by yet another judge. Green was also ordered to attend Alcoholics Anonymous and anger management classes, and pay for additional fees related to his alcohol issues. Green's conviction was based on the fact that he punched Artest and not due to his cup throwing. Green's attorney, Shawn Patrick Smith, responded to the seemingly unfair punishment given to his client in comparison to the sentences the NBA players received by saying, "This is the same thing that goes on every day in the justice system—if you're rich and powerful, you get away with murder" (McCarthy & Upton, 2006, p. 1).

MLB

Baseball's all-time career hits leader, Pete Rose, was sentenced to five months in federal prison for falsification of income tax returns. Rose was ordered to serve three months in a community treatment center, pay a $50,000 fine and complete 1,000 hours of community service (Smith, 1990). Pete Rose was banned from baseball for life by former baseball commissioner A. Bartlett Giamatti following allegations that Rose bet on baseball games. Rose, since admitting betting on baseball games, has continued his national campaign to gain membership into the baseball Hall of Fame.

In 1994, former pitcher for the Colorado Rockies Marcus Moore was charged with first-degree sexual assault, a felony, when his girlfriend accused him of rape. Moore pleaded guilty to misdemeanor assault and was sentenced to two years of probation. He was also ordered to undergo domestic violence counseling and pay $1,650 for the victim's therapy ("Cases Involving," 2004).

Also in 1994, Johnny Ruffin, former pitcher for the Cincinnati Reds, was charged with sexual battery after a woman told police that he had sexually assaulted her in a motel room. He pleaded no contest to a reduced charge of attempted sexual battery. The plea agreement called for him to serve five years' probation, donate $5,000 to a rape crisis center, and perform 500 hours of community service. He also was ordered to pay restitution and the victim's counseling costs ("Cases Involving," 2004).

The increase in on-the-field violence has also led to criminal charges against players. Player-to-player incidents as well as player-to-fan incidents have raised concerns as to why athletes are committing criminal acts during a game. In the 2004 MLB season, for example, Texas Rangers relief pitcher Frank Francisco was charged with aggravated battery (a felony) for throwing a chair, which hit two spectators, into the stands,. One of the fans, Jennifer Bueno, suffered a broken nose as well as cuts to her face. On July 1, 2005, Francisco pleaded no contest to misdemeanor assault and was sentenced 20 days of work detail and was required to attend 26 anger management classes. Francisco was also placed on probation for three years and was ordered to perform 500 hours of community service ("Pitcher sentenced, sent to anger management classes," 2005).

In November 2005, Venezuelan authorities arrested former Florida Marlins relief pitcher Ugueth Urbina for attempted murder. Urbina attacked five farm workers on his property. He injured the men with a machete and poured gasoline on them. In March 2007, Urbina was convicted of attempted murder and was sentenced to 14 years in prison ("Urbina sentenced to prison in Venezuela," 2007).

Former eight-time All-Star Darryl Strawberry was convicted in U.S. District Court of tax evasion and must pay the Internal Revenue Service (IRS) over $430,000 in back taxes ("Strawberry to pay IRS back taxes," 2008). Prior to his tax evasion conviction, Strawberry, in March of 2002, was kicked out of a drug treatment facility for having sex with a female resident, smoking, signing autographs and being disrespectful. Following this incident, Strawberry was imprisoned in 2003 for a 1999 cocaine possession probationary violation. After violating his probation on six separate occasions, he was sentenced to serve 11 months in prison ("Strawberry's stay ends 11 months into 18-month term," 2003). Strawberry won three World Series titles—one in 1986 with the New York Mets, and two with the Yankees in 1996 and 1999.

NHL

In May of 1984, Craig MacTavish, formerly with the Boston Bruins, drove drunk and caused an accident. The driver of the other car died days later. MacTavish served one year in prison. Following his prison time, MacTavish played 14 more seasons in the NHL. In 2000, MacTavish was named head coach for the Edmonton Oilers (Craig MacTavish, 1978 NHL Amateur Draft, n.d.).

In 2000, Marty McSorley, then a member of the Boston Bruins, was found guilty in Canadian court of assault with a weapon. McSorely intentionally swung his hockey stick across the side of Vancouver Canucks forward Donald Brashear's head, sending him falling to the ice. McSorley, a 17-year veteran of the NHL, was given 18 months of probation and barred from playing against Brashear during that time, in both Canada and the United States. The NHL suspended McSorley indefinitely following the incident; he missed the final 23 games of the season. He was required to meet with the NHL commissioner before being considered for reinstatement. The NHL said the case shouldn't have gone to court ("Very major penalty: McSorley found guilty of assault, avoids jail time," 2000).

The NHL's desire to keep the McSorley incident in-house suggests that professional leagues want to keep their players out of the court of law. McSorley's actions, however, were clearly outside the rules of the game and were, therefore, punishable under the law. This incident serves as an example of what can happen when a player's on-the-ice conduct goes beyond the rules of the game such that the victim has an obvious legal cause of action.

There are numerous examples of unacceptable on-the-field conduct, which could have turned into criminal charges against the athlete but instead were handled in-house by the respective leagues. The following NFL example highlights the punitive power that the leagues hold as well as the financial capability of the athlete to settle out of court with victim for an, oftentimes, undisclosed, sum of money.

The NFL suspended Tennessee Titans defensive lineman Albert Haynesworth for an unprecedented five games without pay for stepping on the face of Dallas center Andre Gurode with his cleated foot while Gurode lay on the ground. The injury to Gurode's face caused blurred vision and required 30 stitches to repair all of the cuts ("Haynesworth suspended for unprecedented five games," 2006). This incident is the harshest punishment handed down by the NFL for on-the-field behavior. The five-game suspension cost Haynesworth $190,070 (or 29 percent of his base salary ($646,251) (Maske, 2006). [See Chapter 5 for further information on such instances].

On December 15, 2003, Rob Ramage was found guilty of impaired driving, killing former fellow NHL player Keith Magnuson. Magnuson was killed instantly when Ramage failed to negotiate a curve on a road just north of Toronto. Ramage sustained relatively minor injuries. The two men were former friends. Ramage, who played in the NHL from 1979 and 1993 and was a former first round draft pick, was sentenced in 2007 to four years in prison (Kari, 2007).

Boxing

In 1986, Mike Tyson, one of the most infamous athletes in modern history, became the youngest heavyweight champion in history at age 20, when he knocked out Trevor Berbick. Four years later, in 1990, he lost his title of "champion" when he was knocked out by James "Buster" Douglas ("Tyson gets 24 hours in jail, probation for drug possession, DUI," 2007). Not long after, in 1991, Tyson was charged with the rape of Desiree Washington. The incident, which allegedly occurred in 1991 in an Indianapolis hotel room, ended with Tyson's conviction on the charge of rape and a sentence of six years in prison. Tyson served just three years of his sentence before being released on parole ("Tyson on Washington: 'I just hate her guts'," 2003).

In 1997, while trying to get his boxing career back on track, Tyson infamously bit a piece of Evander Holyfield's ear off during a fight. Following this incident, Tyson's boxing license was suspended, he was fined $3 million, and was banned for one year (Saraceno, 2007). Also in 1999, Tyson pleaded no contest to misdemeanor assault charges in Maryland. In 2007, Tyson pleaded guilty to one felony count of cocaine possession and a misdemeanor DUI count. Because of his violent criminal past, Tyson could have received more than four year in prison but, instead, was sentenced to three years of probation and one day in jail. Tyson also was required to submit to drug testing and serve 360 hours of community service ("Tyson gets 24 hours in jail, probation for drug possession, DUI," 2007).

In 1995, Lawrence Clay-Bey, former United States Olympic team captain, was accused of forcing a woman to perform sexual acts under a threat of violence. He was charged with first-degree sexual assault with a weapon. He pleaded guilty to third-degree sexual assault and was ordered into a court-supervised rehabilitation program ("Cases Involving," 2004).

Jo-el Scott was accused of having sexual contact with three underage girls in 1996 and charged with first-degree rape. He pleaded guilty to reduced charges of attempted rape. He was sentenced to three to six years in prison, which included hit-and-run charges for leaving the scene of an accident in which a 4-year-old boy was critically injured ("Cases Involving," 2004).

In 1996, former heavyweight boxer Anthony Cooks, who failed to appear in court on a charge of possession with intent to distribute cocaine and marijuana, was also charged with the alleged rape of a 14-year-old girl. Cooks pleaded guilty as charged to second-degree rape and was sentenced to three years in prison ("Morrison foe charged," 1996).

In 1997, former World Boxing Association heavyweight champion Bruce Seldon was accused of smoking marijuana and having sex with a 15-year-old girl. He was charged with sexual assault as well as drug and weapons charges. He pleaded guilty to reduced charges of two counts of endangering the welfare of a child. He was sentenced to 364 days in jail and five years of probation. He was ordered to register under New Jersey's Megan's Law statute as a convicted sex offender ("Cases Involving," 2004).

Former heavyweight boxing champion Riddick Bowe was sentenced to 30 days in prison for kidnapping his wife and children. Initially charged with federal kidnapping, Bowe instead accepted a plea bargain and pleaded guilty in 1998 to federal interstate domestic violence charges. Bowe was also fined $5,000 and ordered to serve four years' probation plus six months of house arrest following his release from prison. Regarding the seeming leniency of Bowe's sentence, the judge took into consideration the fact that multiple blows to the boxer's head may have caused brain damage, thereby contributing to Bowe's criminal actions ("Boxer Riddick Bowe sentenced to 30 days in jail for kidnapping wife and kids," 2000).

Tony Ayala Jr. was accused of breaking into a San Antonio home in 2000. Ayala was shot in the shoulder with a handgun by one of the two women in the house. He was charged with burglary with intent to commit sexual assault. He pleaded guilty to reduced charges of burglary and attempt to commit aggravated assault. He was sentenced to 90 days in jail and ten years of probation. He was also ordered into a sexual offender's program to receive treatment to manage his violent tendencies toward women. Prior to this incident, Ayala spent 16 years in prison for a 1983 rape conviction in New Jersey ("Cases Involving," 2004).

Tommy Morrison became the heavyweight champion in 1993 when he knocked out George Foreman. However, his career came to a shocking halt in 1996 when he tested positive for HIV, the virus that causes AIDS. Then, in 2000, Morrison pleaded guilty to drug and weapons charges and was sentenced to two years in prison; Morrison served just 14 months. While serving time in prison, Morrison was again tested for HIV; his test came back negative. Following his release from prison, Morrison obtained a license to fight in West Virginia ("Morrison says error in HIV test hurt career," 2007).

College Football

In 1993, Stan Callender, former defensive lineman for Michigan State, was charged with criminal sexual assault in an off-campus incident involving an 18-year-old student. He pleaded guilty to a misdemeanor charge; the two felony charges were dropped. He was sentenced to two years of probation and six months in jail with all but two weeks suspended ("Cases Involving," 2004).

In 1993, Christian Peter, former defensive tackle for the University of Nebraska, was accused of groping a former Miss Nebraska in a bar. Peter pleaded no contest to a charge of third-degree sexual assault and was sentenced to 18 months' probation ("Cases Involving," 2004).

In 1994, Troy Parker, former University of Toledo standout and MAC (Mid-American Conference) freshman of the year award winner in 1990, was accused of cutting through a screen door and raping a 32-year-old woman. He was convicted of rape, aggravated burglary, felonious sexual penetration, and gross sexual imposition. He was sentenced to terms of 10 to 25 years in prison ("Cases Involving," 2004).

In 1994, former University of Florida player Tony Davis was accused of hitting and sexually assaulting his former girlfriend. Davis was charged with one count of aggravated assault and two counts of sexual battery. He pleaded no contest to two charges of battery and entered a deferred prosecution agreement requiring him to refrain from violating any laws for two years ("Cases Involving," 2004).

Weldon English, Eric Yarbrough, and Calvin Robinson Jr., then members of the Southern Methodist University football team, were accused of raping a 16-year-old girl in 1994 at a motel in Texas. English and Yarbrough pleaded guilty to a reduced charge of sexual assault; each received seven years of probation. Robinson pleaded guilty to a reduced charge of aggravated assault and received four years of probation ("Cases Involving," 2004).

In 1994, Michael Gibson, former Florida State player, received five life sentences—four for rape and one for armed burglary—for an attack on a student whom he raped, robbed, shot and left for dead in her apartment in Tallahassee, Florida. Gibson is also serving two 40-year sentences for two other rapes ("Former RB convicted of rape faces resentencing," 2003).

Former Clemson Tiger Andre Humphrey was accused of assault with intent to commit criminal sexual assault in 1994. He was accepted into a pretrial intervention program that included counseling and 50 hours of community service ("Cases Involving," 2004).

In 1994, DeAnthony Hall, former member of the Arkansas football team, was charged with the attempted rape of an 18-year-old woman in a dormitory for athletes. He pleaded guilty to a reduced charge of public sexual misconduct and was sentenced to one year in jail with six months suspended and fined $1,000 ("Cases Involving," 2004).

Also in 1994, Keith Mills, Jeff Johnson, and Nakia Thompson, then members of the East Tennessee State football team, were accused of having sex with two girls, ages 15 and 13, in a dorm room. All three players were charged with statutory rape. They pleaded guilty to a reduced charge of contributing to the delinquency of a minor (a misdemeanor). They received suspended jail sentences of 11 months and 29 days of probation and were ordered to perform 96 hours of community service ("Cases Involving," 2004).

In 1995, Arthur Turner Jr., a former UNLV football player, was accused of raping an 18-year-old student. He was charged with sexual assault but pleaded guilty to a reduced charge of false imprisonment, a gross misdemeanor ("Cases Involving," 2004).

Rahsetnu Jenkins, former University of Missouri football player, was charged with felony rape in 1995. He pleaded guilty to reduced charges of first-degree sexual misconduct and third-degree assault, both misdemeanors. He was given a one-year suspended sentence and two years of supervised probation on the misconduct charge and 60 days in county jail on the assault charge ("Cases Involving," 2004).

Ike Johnson, Thomas Washington, Sam Carter, and Derrick Carter, all of whom played for Idaho State, were charged with statutory rape in a case involving a 14-year-old girl. They pleaded guilty to a reduced charge of misdemeanor battery in 1995. Each was sentenced to a year of probation and ordered to pay $350 in fines and costs and to serve 10 days of community service ("Cases Involving," 2004).

Brian Edmonds and James Crawford, former Virginia Tech players, were accused of raping a female student in their apartment in 1996. Both players were indicted on rape and attempted sodomy charges. Each conceded that the prosecution had enough evidence to convict them of attempted aggravated sexual battery, but they did not admit guilt. They received one-year suspended sentences ("Cases Involving," 2004).

Michael Mitchell Gooden, Marlon Evis Jones, Dalin Montrell Smith, Emmitt Michael Smith, and Christopher Sorrell, former Grambling State football players, were accused of having sex with a 15-year-old girl in 1996. They were charged with having sex with a juvenile. They pleaded guilty to a reduced charge of contributing to the delinquency of a minor. They received suspended sentences of six months in jail ("Cases Involving," 2004).

In 1998, former Iowa player Robbie Crockett was accused of having sex with a 13-year-old girl and was charged with third-degree criminal sexual conduct. Crockett pleaded guilty to one count of fourth-degree criminal sexual conduct and was sentenced to 90 days in prison and three years of probation. He was also ordered to pay fines and court costs of more than $2,700 and to pay for the victim's counseling ("Cases Involving," 2004).

In 2000, Shevin Wiggins, former Nebraska football player, allegedly fondled a 14-year-old girl. He was charged with a felony count of sexual assault. Wiggins later pleaded guilty to a misdemeanor charge of contributing to the delinquency of a minor ("Cases Involving," 2004).

Three members of the Navy football team, Shaka Amin Martin, Cordrea Brittingham, and Arion Williams, were accused of assaulting a female midshipman and charged with sexual assault in 2001. The players agreed to leave the academy; charges were placed on the inactive docket ("Cases Involving," 2004).

In 2002, former Notre Dame football player, Abram Elam was convicted of sexual battery. He was acquitted on charges of conspiracy to commit rape. Elam received an 18-month suspended sentence and two years' probation ("Cases Involving," 2004).

In 2004, then Virginia Tech quarterback Marcus Vick was sentenced to 30 days in jail after being convicted on charges related to a party with underage girls. Vick was convicted of misdemeanor charges of contributing to the delinquency of a minor. In addition to the jail time, Vick was fined $2,250. Two of Vick's former teammates also were convicted of contributing to the delinquency of a minor. Tailback Mike Imoh, who was 19 at the time, was sentenced to ten days in jail and fined $750. Wide receiver Brenden Hill, also 19, was sentenced to 20 days in jail and fined $1,500 ("Marcus Vick convicted of misdemeanors," 2004).

In October 2007, Northern Colorado backup punter Mitch Cozad was sentenced to seven years in prison for stabbing starting punter Rafael Mendoza the night of September 11, 2006. Cozad was convicted of second-degree assault, but was acquitted of the charge of attempted first-degree murder. Cozad could have been sentenced to the maximum punishment under the law for the assault conviction: 16 years in prison ("Ex-Northern Colorado punter Cozad sentenced to seven years," 2007).

In November 2007, Oklahoma State linebacker, Chris Collins, was sentenced by jury to ten years probation for aggravated sexual assault of a 12-year-old girl. The judge also ordered him to register as a sex offender, perform 750 hours of community service, and pay for one year of counseling for the victim. Collins pleaded guilty one day before his trial was to start and three days after playing in Oklahoma State's 38–35 home loss to Texas. The incident occurred in May 2004 when Collins was 17 years old and the girl was 12. Collins admitted he had sex with the girl at a hotel. Collins did not play his senior year at Texas High School in Texarkana because of the charge against him. A scholarship offer from the University of Texas was rescinded, but in 2006, Oklahoma State offered him a scholarship (Evans, 2007).

College Basketball

In 1995, former Evansville player, Parrish Casebier, was convicted of two felonies—rape and sexual misconduct—with a minor. Casebier was sentenced to eight years in prison ("Cases Involving," 2004).

Michael V. Haley II, former Wright State University basketball player, was convicted of 23 felonies involving a 1995 rape, aggravated robbery and kidnapping in Dayton, Ohio. He was sentenced to 131 to 311 years in prison ("Cases Involving," 2004).

In 1999, Noel Jackson, former Weber State player, pleaded guilty to gross lewdness and was sentenced to three months in jail. He had originally been charged with rape and forcible sexual abuse against a 23-year-old woman ("Cases Involving," 2004).

Former University of Iowa basketball player Pierre Pierce pleaded guilty to a misdemeanor charge of assault causing injury in 2002. He received one year of probation and 200 hours of community service. He was also ordered to get counseling and was forbidden to have contact with the accuser. Pierce was accused of rape, but he was charged with felony sexual assault. Pierce contended that the sex was consensual ("Cases Involving," 2004).

Formerly recruited by Roy Williams, men's basketball coach at the University of North Carolina, Chapel Hill, JamesOn Curry pleaded guilty in 2004 to drug charges and was sentenced to three years' probation. The leading scorer in North Carolina state high school basketball history, Curry had committed to North Carolina until Williams revoked his offer because of the incident ("Curry pleads guilty to drug charges," 2004). Despite his conviction on felony drug charges,

Curry was offered a scholarship at Oklahoma State under coach Eddie Sutton. After playing for Oklahoma for three years, and earning All-Big Twelve honors, the Chicago Bulls drafted Curry with their 51st pick in the NBA draft (Theodore, 2007).

In 2005, former Baylor University basketball player Carlton Dotson was sentenced to 35 years in prison for the murder of former teammate Patrick Dennehy, whose remains were found in a field a few miles from Baylor's campus. Dennehy's death led to an investigation of the men's basketball team after it was found that, then, Head Coach Dave Bliss had given Dennehy and other team members tuition money. Further, evidence surfaced that drug use by some basketball players had not been reported. Ultimately, the Baylor scandals led the resignation of Dave Bliss and Athletic Director Tom Stanton as well as NCAA probation. Dotson is not eligible for parole until he serves at least 17 years in prison (González, 2005).

Females

In 1994, one of the most bizarre sports scandals occurred when it was discovered that ice skating star Tonya Harding engaged in a plot to injure fellow teammate Nancy Kerrigan in order to enhance her own chances of medaling in the upcoming Winter Olympics. Harding's ex-husband, Jeff Gillooly, along with Shawn Eckhardt, Shane Stant and Derrick Smith arranged the assault on Kerrigan. On January 6, 1994, following a practice session, Kerrigan was clubbed just above her right knee by a man using a retractable metal baton as a weapon. Harding pleaded guilty to a felony charge of conspiracy to hinder an investigation and was fined $100,000 and given three years' probation as well as 500 hours of community service. Jeff Gillooly was sentenced to two years in prison and a $100,000 fine; accomplices Shawn Eckhardt, Shane Stant and Derrick Smith were all sentenced to 18 months in prison. Following her conviction, the U.S. Figure Skating Association stripped Harding of her 1994 National Championship title and banned her for life (Teitelbaum, 2005).

One of the only female athletes on record to be accused of murder, San Diego State University track star Latoyonda Promise Mose was charged in July 2002 with the slaying death of her boyfriend, Alan Hardy. Mose claimed that Hardy beat her and she stabbed him to death in self-defense. The court determined that Hardy maintained a history of domestic violence. Mose pleaded guilty to involuntary manslaughter and was sentenced to one year in prison (Teitelbaum, 2005).

Another incident regarding a female athlete and a murder charge is, arguably, the most disturbing incident on record. On August 12, 2007, former Mercyhurst volleyball player Teri Rhodes gave birth to a baby girl and then proceeded to put the newborn in a plastic bag and left it on the floor of the bathtub as she showered. While searching Rhodes' computer, investigators found she had been researching internet topics including, "what can kill a fetus," "alternative methods of ending pregnancy" and "herbal abortion techniques" ("Ex-Mercyhurst athlete guilty in newborn's death," 2008, p. 1). On August 6, 2008, Rhodes pleaded guilty to voluntary manslaughter and faces a maximum of 10 to 20 years in prison. On November 21, 2008, Rhodes was sentenced to 9 to 18 years in prison ("Breaking News: Teri Rhodes Sentenced," 2008).

Once considered one of the best female athletes in the world, Marion Jones was sentenced in January 2008 in a New York federal court to six months in jail for lying in two grand jury investigations about her use of the performance-enhancing steroids. Federal prosecutors handling the Bay Area Laboratory Co-Operative (BALCO) investigation gathered evidence which was used to persuade Jones to plead guilty to making false statements. Jones admitted in court that from September 2000 through July 2001, her former trainer, Trevor Graham, gave her a substance, which he told her was flaxseed oil. In 2001, when Jones realized the substance was actually a performance-enhancing drug, she ended her training relationship with Graham (Wilson & Schmidt, 2007).

Jones won a total of five medals in the 2000 Olympics in Sydney — gold medals in the 100-meter, 200-meter and 1,600-meter relay, and bronze medals in the 400-meter relay and the long jump. She pleaded for a lighter sentence but the U.S. District Judge gave her the maximum term so as to send a message to other high-profile athletes who serve as role models. Additionally, the judge ordered Jones to perform 400 hours of community service during each of her two years of probation. Since her conviction, Jones has returned all of her Olympic medals and the International Olympic Committee has ordered that her records be expunged from its record books. Marion Jones is the first athlete to be convicted and sentenced in a government investigation of steroids use in sports (Neil, 2008).

On April 5, 2008, former U.S. professional team champion cyclist Tammy Thomas was convicted of three counts of perjury and one count of obstruction of justice for lying to a grand jury about her steroid use. In 2002, after testing positive for the previously undetectable steroid *norbolethone*, Thomas received a lifetime competition ban from the U.S. Anti-Doping Agency. In 2003, Thomas testified to a grand jury that she had never taken performance-enhancing drugs or received them from Patrick Arnold, the chemist who worked with BALCO. Thomas's failed drug test, which led to her lifetime suspension, was her second doping offense. On October 10, 2008, Thomas was sentenced to six months house arrest (Vinton, 2008); she had faced one to three years in federal prison (Wilson, 2006).

Summary of Findings

While this chapter does not provide an exhaustive list of athletes who have been convicted of a crime, it highlights numerous criminal athlete convictions. Overall, athletes (n=88) were charged with 146 crimes. The percent distribution for athletes' charges was as follows: sex crime (32 percent); rape (27 percent); assault and/or battery (12 percent); drugs and/or weapons (11 percent); CDM (4 percent); murder (4 percent); homicide (2 percent); tax evasion (2 percent) and, other (6 percent) (see Figure 10.3).

Of the 88 incidents, 77 percent of athletes' charges were reduced. The reduced charges revealed the following: assault and/or battery (35 percent); sex crime (24 percent); CDM (20 percent); rape (3 percent); drugs and/or weapons (3 percent); murder/conspiracy to commit murder (3 percent); tax evasion (2 percent) and, other (10 percent) (see Figure 10.4).

Figure 10.3 Athletes' Charges

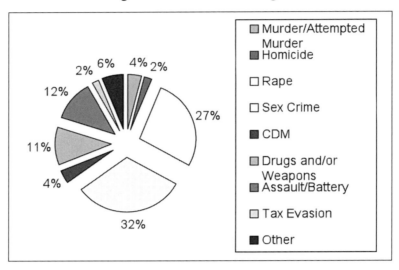

Figure 10.4 Athletes' Reduced Charges

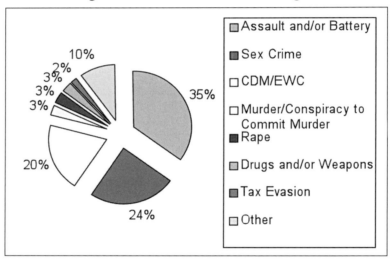

In sum, of the NFL incidents highlighted, a majority of the crimes committed were either sexual in nature, or murder. As for the NBA incidents, half were sexual crimes. Of the MLB incidents, 33 percent were crimes of a sexual nature. The majority of highlighted NHL crimes consisted of impaired driving leading to the death of another person. Of the eight incidents in the sport of boxing, a majority were sexual crimes. NCAA college football and men's basketball incidents were, also, overwhelmingly crimes, sexual in nature. As for the five incidents involving females, two were perjury charges stemming from steroid use; the three other crimes committed were involuntary manslaughter, voluntary manslaughter, and assault/battery.

Why are males committing sexual crimes at such a high rate? Possible explanations for this are discussed below. It is important to recognize, however, that males and females are socialized quite differently about the behaviors that are deemed acceptable or expected in the realm of athletics.

Not only it is interesting to assess criminal trends based on sport and sex, but it is also interesting to note that although males (for example, college football players) were charged with numerous sexual crimes, 89 percent of the perpetrators avoided jail time equal to that of Marian Jones' sentence (6 months in prison) for perjury. This raises an interesting ethical dilemma: which crime should be punished more harshly — violating a person sexually or lying under oath about performance enhancing drug use?

Why do Athletes Commit Crimes?

Researchers have suggested a number of reasons why male athletes might be engaging in criminal behavior. Berry and Smith (2000) offered four sociological explanations for the prominence of crime by athletes: (1) values and norms associated with sports; (2) single-sex environment and sexism; (3) the public's infatuation with athletes; and (4) the absence of regulating crime in sports. Building on the framework of Berry and Smith, it is proposed that the following reasons may explain, in part, why male athletes commit crimes: (1) adherence to a win-at-all cost mentality; (2) male dominance and entitlement; and (3) celebrity status.

What motivates female athletes to commit crimes? Research in this area is lacking; however, with the rise of criminal behavior amongst female athletes scholars must begin to consider the factors that may play a role in a female athlete's decision to engage in criminal activity. Regarding the two female athletes who were convicted of perjury, the notion of blind adherence to "The Sport Ethic" may well have played a role in their decision to deliberately go outside of the rules of the game in order to succeed — this notion is discussed below.

Adherence to a Win-at-All-Cost Mentality

Jay Coakley (2007) defined "**The Sport Ethic**" as *a set of norms that many people in power and performance sports have accepted as the dominant criteria for defining what it means to be an athlete and to successfully claim and identity as an athlete* (p. 168). "What it means to be athlete" includes: making sacrifices for the team, playing through pain, giving *110 percent effort*, and striving for distinction. These qualities, taught in the proper way and learned appropriately by athletes, can be positive. What happens, however, when athletes (as well as coaches) take the notion of striving for distinction to an extreme level? For example, many athletes, oftentimes as a result of encouragement from their coach, adhere to a "whatever it takes" or "win-at-all-cost" mentality in their quest to succeed. When this shift takes place, athletes engage in what has been defined as "gamespersonlike" behavior. **Gamespersonship** *is the art and science of gaining a strategic advantage by morally questionable means.* Athletes who adhere to a "win-at-all-cost" mentality effectively debase the notion of sport and fair competition.

On the flip side, **sportspersonship** *is the adherence to both the letter and the spirit of the rules of the game. A sportsperson respects his/her opponents, the offi-*

cials and the game itself; they display courtesy, fairness, and grace in losing. A sportsperson refuses to seek and unfair advantage. When sportsperson-like behavior gives way to gamesperson-like behavior athletes are, in effect, adhering to a distorted view of what it means to be an athlete. Effectively, athletes believe that engaging in overly aggressive and intimidating acts makes them a better competitor; when in reality, it moves them into a realm of violent behavior, which may have a carryover effect. The carryover effect is the notion that intimidation, aggression and violence in the sport setting *may* carry over into the non-sport setting (Coakley, 2007).

If athletes adhere to a distorted notion of what it means to be an athlete (embracing a "win-at-all-cost" mentality), this can lead to the belief that violent behavior is acceptable in all settings. Consider Chandler and Johnson's (1999) study, which examined the abusive behaviors of college athletes verses those of non-athletes. Results revealed that athletes were more likely to have fondled someone of the opposite sex against his/her will (15 percent) than non-athletes (5 percent) (n=342 athletes; 90 percent African American, 94 percent 18–22 years, 201=male, 141=female). Athletes were also more likely to have forced sex with someone of the opposite sex (7 percent) than non-athletes (2 percent). More athletes than non-athletes characterized the family in which they were raised as physically abusive and also characterized their grade school and high school experiences to be more physically abusive than non-athletes.

In 2003, Smith and Stewart investigated the differences in sexually aggressive attitudes and behaviors among contact sport athletes, non-contact sport athletes and non-athletes (n=282 male undergraduates students at an English university). The results of their study affirmed that men who hold rape-supportive beliefs and who are hostile toward women are more likely to commit rape than those who do not hold such attitudes. Men who believe that rape is the fault of the victim and who find violence against women acceptable are the same men who report actually carrying out such acts of violence.

Results also revealed that men who are more competitive and adhere to a "win-at-all-cost" mentality reported being more sexually aggressive. The common denominator here may well be the notion of dominance. In order to win, athletes perceive that they must dominate (in this case, at any cost). Further, a common motivation behind sexually aggressive behavior is the need for men to dominate women (Smith & Stewart, 2003). Their findings did not, however, support the notion that contact sport athletes are significantly more sexually aggressive than non-contact athletes and non-athletes.

Male Dominance & Entitlement

As was discussed above, male athletes who adhere to a win-at-all-cost mentality tend to be more sexually aggressive toward women (Smith & Stewart, 2003). Taken a step further, Berry and Smith (2000) suggested that when males are socialized, aggressive behavior is oftentimes encouraged and is viewed as being worthy of respect. Furthermore, male aggression has traditionally been accepted as normal and even positive. Such aggressive behavior, when placed in a sex-exclusive setting, may create a heightened level of aggressive behavior. Berry and Smith found that in a mono-sexual environment (a setting or environment consisting of one sex exclusively), males tended to display increased levels of sexually aggressive behaviors toward women.

Do members of athletic teams differ from non-members in their likelihood to commit sexual assault? Crosset, Benedict and McDonald (1995) reported that men in sex-segregated groups (i.e., sports teams) are more likely to engage in group sexual offenses, such as gang rape. Humphrey and Kahn (2000) reported that the likelihood of committing sexual assault depends on the perceived risk of a group. High-risk groups reported significantly higher levels of sexual aggression, hostility, and male peer support for sexual violence toward women than member of perceived low-risk groups. Differences between groups perceived to have low-risk verses high-risk parties was related to subjects' perception of low verses high-risk for sexual assault. For example, a friendlier party, which had an equal number of males and females, where men treated women respectfully, was considered low-risk for sexual assault. Whereas, a high-risk party was one where there was a much greater number of males than females, more segregation based on sex, where men treated women in more degrading ways (Boswell & Spade, 1996). The high-risk setting was also less conducive to conversation (i.e., increased music volume, increased crowds) and as a result more likely to be places where sexual aggression occurred. In such settings where there was a decreased opportunity to talk, men became more aggressive and degrading to women (Humphrey & Kahn, 2000).

The Misrepresentation of African-American Athletes as Criminals

Are African-American athletes *actually* more involved in crime, or are they *presumed* to be more involved in crime? Before examining the scholarly research on this subject, it is important to note that African-Americans constitute about 13 percent of the population, but comprise nearly half of the prison population in the United States (Fulbright, 2007). For years, criminologists have speculated that there is a bias in the criminal justice system against African-Americans. For example, African-Americans are arrested at a rate five times greater than that of their white counterparts. Furthermore, African-Americans are more likely to be charged with serious and multiple offenses, more likely to be convicted, and more likely to be more severely sentenced than whites (Stone, 1999). Does a similar discrepancy exist in the sports world?

Berry and Smith (2000) pointed out that the extensive media coverage given to athletes, especially coverage that emphasizes African-American males solely as athletes, is not necessarily helpful in the movement toward racial equality. Sociologically, seeing African-American males only as successful athletes sends a strong message about opportunities for success that exist for African-American males (i.e., that they can only achieve success through athletics). Widespread coverage in just one area (i.e., the sport setting) creates an extremely limited, and ultimately distorted, picture of what African-American males can actually accomplish in society. For example, how often does the media portray African-American males as doctors, lawyers, CEOs of companies, and other high-ranking positions in society, compared to their portrayal of African-Americans as athletes? As such, while the coverage for African-American males in sport is vast, it reaffirms the existing racial ideology which suggests that whites males hold the ultimate positions of power and authority in society (intellectual capability), whereas black males are gifted athletes (physical capability). Therefore, African-American males who do hold positions of social power in society represent an upset of the social order, a violation of social expectations (Berry & Smith, 2000).

This stereotype must be broken; namely, that African-Americans are solely known and praised for their upward mobility through excellence in sport (Smith, 1995). Further, when an African-American athlete is involved in crime, it reinforces public opinion about, and media portrayals of, African-Americans' disproportionate involvement in crime. Berry and Smith (2000) call this the *politics of representation* — African-American sport figures are represented as criminals, and criminal athletes are represented as African-Americans.

Craig's (2000) research confirms Berry and Smith's (2000) notions that African-American males are more often *perceived* to be the perpetrator of a criminal act than are their white male counterparts. In examining the perceptions of professional athletes who batter, Craig's (2000) results suggested that when subjects were questioned about an incident of assault they in which they perceived the batterer to be Black, they noted it as "a more typical" incident than that in which they perceived the batterer to be White. Craig's results are powerful because they suggest that when faced with a choice between an African-American athlete and a Caucasian athlete as the perpetrator of a crime, people more often perceive the African-American athlete to be the criminal.

The NBA is comprised of 75 percent African-Americans and just 21 percent Caucasians; similarly, African-Americans make up 67 percent of the NFL (Caucasians just 31 percent) (Lapchick, 2007). There is more than a 3:1 difference in the racial make up in the NBA and more than a 2:1 racial ratio difference in the NFL. Recognizing the vast lopsidedness in the racial makeup of the NFL and NBA is necessary in order to accurately assess whether African-American athletes commit more crimes than Caucasian athletes. Statistically, one would expect the ratio of crimes committed to be proportional to that of the size of the group (i.e., since African-American players comprise 75 percent of the NBA, the ratio of athlete crime would, on average, be three incidents of criminal behavior committed by African-Americans to one criminal act committed by a Caucasian). This begs an interesting question: if African-American males constitute just 13 percent of the U.S. population, then why do they make up nearly half of the prison population? Based on these percentages and the work of Berry and Smith (2000), the notion that African-American males are *misrepresented* more often as criminals has legitimacy, especially in light of the existing racial ideology.

Celebrity Status

With all of the media attention they receive, athletes are placed on a pedestal where they are granted a highly privileged status that makes them feel as if they are immune from taking personal responsibility for their actions. When athletes are not punished for their actions, this reinforces the notion that they are above the law (Benedict, 1998a).

In 1997, Benedict and Klien examined the arrest and conviction rates of professional and collegiate athletes accused of sexual assault ($n=217$; from 1986–1995). While allegations of sexual assault against an athlete were far more likely to result in an arrest and in an indictment, they were significantly less likely to be convicted.

> Twenty-one percent of the time no formal action was taken. Of the 172 who were arrested, 32 percent had their charges dismissed. Eight of the remaining 117 athletes who were indicted saw charges against them dismissed prior to trial, while 37 percent reached a plea agreement and 56 percent stood trial before a jury. Fifty (or 76 percent) of the 66 athletes who stood trial were acquitted. Only 10 of the 66 athletes standing trial (15 percent) were found guilty by a jury while 6 (9 percent) ended in a hung jury (Benedict & Klien, 1997, p. 89).

Benedict and Klien discovered a 23 percent discrepancy in the conviction rates between the national sample (54 percent) verses the athletes (31 percent). Why does such a vast difference exist? Two potential hypotheses are offered for this difference:

> (1) the athlete's social environment ... includes the presence of women who appear accessible to athletes ("groupies") and who, as a result, make a consent defense the strategy of preference, and (2) the larger institutional safety net that is available to athletes accused of criminal behavior. The latter includes exceptional financial resources and powerful advocates in the form of coaches, agents, lawyers, and pillars of the community (p. 91).

The professional sports leagues (NFL, NBA, MLB, and NHL) prefer handling the illegal acts of athletes (such as drug and alcohol abuse, and criminal acts of on-the-field violence) in-house. Prior to the new leadership of Commissioner Roger Goodell, the NFL did not take disciplinary action when players committed violent crimes, such as rape, assault, and battery (Benedict, 1998b). What's more, the leagues scarcely punished athletes significantly enough to cause athletes to stop committing such acts. Oftentimes, athletes who had revenue-producing value in the eyes of the league were given a meaningless "slap on the wrist" instead of a deservedly harsh punishment. Under Goodell's watch, however, the NFL has taken a stricter stance against athletes' violent and/or criminal behavior. The NFL's personal conduct policy now specifies behaviors that will not be tolerated ("NFL Players Association," n.d.).

In American society, athletes are viewed as role models—especially for children. When an athlete commits a crime, violent or otherwise, it serves to remind the public that just because athletes are revered does not mean they are immune from behaving in ways that are contrary to what is socially, ethically and legally acceptable. More importantly, when an athlete commits a crime and is not punished by their respective league and/or the legal system, this sends an even more disturbing message to the youth. Misbehavior (in the form of criminal activity) absent of significant consequences is antithetical to what parents teach their children. If a child sees an athlete behave in criminal fashion that results in little or no consequences, then it sends a message to the child that such behavior is acceptable.

The onus of responsibility lies not only on the individual athlete to behave in a way that is ethically responsible and respectful, but also on the leadership of the professional and collegiate sports leagues. When the leagues do not significantly punish an athlete for criminal behavior, they send the message that they value money over what is right or ethical. While, admittedly, we live in a capitalistic society where money holds great value, it certainly should not be held higher than doing what is moral and ethical for the well-being of society. If leagues continue to employ known criminals, then they too have made a deliberate move to adhere to a win-at-costs mentality whereby ethics have been sacrificed in the name of money.

Solutions

Kohlberg's Theory of Moral Development

In 1958, renowned psychologist Lawrence Kohlberg developed "the six stages of moral development." Kohlberg's (1964) research suggested that as people learn to think critically and seek to arrive at the best moral solution to a problem, they develop an increased level of moral awareness.

At stage one, Kohlberg theorized, individuals act solely on behalf of their own interests (egocentric). Further, the only reason for doing what is considered by society to be moral or legal is due to a fear of punishment. During stage two, Kohlberg found that individuals consider their own interests as well as the interests of others (altruism). Altruism is also known simply as *The Golden Rule*, namely, *do unto others as you would have them do to you.*

As people move into stage three, their reasons for behaving ethically center around the desire to please those in their immediate sphere of influence. People acting at stage four have a heightened sense of moral awareness in that their reason for doing the right thing is based on a genuine concern and respect for social systems. At stage five, individuals behave morally based on the notion of a "social contract" (doing the right thing even though others may not). Finally, at stage six, people act in a moral fashion because of what Kohlberg deemed "universal principles." Kohlberg found that people acting at stage six do what is right because they have the utmost respect for the values of human dignity, justice and equality for all.

In examining the decisions athletes make, it is important to assess the stage at which they acting. Are these athletes "stunted" in their moral development and, in effect, acting consistently at stage one? Utilizing Kohlberg's theory of moral development can aid athletes in making better decisions. In difficult situations, athletes should consider why they are doing what they are doing and who they are affecting. Athletes should aim to be making decisions consistently at stages three through six.

Preventative Programs

In 2000, Jackson and Davis introduced a preventative program called PAYS (Power, Attitude, Youth, and Speed—qualities common to highly successful athletes but also qualities which can translate into dominance and aggression). The program takes existing qualities and explains the appropriate setting for displaying such qualities (i.e., on-the-field v. off-the-field). The prevention program begins with communication training, specifically as it relates to the sexual expectations in a relationship. The second stage encourages athletes to utilize principle of "the golden rule" (also known as Kohlberg's stage 2-Altruism) when communicating with their sexual partner (i.e., treat your partner the way you would like to be treated). Finally, PAYS encourages athletes to support each another by holding one another accountable when one member is not acting respectfully. The goal of the PAYS program is to provide male athletes with the tools that will allow them to properly discriminate between behaviors that are appropriate on-the-field verses off-the-field.

Kathy Redmond, who in 1997 settled a Title IX lawsuit against The University of Nebraska and founded The National Coalition Against Violent Athletes (NCAVA), has established another preventative program called *Intercept*. *Intercept* uses sport as a way to develop values such as fairness, accountability, leadership, and tolerance.

Redmond suggests that because playing sport is such a valuable way to socialize children, it is imperative to eliminate criminal behavior among athletes. As role models for America's youth, athletes must display sportsperson-like qualities over those of a gamesperson. The warning that must be heeded is that if youth sport shifts its focus to more closely mirror the win-at-all-cost mentality of college and professional sports, children will inevitably adopt gamesperson-like values as well. As a result of such critical issues, *Intercept* seeks to assess the types of attitudes and environments that contribute to a hostile atmosphere. Furthermore, *Intercept* seeks to promote positive change through education by conducting training and workshops for coaches, athletes, administrators and parents.

Staffo (2001) proposed yet another intervention, suggesting helpful strategies for changing student athletes' attitudes towards violence:

1. Teach unconditional respect for others in order to create an environment where everyone feels valued.
2. Encourage athletes to treat everyone with dignity, from fellow student to referees.
3. Continually reinforce social skills and self-control, and teach athletes how to be less critical and judgmental.
4. Teach the merits and means of good sportspersonship and then, to show that it is truly valued, reward such behavior.
5. Teach stress and anger management and nonviolent conflict resolution, especially among athletes in aggressive contact sports.
6. Provide structure and a clear set of rules, correct inappropriate behavior, and hold students accountable for such behavior.
7. Provide fair, consistent consequences for breaking the stated rules.
8. Develop strategies to reduce the probability of repeated rule-breaking, including stiffer consequences meted out when unacceptable behavior occurs (p. 41).

Further, Staffo (2001) recommended seven ways that schools and universities can better handle issues of athlete misconduct:

1. Systematically assess problems and implement a unified behavior-management and discipline program.

2. Consistently enforce a zero-tolerance policy on violence, along with immediate intervention by school and law-enforcement officials when warning indicators are present.
3. Provide peer counseling, character education, and a mentor program for those who need it.
4. When appropriate, provide information or classes on parenting, child development, child rearing, or living in abusive relationships.
5. Organize a "Student Advocacy Board for Safe Schools," with students who are trained in peer mediation serving as officers.
6. Appoint an "Advisory Council for Safe Schools" to advise the local department of children's affairs.
7. Provide emergency radios for all schools (p. 42).

Athletic administrators have a duty to report incidents of criminal behavior committed by athletes to the proper legal authorities. Masteralexis (1995) stressed the importance of the athletic director handling the situation properly; otherwise, the victim may have a legal cause of action against not only the perpetrator, but also the athletic department and the university. From a practical perspective, it is critical that athletic administrators adhere to university policies, understand criminal as well as sexual harassment laws, and refer the problem to the appropriate university office and/or legal authorities.

Summary

This chapter sought answers to five important questions. First, what kind of crimes are athletes committing? Male athletes are most commonly convicted of sexual assault and/or rape, assault and/or battery, DUI or DWI, theft, and drug related charges. Conversely, since there are only a handful of incidences of criminal acts perpetrated by female athletes, conclusive trends cannot be established. However, in two of the five female cases discussed it does appear that female athletes are also overconforming to "The Sport Ethic" in that they are willing to break the rules (use performance enhancing drugs and lie about it) in order to "win-at-any-cost".

Secondly, what sort of punishments are athletes receiving for their involvement in criminal activity? It appears, based on Benedict and Yaeger's (1998) data that, in the case of professional athletes, about one quarter of the athletes charged with a criminal offense were convicted and/or pleaded guilty, another quarter of the charges were dismissed, and the remaining half were nearly split between pending, reduced charge, acquittal, and no contest. According to Benedict and Klien's (1997) study, criminal complaints against professional and college athletes regarding sexual assault were likely to result in an arrest and indictment; however, they were less likely to be convicted of the crime. This may be due, in part, to the "celebrity status" of athletes.

Thirdly, why are athletes committing crimes? There are a number of factors contributing to an athletes' decision to engage in criminal activity, some of which include: 1) athletes' adherence to a win-at-all costs mentality; 2) male dominance and perceived entitlement; and 3) the "celebrity status" of athletes.

Fourthly, since the NFL and NBA overwhelmingly employ African-American players, is it fair to suggest that African-American athletes commit more criminal acts than their Caucasian counterparts? The media, oftentimes, paints the picture that it is only the African-American athletes who commit crimes. The inaccuracy in this analysis is that since the NBA is comprised of 75 percent African-Americans then, statistically, one would expect the crime ratio to be similar.

Finally, can anything be done to prevent athletes from engaging in criminal activity? The answer is—let's hope so! In order to reduce the number of athletes engaging in criminal activity, an overhaul in the area of moral reasoning needs to take place. Utilization of Kohlberg's theory of moral development provides athletes with a framework by which they can analyze why they are making the decisions they are and who they are affecting. Finally, the PAYS and *Intercept* programs provide preventative strategies that serve as effective ways to reduce the number of criminal acts committed by athletes.

References

Apologetic Vick gets 23-month sentence on dogfighting charges. (2007, December 11). *ESPN.com*. Retrieved April 21, 2008, from http://sports.espn.go.com/nfl/news/story?id=3148549

Benedict, J. (1998b, November 4). Felons don't belong in the NFL. *New York Times*, p. A27.

Benedict, J., & Klien, A. (1997). Arrest and conviction rates for athletes accused of sexual assault. *Sociology of Sport Journal, 14,* 86–94.

Benedict, J., & Yaeger, D. (1998). *Pros and cons: The criminals who play in the NFL*. New York: Warner Books.

Benedict, J.R. (1998a). *Athletes and acquaintance rape*. Thousand Oaks, CA: Sage.

Berry, B., & Smith, E. (2000). Race, sport, and crime: The misrepresentation of African-Americans in team sports and crime. *Sociology of Sport Journal, 17,* 171–197.

Boswell, A.A., & Spade, J.Z. (1996). Fraternities and collegiate rape culture: Why are some fraternities more dangerous places for women? *Gender & Society, 10,* 133–147.

Boxer Riddick Bowe sentenced to 30 days in jail for kidnapping wife and kids. (2000, March 20). *NBET*. Retrieved August 27, 2008, from http://findarticles.com/p/articles/mi_m1355/is_15_97/ai_61487245

Breaking News: Teri Rhodes Sentenced. (2008, November 21). *ErieBlogs*. Retrieved February 2, 2009, from http://www.erieblogs.com/2008/11/21/breaking-news-teri-rhodes-sentenced/

Cases involving athletes and sexual assault. (2004, May 28). *USA Today*. Retrieved April 20, 2008, from http://usatoday.printthis.clickability.com/pt/cpt?action=cpt&title=USATODAY.com+-+Ca

Chandler, S.B., Johnson, D.J., & Carroll, P.S. (1999). Abusive behaviors of college athletes. *College Student Journal, 33(4),* 638.

Coakley, J. (2007). *Sports in society: Issues & controversies* (9th ed.). New York, NY: McGraw Hill.

Craig, K.M. (2000). Defeated athletes, abusive mates? Examining perceptions of professional athletes who batter. *Journal of Interpersonal Violence, 15*(11), 1224–1232.

Craig MacTavish. (n.d.). 1978 NHL amateur draft. Retrieved April 24, 2008, from http://www.hockeydraftcentral.com/1978/78153.html

Crosset, T. W., Benedict, J. R., & McDonald, M. A. (1995). Male student-athletes reported for sexual assault: A survey of campus police departments and judicial affairs offices. *Journal of Sport and Social Issues, 19*(2), 126–140.

Curnutte, M. (2008, August 20). Brown brings Henry back. *Cincinnati.com*. Retrieved August 25, 2008, from http://news.cincinnati.com/apps/pbcs.dll/article?AID=/20080820/SPT02/808200360/1062/spt&referrer=NEWSFRONTCAROUSEL

Curry pleads guilty to drug charges. (2004, April 5). *ESPN.com*. Retrieved April 20, 2008, from http://sports.espn.go.com/espn/print?id=1776102&type=story

Eitzen, S.D., & Sage, G.H. (2003). *Sociology of North American sport* (7th ed.). New York, NY: McGraw-Hill.

Evans, T. (2007, November 8). Oklahoma State player sentenced in sex assault. *New York Times*. Retrieved November 8, 2007, from http://www.nytimes.com/2007/11/08/sports/ncaafootball/08assault.html?ref=sports&page

Ex-Mercyhurst athlete guilty in newborn's death. (2008, August 6). *Pittsburgh Tribune-Review*. Retrieved September 1, 2008, from http://www.pittsburghlive.com/x/pittsburghtrib/news/regional/s_581375.html

Ex-NBA player Newman guilty of domestic battery. (2005, November 16). *ESPN.com*. Retrieved April 21, 2008, from http://sports.espn.go.com/nba/news/story?id=2226136

Ex-Northern Colorado punter Cozad sentenced to seven years. (2007, October 3). *ESPN.com*. Retrieved April 20, 2008, from http://sports.espn.go.com/espn/print?id=3046919&type

Former RB convicted of rape faces resentencing. (2003, September 26). *ESPN.com*. Retrieved August 27, 2008, from http://sports.espn.go.com/ncf/news/story?id=1624267

Fulbright, L. (2007, December 4). Bay area counties toughest on black drug offenders. *San Francisco Chronicle*. Retrieved September 8, 2008, from http://www.sfgate.com/cgi-bin/article.cgi?f=/c/a/2007/12/04/MNHHTNGVJ.DTL

González, A. (2005, June 6). Carlton Dotson sentenced to 35 years for murder of Baylor basketball player. *Associated Baptist Press*. Retrieved April 21, 2008, from http://www.abpnews.com/386.article

Gunman sentenced in Carruth case. (2001, April 6). *New York Times*, p. 7.

Haynesworth suspended for an unprecedented five games. (2006, October 3). ESPN.com. Retrieved August 27, 2008, from http://sports.espn.go.com/espn/print?id=2610577&type=story

Humphrey, S.E., & Kahn, A.S. (2000). Fraternities, athletic teams, and rape: Importance of identification with a risky group. *Journal of Interpersonal Violence, 15*(12), 1313–1322.

Jackson, T.L., & Davis, J.L. (2000). Prevention of sexual and physical assault toward women: A program for male athletes. *Journal of Community Psychology, 28*(6), 589–605.

Kari, S. (2007, October 11). Former NHL player convicted of drunk driving causing death. *CanWest News Service.* Retrieved April 21, 2008, from http://www.canada.com/calgaryherald/news/story.html?id=9536390f-0936-469a-84ed-baece34b17f8

Kohlberg, L. (1964). Development of character and moral ideology. *Review of Child Development Research, 1,* 383–431.

Lapchick, R. (2007). *Racial and gender report card.* University of Central Florida: Institute for Diversity and Ethics in Sport.

Lawyer says Pacman Jones to take deal. (2007, November 14). *New York Times Sport.* Retrieved February 3, 2008, from http://query.nytimes.com/gst/full page.html?res=980CE4DA1631F937A25752C1A9619C8B63&scp=1&sq=pacman+jones&st=nyt

Lipsyte, R. (1995, June 18). Many create the climate for violence. *The New York Times.* Retrieved August 25, 2008, from http://sports.espn.go.com/nfl/news/story?id=2962780

Marcus Vick convicted of misdemeanors. (2004, May 19). *Cable News Network.* Retrieved April 20, 2008, from http://www.cnn.com/2004/LAW/05/19/penalty.box/

Maske, M. (2006, October 3). Haynesworth suspended five games. *The Washington Post.* Retrieved September 9, 2008, from http://www.washingtonpost.com/wp-dyn/content/article/2006/10/02/AR2006100200807.html

Masteralexis, L.P. (1995). Sexual harassment and athletes: Legal and policy implications for athletic departments. *Journal of Sport and Social Issues, 19,* 141–156.

McCarthy, M., & Upton, J. (2006, May 4). Players, fan pay much different prices for brawl. *USA Today.* Retrieved August 27, 2008, from http://www.usatoday.com/sports/2006-05-04-comm-service-brawl_x.htm

Morrison foe charged. (1996, November 1). *The New York Times.* Retrieved August 27, 2008, from http://query.nytimes.com/gst/fullpage.html?res=9C02EFD71E39F932A35752C1A960958260&partner=rssnyt&emc=rss

Morrison says error in HIV test hurt career. (2007, July 22). *The New York Times.* Retrieved August 27, 2008, from http://www.nytimes.com/2007/07/22/sports/othersports/22boxing.html?_r=1&oref=slogin&pagewanted=print

Myers, G. (2008, April 7). Michael Vick playing prison football. *NYDailyNews.com.* Retrieved August 25, 2008, from http://www.nydailynews.com/sports/football/2008/04/05/2008-04-05_michael_vick_playing_prison_football.html

NBA players sentenced in brawl. (2005, September 23). *CBS News.* Retrieved August 27, 2008, from http://www.cbsnews.com/stories/2005/09/23/sportsline/main881281.shtml

Neil, M. (2008, January 11). Marion Jones gets 6 months; Disgraced Olympian lied about steroid use. *ABA Journal*. Retrieved February 3, 2008, from http://www.abajournal.com/news/marion_jones_gets_6_months_disgraced_olympian_lied_about_steroids_use/

NFL Players Association. (n.d). *Personal Conduct Policy*. Retrieved September 1, 2008, from http://www.nflplayers.com/user/template.aspx?fmid=181&lmid=336&pid=0&type=n#1

NFL suspended Lewis for two games. (2005, January 27). *ESPN.com*. Retrieved April 24, 2008, from http://sports.espn.go.com/nfl/news/story?id=1976064

Pacman to make first TNA appearance Thursday. (2007, August 6). *ESPN.com*. Retrieved August 25, 2008, from http://sports.espn.go.com/nfl/news/story?id=2962780

Pitcher sentenced, sent to anger management classes. (2005, June 30). *ESPN.com*. Retrieved August 27, 2008, from http://sports.espn.go.com/mlb/news/story?id=2098227

Plaschke, B. (2007, January 31). Tankful of excuses; Chicago Bears defensive lineman Johnson points the finger at everyone for his multiple run-ins with police and flat-out refuses to apologize. *Los Angeles Times*, p. D1.

Powell, C. (2004, December 19). The different faces of Ray Lewis; Images of Ravens' All-Pro linebacker sometimes seem to conflict. *The Washington Post*, p. E.01.

Pugmire, L. (2006, December 17). Athletes and guns: Special report; Loaded question; Possession, and use, of firearms by athletes has become a hot-button issue, triggering concern for pro leagues such as the NBA and NFL. *Los Angeles Times*, p. D1.

Redmond, K. (n.d.). The national coalition against violent athletes. Retrieved April 21, 2008, from http://www.ncava.org/news.html

Reynolds, T. (2006, October 16). Thomas fired over brawl comments. *TV Analyst*, p.1.

Ritter, K. (2008, January 9). Judge drops NFL's Titans from 'Pacman' Jones lawsuit in Vegas. *Yahoo Sports*. Retrieved February 3, 2008, from http://sports.yahoo.com/ nfl/news?slug=ap-pacmanlawsuit&prov=ap&type=lgns

Saraceno, J. (2007, June 27). Chew on this: Ten years on, Holyfield still fighting. *USA Today*. Retrieved August 27, 2008, from http://www.usatoday.com/sports/columnist/saraceno/2007-06-26-holyfield-tyson-ear_N.htm

Shipley, A., & Whoriskey, P. (2007, November 28). Probe begins in Taylor's death. *The Washington Post*. Retrieved August 25, 2008, from http://www.washington post.com/wp-dyn/content/story/2007/11/27/ST2007112702001.html

Smith, a former Celtic, gets a Split verdict. (1992, March 13). *New York Times*. Retrieved April 24, 2008, from http://query.nytimes.com/gst/fullpage.html?res=9E0CE2DC143AF930A25750C0A964958260

Smith, C. (1990, July 20). Rose sentenced to 5 months for filing false tax returns. The New York Times. Retrieved August 27, 2008, from http://query.nytimes.com/gst/fullpage.html?res=9C0CE7DA1F3EF933A15754C0A966958260

Smith, D., & Stewart, S. (2003). Sexual aggression and sports participation. *Journal of Sport Behavior, 26(4),* 384–396.

Smith, E. (1995). Hope via basketball: The ticket out of the ghetto? *Journal of Sport and Social Issues, 19,* 312–17.

Staffo, D.F. (2001). Strategies for reducing criminal violence among athletes. *Journal of Physical Education, Recreation and Dance, 72(6),* 39–42.

Stone, C. (1999, January). Race, crime, and the administration of justice: A summary of the available facts. *National Institute of Justice Journal, 293,* 26–32.

Strawberry to pay IRS back taxes. (2008, February 12). *MLB.com.* Retrieved August 27, 2008, from http://mlb.mlb.com/content/printer_friendly/mlb/y2008/m02/d12/c2371493.jsp

Strawberry's stay ends 11 months into 18-month term. (2003, April 8). *ESPN.com.* Retrieved August 27, 2008, from http://espn.go.com/mlb/news/2003/0408/1535388.html

Teitelbaum, S.H. (2005). *Sports heroes, fallen idols: How star athletes pursue self-destructive paths and jeopardize their careers.* Nebraska: The University of Nebraska.

Theodore, C. (2007, November 13). Game on for JamesOn. *National Basketball Association News.* Retreived April 20, 2008, from http://www.nba.com/bulls/news/curry_feature_071113.html?rss=true

Tyson gets 24 hours in jail, probation for drug possession, DUI. (2007, November 19). *ESPN.com.* Retrieved August 27, 2008, from http://sports.espn.go.com/espn/print?id=3118757&type=story\

Tyson on Washington: 'I just hate her guts'. (2003, June 4). *ESPN.com.* Retrieved August 27, 2008, from http://espn.go.com/boxing/news/2003/0528/1560271.html

Urbina sentenced to prison in Venezuela. (2007, March 28). *ESPN.com.* Retrieved April 24, 2008, from http://sports.espn.go.com/mlb/news/story?id=2815590

Very major penalty: McSorley found guilty of assault, avoids jail time. (2000, October 7). *Sports Illustrated CNNSI.com.* Retrieved April 24, 2008, from http://sportsillustrated.cnn.com/hockey/nhl/news/2000/10/06/mcsorley_assault_ap

Vinton, N. (2008, October 10). Former cyclist Tammy Thomas sentenced to six months house arrest. *Daily News.* Retrieved February 2, 2009, from http://www.nydailynews.com/sports/more_sports/2008/10/10/2008-10-10_former_cyclist_tammy_thomas_sentenced_to.html

Wilson, D. (2006, December 15). Former American cyclist indicted as Balco inquiry takes new step. *The New York Times.* Retrieved February 5, 2008, from http://www.nytimes.com/2006/12/15/sports/othersports/15balco.html?scp=3&sq=tammy+thomas&st=nyt

Wilson, D., & Schmidt, M. (2007, October 5). Olympic champion acknowledges use of steroids. *New York Times.* Retrieved February 5, 2008, from http://www.nytimes.com/2007/10/05/sports/othersports/05balco.html?pagewanted=1&sq=tammy%20thomas&st=nyt&scp=4

Part VI

Broadening Perspectives

11

Homeland Security/ Disaster Preparedness in Sport Facilities

Christina Merckx, Southeastern Louisiana University

Introduction

The world has changed since September 11, 2001, when four airliners packed with jet fuel and innocent people were used as objects of terror. Before that day ended, roughly 3,000 people were dead and the world, especially America, was questioning how it could happen. Since that fateful day, life in America and around the globe has changed. The world has now become much more aware of terrorist groups, their tactics, and the devastating effect of terrorism on society, economy, and lifestyle. One potential area that has become affected by terrorism is sport and it now behooves the professional sport community to focus on this issue.

Terrorism Defined

Schmid reported in 2004, in his article "Terrorism—The Definitional Problem," that nearly all of the United States Government agencies that deal with counter-terrorism (i.e., The FBI, The State Department and the Department of Defense) use a different definition of terrorism. One reason for this lack of clarity among governmental organizations might be related to the fact that each evaluates terrorism from a different perspective: the FBI seeks out terrorist before an attack, the State Department works with the international organizations to thwart terrorism, and the Department of Defense is called in to address a terrorist attack militarily.

Regardless of the reasons, terrorism would be easier to understand if one common definition were to exist. This is a difficult concept however, rife with complexities and questions. Schmid (2004) again suggests that, "Terrorism is a complex and multidimensional phenomenon and the term is used promiscuously for such a wide range of manifestations (e.g., narco-terrorism, cyber-terrorism) that one wonders whether it is a unitary concept" (p. 380).

The FBI considers terrorist to be criminals. Ironically, even the FBI reports that there is no single definition that is agreed upon nationally or internationally. It seems that perspective is to blame for the inability to define the word because one person may see an act of terrorism as criminal and destructive while another person may see the act as a necessary means for gaining a freedom (i.e., religious, governmental, economic, etc.). The FBI defines terrorism as "the unlawful use of force or violence against persons or property to intimidate or coerce a Government, the civilian population, or any segment thereof, in furtherance of political or social objectives" (Federal Bureau of Investigations, 2008, para. 5).

If terrorism is a criminal activity, whereby the terrorists create fear, destruction and disruption of everyday life to achieve their goal, then the previous definition by the FBI makes great sense. Consequently, this definition can be applied in the sporting world just as easily as any other aspect of society.

For the purpose of this discussion, the following definition will be used to define terrorism: terrorism is the use or threat of violence against persons or property in violation of the criminal laws of the United States to achieve a premeditated objective, usually to draw immediate attention to political, religious, racial, environmental of special interest causes (FEMA, 2008; Hall, Marciani, & Cooper, 2008; Schmid, 2004; U.S. Department of Homeland Security Preparedness Directorate Office of Grants and Training Center for Domestic Preparedness, 2006).

To help with the definitional aspect of sports terrorism, Miller, Veltri, and Gillentine (2008) suggest terrorists are motivated by three specific considerations when evaluating a potential target: economic devastation, the potential for mass casualties, and achieving a high level of attention for a cause. This concept then helps to identify how and where sport enters into the overall terrorism picture. Sport terrorism is defined by what terrorist do.

There is no question that terrorists instill fear or "terror" in their victims; and their victims are not just those who are injured or killed. Anyone who is a target or potential target is a victim of terrorism. Baker, Connaughton, Zhang, and Spengler (2007) suggest that terrorists use threats of terror to create fear, cause citizens to question their government's ability to protect them and get immediate attention for their causes. There is no doubt that sport commands an enormous amount of attention in American society. Every weekend across America, multitudes are engaged at some level of spectator participation dealing with sports. Therefore, if a terrorist organization wanted to elicit immediate attention for their cause, sport would be a superb way to do it.

Sport activities can also be linked economically with government. Examples of this economic association include the Louisiana Superdome to the taxpayers of the State of Louisiana, the Green Bay Packers to the city of Green Bay, Wisconsin, or Little League Baseball with local parks and recreation departments. Miller, et al. (2008) states that, "Sporting events have been consistent targets of terrorism because they are so strongly connected with American economy and culture" (p. 16). They also suggest that the connections between sport/sporting events and major American companies such as Coca-Cola, Anheuser-Busch, and General Motors, for example, creates an economic and cultural platform for terrorists to achieve their objectives against American sporting targets. Currently, sport is a multiple billion dollar industry in the United States and any disruption with this economic engine could cause considerable devastation to the American economy, which is the first objective of a terrorist attack.

According to Hurst, Zoubek, and Pratsinakis (2002), large public gatherings, such as sporting events that celebrate American popular culture, are considered to be potential terrorist targets. Because sport is an extremely important aspect of US society, it brings together thousands of individuals in various localized sites and creates an opportunity for mass casualties. This is the second stated objective of a terrorist attack (Miller, et al., 2008).

Beall (2006) states in an article titled, "Policy Arena Cities, Terrorism and Development," from the perspective of a city planner, terrorists target both the highly visible physical and economic environment.

> The physical environment of the city is important, as is the role of cities in national development, alongside the economics of scale provided by cities in addressing human well-being through public goods and services. All these dimensions are attractive to those seeking maximum impact from their acts of destruction and disruption (Beall, 2006, p. 108).

Beall suggests that terrorists are looking for maximum exposure for their acts. While governments are a main target of terrorism, additional targets include cities associated with sport, colleges and universities whose stadiums can seat as many as 100,000+ people on any given Saturday, professional and other high profile sport settings, and national pastimes, such as the Super Bowl, World Series, and NBA Playoffs, that draw significant levels of attention. In the United States the obsession with sport, combined with the size of stadiums and the tailgating aspects of large-scale sporting events, provides a setting which would host the possibility of a high impact terrorist attack. This demonstrates the third and final aspect of a terrorist attack (Miller, et al., 2008).

In sum, terrorists use fear or terror to achieve their goals, they seek large scale impact for recognition of their demands, they want to disrupt the economic viability of a government or governing body, and want to create as many human casualties as possible as a means to prolong the effects of their actions. Sport terrorism, therefore, can be defined as the use of a highly visible sporting event to create economic devastation, mass casualties and high levels of national and worldwide attention for a terrorist's cause. While these provide reasons as to why terrorist do what they do, it does not define terrorism per se. Terrorism occurs to achieve an outcome, yet we are unable to define the term regardless of the ability to observe the outcome.

History of Terrorism in Sport

The best known act of terrorism in sport occurred on September 5, 1972, during the XXth Olympic Games in Munich Germany. Members of the Palestinian terrorist organization *Black September* permanently changed the Olympic landscape. In the predawn hours of September 5, 1972, five men dressed as athletes jumped a fence at the Olympic Village carrying weapons in gym bags. It was common practice for the security guards to see athletes sneaking back into the Olympic Village late at night or early in the morning, in order to avoid punishment by their coaches or national governing bodies for missing team curfews.

Understanding guards would turn a blind eye to the fence jumping because they saw it as a harmless action by athletes who simply wanted to have fun while in Munich. Little did the guards realize that the terrorists would use their behavior to gain entry into the International Village. Once the terrorists gained access, they took members of the Israeli Olympic team as hostages. After negotiations with the Israeli government to release all Palestinian prisoners broke down, the terrorists eventually killed nine Israeli Olympic team members, a German police officer and a helicopter pilot. Five terrorists also died (Munich massacre remembered, 2002).

Much has been written about this incident, and its outcome was also the subject of a 2005 movie by Stephen Spielberg, called *Munich*. September 5, 1972 has been dubbed the *Munich Massacre* and has left indelible images in the mind of many sport fans, writers, reporters, and media. It has created changes in the planning and preparation of international sporting events to ensure that what happened in Munich in September of 1972 never happens again.

The world of sport has directly felt the sting of terrorism. When interviewed after 9/11, Jim McKay, the famous sportscaster who covered the entire Munich incident, stated that the terrorism which affected the XXth Olympiad in Munich, Germany thirty years ago was the "fuse that started" the modern terrorism era (Connolly, 2002, para. 13).

Many times terrorists use common practices and inherent weaknesses or carelessness to their advantage, which gives them the element of surprise. A confluence of lackadaisical security, the element of surprise, and lack of preparation for such an unsuspected event all lead to the Massacre in Munich. This terrorist attack has changed the security surrounding most international sporting and entertainment events. Since 1972, security of the Olympic Village and Olympic athletes has been a top priority. More and more, the protection of spectators and participants has become the focus of Olympic organizers. With the current worldwide political unrest, ongoing protection is needed to reduce the risk of injury to participants and spectators, as well as ensure the lucrative financial success of these events.

The protection of spectators was called into question during the 1996 Atlanta Olympic Games. The Atlanta Games were among the warmest ever. They were replete with warm Southern hospitality, as well as high temperatures. Consequently, Atlanta Games organizers created a park area where spectators could enjoy cool fountains, good food, evening concerts, and the Olympic Medal ceremonies. Again, a seemingly harmless concept opened the door for another Olympic related act of terrorism, the *Centennial Park Bombing*. On the tenth day of the Atlanta Games (July 27, 1996), a knapsack left near a concert sound tower in Centennial Park, which was packed with homemade explosives, detonated killing two tourists and injury many others. Sharp, Brennan, Keim, Williams, Eitzen, and Lillibridge (1998) reported that this attack was mitigated by the quick response of highly trained military and law enforcement professionals.

Sharp, et al. (1998) reported that the organizers of the 1996 Atlanta Olympic Games should have been prepared for this act of terrorism because of two specific acts of terrorist in the year prior to the Atlanta Olympic Games. The first was the bombing of the Federal Building in Oklahoma City, OK in April of 1995, and the second was the sarin nerve gas attack on a Tokyo Subway (Olson, 1999).

In March of 1995, the Metropolitan Subway in Tokyo, Japan suffered a catastrophic sarin nerve gas attack. During the morning rush hour commute, a terrorist group named Aum Shinrikyo released sarin gas into the underground railway system and exposed 5,000 people to the effects of the nerve gas (Olson, 1999). A month later, in April of 1995, the Alfred P. Murrah Federal Building in Oklahoma City was bombed by convicted homegrown terrorist Timothy McVey, who parked a large, rented box truck filled with fertilizer in one corner of the federal building. Once the vehicle was positioned, McVey used a remote incendiary device to set off the fertilizer, and the ensuing explosion killed 168 American citizens including men, women, and children. At the conclusion of his arrest and trial, McVey was sentenced to death ("The McVeigh trial: After 28 days of 'overwhelming evidence' the jury speaks: Guilty," n.d.).

Because of these two historical terrorist events, Atlanta Olympic organizers began their planning and preparation using heavily practiced multi-faceted terrorist preventative measures (Sharp, et al., 1998). This level of preparation no doubt had a minimizing effect on the *Centennial Park Bombing* incident and the subsequent successful completion of the Atlanta Games. To that end, a new sport management focus and study was opened for the sport management industry dealing with prevention of terrorism in sporting events around the world (Sharp, et al., 1998; Toohey, Taylor, & Lee, 2003).

Prior to 1996, only special military and law enforcement forces were trained in chemical/biological weapons emergency care. The Federal Response Plan for the 1996 Olympic Games involved the United States Marine Corp, the National Center for Environmental Health (NCEH), the Center's for Disease Control (CDC), Emory University's Division of Emergency Medicine, U.S. Army Medical Research Institute of Infectious Diseases, and the Federal Bureau of Investigations (FBI) Assessment Team (Sharp, et al., 1998). This grouping was truly the "dream team" of preventing a terrorist attack.

Even though "the Games served as an unprecedented opportunity to develop and refine integrated response plans through daily interactions, formal planning sessions, tabletop exercise, conferences, and field exercises" (Sharp, et al., 1998, p. 217), the international community realized that expanded measures must be incorporated for all large sporting events across the globe.

Issues of Preparedness — Legal

One issue of preparedness is the legal duty of facility managers and event producers to plan and prevent any act of terrorism. While an act of terrorism may not be expected, it is reasonably foreseeable. Since the possibility of a terrorist attack is real, it is imperative that facility managers and event producers do their best to protect athletes, staff, and fans. In addition, from a monetary standpoint, it is also becoming increasingly important to protect the interests of corporate and event sponsors who stand to suffer significant financial loss if a terrorist attack or threat does not allow an event to occur.

Because of these terrorist events, sport managers must ask primary questions: 1) who will management guard and 2) who will management guard against? Baker, Connaughton, Zhang, and Spengler addressed this matter in a 2007 publication in the *Journal of Legal Aspects of Sport,* wherein they suggested that the legal duty of care standard may be applied to stadium and arena managers through the relationship created by premises liability. Baker, et al., defined the premises liability as, "The duty of care requires those that own or operate sport stadiums to exercise reasonable care in preventing harm to participants and spectators resulting from activities that take place in their facilities" (p. 29). While the focus of this chapter is not specifically risk management, it is an important concept to address. Van Der Smissen (2007) suggests that there are two types of risk – inherent risks and negligent behaviors. She defines inherent risks as "those integral to the activity" (p. 38). Van Der Smissen also defines negligent behaviors as "conduct that is not in accord with the standard of care a prudent professional should give, and hence, the participant is subject to 'unreasonable risk' of injury" (p. 38).

Because acts of terrorism have occurred in sport and sport related events, reasonable foresight would suggest that terrorism could occur at any future sporting event. This foreseeability of terrorism at a sporting event lends itself to the risk of negligent behavior. If the arena/stadium manager does not prepare for foreseeable events, they are subjecting participants to unreasonable risk of injury, death, or financial loss. Therefore it is important for facility and event managers to prepare for a terrorist disaster to avoid liability of negligence.

Issues of Preparedness — Financial

As alluded to earlier, an act of terrorism does more than instill fear. An act of terrorism can also create a financial burden as a means for the terrorist to achieve their goals. This seems to be the case for sporting events, especially those that take place on the world stage (i.e., the Olympic Games, the FIFA World Cup, etc.). The cost of putting on a World Cup, Olympic Games or other international competition is rising (Toohey, et al., 2003). For example, Sophie Hayward (n.d.) of Mindfully.org, reported that cost to prevent and prepare for terrorism at the Los Angeles Olympics of 1984 was $79.4 million. Twenty years later, that cost rose to $1.5 billion for protection against terrorism for the 2004 Olympic Games in Athens (See Figure 11.1).

International sporting events like the Dakar Rally, which bills itself as the "world's most grueling off-road race" across the African Continent (Dakar History, 2008, n.p.), cancelled the 2008 running due to security concerns. A statement of explanation was issued, "Terrorist acts identified by the French authorities threatened the rally directly. On the eve of the start, Etienne Lavigne was forced to announce the cancellation of the 2008 edition" (Dakar History, 2008, n.p.). The cancellation of such a large international event on the night before its start is a fear that faces organizers and event sponsors, who have spent thousands to millions of dollars for the event to occur. These individuals front large sums of money in the hopes of a large return on their investments. Obviously, if events are cancelled, there is no or little return on investment.

Organizers of the Dakar Rally have gone so far as to move the rally to South America in 2009. The effects of this course of action on sponsorship of the Dakar Rally are yet to be seen. The potential implications for canceling and moving an international competition to an entirely different continent could be devastating. Participation in such events takes tremendous resources, and after team sponsors did not get any marketing for the team sponsorship dollars in 2008 they too may

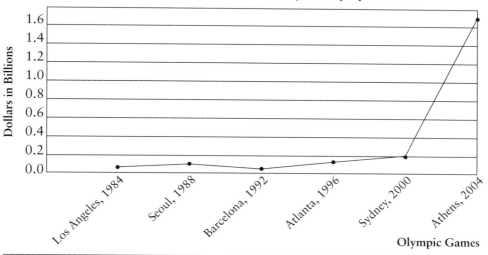

Figure 11.1 The Rising Cost of Security for Olympic Games

Taken from: Wall Street Journal (August 22, 2004) as cited by Hayward, (n.d.).
http://mindfully.org/Reform/2004/Olympic-Games_Security22aug04.htm, para. 1)

pull out, driving the participation rates for the 2009 Dakar Rally down (Dakar History, 2008).

Organizers of the 2002 World Cup also felt the direct effect of financial strain due to terrorism, as Bradford (2006) reported, "that Hamburg-Mannheimer Sports was named as the official insurer of the Cup" (para. 5). However, more than one insurance underwriter had to be called upon to cover the potential loss of revenue to sponsors, hotels/restaurants, promoters, retailers, and others who have a financial interest in the event. Insurance for the World Cup went beyond covering the venues and games themselves in the event of a natural or international incident. Insurance policies were also necessary for sponsors and retailers who had direct marketing ties and promotions associated with the event that was taking place. Bradford (2006) reported that at least 60 percent of the ancillary coverage (insurance needed to protect retailers and sponsors of the event) was provided by a number of private companies and financiers in Europe.

The financial cost associated with terrorism is not purely an issue on the international stage. Professional sport organizations and collegiate sport entities have also felt the impact of the financial burden associated with terrorist activity. The National Football League, which has the largest fan base in the United States, has introduced measures at all of its venues for the prevention of terrorist actions. In June of 2004, Maneval, Merckx, Angelopolus, and Zoeller presented research at the *Panhellenic Association of Sports Economists and Managers* (PASEM) in Athens, Greece, showing that many of the NCAA Division I football stadiums instituted numerous safety precautions to combat the threat of terrorism. These measures come with a price tag, and this is yet another burden that is placed upon sport organizations and the sport loving public.

The *threat* of a terrorist attack alone is enough to cause a serious financial burden. In June 2008, a federal judge sentenced a former grocery clerk to serve six

Table 11.1 Homeland Security Alert System

Red	A red alert means that a *severe risk* of terrorist attack exist
Orange	An orange alert means that a *high risk* of terrorist attack exists
Yellow	A yellow alert means that a *significant risk* of terrorist attack exists
Blue	A blue alert means that a *general risk* of terrorist attack exists
Green	A green alert means that a *low risk* of a terrorist attack exists.

Taken from The Department of Homeland Security website [available at: http://www.dhs.gov]

months in jail and pay $26,750 in restitution for phony threats that he made against NFL Stadiums during the 2006 NFL season (Associated Press, 2008). The 22-year-old native of Wisconsin was sentenced for posting a story on the internet stating that "so-called dirty bombs would be detonated at seven stadiums having games on October 22, 2006 in Miami, Atlanta, Seattle, Houston, Oakland, Cleveland and New York City" (para. 8). The money that the young man must repay will actually be used to reimburse the Cleveland Browns and the New Jersey Sports & Exposition Authority (who operate Giants Stadium in East Rutherford, New Jersey) for costs they incurred because of the fabricated story.

Since both national and international events are potential targets of terrorism, the cost of managing these events will increase. The financial impact of terrorism has been seen in increased insurance premiums for events and increased expenditures by sport organizations. The cost will likely be passed along to the ticket holders. Efforts have been, and will continue to be, made to reduce the financial burden on sport entities from the threat of terror, yet still provide adequate preparations to prevent or thwart such an event. What are some the best practices being utilized to meet the necessary level of protection for the most reasonable expenditure? The following section discusses that very question.

Issues of Preparedness — Best Practices

Ironically, it seems that previous terrorist attacks serve as the starting point for preparedness of future events (i.e., 1996 Centennial Olympics in Atlanta and the Tokyo sarin gas attacks of 1995). Following the terrorist attacks of 9/11, wherein passenger airplanes were the means of destruction, the air space above and around college and NFL football stadiums is now restricted during games. There are many ways to reduce the risk of a terrorist attack in sport: some are costly, some are commonsensical, yet all are necessary in our post 9/11 world.

To help with the preparedness in the United States, the Department of Homeland Security (DHS) was developed. DHS was developed as a mandate of the Homeland Security Act of 2002 by the U.S. Congress and the President of the United States (Office of Homeland Security, 2002). The DHS' purpose is to lead a unified national effort to secure America against terrorist attacks. Following its inception, the DHS developed the Homeland Security Advisory System (HSAS). This system uses a color-coded paradigm to quickly inform the populace as to the likelihood of terrorist attack. A summary of the HSAS color code system is found in Table 11.1.

The United States government has disseminated the HSAS scheme to be utilized by citizens, businesses, public and private agencies, and educational institutions. The HSAS, moreover, should be used as a guideline for athletic events that are held in the United States. This would include everything from recreational league level sport to the largest sporting event, the National Football League's Super Bowl.

In accordance with Federal guidelines, each aspect of the HSAS has a list of suggested courses of action for Federal Agencies and Departments. However, it is wise for sport facility and event managers (many of whom are tied to state and federal funding) to follow the same guidelines when making decisions regarding the risk of terrorist attacks.

For example, if the advisory level is at the *Green/Low* level the Department of Homeland Security suggests that managers do the following:

> Refining and exercising as appropriate preplanned Protective Measures; Ensuring personnel receive proper training on the Homeland Security Advisory System and specific preplanned department or agency Protective Measures; and Institutionalizing a process to assure that all facilities and regulated sectors are regularly assessed for vulnerabilities to terrorist attacks, and all reasonable measures are taken to mitigate these vulnerabilities (Homeland Security Advisory System, 2008, para. 6).

The *Blue/Guarded* level brings a slightly greater level of risk of terrorist attack and the suggestions of:

> Checking communications with designated emergency response or command locations; Reviewing and updating emergency response procedures; and providing the public with any information that would strengthen its ability to act appropriately (Homeland Security Advisory System, 2008, para. 7).

As the colors go from cool greens and blues to the hotter yellow, orange, and red, the risk of terrorist attack increases. Stadium and arena managers should be aware of significant risks of a terrorist attack when the advisory level hits the *Yellow/Elevated* level. The Department of Homeland Security suggests the following:

> Increase surveillance of critical locations; Coordinate emergency plans as appropriate with nearby jurisdictions; Assess whether the precise characteristics of the threat require the further refinement of preplanned Protective Measures; and Implementing, as appropriate, contingency and emergency response plans (Homeland Security Advisory System, 2008, para. 8).

Very few sport managers realize that when the advisory system hits the orange and red levels, it can significantly alter their facility and event planning. When the advisory system reaches *Orange/High Condition* the Department of Homeland Security suggests that managers:

> Coordinate necessary security efforts with Federal, State, and local law enforcement agencies or any National Guard or other appropriate armed forces organizations; Take additional precautions at public events and *possibly considering alternative venues or even cancellation*; Prepare to execute

contingency procedures, threatened facility access to essential personnel only (Homeland Security Advisory System, 2008, para. 9).

If the advisory level reaches *Red/Severe Condition,* sport managers are advised to cancel large scale outdoor events. It is suggested by the Department of Homeland Security that mangers consider the following when the level of risk reaches Red:

> Increase or redirect personnel to address critical emergency needs; Assign emergency response personnel and pre-position and mobilize specially trained teams or resources; Monitor, redirect, or constrain transportation systems; and *Close public and government facilities* (Homeland Security Advisory System, 2008, para. 9).

Because many stadiums and arenas are generally considered to be public/government facilities (especially for state funded university/colleges), managers of such facilities should be aware of the level of risk for a terrorist attack. The risk is updated daily on the Department of Homeland Security website (available at http://www.dhs.gov). Managers should practice emergency action planning during times of low risk. The more the sport organization practices its emergency management protocols the more likely the response to an emergency will run smoothly. It is imperative that the emergency action planning and practice include protocols for a variety of forms of terrorist attacks. This will reduce the risk of negligence and improve the standard of care your organization provides its employees, athletes, spectators and sponsors.

Suggestions from the Field

In 2004, Maneval, et al., evaluated the preparedness of twenty-five NCAA Division I Football Stadiums in light of the terrorist attacks of September 11, 2001, and the development of the Homeland Security Advisory System. Several interesting conclusions and suggestions were offered by stadium managers, athletic directors and police personnel during the course of this investigation. Though given a strict budget, the respondents offered innovative and unique ideas for increasing the anti-terrorist preparedness of college football stadiums. The unique policies and procedures for their athletic departments were placed the Table 11.2, Suggestions from the field.

Summary

Terrorism in sport is a criminal act that has many ramifications. While defining terrorism is difficult, it can be said that terrorism is the use or threat of violence against persons or property in violation of the criminal laws of the United States in order to achieve a premeditated objective, usually to draw immediate attention to political, religious, racial, environmental or special interest causes (FEMA, May 2008; Hall, Marciani, & Cooper, 2008; Schmid, 2004, U.S. Department of

Table 11.2 Suggestions from the Field

- The inclusion of terrorism plans with existing natural disaster plans.
- Establishment of separate plans for every venue, event, and HSAS color level.
- Treat every game day as an orange-alert.
- Inclusion of a federal agent (FBI level or above) who has authority and jurisdiction over land, sea and air space.
- The establishment and hiring of a specialized staff member in charge of disaster preparedness within the athletic department.
- The hiring of specialty firms to handle all game-day procedures.
- Eliminate any and all flyovers and/or parachuting into the stadium.
- Extension of the stadium lock-down from 18 hours to 48–72 hours prior to game-day.
- Modeling of the National Football League's (NFL) terrorist plans.
- Utilization of bomb sniffing canines after the stadium lock-down and at public access gates on game day.
- The use of surveillance cameras in parking, tailgating, spectator, and concession areas.
- Use of metal detectors at all entry points.
- Strictly limiting the issuing of stadium keys to only one approved athletic department representative. Adopt a "single person-one key" approach.
- The establishment of a security perimeter at a minimum distance of one block from the physical location of the stadium.
- Limit access to tailgating areas by only credentialed (picture ID), trusted boosters.
- Publication of evacuation procedures on or in programs, digital display and public address systems.
- Provide evacuation plans for teams, officials, and coaches to include maps, gates, and safe havens in the event of a natural or national disaster.
- Training and practice of evacuation plans for all game-day personnel.
- The establishment of a central command center within the stadium. A top official should represent all parties involved with game-day activities.
- The incorporation of highly visible and numerous security personnel, to include: campus police, local police, highway patrol, sheriff, and national guardsmen.
- Use of barriers on open access roads leading to the stadium. This may include use of team busses as a cost preventative measure.
- Trained ushers for each section of the stadium with bullhorns to direct spectators in the correct direction.

Taken from, Maneval, et al. (2004)

Homeland Security Preparedness Directorate Office of Grants and Training Center for Domestic Preparedness, 2006). The threat or use of violence may have dramatic effects on the sport industry. It has also been an impetus for change within the sport industry.

Terrorists seek to have the greatest possible impact from their criminal acts. Unfortunately, the impact factor related to terrorism in sport is so great that it makes sport and large national and international sporting events an appealing target. National and international sporting events draw major sponsor dollars, national and international media attention, and a multitude of fans. Terrorists see sporting events as a means to create a high level of fear, dismay, or even inflict the greatest number of casualties because of the threat or use of violence at sporting venues and events.

The threat of terrorism has had a direct impact on the cost of managing facilities. The cost is directly related to mitigating a terrorist attack for the benefit of sponsors, owners, and facility and event management personnel. A terrorist attack on a sporting venue or event has a significant financial consequence. Sponsors could lose millions in sponsorship dollars; owners could lose the ability to attract sponsors; and event and facility managers may not be able to recuperate user fees or gate receipts.

The threat of terrorism has both helped and hurt one industry closely associated with risk management in sport. The insurance industry has both benefited and suffered losses related to the threat of terrorism in sport. Because sport is so very costly to produce, sponsors have been called upon to cover sporting events. Sponsors, however, are not interested in being associated with a sporting event that experiences any criminal act, because that may reduce the positive associations their sponsorship brings to the corporation. A criminal event related to terrorism could bring a devastating association with the sponsor and the crime, thus diminishing the positive association with consumers that sponsors usually glean from being associated with sport and sporting events. In an effort to mitigate the risk of financial loss related to crime in sporting events, corporate sponsors have demanded that their financial support be insured against the risk of a terrorist act or the threat of such an act preventing the event from occurring.

Liability and risk management of large sporting events is becoming an industry unto itself. It certainly has created a greater need for qualified facility and event management personnel. A greater need for sport personnel to communicate and work with local, national and international police and military organizations also exists at all levels of sport (local, interscholastic, intercollegiate, professional, and international),. Likewise, specialists in the fields of bio-terrorism, chemical-terrorism, homegrown (national) terrorism, eco-terrorism, and international terrorism are being sought out by sport governing bodies to help prevent disaster.

Acts of terrorism like the Munich and Atlanta Olympics and the 9/11 terrorist attacks have changed the sporting landscape. There is now an impetus for change in a sport minded society that values sport as a major part of the world's economy, lifestyle, and interconnectedness.

References

Associated Press (June 5, 2008). Grocery clerk gets six months in federal prison for Internet hoax. ESPN.com. Retrieved on October 19, 2008, from http://sports.espn.go.com/nfl/news/story?id=3427331

Baker, T.A., Connaughton, D., Zhang, J.J., (2007) Perceived risk of terrorism and related risk management practice of NCAA Division 1A football stadium mangers. *Journal of Legal Aspects of Sport*, 17(1), 27–51.

Beall, J. (2006) Policy arena cities, terrorism and development. *Journal of International Development,* 18, 105–120.

Bradford, M. (June 12, 2006). World Cup kicks off in Germany. *Business Insurance,* 40(24), 3–36. Available EBSCOhost item:193092f57600.

Connolly, M. (September 5, 2002) When sports became life and death. ABC Sports Online. Retrieved on October 19, 2008, from http://espn.go.com/gen/s/2002/0903/1426778.html

Dakar History (2008). Dakar.com Retrieved: February 22, 2008 from http://www.dakar.com/2009/DAK/presentation/us/r1_7-historique.html

Federal Bureau of Investigations.(2008) *FBI policies and Guidelines.* Retrieved August 29, 2008, from http://denver.fbi.gov/nfip.htm

Federal Emergency Management Agency. (2008) Are you ready? General information about terrorism. Retrieved on June 11, 2008, from http://www.fema.gov/areyouready/terrorism_general_info.shtm

Hall, S., Marciani, L., & Cooper, W. (2008) Sport venue security: Planning and preparedness for terrorist-related incidents. *The SMART* Journal, 4(2), 6–15.

Hayward, S. (n.d.). *Securing the Olympic games: $142,857 Security Cost per Athlete in Greece.* Retrieved on October 19, 2008, from http://www.mindfully.org/Reform/2004/Olympic-Games-Security22Aug04.htm

Homeland Security Advisory System — Guidance for Federal Departments and Agencies. [On-Line] Retrieved on October 19, 2008, from http://www.dhs.gov/xinfoshare/programs/gc_1156876241477.shtm

Hurst, R., Zoubek, P., & Pratsinakis, C. (2002) American sports as a target of terrorism: The duty of care after September 11th. *Sport and the Law Journal,* 10(1), 134–139.

Maneval, M.W., Merckx, C.M., Angelopoulos, T.J., and Zoeller, R. (2004). The United States terrorist alert system and its implication for university sport management personnel. *Panhellenic Association of Sports Economists and Managers (PASEM),* Athens, Greece — May, 30–June 2, 2004.

The McVeigh trial: After 28 days of 'overwhelming evidence' the jury speaks: Guilty. (n.d.). CNN.com. Retrieved October 19, 2008 from http://www.cnn.com/US/9706/17/mcveigh.overview/

Miller, J., Veltri, F., & Gillentine, A. (2008) Spectator perception of security at the Super Bowl after 9/11: Implications for sport facility managers. *The SMART Journal,* 4(2), 16–25.

Munich massacre remembered. (2002, September 5). ABC News Online. Retrieved: October 19, 2008, from http://www.abc.net.au/news/indepth/feature items/munich.htm

Office of Homeland Security. (2002, July). *National Strategy for Homeland Security.* Retrieved August, 16, 2008, from http://www.whitehouse.gov/homeland/book/nat_strat_hls.pdf

Olson, K.B. (1999). Aum Shinrikyo: Once and future threat? Emerging Infectious Diseases, 5(4), Centers for Disease Control and Prevention. Retrieved October 19, 2008 from http://www.cdc.gov/ncidod/EID/vol5no4/olson.htm

Schmid, A. (2004). Terrorism—The definitional problem. *Case Western Reserve Journal of International Law,* 36(2/3), 375–419. Available: EBSCOhost Database Item: AN 17481417.

Sharp, T.W., Brennan, R.J., Keim, M., Williams, R.J., Eitzen, E., & Lillibridge, S. (1998). Medical preparedness for a terrorist incident involving chemical or biological agents during the 1996 Atlanta Olympic games. *Annals of Emergency Medicine 32*(2), 214–223.

Toohey, K., Taylor, T., & Lee, C.K. (2003). The FIFA World Cup 2002: The effects of terrorism on sport tourism. *Journal of Sport Tourism,* 8(3), 167–185.

U.S. Department of Homeland Security Preparedness Directorate Office of Grants and Training Center for Domestic Preparedness. (2006). *Weapons of Mass Destruction (WMD) Awareness level training (Student Manual AWR-160).* Washington: Government Printing Office.

Van Der Smissen, B. (2007). Elements of negligence. In D.J. Cotten & J.T. Wolohan (Eds). *Law for Recreation and Sport Managers* (4th ed.). (pp. 36–45). Dubuque, IA: Kendal Hunt.

12

Ticket Scalping: Methods, Issues, and Considerations

Beth A. Cianfrone, Georgia State University
Michael S. Carroll, University of Southern Mississippi

Chapter Overview

The popularity of live sporting events combined with an oftentimes limited supply of tickets has led to ticket scalping. Individuals who purchase tickets and then resell them to fans may be subject to anti-scalping legislation regulated by local jurisdiction or state law. Ticket scalping is now a common practice prior to many sporting events, despite the fact that it may constitute a civil and/or criminal violation. Many forms of ticket scalping exist, and the growing prevalence of Internet usage has led to new challenges facing sport organizations and law enforcement officials trying to regulate ticket sales in what is now referred to as the secondary ticket market. Ticket scalping is often a concern for sport organizations because illegal ticket sales may result in potential crowd control issues, lost income for the sport organization, and/or a disgruntled fan base due to an inability to obtain tickets. The increase in Internet ticket sales has also shifted the attention on the enforcement and legality of reselling tickets in various jurisdictions. This chapter will serve as an introduction to the legalities and issues surrounding ticket scalping. Various methods of legal ticket scalping will be introduced, along with anti-scalping legislation and related case law regarding the regulation of ticket sales. The impact of ticket scalping on sport organizations and consumers, as well as the influence of the Internet on ticket sales and future trends in ticket reselling, will also be discussed.

Introduction

Scalping is "the practice of selling something (especially a ticket) at a price above face value once it becomes scarce (usually just before a high-demand event begins)" (Garner, 2000, p. 1080). The prevalence of ticket scalping is widespread; scalpers standing near an arena or stadium trying to sell tickets to spectators are a common sight before many sporting events. It is difficult to quantify the scope of this practice in a $200 billion event-ticket industry, but industry experts estimate potential revenue generated by the ticket resale market in upwards of $2.5 billion (Geng, Wu, & Whinston, 2007; Heath, 2006). Ticket scalpers represent a substantial part of the sport ticket resale industry and utilize various methods to obtain and resell tickets for profit.

Ticket Scalping Methods

The legalities surrounding ticket scalping depend on the state or municipality in which the act occurs. In certain states, scalping methods are protected by law and do not violate anti-scalping legislation, even though tickets may be sold for a price exceeding the original face value. In other states, however, there are limits on the price a ticket reseller or scalper may charge above the face value of the ticket. The most traditional form of ticket scalping occurs when one person purchases a ticket from the box office or authorized agent (e.g., Ticketmaster) and resells the ticket to another person prior to the event, face to face. These sales often occur immediately outside of the event venue or on street corners near the venue with a large amount of foot traffic to the event. The initial owner of the ticket may sell the ticket to reap a profit, but may also sell simply to get rid of a ticket if he or she cannot attend the event. Many high-profile sporting events draw large crowds and subsequently have a high volume of street and foot traffic leading to the venue. Scalpers selling tickets on these streets can be disruptive, adding to the commotion and chaos, and possibly create safety issues for patrons around the venue (Benitah, 2005; Criscuolo, 1995). Recognizing this public safety concern, states and municipalities have enacted anti-scalping legislation in order to reduce this risk (Gibbs, 2000). Additionally, ticket scalping may create unnecessary and unwanted harassment and annoyance for spectators and fans on their way into a venue. For fans who want to avoid the rush and pre-purchase tickets from a secondary vendor, ticket brokers provide a viable option.

Ticket brokers are a major source of tickets for some consumers. Brokers are agencies that purchase tickets from the box office or team and then resell them. In some states, ticket brokers are exempt from anti-scalping laws and may sell tickets above face value. In an effort to regulate brokers for fair business practices, as well as tax collection purposes, states require that these brokers be registered and licensed. However, legal problems may arise when a ticket broker illegally purchases tickets for resale. Bribing the original ticket sales person would be an example of such an illegal practice (Gibbs, 2000). This could be done at a stadium/venue box office or with an authorized agent or employee of the franchise. Ticket brokers are often criticized for having access to a large amount of tickets and being associated with counterfeit tickets (Cianfrone & Connaughton, 2004). The National Association of Ticket Brokers was created in 1994 to help alleviate some of these concerns by "establishing an industry-wide standard of conduct and creating ethical rules and procedures designed to protect the public and foster a positive public perception of the industry" (National Association of Ticket Brokers, 2008, para. 1).

Similar to ticket brokers, authorized ticket agencies are a common ticket outlet. Unlike brokers, however, authorized agents have a contract with the sporting or event organization to engage in ticket resale. For example, a sport organization may contract with an agency, such as Ticketmaster, to be an exclusive provider of tickets to be sold for a particular game or event (Gibbs, 2000). The authorized agency may be able to add a surcharge above the original face value of the ticket due to their relationship with the sport organization. Oftentimes, this enables authorized ticket agencies to effectively circumvent state anti-scalping legislation. The authorized ticket agencies may be subject to anti-scalping legislation if they sell tickets at prices above the originally contracted price.

Another avenue for ticket scalping is through travel agents, who may sell sporting event tickets for high markups in conjunction with travel packages. Ticket scalping by travel agents is legal because the agencies are state licensed. They can only increase the ticket price, however, if the tickets are included in a hotel and/or travel "package deal" (Cianfrone & Connaughton, 2004; Gibbs, 2000). Travel agents are subject to anti-scalping laws and may face civil and/or criminal charges if they sell the sporting event ticket alone, and not in conjunction with some sort of package.

The popularity of online ticket sales from authorized agents has led to other online ticket opportunities and means of scalping. There are many online auctions and ticket exchanges, such as eBay, StubHub, Inc. (an eBay company), TicketsNow, and London-based Viagogo. Even Facebook, an online social networking site most often associated with college students, allows a fee-free forum for buying and reselling tickets in its online marketplace. The ease of buying and re-selling tickets online has made online auctions and ticket exchanges a very popular form of scalping. This has also created problems for sport organizers and law enforcement officials due to limited control over such sales. Likewise, ticket scalping legislation remains in effect if the person buying or selling the ticket is in a city or state where ticket scalping is regulated. This may be problematic, however, as there is no real consensus as to where the "sale" actually takes place. Questions often arise as to which state legislation has jurisdiction over a ticket bought and sold over the Internet. Tickets are often sold for sporting events that take place in another state. Is the state legislation in which the seller resides the correct legislation to use or the state in which the buyer resides? Perhaps the state in which the event is located is the correct application of legislation. It is easy to see that the emergence and the popularity of cyber-scalping has led to much frustration when determining jurisdictional issues and which laws apply.

Ticket Scalping Legislation

For patrons and would-be attendees at sporting events, ticket scalpers represent a significant source of angst and frustration. They exhaust the oftentimes small box office supply of tickets and then resell them for prices much higher than what the average customer may be able to afford or willing to pay. From a public policy standpoint, everyone should have equitable access to tickets for sporting and entertainment events. Currently, there is no federal legislation aimed at limiting or prohibiting ticket scalping in the United States. In reaction to the problems evident in the sport and entertainment industries due to ticket scalping, state legislatures have passed laws outlawing or restricting ticket scalping and reselling for over 100 years (Siporin, 2004). These laws vary widely from state to state, and time has seen a remarkable evolution in their applicability.

At least twenty-five states have some type of regulation regarding ticket scalping or reselling (see Table 12.1). Generally, state laws governing ticket scalping or reselling place restrictions upon the location, price, and types of events for which tickets may be resold. For example, Arizona holds that a person may not resell a ticket "within two hundred feet of an entry to the stadium, arena, theater or other place where an event is being held, or of the entry to a contiguous parking area" (Ariz. Rev. Stat. Ann. § 13-3718, 2007). Stadiums and arenas may have their own regulations regarding the locations and proximities in which tickets may be resold, as only a small number of these laws impose restrictions based upon location. In South Carolina, tickets may not be resold for more than $1 above the price charged by the original ticket seller, and in Massachusetts, resellers may only charge $2 over the face value of a ticket, plus a reasonable service fee. Indiana, unlike most states, is specific to the type of event ticket regulated, namely a "boxing or sparring match" and may not apply to other types of sporting events (Ind. Code Ann. § 25-9-1-26, 2007). Another point on which these statutes differ is the penalties assessed for a violation. In Rhode Island, a person violating the anti-scalping law is guilty of a misdemeanor and may be fined as much as $1,000 for each offense, whereas in Alabama, no clear penalty is specified, but scalpers must pay a $100 licensing fee. A number of these laws contain certain exceptions, as well. For example, in New Jersey, individuals reselling tickets may only charge up to a 20 percent premium on top of the original ticket price, but an exception is made for licensed ticket brokers who may charge up to a 50 percent premium. Throughout their legal history, inconsistencies among state anti-scalping laws, combined with limited law enforcement resources, have resulted in a general lack of interest in enforcement, which has, in turn, resulted in a number of laws being modified or even abolished. An examination of case law related to ticket scalping serves to illustrate a number of important concepts.

Ticket Scalping Related Case Law

Case law involving ticket scalping often brings into question the constitutionality of the laws themselves. According to Pittman and Osborne (2007), challenges to anti-scalping laws on constitutional grounds are generally unsuccessful, as states are able to rely upon the argument that they have a legitimate interest in protecting the welfare of the public and ensuring access to entertainment and sporting events. Furthermore, anti-scalping laws are rationally related to the stated legitimate goals of curbing scalping activities and maintaining public welfare, and constitute a legitimate exercise of a state's police power. One of the first cases in which the constitutionality of a ticket scalping law was challenged was *Tyson and Brother — United Theatre Ticket Offices v. Banton* (1927), in which the U.S. Supreme Court examined the ticket scalping law in New York, which prohibited the resale of a ticket to any theater for more than fifty cents of face value. The plaintiff in the case was a ticket broker, Tyson and Brother, who operated a licensed business reselling admission tickets for entertainment venues. Tyson and Brother sought to have the court grant

Table 12.1 State Scalping Legislation, as of March 2008

State	Statute	State	Statute
Alabama	Ala. Code § 40-12-167	Montana	
Alaska		Nebraska	
Arizona	Ariz. Rev. Stat. Ann. § 13-3718	Nevada	
Arkansas	Ark. Co. Ann. § 5-63-201	New Hampshire	
California	Cal. Penal Code § 346	New Jersey	N.J. Stat. Ann. §§ 56:8-26 to 8:38
Colorado		New Mexico	N.M. Stat. Ann. § 30-46-1
Connecticut		New York	N. Y Arts & Cult. Aff. § 25. 01 to 25. 35 (partially repealed)
Delaware	11 Del. C. § 918	North Carolina	N.C. Gen. Stat. Ann. § 14-344
Florida		North Dakota	
Georgia	Ga. Code §§ 43-4B-25 to 43-4B-31	Ohio	Ohio Rev. Code Ann. § 715.48
Hawaii	Haw. Rev. Stat. § 440-17	Oklahoma	
Idaho		Oregon	
Illinois	§§ 720 ILCS 375/1 to 375/4	Pennsylvania	
Indiana	Ind. Code Ann. § 25-9-1-26	Rhode Island	R.I. Gen. Laws § 5-22-26
Iowa		South Carolina	S.C. Code Ann. § 16-17-710
Kansas		South Dakota	S.D. Codified Laws § 42-7A-31
Kentucky	Ken. Rev. Stat. Ann. § 518.070	Tennessee	
Maine		Texas	
Louisiana	La. Rev. Stat. § 4:1	Utah	
Maryland	Md. Code Ann., Bus. Reg. § 4-318	Vermont	
Massachusetts	Mass. Gen. Law Ann. Ch. 140 § 185A to 185G	Virginia	Va. Code Ann. § 15.2-969
Michigan	Mich. Comp. Laws Ann. § 750.465	Washington	
Minnesota		West Virginia	
Mississippi	Miss. Code Ann. § 97-23-97	Wisconsin	Wis. Stat. Ann. § 42.07
Missouri		Wyoming	

Note: The above legislation concerns ticket re-sale regulation and not prohibition. Statutes vary state to state. For example, the state of New York allows ticket reselling for above face value but prohibits re-selling within a specified distance from a venue.

an injunction against the revocation of his license and potential prosecution brought by the state for his role in the reselling of tickets in violation of the state law. Having already been ruled against at the District Court level, the plaintiff brought the appeal to the U.S. Supreme Court. The New York ticket scalping law at the time stated that admission prices were "a matter affected with a public interest" and should be regulated by the state "in order to safeguard the public against fraud, extortion, exorbitant rates and similar abuses" (*Tyson*, 1927, p. 427). The court disagreed with this, ruling that a theater or other place of entertainment was not a matter affected with public interest but instead a private enterprise for which legislative regulation was not warranted. As such, the New York law was ruled unconstitutional. This same issue was revisited in *People v. Patton* (1974), when the defendant, Vernon Patton, was charged with re-selling two concert tickets for a price greater than that on the tickets outside of an Illinois arena. Contrary to *Tyson*, the court reasoned that states do have a legitimate interest in regulating the price of tickets to entertainment and amusement events, and therefore, the law was not unconstitutional and not in violation of the 14th Amendment.

Although constitutional challenges to anti-scalping laws have historically been ineffective, this has not stopped a number of states from partially or entirely repealing their ticket scalping laws. In 2007 alone, Connecticut, Minnesota, Missouri, and Pennsylvania all abolished their ticket scalping laws. Just as technology has revolutionized the ways in which companies do business, the secondary ticket market has followed suit, offering a myriad of opportunities to buy and sell tickets online. Having taken notice of this, a number of sport teams and organizations have embraced this trend and developed their own niche within the secondary ticket market. This became a source of contention when consumers recently filed a class action lawsuit against the Chicago Cubs for allegedly scalping their own tickets (*Cavoto v. Chicago Nat'l League Ball Club, Inc.*, 2006). In 2002, the Tribune Company, owners of the Chicago Cubs baseball team, incorporated Wrigley Field Premium Ticket Services, a registered ticket broker in Illinois, and proceeded to sell tickets to Premium, who would then sell them to the public at inflated prices. Under 720 Ill. Comp. Stat. §§ 375/1 to 375/4, selling tickets at a price in excess of face value was explicitly forbidden, unless one of the specified exceptions applied, one of which included status as a registered ticket broker. The Cubs had their own policy that forbade ticket holders from reselling their own tickets and had actually revoked the season tickets of those found to be in violation of this policy. The plaintiffs in this case argued that the dual ownership of the Cubs and Premium violated the Illinois ticket scalping law and other consumer protection statutes, as this arrangement allowed the Cubs to circumvent the law through collusion and then take advantage of consumers. The trial court ruled in favor of the defendants, finding that Premium and the Cubs had not violated the Illinois ticket scalping law nor any consumer protection statutes for the following reasons: (1) the transactions between the Cubs and Premium constituted legal sales, (2) Premium was a licensed ticket broker under Illinois law, and (3) Illinois law did not prohibit the Cubs from selling tickets to its sister corporation, Premium. The Appellate Court subsequently affirmed the decision.

The growth in popularity of the Internet and online ticket auction sites has spurred a number of sport organizations and teams within the National Football League (NFL), Major League Baseball (MLB), National Basketball Association (NBA), and National Hockey League (NHL) to partner with various Internet firms in order to establish themselves within the online secondary ticket market (Heath, 2006). One notable exception, however, occurred when the New England Patriots filed an action against a StubHub, Inc., one of the largest online ticket resellers in the U.S., and individuals identified simply as John Does (*NPS, LLC et al. v. StubHub, Inc. et al.,* 2007). The Patriots claimed that unidentified individuals had engaged in unlicensed resale of tickets, facilitated by StubHub, and sought to require StubHub to provide information that would reveal the identities of those who had bought, sold, or offered to buy or sell tickets on StubHub. The Patriots argued that they had a right to know the identities of the individuals in violation of their own limitations on ticket resale for future purposes, such as canceling season tickets or reporting offenders to authorities. The court ruled that the Patriots had a legitimate interest in knowing the identity of these fans and ordered that StubHub produce documentation disclosing such information. It remains to be seen what action, if any, the Patriot's organization may take against the fans identified in the documentation.

Impact of Scalping on Sport Consumers and Organizations

Cases such as those previously addressed indicate some of the ways scalping can affect sport consumers and organizations. Scalping legislation influences these outcomes to varying degrees. Advocates for legal ticket scalping and brokers argue that these outlets are serving the population who could not obtain tickets through traditional box office means and are simply a form of free market enterprise (Benitah, 2005; Criscuolo, 1995). However, opponents of legal ticket scalping believe scalping raises ticket prices and keeps tickets away from the common sport spectator, as well as creates a nuisance and potential security hazard around a sport venue (Benitah, 2005).

Legalized ticket scalping can be both beneficial and detrimental for sport consumers, depending on the situation. In theory, ticket scalpers provide a ticket resale service to events that are sold out, so sport consumers have another opportunity to purchase these hard to find tickets (Criscuolo, 1995). This is a beneficial avenue for those consumers who could not obtain tickets via traditional box office, phone, or Internet purchasing means. The markup on the ticket is a worthwhile and expected premium for these fans. Some even consider this a free enterprise attitude because the scalpers own the ticket rights and, thus, may resell at any price (Cianfrone & Connaughton, 2004; Diamond, 1992).

Conversely, ticket scalpers and brokers often hold a large share of event tickets, ensuring sport consumers little to no chance of purchasing tickets through the traditional box office or authorized sellers. Major sporting event tickets frequently are sold out within minutes of the initial sale because of brokers, who may have access to high-speed dialing equipment, leaving fans to obtain scalped tickets at higher prices ("Why can't I get tickets?", 1999). Tickets sold by brokers and scalpers also have tremendous markup, so the high prices, in addition to the lack of ticket access, are negative results of legalized ticket scalping for sport consumers.

Sport organizations, like consumers, are affected by scalping legislation both positively and negatively. Through scalping and the laws of supply and demand, the scalped ticket prices can often sell for higher than the original price, and the sport organizations do not receive revenue from this new profit margin. This aspect of ticket scalping is of most concern to sport organizers, owners, and presidents because others are profiting on their product.

However, in some cases, legal scalping can benefit sport organizations. Scalpers and brokers often pre-purchase many tickets, ensuring ticket sales for the team. Sometimes a team falters midseason, has a losing streak, or plays an unpopular opponent, yet scalpers have already pre-purchased many tickets. In this case, the sport organization still profits from the ticket sales, which may not have been otherwise sold. An example of this is shown via StubHub, which reportedly facilitates ticket sales to events at prices below the original face value. StubHub provides sport spectators with a below market value ticket in these situations (StubHub, 2008). Fans who purchase the undesirable tickets at low prices enable seats to be filled for "unattractive games" and contribute to other game day revenue streams such as concessions, licensed merchandise, and parking.

It is interesting to note the effects of scalping laws on face value ticket prices. Williams (1994) studied ticket pricing for NFL teams, comparing cities with anti-scalping legislation to those without the legislation. NFL teams located in cities with some form of anti-scalping legislation had lower ticket prices than NFL teams without scalping laws. The average ticket price was about $1.95 less per ticket in the cities with scalping laws (Williams, 1994). This study suggests teams located in cities with legalized scalping have a better understanding of the true market value of the tickets and, therefore, price their tickets higher. Based on this research, owners would be in favor of legalized scalping. A recent follow-up study by Depken (2006) noted teams located in cities with anti-scalping laws averaged per-game season ticket prices about $10 higher for NFL and $2 higher for Major League Baseball (MLB) teams. Moreover, the results indicated that teams in cities with scalping legislation actually had higher team revenues, and the laws had no effect on attendance. Specifically, based on the increase in ticket prices, Depken figured anti-scalping laws may lead to $2 million per year in revenue for the team owner (Depken, 2006). These studies are important to consider and suggest team owners need to critically assess the potential effect of anti-scalping legislation on their organization's revenue generation. However, these studies do not take into account the online ticket sales, which often circumvent anti-scalping legislation based on buyer and seller location.

Online ticket markets, such as eBay, Viagogo, and StubHub, are subject to scalping legislation depending on the location of the buyer and seller. Online ticket markets provide a great outlet for revenue generation relative to average face value ticket prices, if the demand for the ticket is high. In fact, Forrester Research estimated resale online tickets have become a $2.5 billion business (Isidore, 2007). Super Bowl ticket prices provide an extreme example of this supply and demand. Over the past six years, the average cost of a Super Bowl ticket on StubHub ($3,171) has increased substantially over the average face value cost ($583) (see Figure 12.1). While the true economic effect on ticket scalping legislation remains unclear, the future direction of scalping and scalping legislation appears to be constrained by the online services.

Figure 12.1 Average Super Bowl Ticket Prices — StubHub v. Face Value

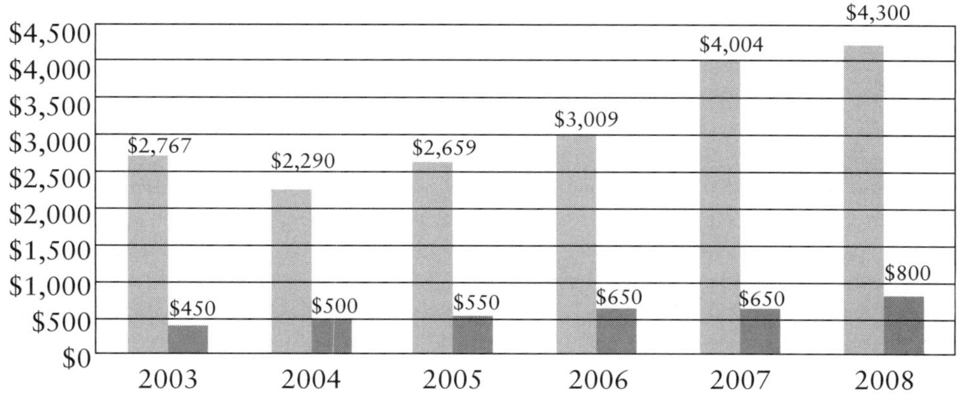

(Associated Press, 2008; "South Florida Super Bowl", n.d.; "Yeah that's the Ticket", 2006)

Future Direction of Scalping, Scalping Legislation, and Ticket Sales

The legal issues regarding ticket scalping remain a dynamic area and state representatives are constantly proposing modifications to current scalping legislation. The popularity of Internet ticket selling sites only further complicates the enforcement of scalping laws. Moreover, the economic and marketing influence of scalping on sport organizations has led to constant review of ticket practices and laws by sport managers.

One effort to combat illegal scalping and counterfeit ticketing has been to create and encourage "fan to fan" ticket exchanges supported by professional teams. Many teams have ticket exchanges set up either through their own team website or via an online authorized agency, such as Ticketmaster. These ticket exchanges allow ticket holders, who may be unable to attend a game, a secure website in which to re-sell their tickets. Likewise, fans unable to purchase tickets originally, or those who decided last minute to attend a game, can purchase tickets via the team-sponsored websites in the convenience of their own home, reducing the fear of counterfeit tickets or fraudulent actions.

Increasingly, more sport organizations have attempted to maximize profits and partially control secondary ticket sales through agreements between online ticket services and sport organizations. The NBA was the first of the major sport leagues to partner with an online ticket service, with an exclusive deal with Ticketmaster (Ante, 2007). In August 2007, StubHub partnered with Major League Baseball Advanced Media LP as the Official Ticket Marketplace of MLB.com (StubHub, 2007). The two companies share ticket resale profits, making baseball tickets the top-selling ticket category on StubHub (Ante, 2007). The deal reportedly cost StubHub $10 million per year for the rights to resell tickets, plus an annual $5 million fee utilized for marketing the teams (Ante, 2007). As of March 2008, the NFL did not have an exclusive league-wide deal, although individual teams had partnerships with various online ticket markets. For example, Viagogo has an exclusive contract to resell tickets for the Cleveland Browns, and StubHub has ticket resale rights for eight NFL teams (Ante, 2007).

Many sport organizations are concerned with season ticket holders' ticket resale and subsequent profits. For example, the New York Jets monitor eBay and other online sites for season ticket holders attempting to resell tickets online (Drury, 2002). The New York Yankees 2008 Season Ticket Renewal Letter indicates that StubHub is the Official Ticket Marketplace of MLB.com and the New York Yankees, and legal resale of tickets on this site is permitted (New York Yankees, 2008). However, illegal ticket resale, or the attempt to resell, will result in the revocation of the season ticket license (New York Yankees, 2008). Many sport organizations have similar policies in place to control the resale of tickets for high profits. It becomes a complicated situation though, when a person legally resells a ticket on StubHub to an unknown consumer, who may subsequently sell the ticket illegally. This may compromise the original season ticket holder's rights to season tickets. It remains to be seen how sport organizations will navigate both their relationship with online ticket sites and season ticket holders.

The National Collegiate Athletic Association (NCAA) has also sought to curb illegal ticket scalping by partnering with RazorGator Experiences for online ticket resale (NCAA, 2007). The NCAA urges fans to sell and buy tickets via RazorGator.com to ensure that some profit is returned back to the NCAA and its member schools (Garcia, 2006). For the NCAA Division I Men's Basketball Championship, Final Four tickets are sold as a package deal for the two semifinals and championship game. Because two of the four teams do not reach the championship game, there is typically an abundance of fans looking to resell their final game tickets. The NCAA also sells a set number of their public allotment tickets, as well as the NCAA "official use" tickets, to RazorGator Experiences for online package deal resale (McCarthy, 2008). The NCAA hopes the partnership will "protect NCAA interests and further its branding surrounding the Division I Men's Basketball Championship; reinforce efforts to preserve the integrity of the championship, and eliminate unauthorized third-party profit on the tournament, which reduces revenue for all NCAA member colleges and universities" (NCAA, 2006, para. 5).

Another form of ticket sales becoming popular among sporting events is an online pre-purchasing reserve system. FirstDIBZ (formerly TicketReserve.com) is an online corporation that sells advanced rights to tickets for major sporting events. For example, a University of Florida football fan can reserve one face value ticket to the NCAA Bowl Championship Series (BCS) National Championship game by purchasing one DIBZ for the game, nearly a year in advance, and naming the Florida Gators in the reservation. If the team actually earned a spot to play in the BCS National Championship game then the fan would be guaranteed a ticket at face value. However, if the Gators did not play in the game, then the fan loses the money that was invested (the DIBZ) for the ticket. Because the ticket rights are purchased in advance, they (the DIBZ) can be sold to another fan midseason, if the team appears to be struggling, the ticket-holder decides not to attend the event, or the fan would like to make a profit on the ticket rights (FirstDibz.com, 2008). For buying and selling DIBZ, there is a 5–7 percent fee to the buyer and a 5–10 percent fee to the seller, both paid to FirstDibz.com, with a minimum $5 transaction fee (FirstDibz.com, 2008). The success of online ticket reserve systems remains to be determined, but it is clear that the future of ticket scalping legislation will need to consider this avenue of ticket sales.

Chapter Review

Sporting event ticket scalping is a growing segment in the $200 billion event-ticket industry (Geng et al., 2007). Scalping methods are dynamic, especially with the increased usage of Internet resale sites. Current anti-scalping legislation has yet to maintain relevancy or have the enforcement needed to uphold these policies. Anti-scalping regulations have been modified over time, but the ever-changing nature of ticket scalping methods suggests the legislation will need further adaptation. Online ticket sales are difficult to monitor and regulate; anti-scalping laws may need to include sanctions dealing with Internet sales or perhaps be eliminated completely, if enforcement cannot control the current methods. Legal and illegal scalping affects sport organizations and consumers in a myriad of ways, so sport managers and fans should be knowledgeable of ticket scalping methods, legislation, and the effects of scalping.

References

Ante, S.E. (2007, December 5). Ticketmaster's Hail Mary pass. *BusinessWeek.com.* Retrieved March 1, 2008, from http://www.businessweek.com/technology/content/dec2007/tc2007125_569284.htm

Ariz. Rev. Stat. Ann. § 13-3718 (2007).

Associated Press. (2008, January 28). Super Bowl tickets being resold at record prices. *ESPN.com.* Retrieved March 1, 2008, from http://sports.espn.go.com/nfl/playoffs07/news/story?id=3217487

Benitah, J.C. (2005). Anti-scalping laws: Should they be forgotten? *Texas Review of Entertainment and Sports Law, 6*(1), 55–78.

Cavoto v. Chicago Nat'l League Ball Club, Inc., 2006 WL 2291181 (Ill. App. 1 Dist. 2006).

Cianfrone, B.A., & Connaughton, D.P. (2004). Legal issues associated with ticket scalping. *SMART Online Journal, 1*(1), 20–25.

Couch, G. (2003, December 31). Cubs, scalpers, government all in it together. *Chicago Sun Times,* p. 135.

Criscuolo, P. J. (1995). Reassessing the ticket scalping dispute: The application, effects and criticisms of current anti-scalping legislation. *Seton Hall Journal of Sport Law, 5*(1), 189–221.

Depken, C. (2006). Another look at anti-scalping: Theory and evidence. *Public Choice, 130*(1–2), 55–72.

Diamond, T. (1992). Ticket scalping: A new look at an old problem. *University of Miami Law Review, 37,* 71–92.

Drury, A. (2002). When it comes to ticket scalping, the Net's the wild west. *USATODAY.com.* Retrieved March 1, 2008 from http://www.usatoday.com/tech/webguide/Internetlife/2002-10-07-e-scalping_x.htm

FirstDibz.com. (n.d.). Help—Frequently asked questions. Retrieved March 1, 2008, from http://www.firstdibz.com/faq_main.html#

Garcia, M. (2006, December 14). NCAA aims to benefit from scalpers' prices. *USA Today*, p. C3.

Garner, B. (Ed.). (2000). *Black's Law Dictionary* (7th ed.). St. Paul: West Group.

Geng, X., Wu, R., & Whinston, A. (2007, April). Profiting from partial allowance of ticket resale. *Journal of Marketing. 71*(2), 183–195.

Gibbs, J. (2000). Cyberscalping: On-line ticket sales. *Toledo Law Review, 31*(3), 471–495.

Happel, S.K., & Jennings, M.M. (1995). The folly of anti-scalping laws. *The CATO Journal, (15)*1. Retrieved March 1, 2008, from http://www.cato.org/pubs/journal/cj15n1-4.html

Heath, T. (2006, July 24). Teams look for their cut among the ticket scalpers. *The Washington Post*, p. E1.

Ind. Code Ann. § 25-9-1-26 (2007).

Isidore, C. (2007, December 29). StubHub's winning ticket. *CNNMoney.com*. Retrieved March 1, 2008, from http://money.cnn.com/2007/12/28/commentary/sportsbiz/ index.htm?section=money_commentary

McCarthy, M. (2008, March 19). NCAA cashes in on Final Four ticket resale; anti-counterfeit measures results in high markups. *USA Today*, p. 1A.

National Association of Ticket Brokers (2008). Retrieved April 23, 2008, from: http://www.natb.org/

NCAA. (2006, December 4). NCAA selects RazorGator experiences as official Fan2Fan ticket exchange and hospitality provider. Retrieved March 1, 2008, from http://www2.ncaa.org/portal/media_and_events/press_room/2006/december/20061204_razorgator_rls.html

New York Yankees. (2008). Season ticket renewal letter. Retrieved March 1, 2008, from http://newyork.yankees.mlb.com/nyy/ticketing/sth_renewal_letter.jsp

NPS, LLC et al. v. StubHub Inc. et al., 22 Mass. L. Rep. 717 (Mass. Super. 2007).

People v. Patton, 309 N.E.2d 572 (Ill. 1974).

Pittman, A., & Osborne, B. (2007). Sport-related crimes: Gambling—ticket scalping—wire and mail fraud. In D.J. Cotton & J.T. Wolohan (Eds.), *Law for recreation and sport managers* (4th ed. pp. 261–272). Dubuque, IA: Kendall/Hunt.

Siporin, M. (2004). *Cavoto v. Chicago Nat'l League Ball Club, Inc.*: Chicago Cubs ticket scalping scandal and the relationship between separate corporate entities owned by a common parent. *DePaul Business & Commercial Law Journal, 2*(4), 723–759.

South Florida Super Bowl Host Committee. (n.d.). Frequently asked questions. Retrieved March 1, 2008, from http://www.superbowlxli.org/hc_faq.html

StubHub. (2007, August 2). StubHub (an eBay Company) and MLB Advanced Media forge long-term online secondary ticketing partnership. Retrieved March 1, 2008, from http://www.stubhub.com/mlb-press-release/.

StubHub. (2008, February 13). Jazz fans finding discount ticket prices despite team success. Retrieved March 1, 2008, from http://www.stubhub.com/sites/corpsite/?gsec=news&gact=press&article_id=7679

Tyson and Brother—United Theatre Ticket Offices v. Banton, 273 U.S. 418 (1927).

Why can't I get tickets? (1999, May 27). *Report on Ticket Distribution Practices.* Retrieved March 1, 2008, from www.oag.state.ny.us/press/reports/scalping/full_text.html

Williams, A.T. (1994). Do anti-ticket scalping laws make a difference? *Managerial and Decision Economics, 15*(5), 503–509.

Yeah, that's the ticket. (2006, May 26). *Sporting News, 230*(21), 32.

Table of Cases

13

Professional Wrestling: Pseudo Sport, Real Death

Jason W. Lee, University of North Florida
Jeffrey C. Lee, Troy University

Introduction

Professional wrestling? Readers may be asking why a text devoted to criminal behavior in *sport* would incorporate a chapter on *professional wrestling*. After all, professional wrestling is just a fake sport that has become a pop culture phenomenon, garnering attention in recent years for a number of controversial aspects. As this chapter will show, professional wrestling, though the outcomes are predetermined, does have certain aspects associated with legitimate sport competition. Professional wrestling also has been fraught with drug scandals on par with, and often superseding that found in, the world of true sport. This chapter will identify these issues and draw parallels to other entities within the world of sport.

Wrestling with Death

Though professional wrestling is not a true sport, it has been riddled with common sport-associated problems. Professional wrestling is no stranger to such drug-related controversies; it is perhaps the most telling of sport-associated entities when it comes to exploring problematic areas involving drug abuse and issues associated with the fallout that can occur in the aftermath of tragedy. The following chapter details scandals, tragedies, and hazards impacting professional wrestling. These problems are further exacerbated by deficiencies in industry standards (no unions, players association, etc.), as well as other contributing factors. To provide a more thorough understanding of professional wrestling, background information pertaining to the history and characteristics of this pseudo sport will be detailed in the subsequent sections.

Professional Wrestling: What is it?

Though it is not a pure sport, per se, wrestling certainly involves many of the elements associated with sport. Whether it's the live crowds, the athletic combatants, the physicality, the fluid movement, or the compelling stories that are being conveyed, professional wrestling has been able to capture the imaginations and interest of its followers for over a century (Lee & Bernthal, forthcoming 2009).

The form of entertainment that is professional wrestling is many things: to some it is a popular entertainment form, and an obsession for its most ardent fans. Others view wrestling as being "low brow" amusement or even trash TV. To others, "it is a spectacle of violence, misogyny and degradation, or merely an entertainment that appeals to the lowest common denominator of human life and entertainment value" (Lee & Bernthal, forthcoming 2009).

"While largely discounted as a genuine sport by most, professional wrestling has evolved from a minor source of 'entertainment' to a culturally powerful multi-media complex" (Atkinson, 2002, p. 47). Much of wrestling's appeal is tied to elements of sport presented in this form of staged violence.

Choreographed Violence

Mazer (1993) stated that "Professional wrestling is a sport that is not, in the literal sense of the word, sporting; a theoretical entertainment that is not theatre" (p. 3). Professional wrestling is encapsulated by sportings a veneer of athleticism over scripted outcomes that read much like a "male soap opera" (though such a categorization would be a misnomer, as wrestling followers are by no means entirely male). This entertainment form has survived, and in the case of companies like World Wrestling Entertainment, thrived. Having attained tremendous popularity in the United States, the "fake sport" has proven to be an extremely popular spectator event.

Pseudo Sport

Though not a true athletic competition, professional wrestling embodies various features associated with true sport. WWE Chairman Vincent K. McMahon has readily referred to his WWE wrestling product as a commodity identified as "sports entertainment," and has compared the professional wrestling industry to a "movie studio" in the wrestling documentary, *Beyond the Mat*. This mind-set is even further demonstrated as his company has further distanced themselves from the term "sport" by commonly referring to their performers simply as "entertainers." Professional wrestling purposefully presents itself as true sport on the surface. Wrestling involves elements of competition, performance, physical exertion, and institutionalization in efforts to entertain audiences through images of athletic violence.

Included in "true sport" imagery provided by professional wrestling are fans routing for the favorites (or against the opposition); winners and losers (though in this case the outcomes are predetermined); competitive athletic endeavors commonly displaying power, skill, and strength; and contests take place in a sport environment (i.e., wrestling rings; also known as the "squared circle").

Thus, wrestling is able to incorporate aspects of performance, competition, physical exertion, and institutionalization in a well-articulated form aimed at entertaining its legions of followers. As Atkinson (2002) stated,

> The athletic moves employed in a professional wrestling match are ... paradoxical. They are competitive expressions of strength and physical dexterity, yet are simultaneously well-rehearsed, manipulated, choreographed, and meticulously planned (p. 60).

Historical Considerations

Professional wrestling has existed in some form for well over a century. Today, professional wrestling is a passion for its most ardent fans, while also being viewed as an uncultured form of amusement, choreographed violence, a morality play, and so on.

The form of entertainment known as professional wrestling began as a legitimate sporting endeavor. Originating as a true sport, early wrestling matches were commonly "long, drawn out affairs that lacked certain elements that kept the paying public inclined to come back for more" (Lee & Bernthal, 2009). Ultimately, wrestling promoters envisioned that the best way to put on an entertaining performance was to implement predetermined results. This mind-set opened the door for an entertainment form that was based on the "performance," rather than pure athletic competition. The staged competitions became part of traveling tours that were similar to carnival circuits during late 1800s and early 1900s.

Eventually, more structured wrestling organizations became established in North America. Different geographic regions held wrestling organizations that became known as "territories" (or wrestling "fiefdoms," as columnist Irv Muschnick (2007) refers to them). For example, wrestling territories that existed in the United States included Florida Championship Wrestling for fans in Florida; World Class Championship Wrestling (or others) catering to fans in Texas and surrounding states; and fans in the northeast had the World Wrestling Federation (WWF, formerly the WWWF).

WWE

Jess McMahon (grandfather of current WWE Chairman, Vincent K. McMahon) and his Capital Sports organization was involved in the promotion of professional wrestling in early days in National Wrestling Alliance (NWA). His involvement evolved into the formation of the World Wide Wrestling Federation (WWWF) in 1963. The company eventually shortened its name to the World Wrestling Federation (WWF) and in 1982, Vincent K. McMahon and his company Titan Sports, Inc. purchased Capital Sports (Wrestling) from his father and his business partners making him the owner of the WWF (Assael & Mooneyham, 2002).

After buying out his father, the younger McMahon embarked on a path that changed the scope of wrestling forever. The prevalence of the territory system quickly diminished as the 1980s moved forward; and by the mid-1980s, the wrestling industry was becoming more centralized.

McMahon expanded his wrestling empire by taking over regional territories and recruiting top regional stars in order to build a collection of wrestling stars as the foundation for his plans of national and global expansion. After taking over the WWF, Vincent K. McMahon burst onto the national scene in unprecedented fashion with the emergence of *Hulkamania*, presenting "Real American Hero" Hulk Hogan. In the aftermath of Hulkamania's genesis, the inaugural *WrestleMania* took place in 1985 at New York City's Madison Square Garden, forever changing professional wrestling and strongly influencing closed circuit broadcasting—which lay a foundation for what is now known as pay-per-view. That same year, WWF spawned a children's Saturday morning cartoon: *Hulk Hogan's Rock 'n' Wrestling*, featuring WWF wrestlers and airing on CBS.

As McMahon's corporation continued expanding, *WWF Monday Night Raw* began airing in 1993. This program remains one of cable programming's highest rated shows. In 1995, World Championship Wrestling (WCW), the WWF's main competitor, began broadcasting *Monday Nitro*, beginning the "Monday Night Wars." The Monday Night Wars sparked a multiple year battle for wrestling supremacy in North America. WCW, originally backed by Ted Turner and his Turner Broadcasting Corporation, was a major force in wrestling. In 1999, WWE premiered its network television offering *SmackDown!* This program is now known as *Friday Night SmackDown!* and has aired on networks such as UPN, CW, and My Network TV.

The year 2001 saw a major shake up in the professional wrestling industry in North America, as the WWF purchased WCW, essentially gaining a monopoly over the major wrestling scene. Since the late 1980s, *World Championship Wrestling* (WCW) was the only formable competition again the WWE juggernaut. Eventually, Turner Broadcasting merged with Time Warner, and subsequently AOL. As a result, Turner's involvement and influence in promoting the WCW brand of wrestling disappeared. After the company dwindled for years, the perfect storm opened up for McMahan and his New York Stock Exchange public corporation. The WWF was able to purchase the WCW brand and its extensive "tape library" for a bargain price of $5 million (this tape library would later be used to enhance the WWE's on-demand television and DVD offerings) (Lovel, 2002).

On the heels of the WCW takeover, WWF became World Wrestling Entertainment (WWE), following a settlement with the World Wildlife Fund. The newly christened WWE then split into two brands in a process identified as "brand extension." During this process, wrestlers were aligned with either the *RAW* brand and its programming or the *SmackDown!* brand and its programming.

WWE as a Commodity

The following statement from *SportsBusiness Journal's* 10 year retrospective encapsulated WWE nicely when it stated:

In the fall of 1998, more 18- to 34-year-old males were watching pro wrestling than were watching "Monday Night Football." The name of the organization may have changed—World Wrestling Federation then, World Wrestling Entertainment now—but as the 74,000 fans who attended this year's WrestleMania in Orlando would tell you, the popularity remains ("Full contact," 2008, n.p.).

In regards to wrestling financial prosperity, Vincent Kennedy McMahon and his brain trust, the World Wrestling Entertainment (WWE), emerged as the premiere force in professional wrestling. The WWE is estimated as being a billion dollar business, and is publicly traded on New York Stock Exchange (NYSE) as "WWE." Prime moments, such as 1985's inaugural WrestleMania broadcast from Madison Square Garden to the 2008 WrestleMania in Orlando's Citrus Bowl, have been a visible popular culture and economic power. WWE's assault on contemporary culture is visible through ventures such as integrated media efforts, which are "used to help to sell television programming and advertisements, pay per view buy rates, DVDs, CDs, posters, t-shirts and almost any other form of merchandising imaginable" (Lee & Bernthal, 2009).

The Wrestling Lifestyle

Aside from the use of performance enhancements that provide a means for developing and maintaining the "real life cartoon figure" appearance, wrestling is associated with various occupational hazards including prevalent injury, travel conditions and scheduling demands, and leading what often is equated to a "rock star" lifestyle.

Appearance Expectations (Maintaining the Look)

Professional wrestling is an image-focused form of entertainment. According to Chris Mannix (2007), "If steroids are common in pro baseball and football, then the drugs are rampant in pro wrestling, which places an enormous emphasis on the size of its athletes" (n.p.). Wrestlers, such as the "Superstars" of the WWE, project an image based on "well-built men of cartoonish and astonishing proportions, meeting in matches that serve as wildly popular soap operas starring human action figures" (Sandomir, 2007, n.p.). With such super-human appearances come the common use and abuse of steroids and other physical enhancement substances; this has been exemplified time and time again through various drug scandals and associated deaths.

Injury

In professional wrestling, drug use and abuse goes far beyond appearance concerns. Wrestlers commonly have relied upon drugs to manage pain, while allowing participants to keep on with show. Use and abuse of painkillers, uppers, sedatives, and others drugs help wresters to deal with pain, wake up, stay awake, relax, sleep, and take part in other life functions. The use of such substances to cope with injury adds to the windfall of drug-associated problems. Such problems are exacerbated by grueling travel demands.

Travel Conditions and Scheduling Demands

In addition to keeping up appearances and attempting to manage pain, wrestlers commonly engage in grueling travel and scheduling demands. Wrestlers cross the country (if not the globe) accumulating astronomical match totals. As wrestlers pile up miles on rental cars and build up a huge accumulation of air miles, their bodies are often denied the chance for appropriate rest and recuperation. The regular pounding that wrestlers accrue is thus exacerbated by a lack of down time.

Living a "Rock Star" Lifestyle

Living the pro wrestler lifestyle provides a life associated with numerous areas of deviance including drug abuse, violence, sexual exploitation, and criminal activity. The occurrence of drug abuse is further categorized into profound performance enhancer use (such as steroids and growth hormones), abuse of painkillers, alcohol, and recreational drugs.

In regards to living the rock star lifestyle, professional wrestling locker rooms have commonly been host to legendary tales. Famed wrestler, Kevin Nash stated, "Rock stars don't party anywhere near what wrestlers do. The quote should be that rock stars party like wrestlers" (Randazzo, 2008, p. 220). Wrestlers may choose to imbibe before, during, and after the wrestling shows. Additionally, wrestlers have been known to have a supply of drugs handy—wrestlers commonly have portable pharmacies (in the form personal bags or fanny packs, etc.).

WWE's Drug Scandals

In regards to drug scandals impacting professional wrestling, there have been a few pivotal moments that are pertinent to issues associated with drugs in professional wrestling. Perhaps the three most pivotal moments are Vince McMahon's steroid indictment in the early 1990s, the death of Eddie Guerrero, and the murder-suicide by Chris Benoit.

McMahon Steroid Trial

Vince McMahon has a multi-faceted personality. His supporters might say that he is an ingenious businessman, who helped to revolutionize professional wrestling (or as he has labeled it, "sports entertainment"), pay-per-view programming, and other aspects of sport and entertainment. He is a self-proclaimed "self-made" billionaire and has turned himself and his company into popular culture icons.

To his detractors, and there are many, Vince McMahon is many things as well. He is more than an evil TV character (his "Mr. McMahon" persona on WWE programming), he is also viewed as an egotistical bully, a shameless promoter of violence and trash TV, and someone who has ruined professional wrestling (at least in the traditional sense of the word) by eliminating his competition at all cost and turning professional wrestling into the "sports entertainment" that can bee seen in WWE programming today.

During the early 1990s, Vince McMahon and his WWF company were embroiled in a major steroid controversy. McMahon and various notable wrestlers were linked to Dr. George Zahorian, who was viewed as a "Dr. Feelgood" for professional wrestlers. After the courts were presented with a mountain of evidence, including a regular pattern of shipments to Vince McMahon, Hulk Hogan, Roddy Piper, and numerous other wrestlers on the WWE payroll, Zahorian was indicted on 15 counts of distributing controlled substances, primarily steroids (Assael & Mooneyham, 2002).

At that time, there were questions about McMahon's involvement and the implications it could have on his wrestling empire. In 1991, under pressure from the looming federal investigation, McMahon decided to institute a drug policy in the WWF. Though McMahon ended up being indicted on charges of possession of steroids and conspiracy to distribute steroids in 1993, he was eventually exonerated of conspiring to distribute steroids to his wrestlers (Mannix, 2007).

Despite being exonerated (unlike Zahorian before him), McMahon's reputation was damaged and there was much speculation pertaining to drug and steroid issues in his company and the wrestling industry as a whole (Miller, n.d.). Additional incriminating testimonies, such as those by Hogan, Piper, and other well-known wrestlers, provided further detail into the apparently prevalent steroid culture in the WWF (Assael & Mooneyham, 2002; Meltzer, 2001).

Randazzo (2008) suggests that Vince McMahon "has probably been the most clearly chemically-enhanced star on WWE TV over the past decade" (p. 268), as he compares Vince McMahon to the bodybuilding legend-turned actor-turned politician, Arnold Schwarzenegger. In this comparison, McMahon is described as still having the "ridiculous jacked-up Schwarzenegger physique," (p. 268) that Arnold himself no longer possesses (McMahon is actually older than the California Governor). This explanation goes on to comment that McMahon has the type of body that a person multiple decades his junior could not have without chemical enhancement.

Aside from the newly instituted drug testing program, there was also a noticeable change in the physiques associated with the WWF top stars. WWF's upper echelon performers were suddenly composed of more moderately physiqued performers like Bret Hart, as opposed to the earlier regime of individuals which displayed the 'roided look (i.e., Hulk Hogan and the Ultimate Warrior). A prime example of this was the sudden departure of top company star, Jim "Ultimate Warrior" Hellwig. Hellwig was even referred to by fellow wrestlers as the "Anabolic Warrior" for all the steroids it took to gain him his superhuman frame (Assael & Mooneyham, 2002; Muschnick, 2007). In addition to Hellwig, another notable wrestler, the "British Bulldog" Davey Boy Smith (Smith will be discussed in further detail later in the chapter), was subsequently fired in 1992 for his involvement with illegal performance enhancers (Meltzer, 2004).

Allegations of further drug activity have continued to surround Vince McMahon. "Considering that Vince McMahon is the CEO, it shouldn't be surprising that chemical dependencies would exist in upper echelons of WWE" (Randazzo,

The three most pivotal moments associated with drug-associated scandals that
have heightened concern over the presence of drug issues impacting the WWE and
the wrestling industry as a whole WWE have been:

1. *The McMahon Trial in the early 1990s.*
2. *The death of Eddie Guerrero, and the subsequent establishment of the
   WWE Wellness Policy.*
3. *The murder-suicide by Chris Benoit (and the associated fallout from this
   horrendous incident).*

2008, p. 300). Randazzo describes McMahon's permissiveness on drug use as
being "legendary." In addition to the McMahon trial, other pivotal moments associated with drug scandals involving the WWE—the deaths of Eddie Guerrero
and Chris Benoit—will be addressed later in the chapter.

Death Watch

Beyond the steroid scandal of the early 1990s, drug abuse in professional
wrestling has resulted in various arrests, suspensions, widespread scandal, and
deaths. Premature wrestling deaths have been occurring in staggering numbers.
Among the casualties have been some of the better known wrestlers to enter the
ring in recent years. The highly visible problem of untimely deaths have been associated with travel, heart attacks and other heart-associated health problems,
performance (in-ring) related deaths, and drug-related fatalities.

The pitfalls associated with wrestling and the high numbers of premature
deaths may be viewed as being the "nature of the beast," or what wrestling legend
"Rowdy" Roddy Piper termed "the sickness" (Piper & Picarello, 2002). As Mannix (2007) stated, "Call professional wrestling sports or call it entertainment, but
whatever you call it, realize that people are dying in it. They are dying because
they believe bigger muscles lead to bigger paychecks. But no one is telling them
that they can't spend a nickel of it if they are dead." (n.p.). The situation was so
bad that some wrestlers would run "dead pools" speculating on who the next casualty would be (Randazzo, 2008). One wrestler, noted for being a heavy drug
user, Scott "Raven" Levy, even attested to being his own selection for next to go
in a wrestlers' dead pool.

When wrestlers consume medications like pain killers, muscle relaxers,
steroids, tranquilizers, and alcohol, it is easy to see how such substances, especially when combined, could lead to a lethal cocktail. Rothstein and Lister (2007)
wrote an article in *The Sun* entitled "105 wrestlers die in a decade." Of the 105
wrestlers listed who died between 1997 and 2007, 42 were identified as being
full-time professionals (individuals who worked regularly for a large North American promotion). The remaining wrestlers were grapplers who worked on a part-
time basis for any of the numerous smaller independent groups operating
throughout the United States and Canada. This account noted that the report fo-

cused on wrestler casualties, not those of other individuals associated with professional wrestling, such as valets, managers, and referees, which would expand the list.

Rothstein and Lister (2007) go on to point out that the premature deaths in wrestling are rarely caused by a single factor—rather, wrestlers die to "a deadly cocktail" of problems, addictions, and stresses. In addition to the heavy use of steroids and growth hormones, the abuse of substances such as painkillers, alcohol, and recreational drugs commonly are at play.

Three years before the feature published by *The Sun*, John Swartz of the *USA Today* wrote a feature on wrestling deaths and steroids in 2004. In his report, profiles were given on the prevalence of drug related deaths that had occurred in the preceding decade. Examining autopsy reports and other data, such as accounts of family members and other wrestlers, Swartz profiled the deaths of well-known wrestling personalities Curt Hennig, Davey Boy Smith, Rick Rude, and Brian Pillman. Each of these noteworthy wrestling deaths will be addressed in the next section.

"Mr. Perfect" Curt Hennig

Given the moniker of "Mr. Perfect," Hennig was one of the biggest wrestling stars of the 1980s and 1990s. He died of acute cocaine intoxication in 2003, at the age of 44. His father (former professional wrestler Larry "the Ax" Hennig) stated that steroids and painkillers also contributed to Hennig's death (Swartz, 2004). At the time of his death, Hennig was still an active wrestler, who was not far removed from his last stint with the WWE. In September of 2008, WWE issued a DVD compilation celebrating the life and career of Hennig, entitled *The Life and Times of Mr. Perfect*.

"The British Bulldog" Davey Boy Smith

Smith died in 2002 at the age of 39 as a result of an enlarged heart. Smith was a powerhouse who was noted for being a heavy drug user, abusing such drugs as steroids, HGH, and a wide assortment of pain medications. His career saw him transition from being a smaller, more technically sound wrestler to his latter day behemoth stature—his 175 pound body bulked up to 270 pounds with the assistance of steroids and HGH (Assael, 2002). His brother-in-law stated that he "paid the price with steroid cocktails and human-growth hormones" (Swartz, 2004, n.p.).

In an article entitled *Overkill*, Shaun Assael (2002) of *ESPN the Magazine* profiled Smith's death, noting how it received little mainstream attention in the U.S. (though more coverage was given in Canada and the U.K.). At the peak of his career, Smith headlined an event attracting 80,000 people to London's Wembly Stadium. Smith's chronic drug use was described as "predictable" by noted wrestling and mixed martial arts columnist Dave Meltzer (2004). Meltzer went on to state that Smith's death was just another in a long succession of unfortunate events that professional wrestlers "had become numb to because the frequency of such stories ... [it was] sadly, almost expected from seeing him during his darkest days" (p. 28).

As a side note, Smith's long time partner, Tom "Dynamite Kid" Billington, has been confined to a wheelchair after years of steroid abuse (Meltzer, 2004). Billington's career was cut short because of injury. His body simply broke down after the rigors of leading an extreme form of the "wrestling life." Interestingly enough, Billington was the childhood hero and wrestling role model for Chris Benoit, who will be discussed in great detail later in this chapter. Smith's son, Harry Smith (who wrestles as D.H. Smith), is a current WWE wrestler. In his short tenure with the company, the youngest Smith has already violated the wellness policy, resulting in a 30-day suspension, seemingly not learning the lessons from his father's tragic tale.

"Ravishing" Rick Rude (Richard Rood)

The man known as "Ravishing" Rick Rude died at the age of 40 from an overdose of "mixed medications" (Swartz, 2004). According to Assael and Mooneyham (2002), Rude "took so many steroids that his heart [gave] out when he turned forty" (p. 98). Several years before his death, Rude was one of the many wrestlers involved in the wrestling scandal in the early 1990s, leading to the indictments of Dr. Zahorian and Vince McMahon. Rude, who was noted for his unusually well-sculpted physique, testified to using steroids for building muscle mass and relieving joint pain.

"The Loose Cannon" Brian Pillman

In 1997, the death of Brian Pillman rocked the wrestling world as the highly popular WWF personality was found dead in his hotel room. Pillman, who was noted for a long history of drug abuse, including steroids, growth hormone, and pain pills, died at the age of 35 (Meltzer, 2001). At the time of his death, Pillman was using human-growth hormone and painkillers (empty bottles of painkillers were found near his body at the site of his death). The official cause of death was cited as heart failure, with cocaine as a contributing factor. In a point of irony, Pillman was in such a state leading up to his death that he was actual one of the few WWF employees that were subject to drug testing. Unfortunately, Pillman was still allowed to compete after failing his tests (Assael & Mooneyham, 2002).

Louie Spicolli

Another "premature" wrestling death profiled in Swartz's report was that of Louie Spicolli (real name Louie Mucciolo). Aside from being the least well known wrestler in Swartz's report, Spicolli was also the youngest of those identified in this expose. At the time of his death at age 27, Spicolli was a regular performer for WCW and was involved in ongoing story lines on the company's televised programming (Swartz, 2004).

Spicolli died in his home of coronary disease (Swartz, 2004). At the time of his death, an empty vial of the male hormone testosterone, pain pills, and an anxiety-reducing drug were found in his home; the coroner's office determined the drugs may have contributed to his heart condition. In the expose *Sex, Lies, and Headlocks* (Assael & Mooneyham, 2002), Spicolli was identified as a recipient of the services of another wrestling "Dr. Feelgood," Dr. Joel Hackett. At the time of Spicolli's death, Hackett's name was found on his medication bottles. Spicolli had ingested 26 somas, and upon arrival to the scene of Spicolli's dead body, police theorized that the effects of the pills could have been multiplied significantly by his earlier wine consumption (Meltzer, 2001). Hackett went on to have his medical license suspended and faced numerous bogus prescription charges. In addition to Spicolli, Hackett has been tied to troubled wrestlers Davey Boy Smith, Brian Pillman (both previously profiled), Scott Hall, and a host of others.

The Death Toll Is Rising

Though the number of premature deaths presented in this chapter are substantial, the WWE was quick to point out that following the Benoit tragedy (detailed later in the chapter), only five wrestlers were under contract at the time of their deaths (Chris Benoit, Eddie Guerrero, Russ Haas [developmental wrestler], Owen Hart [who died following a fall from the rafters of an arena in a theatrical ring entrance mishap], and Brian Pillman). The WWE claim that only five deaths are tied to them is a misnomer; a number of other wrestling casualties occurred within a few years of the wrestler's cessation of employment with the company.

Eddie Guerrero

In 2005, the death of Eddie Guerrero marked a monumental time in the WWE. Guererro was athletic, charismatic, and came from a well-known wrestling family. Not only was Guerrero a former WWE Champion, he was also a highly popular star who had been featured in commercial spots for products like Stacker 2, the dietary supplement company that had partnered with WWE. He was also featured in a UPN network documentary entitled *Cheating Death, Stealing Life: The Eddie Guererro Story*, which featured Guerrero's tragedies and shortcomings (including substance abuse). At the time of its release, Guerrero was celebrated for overcoming his problems and emerging as a triumphant success story. This documentary was later enhanced with more footage and matches and turned into a WWE DVD of the same name. Just when it appeared that Guerrero had overcome his demons and escaped becoming another wrestling casualty, the report came out in various major news outlets that he was found dead in a Minneapolis hotel room. Though his death was not an overdose, he died of heart failure attributed to years of substance abuse. His autopsy showed effects of heart disease tied to drug abuse, due to steroids causing the "heart to work harder to pump blood to an enlarged physique... associated with arterial wear and tear" (Assael, 2007a, n.p.).

The death of WWE Superstar Eddie Guerrero received media attention from news outlets and other entertainment sources. The significant coverage of this event and the subsequent fallout paled in comparison to the widespread attention and media coverage that WWE and the professional wrestling industry as a whole garnered in North America in 2007. Because Guerrero was one of the premiere names on the WWE roster and a former champion for professional wrestling's most noteworthy and profitable organization, great interest and speculation was generated regarding professional wrestling safety and wellness issues, including concerns over drugs aspects. Following the death of Eddie Guerrero, the WWE implemented the WWE Talent Wellness Program.

WWE Talent Wellness Program

In 2006, in the aftermath of Eddie Guerrero's death, WWE initiated its new "wellness policy." The WWE published this announcement as a news alert issue. The alert stated:

> *Effective today, February 27, 2006, WWE is implementing a broad WWE Talent Wellness Program. The Program has two components: 1) an aggressive substance abuse and drug testing policy; and 2) a cardiovascular testing and monitoring program. The Substance Abuse and Drug Testing Policy ("Policy") prohibits the non-medical use and associate abuse of prescription medications and performance-enhancing drugs, as well as the use, possession and/or distribution of illegal drugs by WWE Talent. The use of masking agents and/or diuretics to conceal or obscure the use of prohibited drugs is also prohibited. This Policy will be administered by Dr. David L. Black, Ph.D., D-ABFT, D-ABCC, of Aegis Sciences Corporation, Nashville, Tennessee. Dr. Black will be responsible for scheduling Talent for testing, administering collection of samples, coordinating secure shipment of samples to the testing facility, determining whether any WWE Talent has tested positive and directing the appropriate penalty be imposed* (WWE Talent Wellness Program, 2006).

Since its establishment, the WWE Wellness Policy has claimed various infractors. To date, violators of the policy have been such notable WWE Superstars as Jeff Hardy, William Regal, Kurt Angle, and Randy Orton, among others.

Though some top-billed stars have been caught violating the Wellness Policy, there is still concern that numerous wrestlers with seemingly obvious chemically enhanced physiques have avoided detection. There is also concern associated with how certain performers seem to have made light of the Wellness Policy, even on camera.

The wrestler who goes by the name Triple H (Hunter Hurst Helmsley; real name Paul Levesque) is one example of someone who makes a mockery of the Wellness Policy. Triple H is one of the top stars in the WWE. With a super-human physique, he has managed to be one of the company's main draws for over a decade. During this time, he has become even more intertwined to the inner circle of WWE's upper rankings—he is married to Vince McMahon's daughter, Stephanie. Triple H is noted for his controversial actions and statements. Even the seemingly unapproachable topic of conversation, WWE's Wellness Policy controversies, has been fair game.

For example, on the October 2, 2006 edition of *Monday Night Raw*, Triple H followed up a conversation in which (story line) "General Manager" of *Raw*, Eric Bischoff, was being profiled as a means of promoting his new book. In a backstage skit, Bischoff and wrestler Chris Masters (real name Chris Mordetzky) are shown talking, when Degeneration X (also known as DX; a group composed of Triple H and Shawn Michaels) enters the backstage scene. Triple H asks Masters when is he going to write a book entitled *How to Lose 50 Pounds in Four Weeks*? This was a not-so-veiled reference to Masters' sudden weight and physique loss following a stay in rehab and coming off a Wellness Policy violation suspension.

Triple H has continued to broach the subject of Wellness Violation issues. He recently pretended to be talking to Dr. Black (administrator of WWE drug testing program) as he tried to hand the phone off to Jeff Hardy (a two-time Wellness Policy violator) on the September 5, 2008 edition of *Friday Night SmackDown!* It should be noted that the aforementioned examples are not the only times he has mocked the Wellness Policy on WWE programming.

Beyond this, concern exists over the potential for, as well as previous history of, wrestlers who seem able to avoid detection. Such aspects will be identified in the fallout discussion in the Benoit incident, addressed in the following section.

Chris Benoit

In 2007, the wrestling industry's greatest tragedy occurred: the Benoit incident. After the incident, concerns about wrestling-related deaths and drug issues received unprecedented attention, leading to a number of investigations, second. The Benoit tragedy centered on Chris Benoit, a former World Champion and seemingly "consummate professional wrestler," who killed his wife, former wrestling valet/manager Nancy "Woman" Benoit, and their 7-year-old son, Daniel, in their suburban Atlanta home. Following these murders, Benoit hung himself in his home gym.

Matthew Radazzo (2008) begins the first chapter of his Chris Benoit biography and wrestling expose, *Ring of Hell: The Story of Chris Benoit and the Fall of the Pro Wrestling Industry*, by referencing an ominous quote from Benoit, taken in 2004:

> The world [of wrestling] doesn't push you to the depths of darkness. You do. That drives me nuts.... It's not the world of wrestling that drove [troubled wrestlers] to alcohol, the world of wrestling that drove them to drugs. You do that to yourself." (p. 9).

Radazzo followed up this quote by noting that Benoit was "abusing steroids, painkillers, alcohol, amphetamines, and psychiatric drugs" at the time of the interview (p. 9).

This heinous act brought about unprecedented media coverage for professional wrestling. When the presence of steroids and documentation of Benoit receiving extremely high amounts of prescribed testosterone from a medical physician unfolded, drug concerns regarding professional wrestling were taken to a whole new level. This brought about speculation and commentary regarding concern over lack of industry regulation and even investigations by Congress (to be referenced later). The Benoit tragedy sparked investigations into drug scandals and the effects of head trauma (such as a study by the Sports Legacy Institute).

According to Randazzo (2008), "Benoit's body was in constant pain, and his profoundly damaged brain was further scrambled by years of heavy amphetamine, steroids, alcohol, painkiller, and psychiatric drug abuse" by the age of forty (p. 11). Controversially—and in hindsight, revoltingly—WWE decided to host a three-hour "tribute" to Benoit on its popular *Monday Night Raw* program on the

Following a tribute show to Chris Benoit on *Monday Night Raw*, CEO Vince McMahon made the following statement on the June 27, 2008 episode of the Sci-Fi Network's *ECW* broadcast:

> *Last night on Monday Night Raw, the WWE presented a special tribute show, recognizing the career of Chris Benoit. However, now some 26 hours later, the facts of this horrific tragedy are now apparent.*
>
> *Therefore, other than my comments, there will be no mention of Mr. Benoit tonight. On the contrary, tonight's show will be dedicated to everyone who has been affected by this terrible incident. This evening marks the first step of the healing process. Tonight, the WWE performers will do what they do better than anyone else in the world—entertain you.*

Monday following deaths of the Benoit family. This had become customary; other wrestlers from the main WWE roster had been given tribute shows following their deaths. The Benoit tribute show was broadcast from an empty arena in Corpus Christi, Texas (where the regularly scheduled show was to appear). The show went on prime time television, even though the local police had discovered the Benoit family dead in their home earlier during the day of the broadcast, and there were still many questions about the deaths. This turned out to be a serious lapse of judgment. As further results of the murder suicide were presented, the WWE quickly went in "spin control" mode. They removed virtually all images and mentions of Benoit from their website and issued an apology on the next broadcast show, which took place on the June 26, 2007 edition of *ECW* on the Sci-Fi Network. This scenario was a PR debacle and what Mannix (2007) dubbed a "travesty."

Congressional Involvement

The Chris Benoit murder-suicide case became more significant when, in its aftermath, two congressmen requested that World Wrestling Entertainment provide records pertaining to the WWE's testing policies and practices. This move was similar to that of the investigation into Major League Baseball. It sought details pertaining to "drugs covered by its policies; the entity that conducts its drug testing; the number of tests it conducts annually; the protocols followed after a positive test; and the procedures for awarding exemptions" (Assael, 2007a, n.p.). "If Congress—which has involved itself in the fight against steroid abuse before—is looking for something to do, there is a billion dollar industry with an enormous fan base that needs fixing" (Mannix, 2007, n.p.).

Akin to the investigation that resulted in Major League Baseball's Mitchell Report, Rep. Henry Waxman, chair of the House Committee on Oversight and Government Reform, and ranking minority member Tom Davis sent Vince McMahon a three-page letter asking for the WWE to provide documentation detailing the WWE's drug-testing policy, including information pertaining to test results. These requests were sent because of concerns about the legitimacy of the testing protocol and the worries that the WWE may have been misleading the fans and the general public in regards to the legitimacy of the testing efforts and the motivations behind the procedures. Furthermore, in this letter, WWE wrestlers are were referred to in the letter as being "multimedia stars that have an influence on the behavior and attitudes of the nation's youth" (Assael, 2007a, n.p.). The Congressional investigation also sought to gain "hard figures" regarding the number of tests conducted by the WWE annually, the number of wrestlers tested, positive results for the specific drugs, and the number of positive tests in which the violators were castigated (Assael, 2007a).

The autopsy of Chris Benoit added ammunition to such concern, as the official toxicology report results showed that Benoit's testosterone level was highly elevated (estimated at being approximately 10 times higher than levels allowed under Olympic drug testing guidelines). Aside from extremely high levels of testosterone, the wrestler was also found with amounts of Xanax and hydrocodone in his system at the time of death (Assael, 2007a). These findings, in light of the WWE's claims that Benoit was clean and had not failed recent tests, raised further inquiries and doubts about the apparent room for loopholes and creative use of semantics (such as wrestlers taking testosterone treatments are not taking steroids, etc.) associated with the WWE's wellness policy.

Though the WWE insists that they maintain a strict testing program, randomly testing its athletes at least four times a year, the company and its policy has been criticized for being too soft. With concerns over having an "employee-friendly" policy, the defenders within this process, such as Dr. David Black, the company's hired drug testing administrator, have claimed that "The intention is not to punish [the wrestlers], but to get them [the wrestlers] to engage in a different lifestyle" (Assael, 2007a, n.p.).

Credibility Lost

The WWE has been accused of misleading their fans and the public with information that would lead observers to believe that a stringent testing program was in place (Rothstein, 2007a). Various recent occurrences have helped to shed light on such concerns.

These allegations—which include first-hand reports of steroid use by prominent former wrestlers—have swirled around the WWE for over a decade. Investigations by journalists have described a culture of performance-enhancing drug use in professional wrestling, high fatality rates among young professional wrestlers, and an inability or unwillingness of WWE to address these problems (Assael, 2007a, n.p.).

Following the Benoit tragedy and the WWE's ardent denial of Benoit's steroid use, there were a number of statements made, such as a claim that all that was found in Benoit's system was testosterone (Rothstein, 2007a). WWE lawyer Jerry McDevitt claimed that there was no actual abuse going on, even though the WWE's Wellness Policy states, "The non-medical use of anabolic androgenic steroids (AAS), which include and are based on the natural steroid testosterone, is prohibited" (Mannix, 2007, n.p.). Further validating concerns over the WWE's improper denial were statements by both medical and legal experts clearly identifying testosterone cypionate as an anabolic steroid (Rothstein, 2007).

Sandomir (2007) stated, "By the time Chris Benoit strangled his wife, suffocated his son and hanged himself last month in their home, he had been tested for drugs four times as part of World Wrestling Entertainment's 'talent wellness' program" (n.p.). This included testing negative during a urine test on April 10, 2007 at the site of a WWE event at the Dunkin' Donuts Center in Providence, Rhode Island. This is very conspicuous given the reports of large quantities of steroids that were discovered in his home only a few months later. Reports have shown that Benoit was prescribed 10-month supplies of anabolic steroids every three to four weeks from May 2006 to May 2007 by his physician, Dr. Phil Astin. Dr. Astin has since been indicted for improperly prescribing drugs.

WWE's policy allows for wrestlers to receive a therapeutic exemption if they have damaged their endocrine systems through the abuse of steroids — these wrestlers are allowed to use more steroids for testosterone-replacement therapy, which seems contradictory. The WWE and their testing agents suggest that such allowances are acceptable, since the purpose of the program is not to punish the wrestlers or deprive them a chance to earn a living (Mannix, 2007). However, inconsistencies in placing exemptions and overlooking exemptions in place for several wrestlers, all at the discretion of the program director, raises questions and concern.

Comparatively, WWE's procedures are different than many of sport's governing bodies, where athletes may present their case before a medical board that will make a determination. Dr. Gary Wadler, a WADA consultant and leading expert on performance-enhancing drug issues, points out that such exemptions are something that should be pursued on the front end, rather than a post-facto decision (Sandomir, 2007).

After the Benoit Tragedy

Since the murder-suicide by Chris Benoit, various investigations associated with Benoit, the WWE, and the professional wrestling industry as a whole continue to unfold. This has included investigating questionable and illegal performance enhancement shipments and reports of improper medical practices by the physician that treated Benoit and other wrestlers. Dr. Phil Astin III, who prescribed copious amounts of drugs to Benoit and his wife, was identified being a "pill mill." Astin has been indicted on federal charges of over-prescribing medications (Hollis, 2008). Astin, who was prescribing Benoit a 10-month dosage every month, has also been linked to various other wrestlers since the Benoit deaths, including Benoit's friend Mike "Johnny Grunge" Durham, who died before the age of forty. Durham was described as a wrestler who lived to be loaded (Randazzo, 2008).

Though the Astin situation is troubling (especially in hindsight of the Benoit incident), other "mark doctors" (a term used to refer to medical doctors who are willing to give wrestlers what that are looking for to meet the desired ends) have been documented, in addition to those already identified in this chapter—Astin, Hackett, and Zhahorian. A notable drug abusing wrestler, Lawrence "Lex Luger" Pfhol, admitted to being one of 700 athlete-patients, from an assortment of sports, who receive orders of steroid and human growth hormones (Hollis, 2008). Though Luger did not provide the name of his doctor-supplier in this instance, this is just one example of a doctor illegally providing medications to wrestlers.

Luger, in this same report, went on to provide further details about the ease with which wrestlers receive meds and skirt around testing procedures. He says the key to getting medication is just obtaining a prescription. Once the scripts are obtained, wrestlers have a doctor's excuse for using the given substances. Beyond that, if the "doctor's excuse" is not sufficient, various means can be enacted to get around a dirty drug test result, such masking agents, having samples provided by others, and other dubious methods.

Luger was involved in a scandalous situation when his live-in girlfriend, former wrestling personality Elizabeth "Miss Elizabeth" Hulette, became one of the many tragic wrestling-related deaths. Huelette's persona was the embodiment of the sweet, ladylike goodness that was an exception in the world of wrestling. She died following a variety of problems associated with Lex Luger. At the time of her death, there was a mixture of hydrocodone, Alprazolam (Xanax), steroids, and vodka in her system (Meltzer, 2004). Prior to Huelette's death, police had been called to a domestic dispute that resulted in Luger's arrest (one of multiple arrests for Luger). Luger was arrested again after her death due to the presence of vast amounts of drugs in his body, including: Dianobol, Xanax, Vicodin, somas, and other drugs. Luger was also charged with the sale and distribution of Saizen (a synthetic growth hormone).

Other Deaths

In the wake of the Benoit murder-suicide, the deaths kept coming. Among the wrestlers that died within close proximity to the Benoit incident were Brian Adams, Biff Wellington, Sensational Sherri Martel, Bam Bam Bigelow, Mike Awesome, and John Kronus. While some of these deaths have not been tied to drugs, a number of the most recent deaths have been. In describing the preponderance of drug-associated wrestling deaths, Dr. John Xerogeanes, who serves as the chief of sports medicine at Emory University and as an orthopedic doctor at Georgia Tech, said that drugs in these amounts are indicative of a major problem as "Normal people don't have one of those medications in their body, let alone three of them" (Hollis, 2008, n.p.).

Brian Adams passed away after the Benoit incidence on August 13, 2007. Though Adams was not active on the major professional wrestling scene at the time of his death, (he had last been employed by the WWE in 2001), his death received a significant amount of news coverage due to the windfall of media attention in the aftermath of the Benoit incident. Biff Wellington, Chris Benoit's "Mega-Doses" partner, was found dead of a steroid-induced heart attack the same weekend of the Benoit incident. Prior to Benoit's death, WWE Hall of Fame performer, "Sensational" Sherri Martel died of a drug overdose (Rothstein, 2007b). At the time of her death, Martel had six different drugs in her system, including a lethal concentration of Oxycodone. The trend does not seem to be ending anytime soon. To take a line from former professional Bill Goldberg—Who's Next? It's not a matter of if, but *when* this will happen again.

The Tie-in to "Real" Sport

As reports about wrestling deaths and drug usage emerged, WWE's credibility took further hits. Among the prominent wrestling personalities implicated in these reports were Randy Orton, Adam "Edge" Copeland, Ken "Mr. Kennedy" Anderson, and William Regal (real name Darren Matthews). Additionally, reports implicated Eddy Guerrero and Chris Benoit. The widespread emergence of the reports forced WWE to act: they suspended numerous wrestlers and numerous ongoing story lines were affected, as TV regulars were suddenly written out of the ongoing plots, their disappearances blamed on being "injured," "fired" (story line-wise), or abruptly losing a title.

WWE and the professional wrestling industry were further harmed by former professional wrestling insiders airing dirty laundry in regards to drug abuses and lack of appropriate testing measures (despite the claims of WWE). WWE's credibility was questioned as wrestlers were going to the media and speaking out on the virtues and thoroughness of the WWE Wellness Policy—only to later be named in drug investigations and the ensuing scandals.

Sport's Culture of Chemicals

Professional wrestling has been afflicted by violence, sexual exploitation, and criminal activity (including drug abuse, domestic violence, sex crimes, and homicide). Among the most significant and troubling occurrences revolve around drugs and premature deaths associated with the wrestling industry (the premature deaths are commonly drug-related instances).

Certainly, professional wrestling is not the only sport-associated entity to be impacted by noteworthy scandals. Shockwaves have shifted through the world of sport in the last decade. Examples of this include former National League MVP, the late Ken Cammaniti, and his revelations to *Sports Illustrated*, the controversial statements and allegations of Jose Canseco in his tell-all book, *Juiced*, the allegations and subsequent indictments and prosecutions resulting from the BALCO Laboratories investigations, controversies and scandals associated with mega events such as the Tour de France or the Olympic Games, and various other embarrassments to sport.

Not only has drug abuse in professional wrestling and sport caught the attention of fans and the media, it has also been the focus of several recent law enforcement investigations. In 1990, Anabolic Steroids Control Act was introduced to Congress. This act classifies steroids as a schedule III substance. One of the early investigations was the BALCO (Bay Area Laboratory Co-Operative). In 2004, United States Attorney General John Ashcroft announced a 42-count indictment against BALCO's founders, Victor Conte, James Valante, Remi Korchemny, and Greg Anderson, on charges of conspiracy to distribute and possess with intent to distribute anabolic steroids. The defendants are accused of making and distributing an undetectable steroid that is used by several athletes. Conte pled guilty in 2005 to the conspiracy charge and was sentenced to four months in federal prison ("A Time of Performance-enhancing," 2008).

Llosa and Wertheim (2007) reported that the Drug Enforcement Administration conducted an investigation under the code name "Operation Netroids." This investigation led agents to raid Applied Pharmacy Services in Mobile, Alabama. Applied Pharmacy Services is a compounding pharmacy—a pharmacy that makes its own generic drugs. The raid produced patient records that revealed the names of more than 20 athletes from several sports, including professional wrestling. Dr. Scott Corliss admitted to writing prescriptions for human growth hormones and a variety of steroids for Applied Pharmacy (Kirby, 2008a). Subsequently, Dr. David Wilbirt and Candace Toler have pled guilty to steroid conspiracy charges. Kirby (2008b) reported that Dr. Wilbirt has been linked to wrestler Eddie Guerrero, who died in 2005 of heart disease caused by years of steroid use. It should be noted that as of August 2008, no one from the pharmacy had been charged with a crime (Kirby, 2008b). In September 2008, a New York judge dismissed the indictment of those charges in the Signature Pharmacy case. However, 17 others had already pled guilty (Virtanen, 2008).

In February 2007, officials from multiple law enforcement agencies simultaneously raided the Palm Beach Rejuvenation Center and Signature Pharmacy for illegal distribution of performance enhancing drugs, such as steroids and human growth hormones, for orders placed via the Internet. These raids produced information that led investigators to believe that thousands of clients received a wide array of drugs. The list includes names of prominent athletes (Llosa & Wertheim, 2007).

Also in 2007, the Drug Enforcement Administration conducted a crackdown knows as "Operation Raw Deal." In this operation, agents shut down 26 steroid labs and made in excess of 50 arrests in the United States. Additionally, 37 Chinese factories that produced raw materials for the labs were identified (Assael, 2007c). As intelligence and leads develop from these investigations, it is unknown just how far these law enforcement investigations may reach and what may be revealed in the future.

Is There Any Hope?

Although pro wrestling makes no illusions about its purpose, the countless deaths suggest it's time to scrutinize what goes on there with the same seriousness as in the NBA or NFL. Pro wrestling is still sports entertainment, which doesn't make it all that different from the sports leagues that don't have predetermined outcomes (Hill, 2007, n.p.).

Commercially speaking, the WWE has never ridden higher. Though ratings have been higher at times, the diversity of product offerings has allowed this company to be larger and more visible than ever. Essentially monopolizing the "big time" North American wrestling scene, the WWE is standing strong. The company and the professional industry as a whole are not in danger extinction. Though the WWE is thriving, there are some serious concerns over drug-related problems associated with the WWE, the wrestling industry, and the world of sport as a whole. Various drug related scandals have been identified and explored in this chapter. The implications of such matters in the world of "true sport" have also been discussed. One last question remains: what can be done to clean up, or at least reduce, the problems identified in this chapter?

Randazzo (2008) proposes a four part plan for cleaning up professional wrestling.

1. Breaks in the schedule so that wrestlers could physically recuperate (maintaining long term viability).
2. Comprehensive drug and steroid testing without loopholes.
3. A management decision to not hire unnaturally (chemically) enhanced wrestlers.
4. Comprehensive pension and healthcare programs (Randazzo, 2008, pp. 322–323).

In regards to Radazzo's suggestions, Vince McMahon has the opportunity to be the greatest agent of change for the entire wrestling industry in North America (if not around the world). When it comes to actions that can curb the trend of premature wrestling deaths, it is important that those in positions of power pay heed to and aggressively seek to implement significant changes with wrestling. Changes such as those suggested by Randazzo, enacted by McMahon and others who are influential in the wrestling industry, could easily lighten the load that full time wrestlers endure. Limiting schedules, providing time for recuperation, and not providing a foundation that promotes the use of illegal performance enhancers can go a long way toward righting the wrongs that exist. Such change needs to go beyond certain select individuals taking a "high road" approach and choosing to be clean. There needs to be legitimate deterrence from doing wrong, whether it is tougher testing that does not kowtow to loopholes, selective exemptions, and other potentially problematic areas.

Concern also exists over the implementation of safeguards that support the betterment of performers, both today and in the future. This sentiment is similar to the ongoing battle being waged against the National Football League Player Association. Though the NFL and the WWE are different entities that represent different situations, these wealthy organizations need to ensure that appropriate opportunities are made available for those employees in need—and in the case of wrestling, that includes a significant number. Though such action may be difficult for small-scale independent operations, no such excuse exists for the WWE. Though reports have emerged of the WWE offering rehab arrangements for former employees, there is much more that can and should be done.

Regardless, the very nature of professional wrestling is desperate for an overhaul, especially in regards to how the industry's standard barer, the WWE, moves towards doing what is right for a billion dollar, publicly-held "mega company." The methods for appropriate reform can provide a means for ongoing discussion, but it is apparent that change is needed in order to turn the tide. In conclusion, ESPN's Jemele Hill (2007) hit the nail on the head when she stated, "It seems the drama in pro wrestling isn't as fake as we'd like to believe" (n.p.).

References

Assael, S. (2002, November 18). Overkill. ESPN the Magazine. Retrieved on October 30, 2008, from http://espn.go.com/magazine/vol5no24davey.html

Assael, S. (2007a, July 27). McMahon asked by congressional committee to hand over records. *ESPN the Magazine*. Retrieved on October 30, 2008, from http://sports.espn.go.com/espn/news/story?id=2951586

Assael, S. (2007b, August 31). WWE suspends 10 for violating policy that requires drug tests. ESPN.com. Retrieved on September 8, 2008, from http://sports.espn.go.com/espn/news/story?id=2998062

Assael, S. (2007c, September 24). 'Raw Deal' busts labs across U.S. many supplied by China. *ESPN the Magazine*. Retrieved on September 8, 2008, from http://sports.espn.go.com/espn/news/story?id=3033532

Assael S., & Mooneyham, M. (2002). *Sex, lies, and headlocks: The real story of Vince McMahon and the World Wrestling Federation*. New York: Crown Publishers.

Associated Press (2007, March 20). Orton, other wrestlers linked to probe of pharmacy. Retrieved on August 16,2007 from http://sports.espn.go.com/espn/news/story?id=2805155

Full contact. (2008, n.p.) *SportsBusiness Journal*. Retrieved on September 7, 2008, from http://www.sportsbusinessjournal.com/index.cfm?fuseaction= article.printArticle&articleId=58742

Hill, J. (2007). Pro wrestling has more problem than steroids, ESPN Page 2. Retrieved on September 8, 2008, from http://sports.espn.go.com/espn/page2/ story?page=hill/070628

Hollis, J. (2008). Former wrestlers speak out against sport's culture. Atlanta Journal Constitution. Retrieved on September 8, 2008, from http://www.ajc.com/news/ content/metro/cherokee/stories/2008/06/16/lex_luger_wrestling_culture.html

Kirby, B. (2008a). Prosecutors: Indictments Close in Steroids Case. *Mobile Press Register*. Retrieved on October 28, 2008, from http://www.al.com/press-register/stories/index.ssf?/base/news/1212830130196290.xml&coll=3

Kirby, B. (2008b). Doctor, Fiancée Plead Guilty to Steroid Charges. *Mobile Press Register*. Retrieved on October 28, 2008, from http://www.al.com/press-register/stories/index.ssf?/base/news/1219482917300650.xml&coll=3

Lee, J.W., & Bernthal, M. (in press). Down, but Not Out: World Wrestling Entertainment's Dance with Death. J.W. Lee, (Ed.) In *Branding in sport business* (forthcoming 2009). Durham, NC: Carolina Academic Press

Llosa, L.F., & Wertheim, L.J. (2007, June 26). WWE downplays drug factor. *SI.com*. Retrieved on October 30, 2008, from http://sportsillustrated.cnn.com/ 2007/more/06/26/benoitcase/index.html

Lovel, J. (2002). Black wrestlers to sue Turner. *Atlanta Business Chronicle*. Retrieved on October 31, 2008, from http://www.bizjournals.com/atlanta/stories/ 2002/04/01/story1.html

Mannix, C. (2007, June 26). Should Congress step in? Benoit case latest sign of wrestling's steroid problem. Sports Illustrated.com. Retrieved on October 30, 2008, from http://sportsillustrated.cnn.com/2007/writers/chris_mannix/06/26/benoit/

Meltzer, D. (2001). *Tributes: Remembering some of the world's greatest professional wrestlers*. Etobicoke, ON, Canada: Winding Stair Press.

Meltzer, D. (2004). *Tributes II: Remembering more of the world's greatest professional wrestlers*. Champaign, IL: Sports Publishing L.L.C.

Miller, J. (n.d.) Slam! Sports Wrestling Bios — Vince McMahon. Slam! Sports. Retrieved on October 30, 2008, from http://www.canoe.ca/Slam/Wrestling/Bios/mcmahon-vince.html

Piper, R., & Picarello, R. (2002). *In the Pit with Piper: Roddy Gets rowdy*. New York: Berkley Trade.

Radazzo V.M. (2008). *The story of Chris Benoit and the fall of the pro wrestling industry*. Beverley Hills, CA: Phoenix Books.

Rothstein, S. (2007a, July 20) WWE blasted for drug denial. *The Sun*. Retrieved on September 8, 2008, from http://www.thesun.co.uk/sol/homepage/sport/wrestling/article257356.ece

Rothstein, S. (2007b, September 12). Hillbilly Heroin killed Sherri. *The Sun*. Retrieved on September 8, 2008, from http://www.thesun.co.uk/sol/homepage/sport/wrestling/article293849.ece

Rothstein, S., & Lister, J. (2007, July 26). 105 wrestlers die in a decade, *The Sun*. Retrieved on September 9, 2007, from www.thesun.co.uk/sol/homepage/sport/wrestling/article242058.ece

Sandomir, R. (2007, July 17). WWE's Testing Is Examined after Benoit Murder-Suicide. *The New York Times*. Retrieved on October 30, 2008, from http://www.nytimes.com/2007/07/17/sports/othersports/17wrestling.html

A Time of Performance-enhancing Drugs in Sports. (2008, March 11). *SI.com*. Retrieved on September 8, 2008, from http://sportsillustrated.cnn.com/2008/magazine/03/11/steroid.timeline/index.html

Virtanen, M. (2008, September 11). NY judge drops case against Fla. Pharmacy. *USA Today*. Retrieved on October 28, 2008, from http://www.usatoday.com/_ads/interstitial/2008/page/interstitial.htm?http://www.usatoda y.com/news/nation/2008-09-11-1662118150_x.htm

WWE Talent Wellness Program. (2006). WWE Corporate. Retrieved on October 30, 2008, from http://corporate.wwe.com/documents/TalentWellnessProgram Outline2-27-06CORPweb.pdf

Appendix 1

Drugs and Substance Abuse

Jeffrey C. Lee, Troy University
Brent Paterline, North Georgia College and State University

Overview

It is generally recognized that substance abuse is a worldwide problem facing our society today. There many reasons why people may use substances. Some of the reasons that people use or abuse substances inappropriately include:

1. To go along with the crowd;
2. To feel less afraid or more courageous;
3. To relieve feelings of inferiority or dependency;
4. To relieve feelings of depression, anxiety, or depression;
5. To relax;
6. To escape personal problems;
7. To prepare for stress or endure pain;
8. To improve performance;
9. To increase or reduce appetite;
10. To satisfy a strong psychological craving or compulsion;
11. To experiment; and
12. To rebel.

There are four stages of illicit substance abuse. The first stage is *experimental use*. In this stage, the social experience is more important than the effects of the drug or substance. These substances may be considered "gateway drugs." Substances such as nicotine, alcohol, diet pills, marijuana, and legal stimulants like "No Doze" are often considered gateway drugs. The gateway hypothesis is the contention that use of these substances leads to greater incidence of abuse and the use of more harmful drugs. The next stage is *recreational use*. At this stage, the user views the substance as being important to having a "good time." The next stage is *harmfully involved*. In this stage, users begin to experience substance related problems in their everyday lives. Also at this stage, users begin to take certain risks to use, including using at times and places where they may get caught. The users at this stage often feel that the drugs or substances are helping solve their problems, when in fact they are creating more. The last stage is *chemical dependency*. At this stage, users view that there is no other choice but to use drugs. They often will surround themselves with people that enable their drug use and isolate themselves from nurturing support systems.

There are some common characteristics in people that are labeled as substance abusers. Usually they have very low self-esteem. They secretly feel that they are people with little or no value. They are also people that frequently act impulsively. Substance abusers often find it difficult to plan ahead. Consequences, especially those related to drug abuse, are of little concern, because they "will worry about that later." This characteristic is coupled with an inability to delay gratification. Substance abusers often have a low tolerance for anxiety, pain, or discomfort. They will seek relief from even the most minor conditions. They also find it difficult to tolerate criticism. Substance abusers' reaction to criticism is usually overstated, and the criticism is typically viewed as personal rejection. Substance abusers often have difficulty in forming close intimate relationships with others. They feel it is safer to engage in substance abuse rather than risk getting hurt in a relationship.

Drug Pharmacology

A drug can be defined as any substance that is used legally or illegally for its bodily and psychic effects. Pharmacology is the study of how a drug affects one's body and mind. When examining the effects of a drug, one must remember that all drugs may have multiple effects. For example, marijuana not only causes changes in the brain like time distortion and decline in motor skills, but also causes physical changes such as hunger, dryness of the mouth, redness of the eyes, and may even act as a sexual depressant (Paterline, 2003).

There are many factors that can influence how drugs may affect users. First, the effects of a drug may depend on the amount or dosage an individual has taken. Small doses of cocaine, for example, may give a user an energy boost so he or she becomes talkative and outgoing. However, larger doses of cocaine may make users nervous, paranoid, and unwilling to be around others. Very large doses of cocaine, such as two grams in 30 minutes or less, may cause an overdose in which the drug causes complications in heart rhythms that may lead to sudden death (Paterline, 2003).

The purity of a drug can also influence its effects. Drug dealers often "cut" or mix their drugs with other substances to increase their profits. Because cutting usually involves the diluting of a drug, the effects are often reduced. Heroin sold on the street, for example, is often cut or diluted with such substances as caffeine and various sugars like lactose (Paterline, 2003).

The method of administration is important in determining the effects of drugs on a user. When a drug is taken orally, its effectiveness is diminished because it mixes with food, acid, and digestive enzymes in the gastrointestinal tract. When a drug is smoked, the inhaled substance reaches the brain within five to eight seconds and the effects of the drug are usually relatively short. When drugs are injected intravenously they are administered directly into the bloodstream and are distributed to all the parts of the body in high concentrations in a short period of time. The effects of drugs administered intravenously usually last longer than when inhaled or taken orally. Some drugs, like anabolic steroids, are often injected into muscle tissue, which is known as an intra-muscular injection. Drugs delivered intra-muscularly are absorbed more slowly than those that are administered intravenously because the muscle tissue often serves as a filter.

The effects of a drug may change when it is used or combined synergistically with other drugs. Combining two or more drugs may cause enhancing interactions in which the effects of one drug increase the effects of another drug. This increase in effects may be additive or synergistic. An additive interaction describes a circumstance in which the combined effects of two drugs are simply added together. However, the combination of some drugs may have a synergistic effect, in which the combined effects of both drugs are greater than if they are simply added together. Examples of two drugs that act synergistically are alcohol and barbiturates. One dose of a barbiturate taken with two glasses of wine may result in a more powerful than expected depressant of the central nervous system because of the two drugs' synergism. Often, drugs taken synergistically can be lethal (Paterline, 2003).

The user's tolerance to a drug can also influence how a drug will affect a user. The concept of tolerance refers to the ability of a dosage of a drug to have a gradually diminished effect on the user. With the repeated use of certain drugs, a user may develop a tolerance to the drug in which he or she needs to take more and more of the drug to obtain the same effect. Therefore, the user's body develops a progressive resistance to the effects of the drug so that greater doses of the substance are required to reproduce the original effect. However, as users develop a tolerance to a drug and the amount of a drug required to achieve a desired effect may increase, the amount needed to cause a fatal overdose may not necessarily increase (Paterline, 2003).

Drug Schedules

Congress passed the Comprehensive Drug Abuse Prevention and Control Act, also known as the Controlled Substance Act in 1970. The act was passed in response to a number of diverse and over-lapping drug laws, which require many different agencies to enforce them. This legislation established five schedules (Table A1.1) for the classification of drugs base upon their approved medical uses, potential for abuse, and their potential for producing dependence (Paterline, 2003).

Stimulants

Stimulants are a category of drugs that increase alertness, physical activity, and excitement by speeding up the body's processes. Paterline (2003), reports that stimulants are among the most addictive substances. The pleasurable or desired effects experienced from stimulants often drive users to engage in repeated, often compulsive use, despite the many harmful and self-destructive consequences.

Table A1.1 Drug Schedules

Schedule I	High potential for abuse and no accepted medical use. Research use only and drugs must be stored in secure vaults. Examples: Marijuana, LSD, Mescaline.
Schedule II	High potential for abuse. Some accepted medical use, though use may lead to severe physical or psychological dependence. No prescription renewals are permitted and the drugs must be stored in secure vaults. Examples: Cocaine, Amphetamines, Opium, Morphine, Codeine, Methadone.
Schedule III	Some potential for abuse. Accepted medical use, though use may lead to low-to-moderate physical or psychological dependence. Up to five prescription renewals are permitted within 6 months. Examples: Phencyclidine (PCP), some barbiturates.
Schedule IV	Low potential for abuse. Accepted medical use. Up to five prescription renewals are permitted within six months. Examples: Diazepam (Valium), Phenobarbital.
Schedule V	Minimal abuse potential. Widespread medical use. Minimal controls for selling and dispensing. Examples: prescription cough medicines and substances with small amounts of narcotics.

Abuse is often associated with a pattern of binge use, in which an addict continues to use the drug every few hours until they have depleted their drug supply or reached a point of delirium, psychosis, and physical exhaustion. Once users stop the use of stimulants it is commonly followed by a "crash" where they experience depression, anxiety, drug craving, and extreme fatigue.

Stimulants may be taken orally, sniffed, smoked, and injected. However, sniffing, smoking, or injecting stimulants produce a sudden sensation known as a "rush" (Abadinsky, 2004). The stimulant drugs most frequently abused are cocaine and amphetamines or methamphetamines.

Cocaine

Cocaine is derived from the leaves of the coca shrub, grown in the high-altitude rain forests of Bolivia and Peru in South America. Some common street terms for cocaine are coke, snow, or blow, and it is usually distributed as a white crystalline powder that is sold by the gram. Many users begin their cocaine use by snorting the cocaine powder through the nose where it is absorbed into the bloodstream through the nasal tissues. In order to prevent small amounts of the drug from becoming lodged in the sinus cavities or traveling down the throat, most users chop the cocaine into a fine powder with a razor blade on a hard, flat surface, such as a small mirror. The powder is then arranged into thin lines. Then it is placed in ½ inch to 1 inch long lines and inhaled through a rolled dollar bill or a straw. The cocaine penetrates the small capillaries in the mucous membranes of the nasal lining, enters the blood stream, and then is circulated to the brain and the body (Paterline, 2003).

Crack

Crack is made when sodium bicarbonate (baking soda) and water are added to cocaine. The mixture is heated and cooled, then filtered to collect the crystals.

The substance is then cut in chips or small "rocks" and sold on the street in small, inexpensive dosage units (Paterline, 2003). Abadinsky (2004) describes crack as a drug abusers answer to "fast food." Crack is usually sold on the street in small, glass vials, small bags, or in heavy tinfoil and is typically smoked in a glass pipe that is 3–5 inches long with a metal screen at the top to hold a crack rock. It may also be sprinkled on tobacco or marijuana and smoked in a pipe or stuffed with marijuana into a cigar that is often called a "blunt" on the street. When smoked, the vapors of crack produce an instant and intense rush or high. After the rush, there is a general feeling of euphoria that lasts 5 to 20 minutes. Then there is a low or "crash" characterized by restlessness, irritability, depression, and an intense craving for more of the drug. According to Abadinsky, (2004) this may be accompanied by long periods of sleep. It is the withdrawal or crash, not the euphoric high, that makes crack one of the most addictive drugs currently being used (Paterline, 2003).

Amphetamines and Methamphetamines

Amphetamines and methamphetamines are substances that can be taken orally, smoked, or injected. Some of the effects of amphetamines and methamphetamines are very similar to cocaine. However, there has recently been a significant resurgence in the use of these substances (Levinthal, 2008).

Hallucinogens

Hallucinogens are a group of drugs that cause changes in a user's perception, thinking, emotions, and self-image. These drugs are usually taken orally and are often referred to as mind expansion drugs because they can distort a user's perception of reality. Furthermore, Abadinsky (2004) reports that use of hallucinogens may provide the user access to suppressed or hidden memories. Common effects of these drugs include hallucinations, such as a heightened awareness of sensory input, unreal but vivid images and distortions, and synesthesia or the seeing of sounds and the hearing of visuals. In other words, smells might be felt, and colors may be heard. Many users also describe experiences of heightened emotions and the discovery of profound meanings and emotions. Physically, most hallucinogens dilate a user's pupil and increase blood pressure and pulse rate. LSD (Lysergic Acid Diethylamide) and club drugs like Ecstasy or MDMA are commonly used hallucinogens.

LSD

LSD is a semi-synthetic psychedelic hallucinogenic drug that is derived from a fungus grown on rye called ergot. Its primary street name is "acid." LSD can be sold in tablet, capsule, or liquid forms. LSD is often absorbed into blotter paper and cut into small decorative squares representing a dose. It can also be added to gelatin sheets, which are known as window panes. LSD produces a high that may last as long as 8–12 hours (Abadinsky, 2004).

MDMA

MDMA, or Ecstasy, is a drug that is commonly found in the nightclub or rave scene. It is usually taken orally as a pill or capsule. It produces a high that last for 3–6 hours. Some common effects of MDMA use are illusions, hallucinations, and altered perceptions of time and distance. At the same time, MSMA is reported to have similar properties to stimulants. Some of the physiological effects of the drug are increased blood pressure and heart rates, and dehydration that may lead to heart attacks, strokes, or seizures (Levinthal, 2008).

Depressants

Depressants are a category of drugs that slow down the physical and mental functions of the body. At low doses, these drugs tend to produce a sedative, calming effect by relaxing muscles and relieving feelings of tension and anxiety; but at higher doses they produce drowsiness and may lead to a state resembling sleep. Like alcohol, these drugs can reduce inhibitions in some users, leading to increased sociability or may result in violent behavior. Most depressants are found in the form of a pill or capsule. When taken with alcohol, depressants have a strong synergistic effect and can often lead to accidental or intentional death (Paterline, 2003).

Narcotics

According to Paterline (2003), narcotics are a category of drugs that are also often called opiates because they are derived from the opium poppy plant or made synthetically to have the same drug actions of morphine, a major ingredient of opium. Narcotics are powerful pain relievers and are often used for legitimate medical purposes. Common side effects of narcotics include constipation, constriction of the eye's pupil, and respiratory depression that may lead to irregular breathing. Narcotics are central nervous system depressants and high doses often cause slowing and clouding of mental processes. Unlike other central nervous system depressants, however, there is generally no loss of motor coordination and no slurring of speech. Oxycodone, a time-released pill used in the treatment of chronic pain, is a commonly abused prescription narcotic. Heroin is an illicit narcotic that can be snorted, injected, or smoked and produces a 3–6 hour intense high. Heroin users that are experiencing withdrawal symptoms report a loss of appetite, tremors, panic, cramps, nausea, sweating, and chills (Abadinsky, 2004).

Steroids

Anabolic steroids are drugs patterned after the testosterone molecule that promote masculine changes in the body and increased muscular development. Since the late 1980s anabolic steroids have become popular with competitive athletes and body builders. However, use, overuse, and unsupervised use of these performance enhancing substances have recently received a great amount of attention around the world in professional and amateur sports. Anabolic steroids are typically used orally in a pill form, intramuscular injections, or by a transdermal patch. The abuse of steroids has been known to produce the undesired effect of aggressiveness, mood swings, and liver disease. Men also have been found to have low sperm count, enlarged breast, atrophy of the testicles, and severe acne. Women abusers have been found to experience development of masculine physical characteristics, which may not be reversible. Human Growth Hormone (HGH) is another substance that is not a steroid, but is also used for the ergogenic effect of performance enhancement (Levinthal, 2008).

References

Abadinsky, H. (2004). *Drugs an introduction*. Belmont, CA: Thomson

Levinthal, C.F. (2008). *Drugs, society, and criminal justice*. Boston: Pearson

Paterline, B. (2003). *Drug identification and investigation for law enforcement.* Temecula, CA: Staggs Publishing

Appendix 2

Organized Crime and Sports Wagering: Insider Perspectives with Mike Franzese

Jason W. Lee, University of North Florida

Lee: Mr. Franzese, thank you very much for taking time out of your busy schedule to share your insight on the important issues of sports gambling and the role organized crime in sports gambling. You have a fascinating story. Can you tell us a bit about your background and how you got into organized crime?

Franzese: My dad was the underboss of the Colombo Crime family in the 1960s. When he received a 50 year prison sentence in 1967, I was a pre-med student in college when he went off to do his time in 1970 in Leavenworth Penitentiary. My life changed. I left school. My dad proposed me for membership in the Colombo Family and I was inducted in 1975.

Lee: How high did you rise within the Colombo family (and what did that entail)?

Franzese: I rose in the life by being a good soldier, understanding the politics of the mob life and by making a very significant amount of money. I was appointed a caporegime (captain) in 1980 by the Boss.

Lee: How were you able to get out?

Franzese: Long story here. Combination of knowing the life intimately well, never testifying against my former mob associates and by outlasting almost everyone I knew in the life who is either dead or in prison for life. And, because Jesus Christ had my back! That's the main reason. God had another plan and purpose for my life.

Lee: What safety concerns do you have today?

Franzese: Very few. I don't challenge the guys. I can't go back to Brooklyn to live, but I'm not in fear.

Lee: *Why is sports gambling so attractive to organized crime operations?*

Franzese: Most mobsters love to gamble and love the business of gambling. The concept of risking a little to make a lot is very appealing. Also, mobsters know gambling is a weakness they can exploit in others.

Lee: *What other organized crime groups are heavily associated with sports gambling?*

Franzese: I had personal experience with the Russian mob's involvement in illegal gambling. I also know the Russian mob looks to extort Russian athletes into compromising the outcome of games in which they participate to gain an edge in their gambling operations. La Cosa Nostra does the same, with any athlete they can reach.

Lee: *How significant was sport gambling to your overall business operations?*

Franzese: Very significant to the overall operation of the mob. Fairly significant to my own operations. I was generating millions of dollars per week in the gasoline business. Nothing compared to that in terms of my overall earnings during that time.

Lee: *How does that compare to the status of the profitability of sport gambling today?*

Franzese: I can assure you, there is more money in it today for the mob then during my day, only because of the significant increase in gambling opportunities through the Internet, casinos, and video poker machines.

Lee: *What other criminal activities are tied to sport gambling (and which of these are of greatest concern)?*

Franzese: Extortion and loan sharking are other illegal business activities the mob engages in as a result of its illegal gambling operations.

Lee: *For those not familiar with your work, could you detail what you do, as well some of the organizations, sport and otherwise, that you have worked with and/or been invited to speak to?*

Franzese: Regarding my work with gambling, my objective is to inform and educate athletes and other personnel involved in sports on both the professional and college levels as to the dangers gambling can pose to them personally as well as to the integrity of the sport in which they compete. I currently work regularly with the NBA (National Basketball Association), MLB (Major League Baseball), NCAA (National Collegiate Athletic Association) Division I, II, and III Universities around the country, ATP (Association of Tennis professionals), AFCA (Association of Football Coaches of America), and many high schools nationally.

Lee: What does a typical month look like for you, in regards to travel and appearances?

Franzese: Travelling 2–3 weeks per month. Several appearances all over the country. Writing articles; involved in TV and film productions.

Lee: Explain why such organizations are so interested in having you come in and speak to their athletes?

Franzese: To prevent an athlete, coach, official, or anyone associated with their sport to engage in gambling activity or associate with anyone involved in gambling that might cause them to compromise the integrity of their sport.

Lee: In your opinion, how substantial is America's gambling problem-how does sports gambling stack up to the overall issue gambling in the U.S.?

Franzese: Very substantial and growing rapidly thanks to the Internet, poker on TV, the proliferation of casinos throughout the country. There is an undercurrent of gambling issues people are experiencing in America, as well as throughout the world. Sports gambling is on par with every other form of gambling. Very popular.

Lee: Outside of Nevada, what are the sports gambling hotbeds in the U.S.?

Franzese: Until recently sports gambling was only legal in Las Vegas. As of now, it is the only "hotbed" area for sports gambling in the U.S. However, the Internet picks up the slack across the country, even though gambling on sports is illegal, unlicensed and unregulated on the Internet.

Lee: Do you feel that society takes too lenient of a view on the issue of illegal sport gambling?

Franzese: Yes. They just don't get it unless they get bit by it.

Lee: How prevalent is gambling among athletes on the collegiate level?

Franzese: Very prevalent. Not only among athletes, but among college students in general. Especially on the Internet.

Lee: How does this compare to gambling involvement by professional athletes?

Franzese: The pros are more involved in my experience because they have the money, obviously. Gambling is an extension of their competitive nature.

Lee: Do you see any reason for hope that the status of illegal sports gambling will be able to improve (Why?/Why not?)?

Franzese: No. I see it growing. We now live in a global gambling community. Illegal sports gambling will continue to grow along with the growth of legal gambling. They go hand in hand.

Lee: Do you have any final parting words or advice for our readers?

Franzese: I am not an anti-gambling proponent across the board. My goal is merely to educate and inform people that gambling in its many forms can be dangerous. It can be just as addicting as alcohol or drugs. For those with an addictive or compulsive personality, its "pick your poison," drugs, alcohol, pornography ... gambling. I see no harm in social gambling that does not impact your behavior, or your bank account in a negative way. Unfortunately, I have seen COUNTLESS LIVES destroyed from gambling abuse. Families, friends and business associates of the gambler included.

Young, old, black or white. Doesn't matter. Gambling abuse can be an equal opportunity destroyer. It can creep up on you and get you hooked before you realize what's happening. My advice to those who engage in gambling in any form is to know your limits, understand your own personality and BE CAREFUL!

Appendix 3

Fraud in Non-profit Sport: A Case Study of the Sport Sun State Soccer Association [Optional Teaching Notes]

Jeffrey E. Michelman, University of North Florida
Jason W. Lee, University of North Florida
Bobby E. Waldrup, University of North Florida

Coordinating Class/Group Discussion

To coordinate and stimulate class discussion, professors and instructors may include online resources, such as organizational websites, or solicit verbal discourse of personal involvements pertaining to notable or relevant local non-profit sport organizations. Non-profit sport organizations range from YMCA and Boy's and Girl's Clubs, down to local soccer, football, baseball or any number of other sport providers. Such organizations pose interesting and thought provoking examples of organizations which provide sport activities in various ways to various audiences and consumers. Such organizations have been able to make an impact by various means through providing outlets for children and adults to participate in events, leagues, and so forth. The potential for success of the organizations, countered with the potential for a variety of abuses should be explored, discussed, and analyzed (refer to Exhibit A3.1, "The Fraud Triangle," for further issues associated with the potential for fraud). The dynamic nature of the issues presented in this case can be utilized to stimulate and further enhance discussion efforts on relevant issues.

The existing offerings of non-profit sport organizations are unique and face unique challenges. Students may be asked to evaluate representative non-profit organizations and sample policy issues relative to these organizations. They may be asked to comment on respective non-profit sport organizations that have made an impact or have points of relevance to offer to this discussion from the given geographic area as well.

Exhibit A3.1 The Fraud Triangle

Prerequisite Elements

Opportunity

Pressure   Rationalization

The fraud triangle illustrates three factors that exist in all fraud cases: (1) a pressure or motive, (2) a rationalization of the act, and (3) a perceived opportunity. Every person who commits fraud faces a pressure, whether financial or non-financial, that causes the perpetrator to provoke the action. The element of rationalization refers to the mind set of the perpetrator that allows him to justify the act of fraud. Lastly, the perpetrator must believe that he has an opportunity to commit fraud. The three elements of the fraud triangle are interrelated. That being so, if a person perceives a heightened amount of pressure to commit fraud, the less rationalization he will need to follow through with the act. Fraud prevention implies the removal of one or more of the elements in the fraud triangle, and people who try to prevent fraud usually aim to implement controls that reduce or eliminate the opportunity to commit fraud.

Adapted from Albrecht, S., Albrecht, C., Albrecht, C., & Zimbleman, M. (2008).

Application of Relevant Theoretical Issues

Criminal Behavior; Non-Profit Sport Organizations; Fraud; Theft; Sport Governance; Risk Management; Financial Accountability; Auditing; Bookkeeping; Personal Ethics; Business Ethics

Reference

Albrecht, S., Albrecht, C., Albrecht, C., & Zimbleman, M. (2008). *Fraud examination*. Cincinnati, OH: Thomson/SouthWestern.

Index